W9-COE-115

HEALTH POLICYMAKING IN THE UNITED STATES

Fifth Edition

HEALTH POLICYMAKING IN THE UNITED STATES

Fifth Edition

Beaufort B. Longest, Jr.

Health Administration Press, Chicago, IL
AUPHA Press, Washington, DC

AUPHA
HAP

Your board, staff, or clients may also benefit from this book's insight. For more information on quantity discounts, contact the Health Administration Press Marketing Manager at (312) 424–9470.

This publication is intended to provide accurate and authoritative information in regard to the subject matter covered. It is sold, or otherwise provided, with the understanding that the publisher is not engaged in rendering professional services. If professional advice or other expert assistance is required, the services of a competent professional should be sought.

The statements and opinions contained in this book are strictly those of the author and do not represent the official positions of the American College of Healthcare Executives, the Foundation of the American College of Healthcare Executives, or the Association of University Programs in Health Administration.

15   14   13   12   11   5   4   3   2   1

Library of Congress Cataloging-in-Publication Data

Longest, Beaufort B.
  Health policymaking in the United States / Beaufort B. Longest Jr. — 5th ed.
      p. ; cm.
  Includes bibliographical references and index.
  ISBN 978-1-56793-354-3 (alk. paper)
  1. Medical policy—United States. 2. Health planning—United States. 3. Medical laws
and legislation—United States. 4. Policy sciences—Methodology. I. Title.
  [DNLM: 1. Health Policy—United States. 2. Health Planning—legislation &
jurisprudence—United States. 3. Policy Making—United States. WA 540 AA1 L8h 2009]
  RA395.A3L66 2009
  362.10973—dc22

                                                                    2009036904

The paper used in this publication meets the minimum requirements of American National Standard for Information Sciences—Permanence of Paper for Printed Library Materials, ANSI Z39.48-1984. ∞ ™

Acquisitions editor: Janet Davis; Project manager: Dojna Shearer; Cover designer: Marisa Jackson; Layout: Putman Productions, LLC.

Found an error or a typo? We want to know! Please e-mail it to hap1@ache.org, and put "Book Error" in the subject line.

For photocopying and copyright information, please contact Copyright Clearance Center at www.copyright.com or at (978) 750–8400.

Health Administration Press
A division of the Foundation of the American
   College of Healthcare Executives
One North Franklin Street, Suite 1700
Chicago, IL 60606
(312) 424-2800

Association of University Programs
   in Health Administration
2000 14th Street North
Suite 780
Arlington, VA 22201
(703) 894-0940

For Carolyn

Who understands what a 50/50 partnership means better than anyone I know.

CONTENTS IN BRIEF

CONTENTS IN DETAIL

Appendixes

ACRONYMS AND ABBREVIATIONS

AAFP	American Academy of Family Physicians
AAHSA	American Association of Homes and Services for the Aging
AAMC	Association of American Medical Colleges
AARP	American Association of Retired Persons
AAP	American Academy of Pediatrics
ACHE	American College of Healthcare Executives
ACP	American College of Physicians
ACR	adjusted community rate
ACS	American Cancer Society
	American College of Surgeons
ADA	American Dental Association
	Americans with Disabilities Act
AFDC	Aid to Families with Dependent Children
AHA	American Heart Association
	American Hospital Association
AHCA	American Health Care Association
AHCPR	Agency for Healthcare Policy and Research; now the Agency for Healthcare Research and Quality
AHERA	Asbestos Hazard Emergency Response Act
AHIP	Americas Health Insurance Plans
AHRQ	Agency for Healthcare Research and Quality
AIAMC	Alliance of Independent Academic Medical Centers
AIDS	acquired immunodeficiency syndrome
ALJ	administrative law judge
AMA	American Medical Association
AMWA	American Medical Women's Association
ANA	American Nurses Association
ANRC	American National Red Cross
AoA	Administration on Aging
AUPHA	Association of University Programs in Health Administration

BBA	Balanced Budget Act
BBRA	Medicare, Medicaid, and SCHIP Balanced Budget Refinement Act
BCBSA	Blue Cross and Blue Shield Associations
BIO	Biotechnology Industry Organization
BIPA	Medicare, Medicaid, and SCHIP Benefits Improvement and Protection Act
CA	consortium administrator
CAA	Clean Air Act
CARE	Ryan White Comprehensive AIDS Resources Emergency Act
CBA	cost-benefit analysis
CBO	Congressional Budget Office
CCU	cardiac care unit
CDC	Centers for Disease Control and Prevention
CDER	Center for Drug Evaluation and Research
CEA	cost-effectiveness analysis
CERCLA	Comprehensive Environmental Response, Compensation and Liability Act
CFR	*Code of Federal Regulations*
CHAMPUS	Civilian Health and Medical Program of the Uniformed Services
CHIP	Children's Health Insurance Program
CMS	Centers for Medicare & Medicaid Services
COBRA	Consolidated Omnibus Budget Reconciliation Act
COGR	Council on Governmental Relations
CON	certificate of need
COTH	Council of Teaching Hospitals and Health Systems
CPM	Center for Policy and Management
CPO	Center for Program Operations
CPSC	Consumer Product Safety Commission
CRS	Congressional Research Service
CT	computed tomography
CVD	cardiovascular disease
CWA	Clean Water Act
DHEW	Department of Health, Education, and Welfare
DHHS	Department of Health and Human Services
DME	durable medical equipment
DOJ	Department of Justice
DRA	Deficit Reduction Act
DRG	diagnosis-related group
DSH	disproportionate share hospital

EAB	Environmental Appeals Board
EMS	emergency medical service
EMTALA	Emergency Medical Treatment and Labor Act
EPA	Environmental Protection Agency
EPCRA	Emergency Planning and Community Right-to-Know Act
EPL	effective patient life
EPSDT	early and periodic screening, diagnostic, and treatment
ERISA	Employee Retirement Income Security Act
ESRD	end-stage renal disease
FAHS	Federation of American Hospital Systems
FDA	Food and Drug Administration
FEC	Federal Election Commission
FECA	Federal Election Campaign Act
FFDCA	Federal Food, Drug, and Cosmetic Act
FHSA	Federal Hazardous Substances Act
FIFRA	Federal Insecticide, Fungicide, and Rodenticide Act
FMAP	Federal Medical Assistance Percentage
FPL	federal poverty level
FQHC	federally qualified health center
FR	*Federal Register*
FSA	Federal Security Agency
FY	fiscal year
GAO	Government Accountability Office (Formerly General Accounting Office)
GDP	gross domestic product
GME	graduate medical education
GPO	Government Printing Office
HCBS	home and community-based services
HCFA	Health Care Financing Administration; now Centers for Medicare and Medicaid Services
HHA	home health agency
HHS	Health and Human Services
HI	Hospital Insurance
HIPAA	Health Insurance Portability and Accountability Act
HIV	human immunodeficiency virus
HMO	health maintenance organization
HPNEC	Health Professions and Nursing Education Coalition
HAS	health systems agency
HRSA	Health Resources and Services Administration

ICU	intensive care unit
ICF	intermediate care facility
ICF/MR	intermediate care facility for the mentally retarded
IME	indirect medical education
IOM	Institute of Medicine
IRS	Internal Revenue Service
LEPC	local emergency planning committee
MAACS	maximum allowable actual charges
MA-PD	Medicare Advantage prescription drug plan
MedPAC	Medicare Payment Advisory Commission
MEI	Medicare Economic Index
MIP	Medicare Integrity Program
MIPPA	Medicare Improvement for Patients and Providers Act
MMA	Medicare Prescription Drug, Improvement, and Modernization Act
MN	medically needy
MPRSA	Marine Protection, Research, and Sanctuaries Act
MR	mentally retarded
MRI	magnetic resonance imaging
MSA	Medical Savings Account
NAACP	National Association for the Advancement of Colored People
NACHRI	National Association of Children's Hospitals and Related Institutions
NACOSH	National Advisory Committee on Occupational Safety and Health
NCOA	National Council on Aging
NCQA	National Committee for Quality Assurance
NGT	nominal group technique
NHSC	National Health Service Corps
NIBIB	National Institute of Biomedical Imaging and Bioengineering
NIH	National Institutes of Health
NMA	National Medical Association
NOW	National Organization for Women
OALJ	Office of Administrative Law Judges
OASI	Old Age and Survivors Insurance
OBRA	Omnibus Budget Reconciliation Act

ODA	Orphan Drug Act
OECD	Organization for Economic Co-operation and Development
OIG	Office of the Inspector General
OMB	Office of Management and Budget
OSHA	Occupational Safety and Health Administration
PAC	political action committee
PACE	Programs of All-Inclusive Care for the Elderly
PDP	prescription drug plan
PHP	prepaid health plan
PhRMA	Pharmaceutical Research and Manufacturers of America
PMA	premarket approval
PPRC	Physician Payment Review Commission
PPO	preferred provider organization
PPS	prospective payment system
PRO	peer review organization
ProPAC	Prospective Payment Assessment Commission
PSO	patient safety organization
	provider-sponsored organization
PSRO	professional standards review organization
QDWI	Qualified Disabled and Working Individual
QI	Qualifying Individuals
QIO	quality improvement organization
QMB	Qualified Medicare Beneficiary
R&D	research and development
RBRVS	resource-based relative value scale
RCRA	Solid Waste Disposal Act, as amended by the Resource Conservation and Recovery Act
RIN	regulation identifier number
RN	registered nurse
RO	regional office
RPPO	regional preferred-provider organization
ROE	return on equity
RVS	relative value scale
RWCA	Ryan White Care Act
SCHIP	State Children's Health Insurance Program
SDWA	Safe Drinking Water Act
SERC	state emergency response commission

SGR	sustainable growth rate
SHCC	state health coordinating council
SHPDA	state health planning and development agency
SLMB	Specialized Low-Income Medicare Beneficiary
SMI	Supplementary Medical Insurance
SNF	skilled nursing facility
SNP	Special Needs Plan
SPAP	state pharmaceutical assistance program
SSA	Social Security Administration
SSI	Supplemental Security Income
TANF	Temporary Assistance for Needy Families
TB	tuberculosis
TEFRA	Tax Equity and Fiscal Responsibility Act
TSCA	Toxic Substances Control Act
UPMC	University of Pittsburgh Medical Center
USPHS	United States Public Health Service
VA	Veterans Affairs
WHO	World Health Organization

WEBSITES

Administration on Aging	www.aoa.gov
Agency for Healthcare Research and Quality	www.ahrq.gov
Alliance of Independent Academic Medical Centers	www.aiamc.org
Alliance for Retired Americans	www.retiredamericans.org
America's Health Insurance Plans	www.ahip.org
American Academy of Family Physicians	www.aafp.org
American Academy of Pediatrics	www.aap.org
American Association of Homes and Services for the Aging	www.aahsa.org
American Association of Retired Persons	www.aarp.org
American Cancer Society	www.cancer.org
American College of Healthcare Executives	www.ache.org
American College of Physicians	www.acponline.org
American College of Surgeons	www.facs.org
American Dental Association	www.ada.org
American Health Care Association	www.ahca.org
American Heart Association	www.americanheart.org
American Hospital Association	www.aha.org
American Medical Association	www.ama-assn.org
American Medical Women's Association	www.amwa-doc.org
American Nurses Association	www.ana.org
America's Health Insurance Plans	www.ahip.org
Association of American Medical Colleges	www.aamc.org
Association of University Programs in Health Administration	www.aupha.org
Baxter Healthcare Corporation	www.baxter.com
Biotechnology Industry Organization	www.bio.org
Blue Cross Blue Shield Association	www.bluecares.com
Center for Responsive Politics	www.opensecrets.org
Centers for Disease Control and Prevention	www.cdc.gov
Centers for Medicare & Medicaid Services	www.cms.gov
Congressional Budget Office	www.cbo.gov
Congressional Research Service	www.loc.gov/crsinfo

Consumer Product Safety Commission	www.cpsc.gov
Consortium for Citizens with Disabilities	www.c-c-d.org
Council on Governmental Relations	www.cogr.edu
Council of Teaching Hospitals and Health Systems	www.aamc.org/members/coth
Department of Health and Human Services	www.dhhs.gov
Department of Justice	www.usdoj.gov
Department of Veterans Affairs	www.va.gov
Environmental Protection Agency	www.epa.gov
Families U.S.A.	www.familiesusa.org
Federal Budget	www.gpoaccess.gov/ usbudget/browse.html
Federal Election Commission	www.fec.gov
Federal Register	www.gpoaccess.gov/fr
Federation of American Hospital Systems	www.fahs.com
Food and Drug Administration	www.fda.gov
Government Accountability Office	www.gao.gov
GPO Access	www.gpoaccess.gov/ index.html
Healthy People 2010	www.healthypeople.gov
The Henry J. Kaiser Family Foundation	www.kff.org
House Committee on Appropriations	appropriations.house.gov
House Committee on Energy and Commerce	energycommerce.house.gov
House Committee on Ways and Means	waysandmeans.house.gov
House Office of Legislative Counsel	house.gov/legcoun
Institute of Medicine	www.iom.edu
Joint Commission	www.jointcommission.org
Medicare Payment Advisory Commission	www.medpac.gov
National Association for the Advancement of Colored People	www.naacp.org
National Association of Children's Hospitals and Related Institutions	www.childrenshospitals.net
National Committee for Quality Assurance	www.ncqa.org
National Council of Senior Citizens	www.ncscinc.org
National Institute of Biomedical Imaging and Bioengineering	www.nibib.nih.gov

National Institutes of Health — www.nih.gov
National Medical Association — www.natmed.org
National Organization for Women — www.now.org

Occupational Safety and Health Administration — www.osha.gov
Office of Administrative Law Judges — www.epa.gov/oalj
Office of Management and Budget — www.whitehouse.gov/omb
Organization for Economic Co-operation and Development — www.oecd.org

Pharmaceutical Research and Manufacturers of America — www.phrma.org
President's Commission to Strengthen Social Security — www.csss.gov

Social Security Administration — www.ssa.gov
Senate Committee on Appropriations — appropriations.senate.gov
Senate Committee on Finance — finance.senate.gov
Senate Committee on Health, Education, Labor, and Pensions — help.senate.gov
Senate Office of Legislative Counsel — slc.senate.gov/index.htm

U.S. Public Health Service — www.usphs.gov
University of Pittsburgh Medical Center — www.upmc.com

White House — www.whitehouse.gov
Wisconsin Medical Society — www.wismed.org
World Health Organization — www.who.int

PREFACE

Health is a personal, high-priority goal of most people, and the pursuit of health is of growing significance to the U.S. economy and the nation's system of social justice. Thus, health policy has long received attention from state and federal governments. The nation recently entered a period of unprecedented activism in health policy, especially by the federal government. Under the broad rubric of "health reform," President Obama, in his first year in office, has made changing the healthcare system a central feature of his domestic agenda. He believes strongly that improving the accessibility, affordability, and quality of healthcare is critical to achieving social justice goals. In addition, the president sees controlling healthcare costs as vital to the government's fiscal well-being and the nation's prospects for economic growth and stability.

This textbook is written for those interested in health policy, especially the complicated process by which policy is made. Health policy is defined in this textbook as the set of authoritative decisions made within government that pertain to health and the pursuit of health. The phrase *authoritative decisions* refers to decisions that are made anywhere within the three branches of government—at any level of government—and are within the legitimate purview (i.e., within the official roles, responsibilities, and authorities) of those making the decisions.

Through a long history of incremental and modest steps, an extensive array of authoritative decisions that make up health policy has evolved in the United States. Although dramatic developments in health policy, especially the emergence of Medicare and Medicaid in 1965, and, now, the promise of significant reforms, have occasionally accelerated this history, health policymaking largely takes the form of slow but persistent evolution and modification.

Health policy's role in the pursuit of health is played out in many arenas, because health is determined by many variables: the physical environment in which people live and work, individuals' biology and behavior, social factors, and access to health services. The effects of health policies can be seen in each of these determinants.

At the federal, state, and local levels, governments formulate, implement, and continually modify health policies in an intricately choreographed policymaking process. The purpose of this book is to provide a comprehensive model of this process. An understanding of it is essential to policy competence. For typical health professionals, this topic is at most a secondary interest. However, a sufficient understanding of policymaking will permit people to effectively analyze the public policy environment that affects them and their work and to exert some influence in that environment. This understanding is an increasingly important attribute for those whose professional lives are devoted to the pursuit of better health for society.

I first developed the model of the health policymaking process presented in this book for the benefit of my students, and I have continued to refine it. The usefulness of the model as a framework for students' understanding of the extraordinarily complicated process of health policymaking stimulated me to present it to a broader audience. The result was the first edition of this book. Now in its fifth edition, the book has been and will continue to be used in health policy courses to provide students with an overview of the policymaking process. The model puts the various aspects of policymaking in perspective and serves as a foundation on which students can build a more detailed understanding of the process and how it is related to decisions that affect them and their patients, clients, and customers.

The structure of this textbook largely reflects the model of the policymaking process. Following definitions of health and of health policy in Chapter 1, Chapter 2 lays out the context (the political marketplace) and presents the model. Chapters 3 through 7 describe in detail specific aspects of the policymaking process as outlined in the model. Chapters 3 and 4 cover the agenda-setting and legislation-development aspects of policy formulation, respectively. Chapters 5 and 6 cover the rulemaking and operation aspects of policy implementation, respectively. Chapter 7 addresses policy modification, reflecting the fact that all policies are subject to modification. Chapter 8 is devoted to the development of competence in policymaking. This chapter helps readers develop the dual abilities of analyzing the public policy environment of a health-related organization or interest group and exerting influence in this environment. Competence in these activities is increasingly essential for anyone involved professionally in the pursuit of health.

The book includes 30 appendixes, all of which are intended to enrich the reader's learning experience. Appendixes 1 and 2 provide overviews of Medicare and Medicaid, reflecting the importance of these health policies. Appendix 3 lists chronologically the United States' most important federal laws pertaining to health. In addition to providing synopses of these laws, the chronology illustrates several important characteristics of the nation's health policy. The list clearly shows, for example, that the vast majority of health policies are but modifications of or amendments to previously enacted laws; incrementalism has indeed been a feature of the development of American health policy. Reforms currently underway, while based on significant pieces of legislation will continue the pattern of incrementalism as they evolve. The list of policies in Appendix 3 also shows that health policy mirrors the determinants of health. There are policies that address the environments in which people live, their lifestyles, and their genetics, and there are policies related to the provision of and payment for health services. The remaining appendixes, referred to throughout the book, present excerpts from congressional testimony, examples of rules or proposed rules issued by implementing agencies, and reprints of illustrative letters, executive orders, and other documents that illustrate important aspects of the policymaking process. The intent is to enliven the text and to provide useful and illustrative examples.

Instructor's Resources

An Instructor's Manual is available for instructors who adopt this book. It can be obtained through the Health Administration Press website. For access information, please e-mail hap1@ache.org.

ACKNOWLEDGMENTS

I wish to acknowledge the contributions of several people to this revised book and to thank them for their help. Linda Kalcevic provided superb editorial assistance throughout the revision. Mark Nordenberg, Arthur Levine, Donald Burke, and Judith Lave provided a professional environment conducive to and supportive of scholarship. I have enjoyed a professional home at the University of Pittsburgh for more than 30 years.

I thank Janet Davis, Dojna Shearer, and the rest of the team at Health Administration Press for their professionalism in bringing this book to fruition.

Most of all, however, I want to thank Carolyn Longest. Sharing my life with her continues to make many things possible for me and to make doing them worthwhile.

Beaufort B. Longest, Jr.
Pittsburgh, PA

HEALTH AND HEALTH POLICY

Health and its pursuit are woven tightly into the social and economic fabric of every industrialized nation. Health is essential not only to the physical and mental well-being of people, but also to nations' economies. The United States is expected to spend more than $2.6 trillion in pursuit of health in 2010, which represents 17.7 percent of the nation's gross domestic product (GDP), and to spend more than $4.3 trillion annually, or 20.3 percent of GDP, by 2018 (Centers for Medicare & Medicaid Services 2009d). Thus, it is not surprising that government at all levels is keenly interested in health and how it is pursued. This book explores public policymaking—the intricate process through which government influences the pursuit of health. The primary focus is on the policymaking process at the federal level, although much of the information also applies to state and local government.

This chapter discusses the basic definitions of health and health policy and their relationship to each other. Chapter 2 outlines and describes a model of the public policymaking process and specifically applies this model to health policymaking. Subsequent chapters cover in detail the various interconnected parts of the model.

Health Defined

Health is universally important. In 1948, the World Health Organization (WHO; www.who.int) defined health as the "state of complete physical, mental, and social well-being, and not merely the absence of disease or infirmity." Of course, other definitions of health can be found, including "a dynamic state of well-being characterized by a physical and mental potential, which satisfies the demands of life commensurate with age, culture, and personal responsibility" (Bircher 2005). Rodolfo Saracci (1997) defined health as "a condition of well-being, free of disease or infirmity, and a basic and universal human right." David Byrne (2004), who at the time was European commissioner for health and consumer protection, more recently provided a definition with an important expansion. He views good health as "a state of physical and mental well-being necessary to live a meaningful, pleasant, and productive life. Good health is also an integral part of thriving modern societies, a cornerstone of well performing economies, and a shared principle of European democracies," a definition which can be extended to all democracies.

In fact, health is a priority in all nations, although the resources available for its pursuit vary widely. Current international health expenditure comparisons for the 30 member countries of the Organisation for Economic Co-operation and Development (OECD), all of which share a commitment to democratic government and market economies, are available at www.oecd.org.

The way a nation defines health reflects its values regarding health, the resources it is prepared to devote to the pursuit of health, and how far it would be willing to go to aid or support the pursuit of health among its citizens. A nation that defines health broadly and in positive terms—as in Byrne's definition—will make significant efforts to help its members attain desired levels of health. The range of possible interventions in any society's pursuit of health is enormous, because human health is a function of many variables—or, as they are often called, health determinants.

Health Determinants

For individuals and for a population, health determinants include the physical environments in which people live and work, people's behaviors, their biology (genetic makeup, family history, and acquired physical and mental health problems), social factors (including economic circumstances; socioeconomic position; income distribution; discrimination based on such factors as race/ethnicity, gender, and sexual orientation; and the availability of social networks or social support), and their access to health services (Blum 1983; Evans, Barer, and Marmor 1994; Berkman and Kawachi 2000).

The report *Healthy People 2010* (www.healthypeople.gov), which is currently being revised and updated to *Healthy People 2020*, details comprehensive national health promotion and disease prevention agendas. The following list of health determinants is adapted from its identification and definition of determinants (U.S. Department of Health and Human Services 2000):

- *Biology* refers to the individual's genetic makeup (those factors with which he or she is born), family history (which may suggest risk for disease), and physical and mental health problems acquired during life. Aging, diet, physical activity, smoking, stress, alcohol or illicit drug abuse, injury or violence, or an infectious or toxic agent may result in illness or disability and can produce a "new" biology for the individual.
- *Behaviors* are individual responses or reactions to internal stimuli and external conditions. Behaviors can have a reciprocal relationship with biology; in other words, each can affect the other. For example, smoking (behavior) can alter cells in the lung and result in shortness of breath, emphysema, or cancer (biology), which then may lead an individual to stop smoking (behavior). Similarly, a family history that

includes heart disease (biology) may motivate an individual to develop good eating habits, avoid tobacco, and maintain an active lifestyle (behaviors), which may prevent his or her own development of heart disease (biology).

An individual's choices and social and physical environments can shape his or her behaviors. The social and physical environments include all factors that affect the individual's life—positively or negatively— many of which may be out of his or her immediate or direct control.

- *Social environment* includes interactions with family, friends, coworkers, and others in the community. It encompasses social institutions, such as law enforcement, the workplace, places of worship, and schools. Housing, public transportation, and the presence or absence of violence in the community are components of the social environment. The social environment has a profound effect on individual and community health and is unique for each individual because of cultural customs, language, and personal, religious, or spiritual beliefs. At the same time, individuals and their behaviors contribute to the quality of the social environment.

- *Physical environment* can be thought of as that which can be seen, touched, heard, smelled, and tasted. However, it also contains less tangible elements, such as radiation and ozone. The physical environment can harm individual and community health, especially through exposure to toxic substances, irritants, infectious agents, and physical hazards in homes, schools, and work sites. The physical environment can also promote good health, for example, by providing clean and safe places for people to work, exercise, and play.

- *Policies and interventions* can have a powerful and positive effect on individual and community health. Examples include health promotion campaigns to prevent smoking; policies mandating child restraints and safety belt use in automobiles; disease prevention services, such as immunization of children, adolescents, and adults; and clinical services, such as enhanced mental healthcare. Policies and interventions that promote individual and community health may be implemented by agencies, such as those that oversee transportation, education, energy, housing, labor, and justice, or through places of worship, community-based organizations, civic groups, and businesses.

- *Quality health services* can be vital to the health of individuals and communities. Expanding access to services could eliminate health disparities and increase the quality of life and life expectancy of all people living in the United States. Health services in the broadest sense include not only those received from health services providers but also health information and services received from other venues in the community.

People vary along many dimensions, including their health and health-related needs. The citizenry of the United States is remarkably diverse, varying by age, gender, race/ethnicity, and other factors. Current census data puts the U.S. population at approximately 300 million people; 12.4 percent of them are over 65 years old. By 2020, about 55 million will be older than 65 and about 23 million will be older than 75. Persons of Hispanic or Latino origin make up about 14.8 percent of the population and African Americans constitute approximately 12.8 percent of the population (U.S. Census Bureau 2009). These demographics are important when considering health and its pursuit.

Older people consume relatively more health services, and their health-related needs differ from those of younger people. Older people are more likely to consume long-term-care services and community-based services intended to help them cope with various limitations in the activities of daily living.

African Americans and people of Hispanic or Latino origin are disproportionately underserved for health services and underrepresented in all health professions. They experience discrimination that affects their health and continuing disparities in the burden of illness and death (Krieger 2000; James et al. 2007). "Healthcare disparities" and "health disparities," although related, are not the same. Healthcare disparities refer to differences in such variables as access, insurance coverage, and quality of services received. Health disparities occur when one population group experiences higher burdens of illness, injury, death, or disability than another group.

In recent years, policymakers have paid greater attention to racial/ethnic disparities in care with notable progress. Congress legislatively mandated the Institute of Medicine (IOM; www.iom.edu) to study healthcare disparities and established the National Center on Minority Health and Health Disparities at the National Institutes of Health. Congress also required the Department of Health and Human Services (DHHS; www.dhhs.gov) to report annually, starting in 2003, on the nation's progress in reducing healthcare and health disparities (U.S. Department of Health and Human Services 2008). These steps have established the foundation for better addressing disparities in health and healthcare (James et al. 2007).

The IOM (2002c) study's report, *Unequal Treatment: Confronting Racial and Ethnic Disparities in Health Care*, called for a multilevel strategy to address potential causes of racial/ethnic healthcare disparities, including

- raising public and provider awareness of racial/ethnic disparities in healthcare,
- expanding health insurance coverage,
- improving the capacity and quantity of providers in underserved communities, and
- increasing understanding of the causes and interventions to reduce disparities.

Although the population is diverse, the values that directly affect the basic approach to healthcare in the United States are homogeneous. Many Americans place a high value on individual autonomy, self-determination, and personal privacy and maintain a widespread, although not universal, commitment to justice. Other societal characteristics that have influenced the pursuit of health in the United States include a deep-seated belief in the potential of technological rescue and, although this may be changing, an obsession with prolonging life regardless of the costs. These values shape the private and public sectors' efforts related to health, including the elaboration of public policies germane to health and its pursuit.

Health Policy Defined

Health policy is but a particular version of public policy. There are many definitions of public policy and no universal agreement on which is best. For example, B. Guy Peters (2003) defines public policy as the "sum of government activities, whether acting directly or through agents, as it has an influence on the life of citizens." Thomas A. Birkland (2001, 132) defines it as "a statement by government of what it intends to do or not to do, such as a law, regulation, ruling, decision, or order, or a combination of these." Charles Cochran and Eloise Malone (1999) propose yet another definition: "political decisions for implementing programs to achieve societal goals." Drawing on these and many other definitions, we define public policy in this book as *authoritative decisions made in the legislative, executive, or judicial branches of government that are intended to direct or influence the actions, behaviors, or decisions of others.*

The phrase *authoritative decisions* is crucial. It specifies decisions made anywhere within the three branches of government—and at any level of government—that are within the legitimate purview (i.e., within the official roles, responsibilities, and authorities) of those making the decisions. The decision makers can be legislators, executives of government (presidents, governors, mayors), or judges. Part of these roles is the legitimate right—indeed, the responsibility—to make certain decisions. Legislators are entitled to decide on laws, executives to decide on rules to implement laws, and judges to review and interpret decisions made by others. Exhibit 1.1 illustrates these relationships. A useful source of information about all three branches of the federal government and about state and local governments is www.USA.gov.

In the United States, public policies, whether they pertain to health or to defense, education, transportation, or commerce, are made through a dynamic *public policymaking process.* This process, which is modeled in Chapter 2, involves interaction among many participants in three interconnected phases.

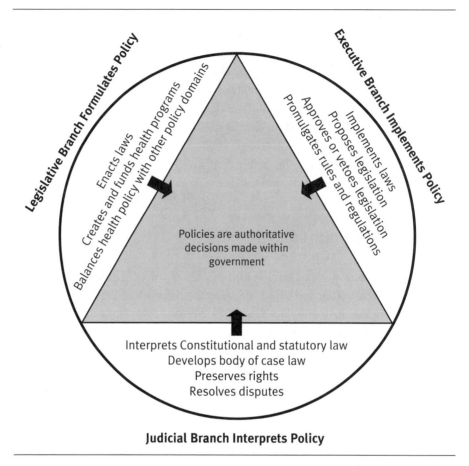

Policies are authoritative
decisions made within
government

Legislative Branch Formulates Policy

Enacts laws
Creates and funds health programs
Balances health policy with other policy domains

Executive Branch Implements Policy

Implements laws
Proposes legislation
Approves or vetoes legislation
Promulgates rules and regulations

Interprets Constitutional and statutory law
Develops body of case law
Preserves rights
Resolves disputes

Judicial Branch Interprets Policy

Public policies that pertain to health or influence the pursuit of health are *health policies*. Health policies are established at federal, state, and local levels of government, although usually for different purposes. Generally, a health policy affects or influences a group or class of individuals (e.g., physicians, the poor, the elderly, children) or a type or category of organization (e.g., medical schools, health plans, integrated healthcare systems, pharmaceutical manufacturers, employers).

At any given time, the entire set of health-related policies made at any level of government constitutes that level's *health policy*. Thus, health policy is a large set of decisions reached through the public policymaking process. Throughout this book, we will say much more about the decisions that form health policy and the process through which these decisions are made. It should be noted at the outset however, that these decisions can be misguided and can have unintended consequences. Some policies fail by worsening the problems they are intended to address or by fostering other problems. For example, through policy changes implemented in 2004, California became the first state to establish nurse staffing ratios in acute care hospitals. The central desired outcome of the policy was improvement in patient outcomes, but there is no evidence that this resulted from the change (Spetz et al. 2009). Although the process of making the decision to impose staffing ratios was contentious, insufficient attention was given to the effect on nurses' wages. In fact, two separate studies designed to estimate the costs of imposing staffing ratios assumed that nurses' wages would be unaffected by the change (Kravitz et al. 2002; Spetz et al. 2000). Implementation of this policy, however, led to significant growth in nurses' wages and in the use of RNs in California hospitals. One study concluded that "wage growth for RNs in California following the implementation of minimum-nurse-staffing legislation outstripped RN wage growth in other states not subject to such legislation" (Mark, Harless, and Spetz 2009). The differences between metropolitan areas inside and outside California were as high as 12 percent. This policy not only failed to achieve its intended purpose, it also generated some surprising and challenging results.

Evidence-based learning can improve policies and minimize such problems, "but learning in complex systems is often weak and slow. Complexity hinders our ability to discover the delayed and distal impacts of interventions, generating unintended 'side effects'" (Sterman 2006, 505). The healthcare system may well be the most complex system in the United States.

Some countries, most notably Canada and Great Britain, have developed expansive, well-integrated policies to fundamentally shape their societies' pursuit of health (Sanders 2002). The United States has a few large health-related policies, including its Medicare program and its regulation of pharmaceuticals, but the U.S. government takes a more incremental or piecemeal approach to health policy. The net result is a very large number of policies, few of which deal with the pursuit of health in a broad, comprehensive, or integrated way. The current efforts to reform the healthcare system may lead to a more comprehensive and integrated health policy. However, as Gawande (2009) has observed, reform has not occurred in one dramatic step in any Western democracy.

Popular opinion holds that the United States is entering a period of major national health reform. The healthcare system is described as "unsustainable" and "flawed." Those making this claim cite uncontrolled costs, variable quality, and millions of uninsured and underinsured people as evidence. Few now contradict these conclusions. However, views on what to do about the problems widely diverge. Furthermore, this is not the first time these problems have stimulated efforts to address them in a comprehensive way. As Hoffman (2009, 1) notes, "The country has been on the verge of national health reform many times before." But the United States has not yet managed the large-scale, comprehensive reforms that would systematically address the cost, quality, and access problems that now characterize its healthcare system.

Policies made through the *public* policymaking process differ from policies established in the *private* sector. Authoritative decisions made in the private sector by executives of healthcare organizations about such issues as their product lines, pricing, and marketing strategies, for example, are private-sector policies. Authoritative decisions made within such organizations as The Joint Commission (www.jointcommission.org), a private accrediting body for health-related organizations, and the National Committee for Quality Assurance (NCQA; www.ncqa.org), a private organization involved in assessing and reporting on the quality of managed care plans, are also private-sector health policies. This book focuses on the public policymaking process and the public-sector health policies that result from this process. Private-sector health policies, however, also play a vital role in the ways society pursues health.

Despite government's substantive role in health policy, which is explored further in subsequent chapters, and its role as a provider of health services in government facilities, most of the resources used in the pursuit of health in the United States are controlled by the private sector. When government is involved in health affairs, it often seeks broader access to health services that are provided predominantly through the private sector. The Medicare and Medicaid programs provide clear examples of this approach. Public dollars purchase services in the private sector for the beneficiaries of these programs. Appendixes 1 and 2, respectively, provide overviews of Medicare and Medicaid. These programs and the policies that guide them are so important to understanding health policy and its effect on health that you may wish to read the overviews now; the information provided will be helpful throughout the book.

Forms of Health Policies

Health policies, which we defined earlier as authoritative decisions, take several basic forms (see Exhibit 1.2). Some policies are decisions made by legislators that are codified in the statutory language of specific pieces of enacted legislation—in other words, laws. Federal public laws are given a number that designates the enacting Congress and the sequence in which the law was enacted. P.L. 89-97, for example, means that this law was enacted by the 89th Congress and was the 97th law passed by that Congress. A briefly annotated chronological list of important federal laws pertaining to health can be found in Appendix 3.

Other policies are the rules and regulations established to implement laws or to operate government and its programs. Still others are the judicial branch's decisions related to health. Examples of health policies include

- the 1965 federal public law P.L. 89-97, which established the Medicare and Medicaid programs;

EXHIBIT 1.2
Forms
of Health
Policies

> Laws
> Rules and Regulations
> Operational Decisions
> Judicial Decisions

- an executive order regarding operation of federally funded health centers;
- a federal court's ruling that an integrated delivery system's acquisition of yet another hospital violates federal antitrust laws;
- a state government's procedures for licensing physicians;
- a county health department's procedures for inspecting restaurants; and
- a city government's ordinance banning smoking in public places within its borders.

Laws

Laws enacted at any level of government are policies. One example of a federal law is the Food and Drug Administration Amendments Act of 2007 (P.L. 110-85), which amended the Federal Food, Drug, and Cosmetic Act to revise and extend the user-fee programs for prescription drugs and medical devices. Another example is the Breast and Cervical Cancer Prevention and Treatment Act of 2000 (P.L. 106-354), which created an optional Medicaid category for low-income women diagnosed with cancer through the Centers for Disease Control and Prevention's (CDC; www.cdc.gov) breast and cervical cancer early detection screening program. State examples include laws that govern the licensure of health-related practitioners and institutions. When laws trigger elaborate efforts and activities aimed at implementing the law, the whole endeavor is called a program. The Medicare program is a federal-level example. Many laws, most of which are amendments to prior laws, govern this vast program.

Appendix 4 provides an example of a complete federal law, the National Institute of Biomedical Imaging and Bioengineering Establishment Act of 2000. This law established the National Institute of Biomedical Imaging and Bioengineering (NIBIB; www.nibib.nih.gov) to accelerate the development and application of biomedical technologies. Electronic versions of this and other federal laws dating back to 1973, the 93rd Congress, can be found at thomas.loc.gov, a website maintained by the Library of Congress that provides access to federal and other legislative information.

Rules and Regulations

Another form policies can take is that of rules and regulations (the terms are used interchangeably in the policy context) established by agencies responsible for implementing laws. The Administrative Procedures Act of 1946 defined "rule" as "the whole or part of an agency statement of general or particular applicability and future effect designed to implement, interpret, or prescribe law," a definition that still stands. Because such rules are authoritative decisions made in the executive branch of government by the organizations and agencies responsible for implementing laws, they fit the definition of public policies. The rules associated with the implementation of complex laws routinely fill hundreds and sometimes thousands of pages. Rulemaking, the processes through which executive branch agencies write the rules to guide law implementation, is an important activity in policymaking and is discussed in detail in Chapter 5.

Rules, in proposed form (for review and comment by those who will be affected by them) and in final form, are published in the *Federal Register* (FR; www.gpoaccess.gov/fr), the official daily publication for proposed and final rules, notices of federal agencies, and executive orders and other presidential documents. The *FR* is published by the Office of the Federal Register, National Archives and Records Administration. Appendix 5 contains the summaries of a proposed rule which would revise parts of the Medicare hospital inpatient prospective payment system and a final rule that modifies and updates certain elements of the Health Insurance Portability and Accountability Act of 1996 (HIPAA). The entire proposed rule and the final rule can be read in the *FR* at www.gpoaccess.gov/fr.

Operational Decisions

When organizations or agencies in the executive branch of any level of government implement laws, they must make operational decisions. These decisions, authoritatively made in the implementing agencies, although different from the formal rules that influence implementation, are policies as well. For example, effectively managing Medicare requires the federal government to undertake a complex and diverse set of management tasks, among them (Gluck and Sorian 2004, 15)

- determining eligibility for Medicare;
- collecting Part B premiums from beneficiaries;
- educating and informing Medicare beneficiaries about their benefits, rights, and options;
- processing and paying Medicare claims;
- implementing Medicare payment policies (i.e., developing and implementing payment methodologies and setting and updating Medicare payment rates)
- administering private Medicare plans;
- selecting and managing Medicare contractors;
- rendering coverage determinations for medical services, procedures, and technologies;

- combating fraud and abuse in Medicare;
- ensuring the quality of services provided to Medicare beneficiaries (i.e., setting standards for healthcare facilities and other providers to participate in Medicare and overseeing quality improvement efforts); and
- supporting Medicare research and demonstration projects.

In carrying out these tasks, the Centers for Medicare & Medicaid Services (CMS; www.cms.gov), the agency responsible for implementing the Medicare and Medicaid programs, must make frequent operational decisions. Again, because they are authoritative, these decisions are policies. Examples of operational decisions can be found in all implementing agencies. For example, the several federal agencies with implementation responsibilities for the Water Quality Improvement Act (P.L. 91-224) establish operational protocols and procedures for dealing with those affected by the provisions of this law. These protocols and procedures are a form of policy because they are authoritative decisions. Appendix 6 provides another example by illustrating ongoing operational decisions made within the federal Food and Drug Administration (FDA; www.fda.gov).

Judicial Decisions

Judicial decisions are another form of policy. An example is the U.S. Supreme Court's ruling in 2000 (by a 5–4 vote) that the FDA cannot regulate tobacco. Another example is the Supreme Court's 2005 decision not to hear an appeal filed by six health insurers in a bid to stop a class-action lawsuit brought by more than 600,000 doctors who claimed the companies underpaid them for treating patients. This decision allowed a lower court's ruling to stand, meaning that a class-action suit could proceed in federal court. A third example is the Supreme Court's 2008 *MetLife v. Glenn* decision regarding how federal courts reviewing claims denials by plan administrators under the Employee Retirement Income Security Act (ERISA) "should take into account the fact that plan administrators (insurers and self-insured plans) face a conflict of interest because they pay claims out of their own pockets and arguably stand to profit by denying claims" (Jost 2008, w430). All three decisions are policies because they are authoritative decisions that direct or influence the actions, behaviors, or decisions of others.

Categories of Health Policies

Another way to consider health policies is to recognize that any type of policy, whether law, rule or regulation, operational decision, or judicial decision, fits into one of several broad categories. Public policies are typically divided into distributive, redistributive, and regulatory categories (Birkland 2001).

Sometimes the distributive and redistributive categories are combined into an allocative category; sometimes the regulatory category is subdivided into competitive regulatory and protective regulatory categories. For our purposes, all of the various forms of health policies fit into two basic categories—allocative or regulatory.

In market economies, such as that of the United States, the presumption is that private markets best determine the production and consumption of goods and services, including health services. Of course, when markets fail, as the financial markets in the United States and worldwide began to do in 2008, government intervention becomes essential. In market economies, government generally intrudes with policies only when private markets fail to achieve desired public objectives. The most credible arguments for policy intervention in the nation's domestic activities begin with the identification of situations in which markets are not functioning properly.

The health sector is especially prone to situations in which markets function poorly. Theoretically perfect (i.e., freely competitive) markets, which do not exist in reality but provide a standard against which real markets can be assessed, require that

- buyers and sellers have sufficient information to make informed decisions,
- a large number of buyers and sellers participate,
- additional sellers can easily enter the market,
- each seller's products or services are satisfactory substitutes for those of their competitors, and
- the quantity of products or services available in the market does not swing the balance of power toward either buyers or sellers.

The markets for health services in the United States violate these requirements. The complexity of health services reduces the consumer's ability to make informed decisions without guidance from the sellers or other advisors. Entry of sellers in the markets for health services is heavily regulated, and widespread insurance coverage affects the decisions of buyers and sellers. These and other factors mean that markets for health services frequently do not function competitively, thus inviting policy intervention.

Furthermore, the potential for private markets on their own to fail to meet public objectives is not limited to production and consumption. For example, markets on their own might not stimulate sufficient socially desirable medical research or the education of enough physicians or nurses without policies that subsidize certain costs associated with these ends. These and similar situations provide the philosophical basis for the establishment of public policies to correct market-related problems or shortcomings.

The nature of the market problems or shortcomings directly shapes the health policies intended to overcome or ameliorate them. Based on their

Appendixes 1 and 2 provide descriptions of the Medicare and Medicaid programs. In addition, the Henry J. Kaiser Foundation publishes useful primers on the Medicare program (www.kff.org/medicare/upload/7615-02.pdf) and the Medicaid program (www.kff.org/medicaid/upload/7334-03.pdf).

primary purposes, health policies fit broadly into allocative or regulatory categories, although the potential for overlap between the two categories is considerable.

Allocative Policies

Allocative policies provide net benefits to some distinct group or class of individuals or organizations at the expense of others to meet public objectives. Such policies are in essence subsidies through which policymakers seek to alter demand for or supply of particular products and services or guarantee certain people access to them. For example, government has heavily subsidized the medical education system on the basis that without subsidies to medical schools, markets would undersupply physicians. Similarly, government subsidized the construction of hospitals for many years on the basis that markets would undersupply hospitals in sparsely populated or low-income areas.

Other subsidies have been used to ensure that certain people have access to health services. The most important examples of such policies, based on the magnitude of expenditures, are the Medicare and Medicaid programs. Medicare expenditures will be approximately $531 billion in 2010 (making up almost 20 percent of the nation's health expenditures) and could reach $884 billion by 2017; Medicaid expenditures will exceed $417 billion in 2010 and could reach $717 billion by 2017 (Centers for Medicare & Medicaid Services 2009).

Federal funding to support access to health services for Native Americans, veterans, and migrant farm workers and state funding for mental institutions are other examples of allocative policies that are intended to help individuals gain access to needed services. Some believe subsidies are reserved for those people who are most impoverished. However, subsidies such as those that support medical education, the Medicare program (the benefits of which are not based primarily on the financial need of the recipients), and the exclusion of employer-provided health insurance benefits from taxable income illustrate that poverty is not necessarily a requirement.

Some of the provisions of the American Recovery and Reinvestment Act of 2009 (P.L. 111-5) provide examples of allocative policy. This law, enacted in response to the global financial crisis that emerged in 2008, contains many health-related subsidies. Exhibit 1.3 lists some examples.

EXHIBIT 1.3 Examples of Health-Related Subsidies Included in the American Recovery and Reinvestment Act of 2009

Continuation of health insurance coverage for unemployed workers	$24.7 billion to provide a 65% federal subsidy for up to 9 months of premiums under the Consolidated Omnibus Budget Reconciliation Act. The subsidy will help workers who lose their jobs to continue coverage for themselves and their families.
Health Resources and Services Administration	$2.5 billion, including $1.5 billion for construction, equipment, and health information technology at community health centers; $500 million for services at these centers; $300 million for the National Health Service Corps (NHSC); and $200 million for other health professions training programs.
Medicare	$338 million for payments to teaching hospitals, hospice programs, and long-term care hospitals.
Medicaid and other state health programs	$87 billion for additional federal matching payments for state Medicaid programs for a 27-month period that began October 1, 2008, and $3.2 billion for additional state fiscal relief related to Medicaid and other health programs.
Prevention and wellness	$1 billion, including $650 million for clinical and community-based prevention activities that will address rates of chronic diseases, as determined by the secretary of health and human services; $300 million to the Centers for Disease Control and Prevention for immunizations for low-income children and adults; and $50 million to states to reduce health care–associated infections.

SOURCE: Reprinted with permission from Steinbrook (2009).

Regulatory Policies

Policies designed to influence the actions, behaviors, and decisions of others by directive are regulatory policies. All levels of government establish regulatory policies. As with allocative policies, government establishes such policies to ensure that public objectives are met. The five basic categories of regulatory health policies are

1. market-entry restrictions,
2. rate- or price-setting controls on health services providers,
3. quality controls on the provision of health services,

4. market-preserving controls, and

5. social regulation.

The first four categories are variations of economic regulation; the fifth seeks to achieve such socially desired ends as safe workplaces, nondiscriminatory provision of health services, and reduction in the negative externalities (side effects) associated with the production or consumption of products and services.

Market-entry-restricting regulations include licensing of health-related practitioners and organizations. Planning programs, through which preapproval for new capital projects by health services providers must be obtained, are also market-entry-restricting regulations.

Although price-setting regulation is generally out of favor, some aspects of the pursuit of health are subject to price regulations. The federal government's control of the rates at which it reimburses hospitals for care provided to Medicare patients and its establishment of a fee schedule for reimbursing physicians who care for Medicare patients are examples.

A third class of regulations are those intended to ensure that health services providers adhere to acceptable levels of quality in the services they provide and that producers of health-related products such as imaging equipment and pharmaceuticals meet safety and efficacy standards. For example, the FDA is charged with ensuring that new pharmaceuticals meet these standards. In addition, the Medical Devices Amendments (P.L. 94-295) to the Food, Drug and Cosmetic Act (P.L. 75-717) placed all medical devices under a comprehensive regulatory framework administered by FDA.

Because the markets for health services do not behave in truly competitive ways, government establishes and enforces rules of conduct for participants. These rules form a fourth class of regulation, market-preserving controls. Antitrust laws—such as the Sherman Antitrust Act, the Clayton Act, and the Robinson-Patman Act—which are intended to maintain conditions that permit markets to work well and fairly, are good examples of this type of regulation.

These four classes of regulations are all variations of economic regulation. The primary purpose of social regulation, the fifth class, is to achieve such socially desirable outcomes as workplace safety and fair employment practices and to reduce such socially undesirable outcomes as environmental pollution and the spread of sexually transmitted diseases. Social regulation usually has an economic effect, but this is not the primary purpose. Federal and state laws pertaining to environmental protection, disposal of medical wastes, childhood immunization, and the mandatory reporting of communicable diseases are examples of social regulations at work in the pursuit of health.

Whether public policies take the form of laws, rules and regulations, operational decisions, or judicial decisions, they are created through a complex process, which is described in Chapter 2. The policymaking model, within which the authoritative decisions that form policies are made, applies at federal and state levels of government, and elements of the model apply at all levels of government. Before examining this model, however, it will be useful to consider how health policies affect health and its pursuit.

The Impact of Health Policy on Health Determinants and Health

From government's perspective, the central purpose of health policy is to enhance health or facilitate its pursuit. Of course, other purposes may be served through specific health policies, including economic advantages for certain individuals and organizations. But the defining purpose of health policy, so far as government is concerned, is to support the people in their quest for health.

Health policies affect health through an intervening set of variables, or health determinants (see Exhibit 1.4). Health determinants, in turn, directly affect health. When examining how it can affect health, consider the role of health policy in the following health determinants:

- physical environments in which people live and work
- behavioral choices and biology
- social factors that affect health, including economic circumstances; socioeconomic position; income distribution within the society; discrimination based on factors such as race/ethnicity, gender, or sexual orientation; and the availability of social networks or social support
- availability of and access to health services

Health Policies and Physical Environments
When people are exposed to harmful agents such as asbestos, dioxin, excessive noise, ionizing radiation, or toxic chemical and biological substances, their health is directly affected. Exposure risks pervade the physical environments of many people. Some of the exposure is through such agents as synthetic compounds that are by-products of technological growth and development. Some exposure is through wastes that result from the manufacture, use, and disposal of a vast range of products. And some of the exposure is through naturally

EXHIBIT 1.4 The Impact of Policy on Health Determinants and Health

occurring agents such as carcinogenic ultraviolet radiation from the sun or naturally occurring radon gas in the soil.

The hazardous effects of naturally occurring agents are often exacerbated by combination with agents introduced by human activities. For example, before its ban, the widespread use of freon in air conditioning systems and other chlorofluorocarbons in aerosolized products reduced the protective ozone layer in Earth's upper atmosphere. This allowed an increased level of ultraviolet radiation from the sun to penetrate to Earth's surface. Similarly, exposure to naturally occurring radon appears to act synergistically with cigarette smoke as a carcinogen.

The health effects of exposure to hazardous agents, whether natural or manmade, are well understood. Air, polluted by certain agents, has a direct, measurable effect on such diseases as asthma, emphysema, and lung cancer and aggravates cardiovascular disease. Asbestos, which can still be found in buildings constructed before it was banned, causes pulmonary disease. Lead-based paint, when ingested, causes permanent neurological damage in infants and young children. This paint is still found in older buildings and is especially concentrated in poorer urban communities.

Over many decades, government has made efforts to exorcise environmental health hazards through public policies. Examples of federal policies include the Clean Air Act (P.L. 88-206), the Flammable Fabrics Act (P.L. 90-189), the Occupational Safety and Health Act (P.L. 91-596), the Consumer Product Safety Act (P.L. 92-573), the Noise Control Act (P.L. 92-574), and the Safe Drinking Water Act (P.L. 93-523).

Health policies that mitigate environmental hazards or take advantage of positive environmental conditions are important aspects of any society's ability to help its members achieve better health. Other determinants provide additional avenues to improved health.

Health Policies and Human Behavior and Biology

As Rene Dubos (1959, 110) observed a half-century ago, "To ward off disease or recover health, men [as well as women and children] as a rule find it easier to depend on the healers than to attempt the more difficult task of living wisely." The price of this attitude is partially reflected in the major causes of death in the United States. Ranked from highest to lowest by the Centers for Disease Control and Prevention (2006), the ten leading causes are heart disease, cancer, stroke, chronic lower respiratory diseases, accidents, diabetes, Alzheimer's disease, influenza/pneumonia, nephritis/nephritic syndrome/ nephrosis, and septicemia.

Behaviors—including choices about the use of tobacco and alcohol, diet and exercise, illicit drug use, sexual behavior, and violence—and genetic predispositions influence many of these causes of death and help explain the pattern. Furthermore, underlying the behavioral factors are such root factors as stress, depression, and feelings of anger, hopelessness, and emptiness, which are exacerbated by economic and social conditions. In short, behaviors are heavily reflected in the diseases that kill and debilitate Americans.

Changes in behaviors can change the pattern of causes of death. The death rate from heart disease, for example, has declined dramatically in recent decades. Although aggressive early treatment has played a role in reducing this rate, better control of several behavioral risk factors—including cigarette smoking, elevated blood pressure, elevated levels of cholesterol, poor diet, lack of exercise, and elevated stress—explain much of the decline. Even with this impressive improvement, however, heart disease remains the most common cause of death and will continue to be a significant cause. Cancer death rates continue to grow, with much of the increase attributable to lung cancer, which is strongly correlated with behavior. Appendix 7 describes the extent of state, commonwealth, and local municipality laws intended to restrict where smoking is allowed.

Health Policies and Social Factors

In addition to their physical environments, behaviors, and genetics, a number of social factors can affect health. Chronic unemployment, the absence of a supportive family structure, poverty, homelessness, and discrimination, among other social factors, affect people's health as surely—and often as dramatically—as harmful viruses or carcinogens.

People who live in poverty experience measurably worse health status (more frequent and more severe health problems) than those who are more affluent (Do and Finch 2008; Phipps 2003). African Americans, Hispanics, and Native Americans, who are disproportionately represented below the poverty line, experience worse health than the white majority (National Center for Health Statistics 2007).

The poor also typically obtain their health services in a different manner. Instead of receiving care that is coordinated, continuing, and comprehensive, the poor are far more likely to receive a patchwork of services, often provided by public hospitals, clinics, and local health departments. In addition, poor people are more often treated episodically, with one provider intervening in one episode of illness and another provider handling the next episode.

The effect of economic conditions on the health of children is especially dramatic (Henry J. Kaiser Family Foundation 2009a; Wood 2003). Impoverished children, on average, have lower birth weights and more conditions that limit school activity than other children. These children are more likely to become ill and to have more serious illnesses than other children because of increased exposure to harmful environments, inadequate preventive services, and limited access to health services.

Economic circumstances are part of a larger set of social factors that unequally affect people in their quest for health. Living in an inner-city or rural setting often increases the challenge of finding health services, because many such locations have too few providers. Lack of adequate information about health and health services is a significant disadvantage, one compounded by language barriers, functional illiteracy, or marginal mental retardation. Cultural backgrounds and ties, especially among many Native Americans, Latinos, and Asian immigrants, for all the support they can provide, can also create a formidable barrier between people and the mainline healthcare system.

An example of health policy intended to address social factors is P.L. 105-33, the Balanced Budget Act of 1997. This policy provided for expanded health insurance coverage of children by establishing the State Children's Health Insurance Program (SCHIP). In 2009, President Obama signed a renewal of this program into law as the Children's Health Insurance Program Reauthorization Act of 2009 (P.L. 111-3). The reauthorization significantly expands coverage to include an additional 4 million children and, for the first time, allows the spending of federal money to cover children and pregnant women who are legal immigrants. This policy, with many others, has addressed some of the social factors that affect health. However, a great deal remains to be done.

Health Policies and Health Services

As shown in Exhibit 1.4, another important determinant of health is availability of and access to health services, which are any of a host of "specific activities undertaken to maintain or improve health or to prevent decrements of health" (Longest and Darr 2008, 232). Health services can be preventive (e.g., blood pressure screening, mammography), acute (e.g., surgical procedures, antibiotics to fight an infection), chronic (e.g., control of diabetes or hypertension), restorative (e.g., physical rehabilitation of a stroke or trauma patient), or palliative (e.g., pain relief or comfort in terminal stages of disease).

The production and distribution of health services require a vast set of resources, including money, human resources, and technology, all of which are heavily influenced by health policies. The organizations and networks that transform these resources into health services and distribute them to consumers are collectively known as the healthcare system. The system itself is also influenced by health policies. Health policies determine the nature of health services through their effect on the resources required to produce the services and on the healthcare system through which the services are organized, delivered, and paid for. Policies' effect on the resources used to provide health services are examined in the next sections.

Money

As Exhibit 1.5 shows, growth of national health expenditures is expected to continue. They may exceed $4.3 trillion by 2018. These expenditures, representing about 17.6 percent of the GDP in 2009, could rise to more than 20 percent of the GDP by 2018 (Sisko et al. 2009). The United States spends more on health than does any other country, in total and on a per capita basis (Organisation for Economic Cooperation and Development 2008; Henry J. Kaiser Family

EXHIBIT 1.5 National Health Expenditures (NHE), Aggregate and per Capita Amounts, and Share of Gross Domestic Product (GDP) for Selected Calendar Years 1993–2018

Spending category	1993	2006	2007	2008[a]	2009[a]	2013[a]	2018[a]
NHE (billions)	$912.5	$2,112.7	$2,241.2	$2,378.6	$2,509.5	$3,110.9	$4,353.2
Health services and supplies	853.1	1,976.1	2,098.1	2,226.6	2,350.1	2,915.8	4,086.2
Personal health care	773.6	1,765.5	1,878.3	1,992.6	2,099.0	2,598.3	3,639.2
Hospital care	317.1	649.3	696.5	746.5	789.4	992.6	1,374.1
Professional services	280.8	661.4	702.1	744.7	785.8	953.7	1,338.1
Physician and clinical services	201.2	449.7	478.8	508.5	539.1	636.1	865.2
Other prof. services	24.5	58.7	62.0	65.8	68.7	84.1	116.8
Dental services	38.9	90.5	95.2	99.9	101.9	121.4	161.4
Other PHC	16.2	62.5	66.2	70.5	76.1	112.0	194.7
Nursing home and home health care	87.3	178.4	190.4	201.8	213.6	269.8	375.8
Home health care[b]	21.9	53.0	59.0	64.4	69.7	92.4	134.9
Nursing home care[b]	65.4	125.4	131.3	137.4	143.9	177.4	240.9
Retail outlet sales of medical products	88.4	276.4	289.3	299.6	310.2	382.1	551.3
Prescription drugs	51.0	216.8	227.5	235.4	244.8	307.8	453.7
Durable medical equipment	13.5	24.2	24.5	25.2	25.2	29.0	38.1
Nondurable medical products	23.9	35.3	37.4	39.0	40.2	45.4	59.5

Foundation 2009b). Other countries have been far more likely to adopt policies such as global budgets for their healthcare systems or to impose restrictive limitations on the supplies of health services (Anderson et al. 2005; Reinhardt, Hussey, and Anderson 2004).

Current health expenditures and projected future increases have significant implications. The increasing expenditures, in part, reflect higher prices.

EXHIBIT 1.5 (Continued)

Spending category	1993	2006	2007	2008[a]	2009[a]	2013[a]	2018[a]
Program admin. and net cost of private health insurance	52.8	150.4	155.7	165.6	178.8	225.2	315.0
Government public health activities	26.8	60.2	64.1	68.3	72.3	92.3	132.0
Investment	59.3	136.6	143.1	152.0	159.4	195.2	267.0
Research[c]	16.4	41.3	42.4	43.6	44.5	52.2	70.2
Structures and equipment	42.9	95.2	100.7	108.4	114.9	142.9	196.8
NHE per capita	$3,468.3	$7,062.3	$7,420.8	$7,804.3	$8,160.3	$9,767.3	$13,100.3
Population (millions)	263.1	299.1	302.0	304.8	307.5	318.5	332.3
GDP, billions of dollars	$6,657.4	$13,178.4	$13,807.5	$14,290.8	$14,262.2	$17,072.6	$21,479.9
NHE as percent of GDP	13.7%	16.0%	16.2%	16.6%	17.6%	18.2%	20.3%

SOURCES: Centers for Medicare and Medicaid Services, Office of the Actuary, National Health Statistics Group; and U.S. Department of Commerce, Bureau of Economic Analysis and Bureau of the Census.

NOTES: Numbers might not add to totals because of rounding; 1993 marks the beginning of the shift to managed care.
[a]Projected.
[b]Freestanding facilities only. Additional services are provided in hospital-based facilities and counted as hospital care.
[c]Research and development expenditures of drug companies and other manufacturers and providers or medical equipment and supplies are excluded from "research expenditures" but are included in the expenditure class in which the product falls.

These higher prices have reduced access to health services by making it more difficult for many people to purchase the services or the insurance needed to cover those services. Increases in health expenditures have absorbed much of the growth of many workers' real compensation, meaning that as employers spend more to provide health insurance benefits, wages decrease. Some employers have dropped health insurance altogether. With the nation working its way through the worst economic downturn since the Great Depression, declining employment is dramatically affecting the number of uninsured. A 1 percent rise in unemployment has been estimated to increase the number of uninsured by 1.1 million and to drive another 1 million people onto the Medicaid rolls (Henry J. Kaiser Family Foundation 2009c). The number of people without health insurance in the United States grew from about 40 million in

2000 to about 46 million, or 18 percent of the population under the age of 65, in 2007 (DeNavas-Walt, Proctor, and Smith 2008).

Because federal and state governments now spend so much on health, rising health expenditures have put substantial pressures on their budgets. As health expenditures consume a growing portion of government resources, it becomes more difficult for government to support other priorities such as education or homeland security (Congressional Budget Office 2009). Appendix 8 reproduces a brief perspective on this issue from the director of the Congressional Budget Office (CBO; www.cbo.gov).

Human Resources   The talents and abilities of a large and diverse workforce make up another basic resource used to provide health services. Human resources are directly affected by health policies. There are more than 14 million healthcare workers in the United States, the largest number in any industry, and 7 of the 20 occupations projected to grow the fastest over the next several years are concentrated in healthcare. Healthcare will generate about 3 million new jobs between 2006 and 2016, again leading all industries (U.S. Department of Labor 2009). The effect of policies on health-related human resources can be seen clearly in the nation's supply of physicians and registered nurses.

There are about 817,000 active physicians in the United States. Slightly more than one third are generalists (family practice, general pediatrics, or general internal medicine); the remaining two thirds are specialists (National Center for Health Workforce Analysis 2006). The number of physicians doubled from the mid-1960s to the mid-1990s. To a considerable extent, this was due to federal policies intended to increase their supply, including the Health Professions Educational Assistance Act of 1963 (P.L. 88-129) and its amendments of 1965, 1968, and 1971.

Studies by the National Center for Health Workforce Analysis demonstrate a serious shortage in the supply of RNs and project the shortage to increase in future years. As Exhibit 1.6 shows, "by 2020 the national shortage is projected to increase to more than 1 million FTE RNs if current trends continue, suggesting that only 64 percent of projected demand will be met" (National Center for Health Workforce Analysis 2009, 26).

Concerted efforts have and will continue to be made to alleviate the shortage. The main federal response to date is the Nurse Reinvestment Act of 2002 (PL 107-205), which authorized the following provisions:

- loan repayment programs and scholarships for nursing students
- public service announcements to encourage more people to enter the nursing profession
- career ladder programs for those who wish to advance within the profession
- best practice grants for nursing administration

	2005	*2010*	*2015*	*2020*
Supply	1,942,500	1,941,200	1,886,100	1,808,000
Demand	2,161,300	2,347,000	2,569,800	2,824,900
Shortage	(218,800)	(405,800)	(683,700)	(1,016,900)
Supply ÷ Demand	90%	83%	73%	64%
Demand shortfall	10%	17%	27%	36%

EXHIBIT 1.6
Projected U.S. FTE RN Supply, Demand, and Shortages, 2005–2020

SOURCE: Adapted from National Center for Health Workforce Analysis (2009, 27).

- long-term care training grants to develop and incorporate gerontology curriculum into nursing programs
- a fast-track faculty loan repayment program for nursing students who agree to teach at a school of nursing

In addition to federal policy, some states have enacted laws requiring minimum patient-to-nurse staffing ratios and prohibiting mandatory overtime to ensure safer working conditions for nurses. Such conditions help retain current nurses and attract those who left nursing careers back to the workforce. As federal and state policymakers continue to address this problem, their efforts to establish effective policies will require consideration of the following questions (Henry J. Kaiser Family Foundation 2008):

- How and why is this current nursing shortage different from previous shortages? Do the policy options address the current problems, or are they responding to historical problems?
- How does the nursing shortage affect the quality of patient care?
- Is ensuring an adequate nurse workforce a federal responsibility? What is the correlation, if any, between the availability of nurses in the health workforce and the nature and funding of federal discretionary nursing programs?
- What other federal policies affect the demand for and supply of nurses?
- What is the nature of states' "safe staffing" legislation? Why are states addressing the nursing shortage this way? Does this policy have potential unintended consequences? Will an inability to find enough qualified RNs force hospitals to eliminate beds and reduce access to care?
- Do state nursing policies affect the supply of nurses from state to state? If so, how?

Technology

A third type of resource that health policies significantly affect is health-related technology (Longest and Darr 2008). Broadly defined, technology is the application of science to the pursuit of health. Technological advances result in better pharmaceuticals, devices, and procedures. A major influence on the pursuit of health in the United States, technology has helped eradicate some diseases and has greatly improved diagnoses and treatment for others. Diseases that once were not even diagnosed are now routinely and effectively treated. Advancing technology has brought medical science to the early stages of understanding disease at the molecular level and intervening in diseases at the genetic level.

The United States produces and consumes more health-related technology than does any other nation, and it spends far more on it. It has provided technology with a uniquely favorable economic and political environment. As a result, health-related technology is widely available in the United States.

Health policy provides funding for the research and development (R&D) that leads to new technology, although the private sector also pays for a great deal of R&D. The United States has a long history of support for the development of health-related technology through policies that support biomedical research and encourage private investment in such research. The National Institutes of Health (NIH; www.nih.gov) invests more than $29 billion annually in medical research. About 80 percent of the NIH's funding is awarded through almost 50,000 competitive grants to more than 325,000 researchers at over 3,000 universities, medical schools, and other research institutions in every state and around the world. About 10 percent of the NIH's budget supports projects conducted by nearly 6,000 scientists in its own laboratories, most of which are on the NIH campus in Bethesda, Maryland (National Institutes of Health 2009).

Encouraged by policies that permit firms to recoup their investments, private industry also spends heavily on biomedical R&D. In fact, the Pharmaceutical Research and Manufacturers of America (PhRMA; www.phrma.org), which represents the nation's leading pharmaceutical research and biotechnology companies, reports that industry-wide research investment was $58.8 billion in 2007 (Pharmaceutical Research and Manufacturers of America 2009).

Health policy also affects technology through the application of regulatory policies, such as those promulgated by the FDA to ensure technology's safety and efficacy. The FDA is responsible for protecting the public health by assuring the safety, efficacy, and security of human and veterinary drugs, biological products, medical devices, the food supply, cosmetics, and products that emit radiation (U.S. Food and Drug Administration 2009). The following are laws the FDA is responsible for, or partially responsible for, implementing, including writing rules for implementation:

- Food, Drug, and Cosmetic Act of 1938 (P.L. 75-717)
- Infant Formula Act of 1980 (P.L. 96-359)
- Orphan Drug Act of 1983 (P.L. 97-414)
- Federal Anti-Tampering Act of 1983 (P.L. 98-127)
- Drug Price Competition and Patent Term Restoration Act of 1984 (P.L. 98-417)

- Prescription Drug Marketing Act of 1987 (P.L. 100-293)
- Generic Animal Drug and Patent Term Restoration Act of 1988 (P.L. 100-670)
- Sanitary Food Transportation Act of 1990 (P.L. 101-500)
- Nutrition Labeling and Education Act of 1990 (PL 101-535)
- Safe Medical Devices Act of 1990 (P.L. 101-629)
- Medical Device Amendments of 1992 (P.L. 102-300)
- Prescription Drug Amendments of 1992 (PL 102-353)
- Mammography Quality Standards Act (MQSA) of 1992 (P.L. 102-539)
- Prescription Drug User Fee Act (PDUFA) of 1992 (P.L. 102-571)
- Animal Medicinal Drug Use Clarification Act (AMDUCA) of 1994 (P.L. 103-396)
- Dietary Supplement Health and Education Act of 1994 (P.L. 103-417)
- FDA Export Reform and Enhancement Act of 1996 (P.L. 104-134)
- Food Quality Protection Act of 1996 (P.L. 104-170)
- Animal Drug Availability Act of 1996 (P.L. 104-250)
- Food and Drug Administration Modernization Act (FDAMA) of 1997 (P.L. 105-115)
- Best Pharmaceuticals for Children Act of 2002 (P.L. 107-109)
- Medical Device User Fee and Modernization Act (MDUFMA) of 2002 (P.L. 107-250)
- Public Health Security and Bioterrorism Preparedness and Response Act of 2002 (P.L. 107-188)
- Animal Drug User Fee Act of 2003 (P.L. 108-130)
- Pediatric Research Equity Act of 2003 (P.L. 108-155)
- Project BioShield Act of 2004 (P.L. 108-276)
- Minor Use and Minor Species Animal Health Act of 2004 (P.L. 108-282)
- Food Allergen Labeling and Consumer Protection Act of 2004 (P.L. 108-282)
- Dietary Supplement and Nonprescription Drug Consumer Protection Act of 2006 (P.L. 109-462)
- Food and Drug Administration Amendments Act of 2007 (P.L. 110-85)

Advances in technology have caused the costs of health services to rise as the new technology is used and paid for. One paradox of advancing health-related technology is that as people live longer because of these advances, they then may need additional health services. The net effect drives up health expenditures for the new technology and for other services consumed over a longer life span. The costs associated with use of technology generate policy issues of their own. An example of this is how Medicare policies guide the determination of whether it will pay for new services, treatments, and technologies. Using a complex process, consideration is given to whether the item is safe, effective, and appropriate; whether it leads to improved health outcomes; and the quality of available evidence (Neumann, Kamae, and Palmer 2008). An overview of this decision-making process can be found in "An Introduction to How Medicare Makes Coverage Decisions" (Medicare Payment Advisory Commission 2003, 245-50). Hlatky, Sanders, and Owens (2005) provide a specific example with their discussion of Medicare's decision to cover implantable cardioverter defibrillators (ICDs).

The Role and Importance of Policy Competence in the Pursuit of Health

Because there is a powerful connection between health policy and health, anyone professionally involved in the pursuit of health through any of the determinants shown in Exhibit 1.4 has a vested interest in understanding how health policy is made at all levels of government. An understanding of the context and the decision-making process leads to a higher degree of policy competence.

DeBuono, Gonzalez, and Rosenbaum (2008, 206) state the challenge and importance of engagement in the policymaking arena as follows:

> Many public health practitioners fear getting involved with the policy world. There is no question that public health practice is valuable and fulfilling when the task is to gather data, issue reports, and find solutions that modify individual behavior. However, if the nation is ever to achieve optimal population health, then the public health dialogue must include the policy dimension. To advance the health of the population, the public health system must train a work force capable of, and ready to embrace, policy leadership as an inherent and critical element of the profession.

Similar conclusions apply to healthcare managers, physicians, nurses, and other health professionals. It is entirely possible that, with sufficient policy competence, these professionals can contribute as much or more to improving health through their efforts to improve and enhance the nation's health policy as they do through the more routine practice of their professions.

In many ways, this book is about enhancing the policy competence of healthcare managers and other health professionals. We discuss policy competence more thoroughly in the final chapter, but in this chapter it is sufficient to say that policy competence is made up of the dual abilities to (1) analyze the impact of public policies on one's domain of interest or responsibility and (2) exert influence in the public policymaking process.

The single most important factor in policy competence—including the ability to analyze the impact of public policies or to exert influence in the policymaking process—is to understand the public policymaking process as a *decision-making* process. Public policies, including health policies, are decisions, albeit decisions made in a particular way by particular people. Thus, understanding policymaking means understanding a particular type of decision making, including its context, participants, and processes.

As we discuss throughout the book, the public policymaking process includes three tightly interwoven and interdependent phases: formulation, implementation, and modification. The phases do not unfold in neat sequence. Instead, they blend together in a gestalt of actors, actions, and, sometimes, inactions that yield policies. Exhibit 1.7 illustrates the relationships among the phases of policymaking.

This illustration of the policymaking process emphasizes the cyclical character of public policymaking and shows it as an ongoing phenomenon, one without a definitive beginning or end. In this view of public policymaking, policy formulation (making the decisions that are policies) is inextricably connected to policy implementation (taking actions and making additional decisions, which are themselves policies, necessary to implement policies). Neither phase is complete without the other. Because neither formulation nor implementation achieves perfection or exists in a static world, policy modification is vital. Modifications to previously formulated and implemented policies can range from minor alterations in implementation, to new rules and regulations for implementation, to modest amendments to existing legislation, to fundamental policy changes reflected in new public laws.

Policy competence is increasingly important to those who wish to be effectively involved in the pursuit of health. Many participants in the political marketplace seek to further their objectives by influencing the outcomes of this process and by more accurately predicting those outcomes. An adequate degree of policy competence is necessary to understand what effect the policymaking process might have on a vital interest. Through competent participation, one can influence future health policies and, thus, the determinants of health and ultimately health itself.

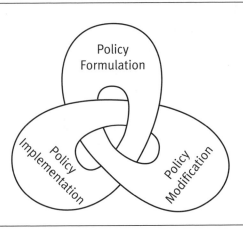

EXHIBIT 1.7

The Intertwined Relationships Among Policy Formulation, Implementation, and Modification

Summary

Good health is "a state of physical and mental well-being necessary to live a meaningful, pleasant and productive life. Good health is also an integral part of thriving modern societies, a cornerstone of well performing economies, and a shared principle of European democracies," a definition that can readily be extended to all democracies (Byrne 2004). Considering health in this way emphasizes the need to address many health determinants: the physical environments in which people live and work; their behaviors and genetics; social factors, including economic circumstances, socioeconomic position, income distribution, discrimination based on factors such as race/ethnicity, gender, or sexual orientation, and the availability of social networks or social support; and the type, quality, and timing of health services that people receive.

Health policies are authoritative decisions made within government that are intended to direct or influence the actions, behaviors, or decisions of others pertaining to health and its determinants. These policies are the principal means through which government in a developed society helps shape the pursuit of health. These decisions can take the form of laws, rules, and operational decisions made in the context of implementing laws and judicial decisions. Health policies, like other public policies, can fit into broad allocative or regulatory categories.

Policy competence is made up of the dual abilities to analyze the impact of public policies on one's domain of interest or responsibility and exert influence in the public policymaking process. This competence begins with an understanding of the public policymaking process and the context in which it takes place. Policy competence can be valuable to healthcare managers and other health professionals, who can use it to affect health by affecting the determinants of health.

Review Questions

1. Define health. What are the determinants of health in humans?
2. Define public policies and health policies.
3. What forms do health policies take? Give an example of each.
4. Compare and contrast the two basic categories of health policies.
5. Discuss the connection between health policies, health determinants, and health.
6. What is policy competence? Why is it important to anyone who is interested in being involved in the pursuit of health?

THE CONTEXT AND PROCESS OF HEALTH POLICYMAKING

Whether health policies take the form of laws, rules or regulations, operational decisions, or judicial decisions, all policies are decisions made through a complex process. With certain variations, policies at the federal, state, and local levels of government are made through similar processes. Furthermore, the structure of the decision-making process is the same for all policy domains, whether health, education, defense, taxes, welfare, or another area.

The domain of health policy is broad, because health, as discussed in Chapter 1, is a function of multiple determinants: the physical environment in which people live and work, their behaviors and biology, social factors, and the health services to which they have access. The health domain also overlaps with other policy domains. For example, it is impossible to consider health policy apart from its relationship to tax policy. Health policy cannot be separated from the fact that government finances, essentially through taxes, many of the services or programs health policy establishes. At a minimum, any dollars spent as a result of public health policies have alternative uses in other domains.

Another example of overlapping policy domains is the 1996 Personal Responsibility and Work Opportunity Reconciliation Act (P.L. 104-193), also known as the Welfare Reform Act, which had significant health implications. In addition to the obvious effect of changes to the nation's welfare policy regarding such health determinants as the social and economic environments affected people face, this law fundamentally affected eligibility for Medicaid. Since the establishment of the Medicaid program in 1965, families receiving Aid to Families with Dependent Children (AFDC) have been automatically enrolled in the Medicaid program. The Welfare Reform Act, however, replaced AFDC with the Temporary Assistance to Needy Families (TANF) block grant. Under the provisions of the TANF block grant, states were given broad flexibility to design income support and work programs for low-income families with children and were required to impose federally mandated restrictions, such as time limits, on federally funded assistance.

The Welfare Reform Act provided for children and parents who would have qualified for Medicaid based on their AFDC eligibility to continue to be eligible for Medicaid. But in the absence of AFDC, states found it necessary to use different mechanisms to identify and enroll former AFDC recipients in their Medicaid programs. This example is typical of the overlap between policies in different domains. A former European Commissioner for Health and Consumer Protection describes this relationship as follows: "To achieve good health, we need to look at the grass root problems—poverty, social exclusion, healthcare access. We need to understand how different socio-economic and environmental factors affect health. And then we need to make all these factors work together for good health. Good health must become the driving force behind all policy-making" (Byrne 2004, 7).

The main purposes of this chapter are to provide a description of the political context within which health policymaking takes place and to present a model of the public policymaking process. The political context is discussed first, beginning with the fact that health policymaking is both a federal and a state responsibility. Subsequently, we describe features of the political marketplace and present a model of the policymaking process.

The Context of Health Policymaking: Federal and State Governments Make Health Policy

Health policy is a joint federal-state responsibility. Although much of this book is devoted specifically to policymaking at the federal level, almost all of the content applies equally at the state level. The two levels have somewhat different health policy responsibilities, but their organization, structure, and policymaking process are similar. As Weissert and Weissert (2006, 250–51) point out, each state has a constitution and a bill of rights. These documents set forth the structure and function of the state government and of the local governments within their boundaries. Each state has three branches of government, and the duties of each branch are essentially the same as those in the federal government. The legislative branch passes laws and oversees the executive branch, which implements the laws. The judiciary branch determines the constitutionality of laws and adjudicates violations of them at both levels.

An unsettled debate over the appropriate distribution of health policy responsibilities between federal and state governments dates from the nation's founding. Over the years, the balance has occasionally shifted, with the federal government dominating health policy for most of the period since the mid-1960s. Recent changes in states' responsibilities for operating the Medicaid program and the failure in the early 1990s of federally led attempts at comprehensive health reform have reinforced the states' traditional health policy roles, and some states have undertaken new, broader roles.

States' Roles in Health Policy
The states' role in protecting and ensuring the public's health is their fundamental responsibility in the pursuit of health. However, states' health policy roles have expanded (Leichter 2008; King 2005). The key health policy responsibilities of

Current information about state health policy can be found at the Kaiser Family Foundation website (www.kff.org) in the section on State Health Policy. State-level data on demographics, health, and health policy, including health coverage, access, financing, and state legislation and budgets, are available at www.statehealthfacts.org.

states are briefly summarized in the following sections, beginning with the states' continuing role as guardians of the public's health.

States were granted constitutional authority to establish laws that protect the public's health and welfare. This responsibility engages states in protecting the environment; ensuring safe practices in workplaces and food service establishments; mounting programs to prevent injuries and promote healthy behaviors; and providing health services such as public health nursing and communicable disease control, family planning and prenatal care, and nutritional counseling. Since the attacks of September 11, 2001, state and regional public health departments have become vital participants in protecting the public from the health consequences of terrorist attacks.

States as Guardians of the Public's Health

Typically, the state government is the largest purchaser of healthcare services in a state (King 2005). States assume significant responsibility for funding their Medicaid programs. Although the costs of these programs are shared with the federal government, this program typically consumes 17–20 percent of state budgets (Kaiser Commission on Medicaid and the Uninsured 2009; National Governors Association and National Association of State Budget Officers 2009). Medicaid is among the highest policy—let alone health policy—priorities for the states. In addition to their Medicaid funding roles, the states also typically pay the costs of providing health insurance benefits to state employees and their dependents and, in many states, for other public-sector workers, such as teachers. The states also purchase services under the Children's Health Insurance Program (CHIP), and many have established state-only programs to assist the uninsured. Examples include Pennsylvania's AdultBasic plan, which expands coverage to more of the state's uninsured adults, and Oregon's Family Health Insurance Program, aimed at low-income working citizens and their dependents. States will likely continue to play increasingly important funding roles as part of their health policy responsibilities.

States as Purchasers of Healthcare Services

States as Regulators

States have legal authority to regulate almost every aspect of the healthcare system and many aspects of the overall pursuit of health. The states license and regulate health professionals through the provisions of their practice acts, and they license and monitor health-related organizations. States also establish and monitor compliance with environmental quality standards.

A particularly important aspect of the role of states in health-related regulation is their responsibility for the health insurance industry as it operates within their boundaries. States control the content, marketing, and price of health insurance products and health plans because the 1945 McCarran-Ferguson Act (P.L. 79-15) left most insurance regulation to the states. However, recent changes in federal law illustrate the tenuous line between federal and state regulation of this industry and portend continued vagueness in this relationship.

For example, the 1974 Employee Retirement Income Security Act (P.L. 93-406), commonly known as ERISA, preempts the states' regulation of pensions and self-insured employer health plans. The 1985 Consolidated Omnibus Budget Reconciliation Act (P.L. 99-272), also known as COBRA 1985, gives people leaving a job in any state the right to retain their existing employer-provided health insurance for up to 18 months by paying the premiums directly, plus a small surcharge. The 1996 Health Insurance Portability and Accountability Act (P.L. 104-191), also known as HIPAA, guarantees access to health insurance to employees who work for companies that offer health insurance benefits if and when they change jobs or become unemployed. The legislation also guarantees renewability of health insurance coverage so long as premiums are paid.

States as Safety Net Providers

States provide safety nets—although these are often porous—through their support for community-based providers, hospitals that provide charity care, local health departments and clinics that serve low-income people, and other programs that ensure access to appropriate healthcare services (King 2005).

An especially important category of community-based providers are the federally qualified health centers (FQHCs). These can be community health centers, migrant health centers, healthcare for the homeless programs, and other service providers. FQHCs receive much of their funding from federal grants but also depend in part on Medicaid and Medicare patients to subsidize care for their uninsured patients.

States as Educators

States subsidize medical education, often but not exclusively in state-supported medical schools. They also subsidize graduate medical education (GME) through Medicaid payments to teaching hospitals, state appropriations, and scholarship and loan programs. Most states provide incentives such as student loan repayments to students who help the state achieve its goals—for example, by choosing nursing or family practice or serving in low-income or rural areas.

More broadly, states provide funding and expertise for large-scale campaigns to improve population health through such educational programs as informing parents about immunization benefits and requirements or encouraging the general public to use seat belts and motorcycle helmets. They also provide funding to schools to support efforts to encourage healthy lifestyles by addressing such topics as nutrition, sex education, and drug and alcohol abuse among students.

In the health policy domain, the popular view considers states laboratories in which experimentation with such policy ideas as comprehensive approaches to health reform take place. According to this view, states try various solutions to problems, and the results demonstrate the usefulness of these solutions for other states and, in some instances, for federal policymakers.

States as Laboratories

Other views of this role are less positive. For example, Davidson (1997, 894), speaking of the states' efforts at comprehensive reform of their healthcare systems, notes, "On the one hand, we have fifty individual political markets which, implicitly, act or fail to act for their own reasons; on the other hand, we have the phenomenon of many, if not most, states taking up the same thorny topic in the same period." In other words, a variety of states, each pursuing solutions to the same problem in idiosyncratic ways under unique sets of reasons in the same time frames, are unlikely to treat each other as laboratories or to benefit much from the others' experiences. Oliver and Paul-Shaheen (1997, 721) support this view. They concluded from their study of six states that enacted major health reform legislation that the wide variation among their approaches to reform "casts doubt on the proposition that states can invent plans and programs for other states and the federal government to adopt for themselves."

Whether or not the states are particularly good laboratories for other states or for the federal government, their roles in health policy innovation are expanding. In the absence of federal solutions, some states have found at least partial solutions to some of the health policy challenges they face.

The Context of Health Policymaking: The Political Marketplace

The political marketplace for health policies has characteristics in common with a traditional economic market. Many different products and services, including those used in the pursuit of health, are bought and sold in the context of economic markets. Willing buyers and sellers enter into economic exchanges in which each party attains something of value. One party demands, and the other supplies. By dealing with each other through market transactions, individuals and organizations buy needed resources and sell their outputs. These relationships are summarized in Exhibit 2.1.

EXHIBIT 2.1

Relationships
in the Political
Marketplace

Sellers   Economic exchanges in market transactions   Buyers

(Suppliers)   (Demanders)

Negotiation in Markets

Because people are calculative regarding the relative rewards and costs of market exchanges, they negotiate. Negotiation, or bargaining, involves two or more parties attempting to settle what each shall give and take (or perform and receive) in an economic transaction. The next section shows a parallel between this feature of economic markets and the operation of political markets. In the negotiations that take place in an economic market, the parties seek a mutually acceptable outcome in a situation where their preferences are usually negatively related (e.g., buyers prefer lower prices, while sellers prefer higher prices). Indeed, if the preferences for outcomes are positively related, an agreement can be reached almost automatically.

More typically, at least two types of issues must be resolved through the negotiations. One type involves the division of resources—the so-called tangibles of the negotiation, such as who will receive how much money and what products or services. Another type centers on the resolution of the psychological dynamics and the satisfaction of personal motivations of the negotiating parties. These issues are the intangibles of the negotiation and can include such notions as appearing to win or lose, to compete effectively, and to cooperate fairly.

Negotiations in economic exchanges usually follow one of two strategic approaches: cooperative (win/win) or competitive (win/lose) strategies. The better negotiating strategy in a particular situation is a function of the interaction of several variables (Watkins 2006). Greenberger and colleagues (1988) contrast the optimal conditions for cooperative negotiating strategies with the optimal conditions for competitive strategies as follows.

Cooperative negotiating strategies work best when

- the tangible goal of both negotiators is to attain a specific settlement that is fair and reasonable;
- sufficient resources are available in the environment for both negotiators to attain their tangible goal, more resources can be attained, or the situation can be redefined so that both negotiators can "win";
- each negotiator thinks it is possible for both to attain their goals through the negotiation process; or
- the intangible goals of both negotiators are to establish a cooperative relationship and to work together toward a settlement that maximizes their joint outcomes.

Competitive negotiating strategies work best when

- the tangible goal of both negotiators is to attain a specific settlement or to get as much as they possibly can;
- the available resources are not sufficient for both negotiators to attain their goals, or their desire to get as much as possible makes it impossible for one or both to actually attain their goals;
- both negotiators think it is impossible for both to attain their goals simultaneously; or
- the intangible goal of each negotiator is to beat the other.

The Operation of Political Markets

Health policies—indeed, all public policies—are made in the context of political markets, which in many ways operate like traditional economic markets. However, there are notable differences. The most fundamental is that buyers or demanders in economic markets express their preferences by spending their own money. That is, they reap the benefits of their choices, and they directly bear the costs of those choices. In political markets, on the other hand, the link between who receives benefits and who bears costs is less direct. Feldstein (2006), for example, observes that public policies that impose costs on future generations are routinely established. The nature of the political marketplace dictates that many decisions made by contemporary policymakers are influenced by the preferences of current voters, perhaps to the detriment of future generations. Such allocative policies as Medicare and Social Security are examples of this phenomenon. In the case of Social Security, outlays are projected to exceed revenues in the future; it is currently projected that this could occur first in 2019 (Congressional Budget Office 2008b).

The CBO (2008b) suggests that there are only four approaches to closing that gap, each of which has substantial drawbacks:

1. The benefits that are scheduled to be paid to future recipients under current law could be reduced, lowering Social Security's contribution to their income.
2. The taxes that fund Social Security could be raised to draw additional resources from the economy to the program.
3. The resources consumed by other federal programs could be reduced to cover the gap between Social Security's outlays and revenues.
4. The federal government's borrowing could be increased, which would be another way to draw more resources from the economy to Social Security. That borrowing would need to be repaid by future generations, however, either through increased taxes or reduced federal spending.

Of course, Social Security is not the only source of pressure on the federal budget. The financial crisis that engulfed the United States and most of the world beginning in late 2008 is causing an unprecedented increase in the federal deficit as government seeks a resolution. In addition, the aging of the U.S. population—which is the main cause of the projected increase in Social Security spending—will raise costs for other entitlement programs. In particular, the CBO projects that Medicare and Medicaid expenditures will grow even faster than Social Security outlays because of rising healthcare costs. Unless taxation reaches much higher levels in the United States, current spending policies are likely to prove financially unsustainable over the long term. The resulting burden of federal debt will have a corrosive and potentially contractionary effect on the economy.

Feldstein (2006) also points out that decision makers in political markets use different criteria from those used in traditional economic markets. In both markets, thoughtful decision makers take benefits and costs into account. In political markets, however, decision makers may use different time frames. Because legislators stand for periodic reelection, they typically favor policies that provide immediate benefits to their constituencies, and they tend to weigh only, or certainly more highly, immediate costs. Unlike most decision makers in economic markets, who consider costs and benefits over the long run, decision makers in political markets are more likely to base decisions on immediate costs and benefits. An obvious consequence of this is policies with immediate benefits but burdensome future costs.

In political markets, suppliers and demanders stand to reap benefits or incur costs because of the authoritative decisions called policies. Policies are therefore valued commodities in the political marketplace. These relationships are shown in Exhibit 2.2.

Given that demanders and suppliers will enter into exchanges involving policies, it is helpful to know who the demanders and suppliers are and what motivates their decisions and actions in political markets.

EXHIBIT 2.2 The Operation of Political Markets

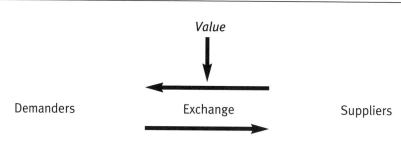

Structurally and operationally, a political market is much like an economic market.

Demanders and Suppliers of Health Policies

As we noted, political markets operate similarly to economic markets. In both markets, something of value is exchanged between suppliers and demanders. Considering political markets in this way permits us to view public policies as a means of satisfying certain demanders' wants and needs in much the same way that products and services produced and sold in economic markets serve to satisfy demanders (or, in an economic context, consumers). In commercial markets, demanders seek products and services that satisfy them. In political markets, demanders seek public policies that satisfy their preferences. Policymakers are in a position to supply the public policies that demanders seek.

The Demanders of Health Policies

Broadly, the demanders of health policies can include (1) anyone who considers such policies relevant to the pursuit of their own health or that of others about whom they care and (2) anyone who considers such policies a means to some other desired end, such as economic advantage. These desires motivate participation in political markets, just as desires motivate participation in economic markets.

For individuals, however, effective participation in the political marketplace presents certain problems and limitations. To participate effectively, individuals must acquire substantial policy-relevant information, which can require considerable time and money. Beyond this, individual participants or demanders often must be prepared to expend additional time and money in support of achieving desired policies. Any particular health policy might have significant, or even noticeable, benefits for only a few individuals. Consequently, individual demander participation is limited in the political markets for policies.

Organizations, such as large health systems, health insurance companies, and technology suppliers, have a significant advantage over individuals in the political marketplace. They may have the necessary resources to garner needed policy-relevant information and to support their efforts to achieve desired policies. In addition, an organization's health policy interests may be concentrated. A change in Medicare policy that results in an increased deductible of $100 per year for certain individuals is one thing; a policy change that results in several million dollars of revenue for a health services organization is quite another. Organizations tend to be more effective demanders of health policy than individuals, in part because the stakes for them tend to be higher.

The most effective demanders of policies, however, are well-organized interest groups. These are groups of people or organizations with similar policy goals that enter the political process to try to achieve those goals. By combining and concentrating the resources of their members, interest groups can have a much greater impact than individuals or organizations alone.

In effect, interest groups provide their members—whether individuals or organizations—with greater opportunities to participate effectively in the political marketplace (McGarity and Wagner 2008; Cigler and Loomis 2007). This is what the American Medical Association (AMA; www.ama-assn.org) does for individual physicians, what the American Association of Retired Persons (AARP; www.aarp.org) does for older individuals, and what PhRMA does for its member companies. Because of their power in political markets, interest groups, as demanders of health policy, are described more fully in the next section.

Interest Groups in the Political Marketplace

Interest groups (also called advocacy groups, lobby groups, pressure groups, or special interest groups) arise in democratic societies because the opportunities to achieve particular outcomes are enhanced through collective action in the political marketplace, specifically through influencing the public policymaking process. They are ubiquitous in the United States, in the health policy domain as in any other. However, as Exhibit 2.3 shows, the relative influence of interest groups in political markets varies by state.

The First Amendment to the U.S. Constitution guarantees the American people the right "peaceably to assemble, and to petition the Government for a redress of grievances." However, constitutional guarantees notwithstanding, political theorists from the nation's beginning to the present day have disagreed about whether interest groups play positive or negative roles in American political life (Ornstein and Elder 1978; Moe 1980; Cigler and Loomis 2007; Peters 2003; Edwards, Wattenberg, and Lineberry 2009).

James Madison, writing in the *Federalist Papers* in 1787, discusses the relationship of groups, which he called "factions," to democratic government. In *Federalist* Number 10, he defines a faction as "a number of citizens, whether amounting to a majority or a minority of the whole, who are united and actuated by some common impulse of passion, or of interest, adverse to the rights of citizens, or to the permanent and aggregate interests of the community." Madison felt strongly that factions, or interest groups, were inherently bad. He also believed, however, that the formation of such groups was a natural outgrowth of human nature (he writes in *Federalist* Number 10 that "the latent causes of faction are sown into the nature of man") and that government should not seek to check this activity.

Madison felt that what he called the "mischiefs of faction" could and should be contained by setting the "ambition" of one faction against the selfish preferences and behaviors of others. So began the uncertainty about and ambiguity toward the role of interest groups in public policymaking in the United States. One point about which there is neither uncertainty nor ambiguity,

Dominant (4)	Dominant/ Complementary (26)	Complementary (15)	Complementary/ Subordinate (5)	Subordinate (0)	**EXHIBIT 2.3** Comparing Interest Group Strength Across the States
Alabama	Alaska	Colorado	Kentucky		
Florida	Arizona	Connecticut	Michigan		
Hawaii	Arkansas	Indiana	Minnesota		
Nevada	California	Maine	South Dakota		
	Delaware	Massachusetts	Vermont		
	Georgia	Montana			
	Idaho	New Hampshire			
	Illinois	New Jersey			
	Iowa	New York			
	Kansas	North Carolina			
	Louisiana	North Dakota			
	Maryland	Pennsylvania			
	Mississippi	Rhode Island			
	Missouri	Washington			
	Nebraska	Wisconsin			
	New Mexico				
	Ohio				
	Oklahoma				
	Oregon				
	South Carolina				
	Tennessee				
	Texas				
	Utah				
	Virginia				
	West Virgina				
	Wyoming				

NOTE: This classification of interest group strength across the states is a composite of the judgments of experienced political observers in each state. Interest groups have an overwhelming influence in dominant states. In dominant/complementary states, interest group influence is strong but limited by the influence of other political actors such as party organizations, governmental institutions, or the electorate. In complementary states, interest group influence strikes a balance with other political actors. In complementary/subordinate states, interest group influence is secondary to the influence of other political actors. To be placed in the subordinate category, interest group influence in a state would have to be weak or inconsequential—a situation not apparent in any of the states.

SOURCE: Adapted from A. J. Nownes, C. S. Thomas, and R.J. Hrebenar (2008).

however, is that interest groups play an active role in the public policymaking process. Reflecting widely divergent views on the manner in which interest groups play their role in this process, two distinct perspectives on ways in which groups influence policymaking have emerged: the pluralist and the elitist models.

The Pluralist Perspective

People who hold the pluralist perspective on the role of interest groups in policymaking believe that because so many interest groups are operating, everyone's interests can be represented by one or more of them. Adherents to the pluralist model usually maintain that interest groups play an essentially positive role in public policymaking. They argue that various interest groups compete with and counterbalance each other in the political marketplace. Pluralists do not question that some groups are stronger than others. However, they contend that as groups seek their preferred outcomes, power is widely dispersed among competing groups, with each group winning some of the time and losing some of the time.

Pluralist theory about how the policymaking process works includes several interconnected arguments that, taken together, constitute what has come to be called a group theory of politics (Truman 1992). The central tenets of the group theory include the following:

- Interest groups provide essential links between people and their government.
- Interest groups compete among themselves for outcomes, with the interests of some groups counterbalanced by the interests of others.
- No group is likely to become too dominant in the competition; as groups become powerful, other countervailing interests organize or existing groups intensify their efforts. An important mechanism for maintaining balance among the groups is their ability to rely on various sources of power. Groups representing concentrated economic interests may have money, but consumer groups may have more members.
- The competition among interest groups is basically fair. Although there are exceptions, groups typically play by the rules of the game.

Some observers have concluded that the pluralist approach is out of control. There are more than 11,000 associations of national scope today and another 16,000 state or regional associations in such domains as business, education, religion, science, and health—all actively pursuing a variety of policy interests on behalf of their members (Concept Marketing Group, Inc. 2009). The problem, according to the critics of pluralism, is not merely the large number of groups but also the fact that government seems to consider the demands and preferences of all interest groups to be legitimate. There is little debate that government does attempt to satisfy the preferences of many interests, sometimes in conflicting ways.

Critics of the pluralist approach to the role of interest groups in the public policymaking process strongly agree on two points:

1. Interest groups have become too influential in the policymaking process. Satisfying their multiple and often conflicting demands seems to drive government rather than government being driven by a desire to

base policy decisions on considerations of what is best for the nation as a whole—that is, on the public interest.

2. Seeking to satisfy the multiple and often conflicting demands of various interest groups leads to confusion, contradiction, and even paralysis in the policymaking process. Rather than making a difficult choice between satisfying X or Y, government seems frequently to pretend that there is no need to make the choice and seeks to satisfy both X and Y.

In addition to those who criticize the pluralist approach as dysfunctional and out of control are those who believe that the perspective itself is misguided, or even wrong. Instead of everyone having a chance to influence the policymaking process through one group or another, some people believe that such influence actually resides only in the hands of an elite few.

Whereas pluralists point with pride to the remarkable number of organized groups actively and aggressively participating in the American process of public policymaking, elitists point out how most groups are fairly powerless and ineffectual. The elitist perspective on the role of interest groups, which is the opposite of the pluralist viewpoint, grows out of a power elite model of American society.

The Elitist Perspective

This model is based on the idea that real political power in the United States is concentrated in the hands of the small proportion of the population that controls the nation's key institutions and organizations and much of its wealth. In the elitist perspective, these so-called "big interests" look out for themselves in part by disproportionately influencing, if not controlling, the public policymaking process. It is debatable whether this model accurately reflects the American political marketplace, but it does represent the opinions of a growing majority of Americans concerning which members of the society have the most influence.

The elitist theory holds that a power elite, often referred to as "the establishment," acts as a gatekeeper to the public policymaking process. Unless the power elite considers an issue important, the issue does not get much attention in policymaking circles. Furthermore, the theory holds, once an issue is on the policy agenda, public policies made in response reflect the values, ideologies, and preferences of this governing elite (Dye 2008). Thus, the power elite dominates public policymaking through its superior position in society. Its powerful roles in the nation's economic and social systems allows the elite to shape the formulation of policies and control their implementation. It has been argued that the nation's social and economic systems depend on the power elite's consensus regarding the system's fundamental values, and the only policy alternatives that receive serious consideration are those that fall within the shared consensus (Dye 2002).

The central tenets of the power elite theory stand in stark contrast to the pluralist perspective. These tenets are as follows (Dye and Zeigler 2009; Edwards, Wattenberg, and Lineberry 2009):

- Real political power resides in a very small number of groups; the large number of interest groups is practically meaningless because the power differentials among them are so great. Other groups may win minor policy victories, but the power elite always prevails on significant policy issues.
- Members of the power elite share a consensus or near consensus on the basic values that should guide public policymaking: private property rights, the preeminence of markets and private enterprise as the best way to organize the economy, limited government, and the importance of individual liberty and individualism.
- Members of the power elite have a strong preference for incremental changes in public policies. Incrementalism in policymaking permits time for the economic and social systems to adjust to changes without feeling threatened, with minimal economic dislocation or disruption and with minimal alteration in the social system's status quo.
- Elites protect their power bases. Some limited movement of non-elites into elite positions is permitted to maintain social stability, but only after non-elites clearly accept the elites' consensus values.

Which Perspective Is Correct?

Those who hold the power elitist perspective challenge those who hold the pluralist perspective by pointing to the highly concentrated and interlocked power centers in American society. Studies of the concentration of power do find that many of the top leadership positions in the United States—on corporate, foundation, and university governing boards, for example—are held by people who occupy more than one such position (Domhoff 2009).

Those who prefer the pluralist perspective, however, are equally quick to cite numerous examples in which those who traditionally have been grossly underrepresented in the inner circles of the power elite have succeeded in their collective efforts to significantly influence the public policymaking process. African Americans, women, and consumers in general provide examples of the ability of groups once ignored by policymakers to organize as effective interest groups and redirect the course of the public policymaking process.

Neither the pluralist nor the elitist perspective alone fully explains how the interests of individuals or organizations relate to the public policymaking process. The results of that process affect the interests of all individuals and all organizations to varying degrees. Many, if not all, individuals and organizations with interests can influence the policymaking process, although, again, not to equal degrees. The elitist and pluralist approaches each have something to contribute to an understanding of the roles interest groups play in the marketplace for public policies. Whether such groups work proactively, by seeking to stimulate new policies that serve the interests of their members, or reactively, by seeking to block policy changes that they do not believe serve their members' best interests, they are intrinsic to the public policymaking process. Interest groups provide their members with a way to link their policy preferences into a more powerful, collective voice that greatly increases the likelihood of a significant influence on policymaking.

The Suppliers of Health Policies

Because policies are made in the executive, legislative, and judicial branches of government, the list of potential policymakers is lengthy. Members of each branch of government supply policies in the political market, although each branch plays its role differently.

Legislators as Suppliers

One important group of public policy suppliers is elected legislators, whether members of the U.S. Congress, state legislatures, or city councils. Few aspects of the political marketplace are as interesting, or as widely observed and studied, as the decision-making behaviors of legislators and the motives and incentives behind those behaviors. To a large extent, this intense interest in the motivations of policy suppliers reflects the desire of policy demanders to exert influence over the suppliers.

Although neither extreme fully reflects the motivations of legislators, the end points on a continuum of behaviors that policymakers might exhibit can be represented by those who seek to maximize the public interest on one end and by those who seek to maximize self-interest on the other end. A legislator at the public interest extreme would always seek policies that maximize the public interest, although the true public interest might not always be easy to identify. A legislator whose motivations lie at the self-interest extreme would always behave in a manner that maximizes self-interest, whether that interest is reelection, money, prestige, power, or whatever appeals to the self-serving person.

In the political marketplace, legislators can be found all along the continuum between extreme public-interest and extreme self-interest motivations. Although some people incorrectly ascribe dominant self-interest motives to all legislators, the actions and decisions of most legislators reflect a complex mixture of the two motivations, with exclusively self-interested or public-interested motives only rarely dominating decisions.

Motives aside, legislators at all levels of government are key policy suppliers, especially of policies in the form of laws. For example, only Congress can enact new or amend existing public laws. In political markets, legislators constantly calculate the benefits and costs of their policymaking decisions and consider who will reap these benefits and bear these costs. Factoring in the interests they choose to serve, they make their decisions accordingly. Their calculations are complicated by the fact that the costs and benefits of a particular decision often affect many people in different ways.

In effect, policies typically create winners and losers. The gains some people enjoy come at the financial expense of others, or at least at the expense of having someone's problems ignored or someone's preferred solutions postponed. Most of the time, most legislators seek to maximize their own net political gains through their policy-related decisions, because reelection is an abiding objective.

In view of the reality that most policies create winners and losers, legislators may find that their best strategy is to permit the winners their victory, but not by a huge margin, and in so doing cushion the impact on the losers. For example, suppose a legislator is considering a policy that would increase health services for an underserved population at the expense of higher taxes on others. Options include various policies with the following outcomes: (1) few services at relatively low cost, (2) more services at higher cost, and (3) many services at very high cost. Facing such a decision, and applying the concept of net political gain, policymakers might opt for the provision of a meaningful level of services, but one far below what could have been provided and at a cost below what would have been required for a higher level of services. The "winners" receive more services, but the expense for the "losers," who have to pay for the new services, is not as great as it might have been. Through such calculations and determinations legislators routinely seek to maximize their net political gains.

Executives and Bureaucrats as Suppliers

At all levels of government, members of the executive branch are important policy suppliers, although their role differs from that of legislators (see Exhibit 1.1). Presidents, governors, mayors, and other senior public-sector executives offer policies in the form of legislative proposals and seek to have legislators enact their preferred policies. Chief executives and those in charge of government departments and agencies are directly responsible for policies in the form of rules or regulations used to guide the implementation of laws and operational protocols and procedures for the policies they implement. Career bureaucrats who participate in these activities and thus become suppliers of policies in the political marketplace join elected and appointed executives and managers in their rulemaking and operational duties.

Elected and appointed officials of the executive branch are often affected by the same self-interest/public-interest dichotomy that affects legislators; reelection concerns in particular often influence their decisions. Like legislators, elected and appointed members of executive branches are apt to calculate the net political gains of their policy-related decisions and actions. As a result, their motivations and behaviors in the political marketplace can be similar to those of legislators. However, the behaviors of members of the executive branch of a government and members of its legislative branch show some important differences.

The most fundamental difference derives from the fact that the executive branch generally bears greater responsibility than the legislative branch for the state of the economy, and it is widely perceived to bear even more responsibility than it actually does. Presidents, governors, and mayors, along with their top appointees, are held accountable for economic conditions much more explicitly than are Congress, state legislatures, or city councils. Although legislators do not escape this responsibility altogether, the public typically lays most of the responsibility at the feet of the executive branch. This can be seen in the financial crises facing the United States and much of the world beginning in 2008. The executive branch, especially the president, is expected to spur development of legislation to rescue the nation from this circumstance. When people do blame the legislative branch, they tend to hold the entire Congress or the state or city legislature collectively responsible rather than to blame individual legislators.

The concentration of responsibility for the economy in the executive branch influences the decision making that takes place there. Because of the close connection between government's budget and the state of the economy, the budget implications of policy decisions are carefully weighed in the executive branch. Not infrequently, the legislative and executive branches will hold different positions on health policies because members in the two branches give different weight to the budget implications of the policies they are considering.

Career bureaucrats, or civil servants, in the executive branch also participate in policymaking in the legislative branch when they collect, analyze, and transmit information about policy options and initiate policy proposals in their areas of expertise. However, the motivations and behaviors of career bureaucrats tend to differ from those of legislators and those of members of executive branches.

The behaviors and motivations of career bureaucrats in the public sector are often analogous to those of employees in the private sector. Workers in both settings typically seek to satisfy certain personal needs and desires through their work. This can obviously be categorized as self-serving in both cases. But government employees are no more likely to be totally motivated by self-interests than are private sector workers. Most workers in both sectors are motivated by blends of self-interest and interest in what is good for the larger society.

However, most career bureaucrats watch a constantly changing mix of elected and senior government officials—with an equally dynamic set of policy preferences—parade past, while they remain as the most permanent human feature of government. It should surprise no one that career bureaucrats develop a strong sense of identification with their home department or agency or that they become protective of it. This protectiveness is most visible in the relationships between government agencies or departments and those with legislative oversight of them, including authorization, appropriation, and performance review responsibilities. Many career bureaucrats equate the well-being of their agencies, in terms of their size, budgets, and prestige, with the public interest. Obviously, this is not always the case.

The Judiciary as Supplier

The judicial branch of government is also a supplier of policies. For example, whenever a court interprets an ambiguous law, establishes judicial procedure, or interprets the U.S. Constitution, it makes a policy. These activities are conceptually no different from those involved when legislators enact public laws or when members of the executive branch establish rules and regulations to guide implementation of laws or make operational decisions regarding their implementation. All of these activities are policymaking, because they lead to authoritative decisions made within government for the purpose of influencing or directing the actions, behaviors, and decisions of others.

Policymaking in the judicial branch, however, differs from that in the legislative and executive branches, not only in focus but also in operation. The responsibilities of courts require them to focus narrowly on the issues involved in specific cases or situations. This stands in stark contrast to the wide-open political arena in which most other public policymaking occurs.

The courts are involved in numerous and diverse aspects of health policy, reflecting the entire range of health determinants (i.e., physical environment, behavior and genetics, social factors, and health services). For example, in a 1980 opinion in what is called the benzene case, the U.S. Supreme Court invalidated an Occupational Safety and Health Administration (OSHA; www.osha.gov) rule limiting benzene to no more than one part per million in the air in workplaces. In the court's view, OSHA had not found a significant risk to workers' health before issuing the rule.

In a 1905 landmark ruling in *Jacobson v. Massachusetts*, the U.S. Supreme Court upheld compulsory vaccination as an appropriate use of state police power to protect the health, welfare, and safety of a state's citizens. Police powers granted to the states by the U.S. Constitution provide the legal basis for state authority in the field of public health. This case involved a compulsory vaccination regulation of the Cambridge, Massachusetts, Board of Health. Defendant Jacobson refused to be vaccinated and contended that the requirement invaded his liberty. The Court held, however, that

> the liberty secured by the Constitution to every person...does not import an absolute right in each person to be at all times and in all circumstances wholly freed from restraint...it was the duty of the constituted authorities primarily to keep in view the welfare, comfort and safety of the many, and not permit the interests of the many to be subordinated to the wishes or convenience of the few.

Furthermore, the Court stated that

> it is equally true that in every well-ordered society charged with the duty of con-
> serving the safety of its members the rights of the individual in respect of his liberty
> may at times, under the pressure of great dangers, be subjected to such restraint,
> to be enforced by reasonable regulations, as the safety of the general public may
> demand... .

The heart of the judiciary's ability to supply policies lies in its role in interpreting the law. The courts can exercise the powers of nullification, interpretation, and application to the rules and regulations established by the executive
branch in carrying out its implementation responsibilities. This includes the
power to declare federal and state laws unconstitutional—that is, to declare
laws enacted by the legislative branch to be null and void. This role of the
courts is clearly illustrated in a ruling by the 9th U.S. Circuit Court of Appeals
that overturned Arizona legislation requiring abortion clinics in that state to
submit to warrantless searches and to make patient files available to state regulators. These onerous state regulations had been established following the
death of a patient having a clinic abortion. The appeals court based its ruling
on an interpretation that the regulations violated constitutional restrictions on
searches and seizures and that requiring the clinics to submit patient files to
state regulators on demand violated the patients' privacy rights (Kravets 2004).

Another example of the interpretative role of the courts in health policymaking is the ruling by the U.S. Supreme Court in April 1995 that ERISA
(P.L. 93-406) does not preclude states from setting hospital rates. The case
that resulted in this ruling arose out of New York's practice of adding a surcharge to certain hospital bills to help pay for health services for some of the
state's low-income citizens. The state's practice was challenged by a group of
commercial insurers and HMOs and by New York City (Green 1995). A number of health-related interest groups filed a joint *amicus curiae* (friend of the
court) brief in which they asserted that Congress, in enacting ERISA, never
intended for it to be used to challenge state health reform plans and initiatives.
The Supreme Court's ruling is generally seen as supportive of state efforts to
broaden access to health services for their poorer residents through various reforms and initiatives.

Health policymaking within the judicial branch is far more prevalent in
state courts and lower federal courts than in the U.S. Supreme Court. A state-
level example of courts making important health policy can be seen in
Pennsylvania cases involving the tax-exempt status of healthcare organizations. In one 1995 case, for example, the Indiana County, Pennsylvania,
Court of Common Pleas rebuffed the leaders of Indiana Hospital in their appeal to have the hospital's tax-exempt status restored after the exemption had
been revoked by the county in 1993. In making its ruling, the court held that
the hospital failed to adequately meet one of the state's tests through which

an organization qualifies for tax exemption. Among other criteria, at the time of this case, the state required a tax-exempt organization "to donate or render gratuitously a substantial portion of its services."

In making its ruling, the Indiana County court took note of the fact that Indiana Hospital's uncompensated charity care in fiscal year 1994 had amounted to approximately 2 percent of its total expected compensation and contrasted this with an earlier case resulting from the revocation of the tax-exempt status of a nursing home in the state. The state supreme court decision in the St. Margaret Seneca Place nursing home case (*St. Margaret Seneca Place v. Board of Property Assessment Appeals and Review, County of Allegheny, PA*) had been that the nursing home did meet the state's test because it demonstrated that it bore more than one-third of the cost of care for half of its patients.

The variation in these and several other Pennsylvania cases in the courts' interpretation of the state's partial test for tax-exempt status (i.e., the requirement that a tax-exempt organization is "to donate or render gratuitously a substantial portion of its services") led to enactment in 1997 of clarifying legislation on this and other points regarding the determination of tax-exempt status. Late in that year, the governor of Pennsylvania signed into law House Bill 55, known as the Institutions of Purely Public Charity Act, or Act 55. This act permits an institution to meet the charitable purpose test and qualify for tax exemption if it has a charitable mission, is free of private profit motive, is designated a 501(c)(3) by the federal government, and is organized for any of the following reasons:

- relief of poverty
- advancement and provision of education, including secondary education
- advancement of religion
- prevention and treatment of disease or injury, including mental retardation and mental illness
- government or municipal purposes
- accomplishment of a purpose that is recognized as important and beneficial to the public and that advances social, moral, or physical objectives

The act specifically clarified, quite liberally, how an institution could meet the requirement for donating or rendering gratuitously a substantial portion of its services. Act 55 established 3 percent of an institution's total operating expenses as the necessary contribution of charitable goods or services. In this instance, court decisions were policies themselves, and the impact of the decisions eventually led to a significant change in Pennsylvania's public laws.

It is generally acknowledged that, because the pursuit of health in the United States is so heavily influenced by laws and regulations, the courts are a major factor in the development and implementation of health policies (Rosenblatt 2008; Gostin 2008). The courts include not only the federal court system but also the court systems of the states and the territories. Each of these systems has developed in idiosyncratic ways, and each has a constitution to guide it, specific legislation to contend with, and its own history of judicial decisions. A great deal of information on the structure and operation of the U.S. legal system can be found in the outline of the legal system provided by the U.S. Department of State (2004).

Although the federal and state courts play significant roles as policy suppliers, their behaviors, motivations, and roles differ significantly from those of participants in the legislative and executive branches. In their wisdom, the drafters of the U.S. Constitution created the three branches, and Article III ensured the judicial branch's independence, at least mostly so, from the other branches.

An independent judiciary facilitates adherence to the rules all participants in the policymaking process must follow. Federal judges are appointed rather than elected, and the appointments are for life. Consequently, federal judges are not subject to the same self-interest concerns related to reelection that many other policymakers face. This enhances their ability to act in the public interest, although judges, like all policymakers, vary in their personal commitments to this objective (Cass 2008).

Interplay Among Demanders and Suppliers in the Political Marketplace

In the political marketplace, demanders and suppliers of policies seek to further their objectives. These objectives can be based on self-interest and involve some health or economic advantage, or they can be based on what is best for the public, or at least some subset of society, such as the elderly, poor, or medically underserved. In either case, the outcome depends on the relative abilities of some participants in the marketplace to influence the actions, behaviors, and decisions of other participants.

Power and Influence in Political Markets
Influence in political markets, just as in private economic markets, is defined as "actions that, either directly or indirectly, cause a change in the behavior and/or attitudes of another individual or group" (Shortell and Kaluzny 2006, 533). But to have influence, one must also have power. More power means more potential to influence others. Therefore, an understanding of influence requires an understanding of power.

Those who wish to exert influence in the political marketplace must first acquire power from the sources available to them (Alexander et al. 2006). The classic categories for sources of interpersonal power include legitimate, reward, coercive, expert, and referent (French and Raven 1959). These bases of interpersonal power apply to individuals, organizations, and interest groups in political markets.

Legitimate power, for example, derives from one's relative position in a social system, organization, or group; this form of power is also called *formal power* or authority. It exists because assigning or ascribing certain powers to individuals, organizations, or groups better enables them to fulfill their duties or perform their work effectively. Elected officials, appointed executives, judges, health professionals, corporation executives, union leaders, and many other individual participants in the political marketplace, possess legitimate power that accompanies their social or organizational positions. Suppliers and demanders of policies possess legitimate power. That is, they can exert influence in the policymaking process because they are recognized as legitimate in the process.

Reward power is based on the ability of one person, organization, or group to reward others for their decisions and actions. Reward power stems in part from legitimate power. It comes from many sources and takes many forms. Within organizations, it includes the obvious: control over pay increases, promotions, work and vacation schedules, recognition of accomplishments, and such status symbols or perks as club memberships and office size and location. In economic markets, the buying power of consumers is a form of reward power. In political markets, reward power is more likely to take the form of favors that can be provided or exchanged, specific influence with particular individuals or groups, and whatever influence can be stored for later use. *Coercive power* is the opposite of reward power and is based on the capacity to withhold or to prevent someone from obtaining desired rewards.

Expert power tends to reside in individuals but can also reside in a group or organization. It derives from possessing expertise valued within the political marketplace, such as expertise in solving problems or performing crucial tasks. People with expert power often occupy formal positions of authority, transferring some of the expert power to the organization or group. People who can exercise their expert power in the policymaking arena may also be trusted advisers or associates of other participants in the political marketplace.

Referent power derives from the influence that results from the ability of some people, organizations, and interest groups to engender admiration, loyalty, and emulation from others. In the marketplace for policies, this form of power, when it pertains to individuals, is called *charismatic power*. Charismatic power usually belongs to a select few people who typically have strong convictions about the correctness of their preferences, have great self-confidence in their own abilities, and are widely perceived to be legitimate agents of change. It is rare for a person, organization, or interest group to gain sufficient power to heavily influence policymaking simply from referent or charismatic power, even in political markets where charisma is highly valued.

But it can certainly give the other sources of power in the political marketplace a boost.

The bases of power in the political marketplace are interdependent. They can and do complement and conflict with each other. For example, people, organizations, or groups that are in a position to use reward power and who do so wisely can strengthen their referent power. Conversely, those who abuse coercive power might quickly weaken or lose their referent power. Effective participants in the marketplace for policies—those individuals, organizations, and groups that succeed at translating their power into influence—tend to be fully aware of the sources of their power and to act accordingly. They seem to understand intuitively the costs and benefits of using each kind of power and can draw on them appropriately in different situations and with various people they wish to influence.

Power and Influence of Interest Groups: Breaking the Iron Triangles

Some interest groups, including several in the health domain, are extraordinarily powerful and influential in demanding public policies. To fully appreciate their power and the influence it permits, it is necessary to understand *iron triangles*, a model of the relationships that sometimes exist among participating individuals, organizations, and groups in the political marketplace.

Any policy domain attracts a set of participating individuals, organizations, and groups. Each participant has some stake in policies affecting the domain and thus seeks to influence policymaking. Some of the participants, or stakeholders, in a domain demand policies; others supply policies. Collectively, these stakeholders form a *policy community*.

Traditionally, the policy community formed around a particular policy domain (such as health) has included any legislative committees with jurisdiction in the domain, the executive branch agencies responsible for implementing public laws in the domain, and the private-sector interest groups involved in the domain. The first two categories are suppliers of the policies demanded by the third category. This triad of organized interests has been called an iron triangle because when all three sides are in accord, the resulting stability allows the triad to withstand attempts to make undesired changes.

A policy community that could be appropriately characterized as a strong and stable iron triangle dominated the health policy domain until the early 1960s, when battle lines began to be drawn over the eventual shape of the Medicare program. This triangle featured a few powerful interest groups with concordant views that, for the most part, had sympathetic partners in the legislative committees and in the relevant implementing agencies of government.

During this period, the private-sector interest group members of the iron triangle that dominated health policy, notably AMA and the American

Hospital Association (AHA; www.aha.org), joined later by the American College of Physicians (ACP; www.acponline.org) and the American College of Surgeons (ACS; www.facs.org), generally held a consistent view of the appropriate policies in this domain. Their shared view of optimal health policy was that government should protect the interests of health services providers and not intervene in the financing or delivery of health services (Peterson 1993). Under the conditions and expectations extant in these largely straightforward relationships, it was relatively simple for the suppliers and demanders of policies to satisfy each other. This triangle was unbreakable into the second half of the twentieth century.

The dynamics of the situation began to change dramatically with the policy battles over Medicare, and they worsened with the addition of Medicaid to the debate. Fundamental differences emerged among the participants in the health policy community in terms of their views of optimal health policy. Today, there is rarely a solid block of concordant private sector interests driving health policy decisions. For example, differences over questions of optimal policy shattered the accord between AMA and AHA. Splintering within the memberships of these groups caused even more damage. For example, the medical profession no longer speaks through the single voice of AMA; organizations such as ACP and the American Academy of Family Physicians (AAFP; www.aafp.org) can and sometimes do support different policy choices. Similarly, AHA is now joined in policy debates by organizations with diverse preferences representing the specific interests of teaching hospitals, public hospitals, for-profit hospitals, and other hospital subsets. These changes have eroded the solidarity among private-sector interest groups and the public-sector members of the health policy community.

Rather than an iron triangle, the contemporary health policy community is far more heterogeneous in its membership and much more loosely structured. At most, this community can be thought of as a group of members whose commonality stems from the attention they pay to issues in the health policy domain. There is an important difference, however, between shared attentiveness to health policy issues and shared positions on optimal health policy or related issues. The loss of concordance among the members of the old iron triangle has somewhat diminished the power of certain interest groups. Nevertheless, they remain highly influential, and other interest groups have also been able to assume influential roles in health policymaking.

Ethics in the Political Marketplace

Ethics in policymaking is covered in more detail in Chapter 8, but it is essential to any discussion of the political marketplace. Humans control political markets. Thus, various mixes of altruism and egoism influence what takes place. Human control of the public policymaking process means that its operation, outcomes, and consequences are directly affected by the ethics of those who participate in the process. Ethical considerations help shape and guide the development of new policies by contributing to definitions of problems and the structure of policy solutions.

Having considered the context within which health policies are made, especially the structure and operations of political markets, and having identified the demanders and suppliers who interact in these markets and the important operational and ethical aspects of these interactions, it is now possible to consider the intricate process through which public policies are made. The consideration begins in this chapter at the conceptual level; applied discussions of the component parts of the policymaking process follow in subsequent chapters.

A Conceptual Model of the Public Policymaking Process

The most useful way to conceptualize a process as complex and intricate as the one through which public policies are made is through a schematic model. Although such models, like the one presented here, tend to be oversimplifications, they can accurately reflect the component parts of the process and their interrelationships. Exhibit 2.4 is a model of the public policymaking process in the United States. We discuss the component parts of the model in greater detail in subsequent chapters. Several key features of the policymaking process as reflected in this model are helpful in understanding the policymaking process.

Policymaking Is a Cyclical Process

As Exhibit 2.4 illustrates, the policymaking process is a continuous cycle in which all decisions are subject to modification. Public policymaking is a process within which numerous decisions are reached and then revisited as circumstances change. The cyclical nature of health policymaking can be seen in the pattern of Medicare policy presented in Appendix 9.

Policymaking Is Influenced by External Factors

Another important feature of the public policymaking process shown in Exhibit 2.4 is the influence of factors external to the process itself. The policymaking process is an *open system*, one in which the process interacts with and is affected by events and circumstances in its external environment. This important phenomenon is shown in the model by the effect of the preferences of individuals, organizations, and interest groups that are affected by policies—along with biological, cultural, demographic, ecological, economic, ethical, legal, psychological, social, and technological inputs—on the policymaking process.

As we discussed in Chapter 1, legal inputs, which include decisions made in the courts, are themselves policies. In addition, however, decisions

Exhibit 2.4 Model of the Public Policymaking Process in the United States

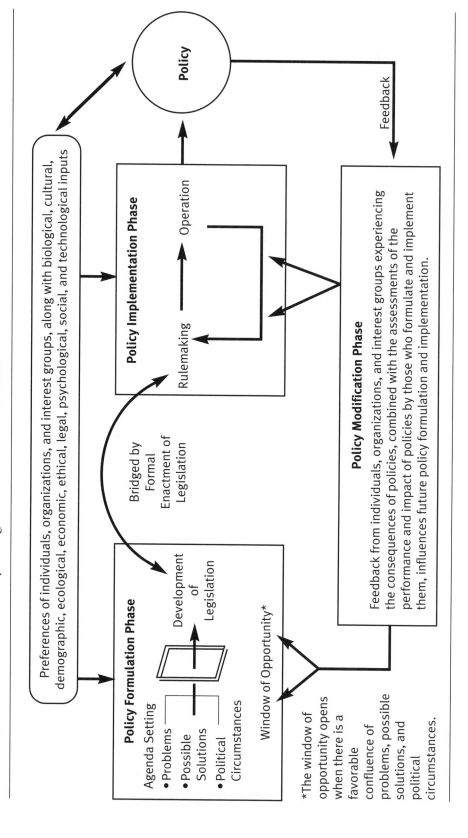

Policy

Policy Implementation Phase

Rulemaking → Operation

Preferences of individuals, organizations, and interest groups, along with biological, cultural, demographic, ecological, economic, ethical, legal, psychological, social, and technological inputs

Feedback

Bridged by Formal Enactment of Legislation

Policy Formulation Phase

Agenda Setting
• Problems
• Possible Solutions
• Political Circumstances

Development of Legislation

Window of Opportunity*

Policy Modification Phase

Feedback from individuals, organizations, and interest groups experiencing the consequences of policies, combined with the assessments of the performance and impact of policies by those who formulate and implement them, influences future policy formulation and implementation.

*The window of opportunity opens when there is a favorable confluence of problems, possible solutions, and political circumstances.

made within the legal system influence other decisions made within the policymaking process. Legal inputs help shape all other policy decisions, including by reversing them when they are unconstitutional.

Technology provides another example of the effect of external factors on the policymaking process. The United States is the world's major producer and consumer of health-related technology. As the policymaking model shows, technological inputs flow into the policymaking process. Along with other effects, the costs of new technologies must be factored into public and private insurance programs (Congressional Budget Office 2008a). As Elmendorf (2009) noted, "given the central role of medical technology in cost growth, reducing or slowing spending over the long term would probably require decreasing the pace of adopting new treatments and procedures or limiting the breadth of their application."

The Components of the Policymaking Process Are Interactive and Interdependent

While the model emphasizes the various distinct component parts or phases of the policymaking process, it also shows that they are highly interactive and interdependent. The public policymaking process modeled in Exhibit 2.4 includes the following three interconnected phases:

1. policy formulation, which incorporates activities associated with setting the policy agenda and, subsequently, with the development of legislation
2. policy implementation, which incorporates activities associated with rulemaking that help guide the implementation of policies and the actual operationalization of policies
3. policy modification, which allows for all prior decisions made within the process to be revisited and perhaps changed

Once enacted as laws, policies remain to be implemented. The formulation phase (making the decisions that lead to public laws) and the implementation phase (taking actions and making additional decisions necessary to implement public laws) are bridged by the formal enactment of legislation, which shifts the cycle from the formulation to the implementation phase.

Implementation responsibility rests mostly with the executive branch, which includes DHHS and the Department of Justice (DOJ; www.usdoj.gov), and independent federal agencies, such as the Environmental Protection Agency (EPA; www.epa.gov) and the Consumer Product Safety Commission (CPSC; www.cpsc.gov). These and many other departments and agencies in the executive branch exist primarily to implement the policies formulated in the legislative branch. This relationship between policy formulation and implementation is illustrated by the list of major federal laws for which the EPA is responsible in Appendix 10.

Some of the decisions made in the course of policy implementation become policies themselves. Rules and regulations promulgated to implement a law and operational protocols and procedures developed to support a law's implementation are policies as surely as is the law itself. Similarly, judicial decisions regarding the applicability of laws to specific situations or regarding the appropriateness of the actions of implementing organizations are public policies. Policies are established within the formulation and the implementation phases of the overall process.

The policy modification phase exists because perfection cannot be achieved in the other phases and because policies are established and exist in a dynamic world. Suitable policies made today may become inadequate with future biological, cultural, demographic, ecological, economic, ethical, legal, psychological, social, and technological changes. Pressure to change established policies may come from new priorities or the perceived needs of individuals, organizations, and interest groups affected by the policies.

Policy modification, which is shown as a feedback loop in Exhibit 2.4, may entail only minor adjustments in the implementation phase or modest amendments to existing public laws. In some instances, however, the consequences of implementing certain policies can feed all the way back to the agenda-setting stage. For example, formulating policies to contain the costs of providing health services—a key challenge facing policymakers today—is to a large extent an outgrowth of previous policies that expanded access and increased the supply of human resources and advanced technologies to be used in providing health services.

Policymaking Is a Highly Political Process

One feature of the public policymaking process that the model presented in Exhibit 2.4 cannot adequately represent—but one that is crucial to understanding the policymaking process—is the political nature of the process in operation. While many people believe—and still others naively hope—that public policymaking is a predominantly rational decision-making process, this is not the case.

The process would no doubt be simpler and better if it were driven exclusively by fully informed consideration of the best ways for policy to support the nation's pursuit of health, by open and comprehensive debate about potential policies, and by rational selection from among policy choices strictly on the basis of ability to contribute to the pursuit of health. Those who are familiar with the policymaking process, however, know that a wide range of other factors and considerations influence the process. The preferences and influence of interest groups, political bargaining and vote trading, and ideological biases are among the most important of these factors. This is not to say that rationality plays no part in health policymaking. On a good day, it will gain a place among the flurry of political considerations, but "it must be a very good and rare day indeed when policymakers take their cues mainly from scientific knowledge about the state of the world they hope to change or protect" (Brown 1991, 20).

The highly political nature of the policymaking process in the United States accounts for competing theories about how this process plays out. At the opposite ends of a continuum sit strictly public-interest and strictly self-interest theories of how policymakers behave. Policies made entirely in the public interest would be the result of all participants acting according to what they believe to be the public's interest. Alternatively, policies made entirely through a process driven by self-interests would reflect the interplay of the various self-interests of the diverse participants. Policies resulting from these two hypothetical extremes would indeed be very different.

In reality, however, health policies always reflect a mix of public-interest and self-interest influences. The balance between the public and self-interests being served is important to the ultimate shape of health policies. For example, the present coexistence of the extremes of excess (the exorbitant incomes of some physicians and health plan managers, esoteric technologies, and various overcapacities in the healthcare system) and deprivation (lack of insurance for millions of people and inadequate access to basic health services for millions more) resulting from or permitted by some of the nation's existing health policies suggests that the balance has been tipped too often toward the service of self-interests.

This aside, public policymaking in the U.S. health domain is a remarkably complex process, although clearly an imperfect one. The intricacies of the process are explored more thoroughly in subsequent chapters. In general, policymaking is a highly political process. It is continual and cyclical in its operation, it is heavily influenced by factors external to the process, and the component phases and activities within the phases of the process are highly interactive and interdependent.

Summary

Health policies, like those in other domains, are made within the context of the political marketplace, where demanders for and suppliers of policies interact. The federal and state governments have important health policy roles, and their policymaking processes are quite similar.

The demanders of policies include those who view public policies as a mechanism for meeting their health-related objectives or other objectives, such as economic advantage. Although individuals alone can demand public policies, the far more effective demand emanates from organizations and especially from organized interest groups. The suppliers of health policy include elected and appointed members of all three branches of government and the civil servants who staff the government.

The interests of the various demanders and suppliers in this market cannot be completely coincident—often, they are in open conflict—and the decisions and activities of any participant always affect and are affected by the activities of other participants. Public policymaking in the health domain is a human process, a fact with great significance for the outcomes and consequences of the process and one that argues for ethical behavior by all involved in the process.

The policymaking process itself is a highly complex, interactive, and cyclical process that incorporates formulation, implementation, and modification phases. These phases are discussed in detail in subsequent chapters.

Review Questions

1. Compare and contrast the operation of traditional economic markets with that of political markets.
2. Discuss the roles of states in health policy.
3. Who are demanders and suppliers of health policies? What motivates each in the political marketplace?
4. Compare and contrast the pluralist and elitist perspectives on interest groups in the political marketplace.
5. Define power and influence. What are the sources of power in political markets?
6. Draw a schematic model of the public policymaking process.
7. Describe the general features of the model drawn in question 6.

POLICY FORMULATION: AGENDA SETTING

This chapter and the four that follow examine in greater detail the three distinct phases of the health policymaking process described in Chapter 2. This chapter focuses on the agenda setting that occurs in the policy formulation phase. Chapter 4 focuses on the development of legislation that also occurs in that phase. Chapter 5 describes the rulemaking aspects of the policy implementation phase, and Chapter 6 describes the operation aspects of the policy implementation phase. Chapter 7 discusses the policy modification phase. These chapters apply the model to health policymaking almost exclusively at the national level of government. However, as is true of previous chapters, much that is said here about the process of public policymaking also applies at the state and local levels. The contexts, participants, and specific mechanisms and procedures obviously differ among the three levels, but the core process is similar (see Exhibit 3.1).

Overview of the Policy Formulation Phase

The formulation phase of health policymaking is made up of two distinct and sequential parts: agenda setting and legislation development (see the shaded portion of Exhibit 3.1). Each part involves a complex set of activities in which policymakers and those who would influence their decisions and actions engage.

The formulation phase of policymaking results in policy in the form of new public laws or amendments to existing laws. The public laws or amendments pertaining to health are initiated by the interactions of diverse health-related problems, possible solutions, and dynamic political circumstances that relate to the problems and to their potential solutions. Before the policymaking process can progress, some mechanism must initiate the emergence of certain problem/solution combinations and their subsequent movement through the development process.

At any given time, there are many problems or issues related to health. Many of them have possible solutions that are apparent to policymakers. Often these problems have alternative solutions, each of which has its supporters and detractors. Diverse political interests overlay the actual problems and potential solutions. *Agenda setting*, a crucial initial step in the policymaking

EXHIBIT 3.1 A Model of the Public Policymaking Process in the United States: Agenda Setting in the Policy Formulation Phase

Preferences of individuals, organizations, and interest groups, along with biological, cultural, demographic, ecological, economic, ethical, legal, psychological, social, and technological inputs

Policy

Policy Implementation Phase

Rulemaking → Operation

Feedback

Bridged by Formal Enactment of Legislation

Policy Formulation Phase

Agenda Setting
• Problems
• Possible Solutions
• Political Circumstances

Development of Legislation

Window of Opportunity*

Policy Modification Phase

Feedback from individuals, organizations, and interest groups experiencing the consequences of policies, combined with the assessments of the performance and impact of policies by those who formulate and implement them, influences future policy formulation and implementation.

*The window of opportunity opens when there is a favorable confluence of problems, possible solutions, and political circumstances.

process, describes the process by which particular problems emerge and advance to the next stage.

Once a problem that might be addressed through public policy rises to a prominent place on the political agenda—through the confluence of the problem's identification, the existence of possible policy solutions, and the political circumstances surrounding the problem and its potential solutions—it can, but does not necessarily, proceed to the next point in the policy formulation phase, development of legislation. Kingdon (1995) describes the point at which problems, potential solutions to them, and political circumstances converge to stimulate legislation development as a *window of opportunity* (see Exhibit 3.1).

At this second step in policy formulation, policymakers propose specific legislation. One can think of these proposals as hypothetical or unproven solutions to the problems they are intended to address. The proposals then go through carefully prescribed steps that can, but do not always, lead to policies in the form of new public laws or, more often, amendments to previously enacted laws.

Only a small fraction of the problems that might be addressed through public policy ever emerge from agenda setting with sufficient impetus to advance them to this point. And even when they do, only some of the attempts to enact legislation are successful. The path of legislation—that is, of policy in the form of public laws—can be long and arduous (Hacker 1997). The details of this path that pertain to agenda setting are described in this chapter, and those that pertain to the development of legislation are discussed in Chapter 4.

Agenda Setting

Kingdon (1995) describes agenda setting in public policymaking as a function of the confluence of three streams of activity: problems, possible solutions to the problems, and political circumstances. (Some people prefer the term "issue" to refer to something that might trigger policymaking [e.g., Gormley and Boccuti 2001]. We use "problem" to be consistent with Kingdon's terminology.) According to Kingdon (1995, 166), when problems, possible solutions, and political circumstances flow together in a favorable alignment, a "policy window" or "window of opportunity" opens. When this happens, a problem/potential solution combination that might lead to a new public law or an amendment to an existing one emerges from the set of competing problem/possible solution combinations and moves forward in the policy-making process (see Exhibit 3.2).

Current health policies in the form of public laws, such as those pertaining to environmental protection, licensure of health-related practitioners

EXHIBIT 3.2
Agenda Setting
as the
Confluence
of Problems,
Possible
Solutions,
and Political
Circumstances

Problems
Possible Solutions
Political Circumstances

A Place on the Policy Agenda

and organizations, funding for AIDS research or women's health, and regulation of pharmaceuticals, exist because problems or issues emerged from agenda setting and triggered changes in policy. However, the mere existence of these problems was not sufficient to trigger the development of legislation intended to address them.

The existence of health-related problems, even very serious ones such as inadequate health insurance coverage for millions of people or the continuing widespread use of tobacco products, does not always lead to policies intended to solve or ameliorate them. There also must be potential solutions to the problems and the political will to enact specific legislation to implement those solutions. Agenda setting is best understood in the context of its three key variables: problems, possible solutions, and political circumstances.

Problems

The breadth of problems that could initiate agenda setting is reflected in the range of possible health policies. Chapter 1 discussed how health is affected by several determinants: the physical environments in which people live and work; their behaviors and biology; social factors; and the type, quality, and timing of health services they receive.

Beyond these determinants, as shown in Exhibit 3.1, the preferences of individuals, organizations, and interest groups and the biological, cultural, demographic, ecological, economic, ethical, legal, psychological, social, and technological aspects of American life affect policymaking throughout the process. These inputs join with the consequences of the policies produced through the ongoing policymaking cycle (see the feedback loop in Exhibit 3.1) to continuously supply agenda setters with a massive pool of contenders for a place on that agenda. From among the contenders, certain problems find a place on the agenda, while others do not.

Problems That Drive Policy Formulation

The problems that eventually lead to the development of legislation are generally those that policymakers broadly identify as important and urgent. Problems that do not meet these criteria languish at the bottom of the list or never find a place on the agenda at all. Price (1978) argues that whether a problem receives aggressive congressional intervention in the form of policymaking depends on its public salience and the degree of group conflict surrounding it. He defines a publicly salient problem or issue as one with a high actual or potential level of public interest. Conflictive problems or issues are those that stimulate intense disagreements among interest groups or those that pit the interests of groups against the larger public interest. Price contends that the incentives for legislators to intervene in problems or issues are greatest when salience is high and conflict is low. Conversely, incentives are least when salience is low and conflict is high. Appendix 11 illustrates the difficulty of legislative intervention when the conflict surrounding a problem is high.

Problems that lead to attempts at policy solutions find their place on the agenda along one of several paths. Some problems emerge because trends in certain variables eventually reach unacceptable levels—at least, levels unacceptable to some policymakers. Growth in the number of uninsured and cost escalation in the Medicare program are examples of trends that eventually reached levels at which policymakers felt compelled to address the underlying problems through legislation.

Another problem that emerged in this way and led to specific legislation was that a large number of people felt locked into their jobs because they feared that preexisting health conditions might prevent them from obtaining health insurance if they changed jobs. In response to this problem, the Health Insurance Portability and Accountability Act of 1996 (HIPAA; P.L. 104-191) significantly limits the use of preexisting-condition exclusions and enhances the portability of health insurance coverage when people change jobs. Other provisions in this law guarantee availability and renewability of health insurance coverage for certain employees and individuals and an increase in the tax deduction for health insurance purchased by the self-employed.

Problems also can be spotlighted by their widespread applicability (e.g., the high cost of prescription medications to millions of Americans) or by their sharply focused impact on a small but powerful group whose members are directly affected (e.g., the high cost of medical education).

Some problems gain their place on the agenda or strengthen their hold on a place because they are closely linked to other problems that already occupy secure places. Efforts by the legislative and executive branches of the federal government to address the nation's budget deficit problem, at least in part through reduced expenditures on the Medicare program, are a recurring example of the link between one problem (cost increases in the Medicare program) and another (growth of the federal deficit). Linking these two problems significantly strengthened political prospects for the development of legislation intended to curtail Medicare program expenditures, as the Balanced Budget Act of 1997 (P.L. 105-33) demonstrated. This legislation called for reductions in the growth of Medicare expenditures of $385 billion from 1998 through 2007.

Problems also can emerge more or less simultaneously along several paths. Typically, problems that emerge this way become prominent on the policy agenda. For example, the problem of the high cost of health services for the private and public sectors has long received attention from policymakers. This problem emerged along a number of mutually reinforcing paths. In part, the cost problem has been prominent because the cost trend data disturbs many people. The data contribute to and reinforce a widespread acknowledgment of the problem of health costs in public poll after public poll and have attracted the attention of some of those who pay directly for health services through the provision of health insurance benefits, especially the politically powerful business community. Finally, the health cost problem, as it relates to public expenditures—for the Medicare and Medicaid programs especially—has also been linked at times to the need to control the federal budget.

The importance of these variables has been magnified greatly in the context of the global financial crisis engulfing the world beginning in 2008 (Shah 2009). The variables of healthcare costs and the escalating federal budget form a *combination* of circumstances. The health cost problem reinforces each of these circumstances, which is why this problem remains perennially prominent in the minds of many policymakers. Add to this the financial crisis, and it seems clear that healthcare costs will receive renewed attention in the years ahead. The persistence of this problem since long before the current financial crisis began has more to do with the nature of potential solutions than with the identification of health costs as a problem.

Possible Solutions

The second variable in agenda setting (see Exhibit 3.2) is the existence of possible solutions to problems. Problems themselves—even serious, fully acknowledged ones with widespread implications, such as high costs, poor quality, and uneven access to needed health services—do not invariably lead to policies. Potential solutions must accompany them. The availability of possible solutions depends on the generation of ideas and, usually, a period of idea testing and refinement. As Appendix 12 illustrates, numerous ideas might serve as solutions to problems, either in single application or in various combinations.

While the menus of alternative solutions vary in size and quality, alternative solutions almost always exist. An excessive number of alternatives can slow the problem's advancement through the policymaking process as the relative merits of the competing alternatives are considered. Without at least one solution believed to have the potential to solve it, however, a problem does not advance, except in some spurious effort to create the illusion that it is being addressed.

When alternatives exist, policymakers must decide whether the potential solutions are worth developing into legislative proposals. Frequently, multiple solutions to a particular problem will be considered worthy of such action, resulting in the simultaneous development of several competing proposals. This tends to make agenda setting rather chaotic, although rigorous research and analysis can sometimes provide more clarity.

Health services research is "the multidisciplinary field of scientific investigation that studies how social factors, financing systems, organizational structures and processes, health technologies, and personal behaviors affect access to healthcare, the quality and cost of healthcare, and ultimately our health and well-being. Its research domains are individuals, families, organizations, institutions, communities, and populations" (AcademyHealth 2009). The Agency for Healthcare Research and Quality (AHRQ; www.ahrq.gov) defines health services research more simply as "scientific inquiry into the ways in which health services are delivered to various constituents" (AHRQ 2009). Health services researchers seek to understand how people obtain access to healthcare services, the costs of the services, and the results for patients of using this care. The main goals of this type of research include identifying the most effective ways to organize, manage, finance, and deliver high quality care and services and, more recently, how to reduce medical errors and improve patient safety (AHRQ 2009). Health services research, along with much biomedical research, contributes to problem identification and specification and the development of possible solutions. Thus, research can help establish the health policy agenda by clarifying problems and potential solutions. Well-conducted health services research provides policymakers with facts that might affect their decisions.

The Role of Research and Analysis in Defining Problems and Assessing Alternatives

Policymakers value the input of the research community sufficiently to fund much of its work through NIH, AHRQ, and other agencies. AHRQ, the health services research arm of DHHS, complements the biomedical research mission of its sister agency, NIH. AHRQ is the federal government's focal point for research to enhance the quality, appropriateness, and effectiveness of health services and access to those services.

Research plays an important documentation role through the gathering, cataloging, and correlating of facts related to health problems and issues. For example, researchers have documented the dangers of tobacco smoke; the presence of HIV; the numbers of people living with AIDS, a variety of cancers, heart disease, and other disease; the effect of poverty on health; the number of people who lack health insurance coverage; the existence of health disparities among population segments; and the dangers imposed by exposure to various toxins in the physical environment. Quantification and documentation of health-related problems give the problems a better chance of finding a place on the policy agenda.

The second way research informs, and thus influences, the health policy agenda is through analyses to determine which policy solutions may work. The fundamental contribution of biomedical research to the development of medical and health technology in the United States is well established. This research has made possible the diagnosis and treatment of previously untreatable diseases. Health services research provides valuable information to policymakers as they propose, consider, and prioritize alternative solutions to problems.

Potential solutions that might lead to public policies—even if the policies themselves are formulated mainly on political grounds—must stand the test of plausibility. Research that supports a particular course of action or attests to its likelihood of success—or at least to the probability that the course of action will not embarrass policymakers—can make a significant contribution to policymaking by helping to shape the policy agenda.

What research cannot do for policymakers, however, is make decisions for them. Every difficult decision regarding the health policy agenda ultimately rests with policymakers.

Making Decisions About Alternative Possible Solutions

Problems that require decisions and alternative possible solutions to them are two prerequisites for using the classical, rational model of decision making outlined in Exhibit 3.3. This model shares the basic pattern of the organizational decision-making process typically followed in the private and public sectors. However, differences between the two sectors in the use of this model typically arise with the introduction of the *criteria* used to evaluate alternative solutions.

Some of the criteria used to evaluate and compare alternative solutions in the private and public sectors are the same or similar. For example, the criteria set in both sectors usually includes consideration of whether a particular

EXHIBIT 3.3
The Rational Model of Decision Making

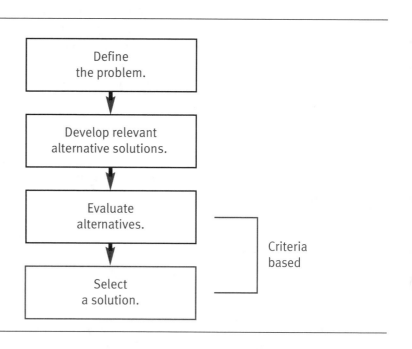

solution will actually solve the problem, whether it can be implemented within available resources and technologies, its costs and benefits relative to other possible solutions, and the results of an analysis of the alternatives.

In both sectors, high-level decisions have scientific or technical, political, and economic dimensions. The scientific or technical aspects can be more difficult to factor into decisions when the evidence is in dispute, as it often is (Atkins, Siegel, and Slutsky 2005; Steinberg and Luce 2005). The most pervasive difference between the criteria sets used in the two sectors, however, is in the roles political concerns and considerations play. Decisions made by public sector policymakers must reflect greater political sensitivity to the public at large and to the preferences of relevant individuals, organizations, and interest groups. This helps explain the importance of the third variable in agenda setting in the health policymaking process, political circumstances.

Political Circumstances

A problem that might be solved or lessened by a policy change, even in combination with a possible solution to that problem, is not sufficient to move the problem/solution combination forward in the policymaking process. A political force, or what is sometimes called political will, is also necessary.

Thus, the political circumstances surrounding each problem/potential solution form the crucial third variable in creating a window of opportunity through which problems/potential solutions move toward development of legislation. This variable is generally as important as the other two variables in this complex equation (see Exhibit 3.2), and in times of crisis such as the global financial crisis that emerged in 2008, political circumstances can be by far the most significant factor in stimulating policy changes. The American Recovery and Reinvestment Act of 2009 (P.L. 111-5) is an example of this phenomenon. The establishment of a political thrust forceful enough to move policymakers to act on a health-related problem is often the most challenging variable in the problem's emergence on the policy agenda.

Whether the political circumstances attendant on any problem/potential solution combination are sufficient to actually open the window of opportunity depends on the competing entries on the policy agenda. The array of problems is an important variable in agenda setting. When the nation is involved in serious threats to its national security or its civil order, for example, or when a state is in the midst of a sustained recession, health policy will be treated differently. In fact, health policy, which is often a high priority for the American people, can be pushed to a secondary position at times. Appendix 13 shows that health issues and policies have become lower priorities than they were in recent years.

The political circumstances surrounding any problem/potential solution combination include such factors as the relevant public attitudes, concerns, and opinions; the preferences and relative ability to influence political decisions of various groups interested in the problem or the way it is addressed; and the positions of involved key policymakers in the executive and legislative branches of government. Each of these factors can influence whether a problem is addressed through policy and the shape and scope of any policy developed to address the problem.

Two factors in particular exert great influence in establishing the policy agenda. These are interest groups and the chief executive (president, governor, or mayor). The role of each in agenda setting is discussed in the next two sections.

Interest Group Involvement in Agenda Setting

As we discussed in Chapter 2, interest groups are ubiquitous in the political marketplace. Perhaps nowhere in the policymaking process is the influence of interest groups more powerful than in the agenda-setting activities of the formulation phase (see Exhibit 3.1).

To fully appreciate the role of interest groups in setting the policy agenda, consider the role of individual Americans. In a representative form of government, such as that of the United States, individual members of society, unless they are among the elected representatives, usually do not vote directly on policies. They can, however, vote on policymakers. Thus, policymakers are interested in what individuals want, even when that is not easy to discern.

However, one of the great myths about democratic societies is that their members, when confronted with tough problems such as the high cost of healthcare for everyone, the lack of health insurance for many, or the existence of widespread disparities in health among segments of the society, ponder the problems carefully and express their preferences to their elected officials, who then factor these opinions into their decisions about how to address the problems through policy. Sometimes these steps take place, but even when the public expresses its opinions about an issue, the result is clouded by the fact that the American people are heterogeneous in their views. Opinions are mixed on health-related problems and their solutions. Public opinion polls can help sort out conflicting opinions, but polls are not always straightforward undertakings. In addition, individuals' opinions on many issues are subject to change.

Yankelovich (1992) points out that the public's thinking on difficult problems that might be addressed through public policies evolves through predictable stages, beginning with awareness of the problem and ending with judgments about its solution. In between, people explore the problem and alternative solutions with varying degrees of success. The progress of individuals through these stages is related to their views on the problems and solutions.

The diversity among members of society and the fact that individual views on problems and potential solutions evolve over time explain in large part the greater influence of organizations and interest groups in shaping the policy agenda. Interest groups in particular can exert extraordinary power and influence in the political marketplace for health policies, as we discussed in Chapter 2.

Whether made up of individuals or organizations, interest groups are often able to present a unified position to policymakers on their preferences regarding a particular problem or its solution. A unified position is far easier for policymakers to assess and respond to than the diverse opinions and preferences of many individuals acting alone. Although individuals tend to be keenly interested in their own health and the health of those they care about, their interests in specific health policies tend to be diffuse. This stands in contrast to the highly concentrated interests of those who earn their livelihood in the health domain or who stand to gain other benefits there. This phenomenon is not unique to health. In general, the interests of those who earn their livelihood in any industry or economic sector are more concentrated than the interests of those who merely use its outputs.

One result of the concentration of interests is the formation of organized interest groups that seek to influence the formulation, implementation, and modification of policies to some advantage for the group's members. Because all interest groups seek policies that favor their members, their own agendas, behaviors, and preferences regarding the larger public policy agenda are often predictable.

Feldstein (2006) argues, for example, that all interest groups representing health services providers seek through legislation to increase the demand for members' services, limit competitors, permit members to charge the highest possible prices for their services, and lower their members' operating costs as much as possible. Likewise, an interest group representing health services consumers logically seeks policies that minimize the costs of the services to its members, ease their access to the services, increase the availability of the services, and so on. Essentially, this is human nature at work.

As we noted earlier, interest groups frequently play powerful roles in setting the nation's health policy agenda, as they subsequently do in the development of legislation and the implementation and modification of health policies. These groups sometimes proactively seek to stimulate new policies that serve the interests of their members. Alternatively, they sometimes reactively seek to block policy changes that they believe do not serve their members' best interests.

Opportunities to join interest groups are widely available. As we discussed in Chapter 2, individual physicians can join and have some of their interests represented by AMA. Nurses can join the American Nurses Association (ANA; www.ana.org). Not only can hospitals join the AHA, but teaching hospitals can join the Association of American Medical Colleges' (AAMC; www.aamc.org) Council of Teaching Hospitals and Health Systems; children's hospitals can join the National Association of Children's Hospitals and Related Institutions (NACHRI; www.childrenshospitals.net); and investor-owned hospitals can join the Federation of American Hospital Systems (FAHS; www.fahs.com). Health insurers can join America's Health Insurance Plans (AHIP; www.ahip.org).

Even subsets of the general population can join a group that seeks to serve their health-related interests. For example, the AARP is a powerful interest group representing the interests of many of the nation's older citizens. Other consumer-oriented interest groups include the Alliance for Retired Americans (www.retiredamericans.org); Families U.S.A. (www.familiesusa.org), which describes itself as the "voice of healthcare consumers"; and the Consortium for Citizens with Disabilities (www.c-c-d.org).

Tactics of Interest Groups in Agenda Setting

As influential participants in U.S. public policymaking, interest groups are integral to the process. And they are especially ubiquitous in the health domain. But how do they exert their influence? Interest groups rely heavily on four tactics: lobbying, electioneering, litigation, and, especially recently, shaping public opinion so that it might in turn influence the policymaking process to the groups' advantage (Edwards, Wattenberg, and Lineberry 2009). Each of these tactics is described in the following sections.

Lobbying This widely used influencing tactic has deep roots in U.S. public policymaking, and its use is growing. Lobbying expenditures on health issues at the federal level reached more than $480 million dollars in 2008 (Center for Responsive Politics 2009). In that year, 495 lobbyists sought to influence the Centers for Medicare & Medicaid Services, and another 282, representing such clients as the Biotechnology Industry Organization, Johnson & Johnson, and the United Fresh Produce Association, lobbied the FDA (Center for Responsive Politics 2009).

In the minds of many people, lobbying conjures a negative image of money exchanging hands for political favors and backroom deals. But ideally it is nothing more than communicating with public policymakers for the purpose of influencing their decisions to be more favorable to, or at least consistent with, the preferences of the lobbyist (Andres 2009; Herrnson, Shaiko, and Wilcox 2005).

"Lobbying," the word for these influencing activities, and "lobbyists," the word for people who do this work, arose in reference to the place where such activities first took place. Before members of Congress had offices or telephones, people who sought to influence their thinking waited for the legislators and talked to them in the lobbies of the buildings they frequented. The original practitioners of this influencing tactic spent so much time in lobbies that they came, naturally enough, to be called lobbyists, and their work, lobbying.

The vast majority of lobbyists operate in an ethical and professional manner, effectively representing the legitimate interests of the groups they serve. However, the few who behave in a heavy-handed or even illegal manner have to some extent tarnished the reputations of all who do this work. Their image is further affected by the fact that their work, properly done, is essentially selfish in nature. Lobbyists seek to persuade others that the position of the interests they represent is the correct one. Lobbyists' whole professional purpose is to persuade others to make decisions that are in the best interests of those who employ or retain them.

Opinions and results of studies on the effectiveness of lobbying are mixed at best (Bergan 2009). Some ambivalence over the role of lobbying derives from the inherent difficulty in isolating its effect from the other influencing tactics discussed later. There is no doubt that lobbying affects the policymaking process, but it seems to work best when applied to policymakers who are already committed, or at least sympathetic, to the lobbyist's position on a public policy issue (Edwards, Wattenberg, and Lineberry 2009). Lobbyists certainly played a prominent role in the enactment of the Medicare Prescription Drug, Improvement, and Modernization Act of 2003 (P.L. 108-173) and in other health policies (Kersh 2008; Weissert and Weissert 2006). Appendix 14 provides an example of highly focused and cooperative lobbying.

The influence lobbyists exert on policymaking is facilitated by several well-recognized sources (Ornstein and Elder 1978; Herrnson, Shaiko, and Wilcox 2005).

- Lobbyists are an important source of information for policymakers. Although most policymakers must be concerned with many policy issues simultaneously, most lobbyists can focus and specialize. They can become expert and can draw on the insight of other experts in the areas they represent.
- Lobbyists can assist policymakers with the development and execution of political strategy. Lobbyists typically are politically savvy and can provide what amounts to free consulting to the policymakers they choose to assist.
- Lobbyists can assist elected policymakers in their reelection efforts. (More is said about this in the next section, on electioneering.) This assistance can take several forms, including campaign contributions, votes, and workers for campaigns.
- Lobbyists can be important sources of innovative ideas for policymakers. Policymakers are judged on the quality of their ideas as well as their abilities to have those ideas translated into effective policies. For most policymakers, few gifts are as valued as a really good idea, especially when they can turn that idea into a bill that bears their name.
- Finally, lobbyists can be friends with policymakers. Lobbyists are often gregarious and interesting people in their own right. They entertain,

sometimes lavishly, and they are socially engaging. Many of them have social and educational backgrounds similar to those of policymakers. In fact, many lobbyists have been policymakers earlier in their careers. It is neither unusual nor surprising for lobbyists and policymakers to become friends.

Electioneering   The effectiveness of electioneering in influencing the policymaking process is based on the simple fact that policymakers who are sympathetic to a group's interests are far more likely to be influenced than are policymakers who are not sympathetic. Thus, interest groups seek to elect and keep in office policymakers whom they view as sympathetic to the interests of the group's members. Electioneering, or using the resources at their disposal to aid candidates for political office, is a common means through which interest groups seek to influence the policymaking process. Many groups have considerable resources to devote to this tactic.

Interest groups have, to varying degrees, a set of resources that involve electoral advantages or disadvantages for political candidates. "Some groups—because of their geographical dispersion in congressional districts throughout the country; their ability to mobilize their members and sympathizers; and their numbers, status, or wealth—are thought to have an ability to affect election outcomes" (Kingdon 1995, 51).

One of the most visible aspects of electioneering is the channeling of money into campaign finances. Exhibit 3.4 shows the extent of this activity in the 2008 election cycle. Health-related interest groups participate heavily in this form of electioneering. Appendix 15 describes groups permitted to engage in political activity.

In 1975, Congress created the Federal Election Commission (FEC; www.fec.gov) to administer and enforce the Federal Election Campaign Act (FECA)—the law that governs the financing of federal elections. The duties of FEC, which is an independent regulatory agency, are to disclose campaign finance information; enforce the provisions of the law, such as the limits and prohibitions on contributions; and oversee the public funding of presidential elections.

The Center for Responsive Politics, a nonpartisan, not-for-profit research group based in Washington, DC, is a rich source of information on the use of money in politics and its effect on elections and public policymaking. The center's website (www.opensecrets.org) provides extensive, detailed information on the flow of money in the political process.

Although participation in campaign financing is an important source of influence for interest groups, the most influential groups are those who exert their influence through lobbying and electioneering activities. The hospital industry is a notable example. The AHA is a leading campaign contributor through its political action committee (PAC). Furthermore, it has many additional resources at its disposal. As Kingdon (1995) points out, every congressional

EXHIBIT 3.4 Money Raised in the 2008 Election Cycle

House

Party	No. of Candidates	Total Raised	Total Spent	Total Cash on Hand	Total from PACs	Total from Individuals
All	1372	$977,054,868	$935,672,848	$195,260,540	$323,012,410	$531,115,597
Democrats	674	$532,197,663	$489,210,419	$126,473,381	$195,416,938	$287,474,388
Republicans	622	$440,264,569	$442,443,242	$68,295,682	$127,292,703	$240,794,351

Senate

Party	No. of Candidates	Total Raised	Total Spent	Total Cash on Hand	Total from PACs	Total from Individuals
All	169	$410,509,962	$419,908,768	$43,796,265	$80,898,314	$270,334,968
Democrats	82	$216,315,667	$218,147,947	$29,167,591	$34,951,737	$148,206,580
Republicans	68	$193,611,964	$201,179,861	$14,615,750	$45,937,331	$121,758,548

President

Party	No. of Candidates	Total Raised	Total Spent	Total Cash on Hand	Total from PACs	Total from Individuals
All	27	$1,810,183,166	$1,759,269,261	$49,540,234	$5,739,032	$1,388,394,897
Democrats	12	$1,147,473,276	$1,122,625,803	$21,878,538	$2,982,716	$965,964,800
Republicans	11	$656,298,931	$630,350,412	$27,500,295	$2,748,049	$417,307,576

SOURCE: Center for Responsive Politics (2009). [Online statistics; retrieved 2/13/09.] www.opensecrets.org/bigpicture/stats.php. Reprinted with permission.

district has hospitals whose trustees are community leaders and whose managers and physicians are typically articulate and respected in their community. These spokespersons can be mobilized to support sympathetic candidates or to contact their representatives directly regarding any policy decision.

As Ornstein and Elder (1978, 74) observe, "The ability of a group to mobilize its membership strength for political action is a highly valuable resource; a small group that is politically active and cohesive can have more political impact than a large, politically apathetic, and unorganized group." The ability to mobilize people and other resources at the grassroots level helps explain the capabilities of various groups to influence the policymaking process. The most influential health interest groups, including AHA and AMA, have particularly strong grassroots organizations to call into play in their lobbying and electioneering tactics.

Litigation

A third tactic interest groups can use to influence the policymaking process is litigation. Interest groups, acting on behalf of their members, seek to influence the policy agenda and the larger policymaking process through litigation in which they challenge existing policies, seek to stimulate new policies, or try to alter certain aspects of policy implementation. Use of the litigation tactic in state and federal courts is widespread, and interest groups increasingly employ it in their efforts to influence policymaking in the health domain.

Although interest groups are more likely to seek to influence legislative and executive branch decisions, they can and do pursue their policy goals in the courts. This tactic is especially attractive when interest groups do not have the economic resources to mount a large lobbying effort or do not have large and influential memberships. In these circumstances, groups may find the judicial branch a more fertile ground for their efforts. When interest groups turn to the courts, they are likely to use one of two strategies: test cases and *amicus curiae* ("friend of the court") briefs.

Because the judiciary engages in policymaking only by rendering decisions in specific cases, interest groups may attempt to ensure that cases that pertain to their interests are brought before the courts. This is the test-case strategy. A particular interest group can initiate and sponsor a case, or it can participate in a case initiated by another group which is pertinent to its interests. The latter strategy involves filing an *amicus curiae* brief and is the easiest way for interest groups to become involved in cases. This strategy, which is used in federal and state appellate courts rather than trial courts, permits groups to get their interests before the courts by filing the briefs even when they do not control the cases in which they participate. To file a brief, a private group must obtain permission from the parties to the case or from the court. This requirement does not apply to government interests. In fact, the solicitor general of the United States is especially important in this regard, and in some situations the U.S. Supreme Court invites the solicitor general to present an *amicus* brief.

Friend-of-the-court briefs are often intended not to strengthen the arguments of one of the parties but to assert to the court the filing group's preferences as to how a case should be resolved. *Amicus curiae* briefs are often filed to persuade an appellate court to either grant or deny review of a lower-court decision (U. S. Department of State 2004).

In Chapter 2, we cited a case in which a group of commercial insurers and HMOs in New York City challenged the State of New York's practice of adding a surcharge to certain hospital bills to raise money to help fund health services for indigent people (Green 1995). The U.S. Supreme Court heard this case. Because the outcome was important to their members, a number of health interest groups filed *amicus* briefs in an effort to influence the court's decision. Through such written depositions, groups state their collective position on issues and describe how the decision will affect their members. This practice is widely used by interest groups in health and other domains. It has made the Supreme Court accessible to these groups, who, in expressing their views, have helped determine which cases the court will hear and how it will rule on them (Collins 2008). This practice is also frequently and effectively used by interest groups in lower courts to help shape the health policy agenda.

The use of litigation is not limited to attempts to shape the policy agenda, however. One particularly effective use of this tactic is seeking clarification from the courts on vague pieces of legislation. This practice provides opportunities for interest groups to exert enormous influence on policymaking overall by influencing the rules, regulations, and administrative practices that guide the implementation of public statutes or laws. We will say more about this in the next chapter, where the discussion turns specifically to rulemaking in the overall public policymaking process. For now, recall from Chapter 1 that the rules and regulations established to implement laws and programs are themselves authoritative decisions that fit the definition of public policies.

Shaping Public Opinion

Because policymakers are influenced by the electorate's opinions, many interest groups seek to influence the policymaking process by shaping public opinion (Brodie and Blendon 2008). A good example of this can be seen in some of the activities of the Coalition to Protect America's Health Care (2009). The coalition describes itself as "a unique organization of hospitals, national, state, regional and metropolitan associations united with the business community behind one goal: to create television, radio and print advertising that seeks to protect and preserve the financial viability of America's hospitals."

This tactic, of course, is not new. It was used extensively in the congressional debate over national health reform in 1993 and 1995. Interest groups spent more than $50 million seeking to shape public opinion on the issues involved. For example, many thought the health insurance industry's ubiquitous

"Harry and Louise" ads were effective during the debate (Hacker 1997). This was not the first use of this public opinion tactic by healthcare interest groups, however.

Intense opposition in some quarters to the legislation, especially by AMA, fueled the congressional debate over the Medicare legislation in the 1960s. The American public had rarely, if ever, been exposed to so feverish a campaign to shape opinions as it experienced in the period leading up to its enactment in 1965.

Among the many activities undertaken in that campaign to influence public opinion (and through it, policymakers), perhaps none is more entertaining in hindsight—and certainly few better represent the campaign's tone and intensity—than one action taken by AMA. As part of its campaign to influence public opinion on Medicare, AMA sent every physician's spouse a recording and advised him or her to host friends and neighbors and play the recording for them. The idea was to encourage these people to write letters to their representatives in Congress in opposition to the legislation. Near the end of the recording, narrated by Ronald Reagan, the following words can be heard (as quoted in Skidmore 1970, 138):

> Write those letters now; call your friends and tell them to write them. If you don't, this program, I promise you, will pass just as surely as the sun will come up tomorrow. And behind it will come other federal programs that will invade every area of freedom as we have known it in this country. Until one day...will awake to find that we have socialism. And if you don't do this, and I don't do it, one of these days you and I are going to spend our sunset years telling our children and our children's children what it was like in America when men were free.

Although the effect of the appeals to public opinion made by interest groups on policymaking is debatable, the extent and persistence of the practice suggests that interest groups believe that it does make a difference. One factor clearly mitigates the usefulness of this tactic and makes difficult its use by interest groups: the heterogeneity of the American population's perceptions of problems and preferred solutions to them. For example, in the congressional debate over major health reform in the 1990s, the majority viewpoint at the beginning of the debate was that health reform was needed. However, at no time during the debate was a public consensus achieved on the nature of that reform. No feasible alternative for reform ever received majority support in any public opinion poll. During most of the debate, in fact, public opinion was approximately evenly divided among the possible reform options (Brodie and Blendon 1995).

Interest Group Resources and Success in Influencing the Policy Agenda

Using lobbying, electioneering, litigation, and efforts to shape public opinion, interest groups seek to influence the policy agenda and the larger public policymaking process to the strategic advantage of their members. The degree of success they achieve depends on the resources at their disposal. Ornstein and Elder (1978) categorize the resources of interest groups into the following categories:

- physical resources, especially money and the number of members
- organizational resources, such as the quality of a group's leadership, the degree of unity or cohesion among its members, and the group's ability to mobilize its membership for political purposes
- political resources, such as expertise in the intricacies of the public policymaking process and a reputation for influencing the process ethically and effectively
- motivational resources, such as the strength of ideological conviction among the membership
- intangible resources, such as the overall status or prestige of a group

An especially important physical resource is the size of a group's membership and the relative proportion of potential members who are actual members. "Part of a group's stock in trade in affecting all phases of policymaking—agendas, decisions, or implementation—is its ability to convince government officials that it speaks with one voice and truly represents the preferences of its members" (Kingdon 1995, 52). Larger groups can obviously have more financial resources, but perhaps even more importantly, size might provide an advantage simply because the group's membership is spread through every legislative district. However, the costs of organizing a large group, especially if their interests are not extremely concordant and focused, can be high.

The mix of physical, organizational, political, motivational, and intangible resources available to an interest group, and how effectively the group uses them, helps determine the group's influence on the policy agenda and other aspects of the policymaking process. A particular group's performance is also affected by its access to resources compared with groups that may be pursuing competing or conflicting policy outcomes (Feldstein 2006; Kingdon 1995; Edwards, Wattenberg, and Lineberry 2009). The political marketplace, as we discussed in Chapter 2, is a place where many people and groups promote their policy preferences.

The Influential Role of Chief Executives in Agenda Setting

The chief executive—the president, governor, or mayor—also influences the policy agenda, including the agenda for policy in the health domain. Popular chief executives can do this easily (Aberbach and Peterson 2006). Kingdon (1995) attributes the influence of presidents (and his point also applies to other chief executives) to certain institutional resources inherent in the executive office. Speaking specifically about presidents and their roles at the federal level, Blumenthal and Morone (2008, 95) state that "presidents energize healthcare policy—they set the political agenda, propose solutions, and organize programs. Bold health policies almost always require presidential leadership."

Political advantages available to chief executives include the ability to present a unified administration position on issues—which contrasts with the legislative branch, where opinions and views tend to be heterogeneous—and the ability to command public attention. Properly managed, the latter ability can stimulate substantial public pressure on legislators. Chief executives can even rival powerful interest groups in their ability to shape public opinion around the public policy agenda.

Lammers (1997) emphasizes the ability of chief executives to perform "issue-raising activities" as crucial to their influence on agenda setting. He notes that the development of legislation is "generally preceded by a variety of actions that first create a widespread sense that a problem exists that needs to be addressed" (Lammers 1997, 112). Chief executives can emphasize problems and preferred solutions in a number of ways, including press conferences, speeches, and addresses. This may be an especially potent tactic in such highly visible contexts as a president's state of the union address or a governor's state of the state address.

Candidates for the presidency are often specific in their campaigns on various health policy issues, sometimes even to the point of endorsing specific legislative proposals (Fishel 1985). Examples include the emphasis presidents Kennedy and Johnson gave to enactment of the Medicare program in their campaigns and President Clinton's highly visible commitment to fundamental health reform as a central theme of his 1992 campaign. President Bush made enactment of the Medicare Prescription Drug, Improvement, and Modernization Act of 2003 a priority as he entered the campaign for his second term in 2004. In his 2008 campaign, President Obama made health reform one of the highest priorities for his anticipated administration.

Another issue-raising mechanism some chief executives favor is the appointment of special commissions or task forces (Linowes 1998). President Clinton used this tactic in the 1993 appointment of the President's Task Force on Health Care Reform (Johnson and Broder 1996), as did President Bush in the creation of the President's Commission to Strengthen Social Security (www.csss.gov) in 2001.

Governors can also use commissions and task forces to elevate issues on the policy agenda. For example, Massachusetts made history when its Gay and Lesbian Student Rights Law was signed by Governor William F. Weld. He established the nation's first Governor's Commission on Gay and Lesbian Youth, which helped lead the state legislature to enact the law. This law prohibits discrimination in public schools on the basis of sexual orientation. Gay students are guaranteed redress if they encounter name-calling, threats of violence, and unfair treatment in school. In another example, Governor Robert Ehrlich of Maryland appointed the Governor's Task Force on Medical Malpractice and Health Care Access in June 2004 to address the crisis created by the cost of malpractice insurance.

Chief executives occupy a position that permits them to influence each phase of the policymaking process. In addition to their issue-raising role in agenda setting, they are well positioned to focus the legislative branch on the development of legislation and to prod legislators to continue their work on favored issues even when other demands compete for their time and attention. In addition, chief executives are central to the implementation of policies by virtue of their position atop the executive (or implementing) branch of government, as we discuss in Chapter 6, and they play a crucial role in modifying previously established policies, as we discuss in Chapter 7.

The Nature of the Health Policy Agenda

The confluence of problems and potential solutions and the political circumstances that surround them invariably shapes the health policy agenda. This agenda, however, is extraordinarily dynamic, literally changing from day to day. In addition, the nation's health policy agenda coexists with policy agendas in other domains, such as defense, welfare, education, and homeland security. The situation is further complicated by the fact that in a pluralistic society where difficult problems exist and clear-cut solutions are rare, every problem and potential solution has different "sides," each with its supporters and detractors. The number, ratio, and intensity of these supporters and detractors are determined by how much the problem and its solution affect them. One consequence of this phenomenon is severe crowding and confounding of the health policy agenda. It is impossible to describe this agenda in its full form at any point in time; it is enormous and in constant flux.

As policymakers seek to accommodate the needs and preferences of different interests in particular problem/potential solution combinations, the inevitable result is a large and diverse set of policies that are riddled with incompatibilities and inconsistencies. The subset of U.S. policies on the production and consumption of tobacco products—a mix that simultaneously facilitates and discourages tobacco use—provides a good example of the coexistence of public policies at cross-purposes.

Another example can be seen in the health policy agenda, and in the eventual pattern of public policies, related to medical technology. Policymakers have sought to spread the benefits of new medical technology and at the same time to protect the public from unsafe technologies and slow the growth in overall health costs through controlling the explosive growth of new technologies. The result is a large group of technology-related policies that seek to foster (e.g., NIH, National Science Foundation, other biomedical funding, tax credits for biomedical research in the private sector), to inhibit (e.g., state-run certificate-of-need programs that restrain the diffusion of technology), and to control (e.g., Food and Drug Administration regulation and product liability laws) the development and use of medical technology in the United States.

Its complexity and inconsistency aside, the most important aspect of the health policy agenda is that when a problem is widely acknowledged, when possible solutions have been identified and refined, and when political circumstances are favorable, a window of opportunity opens, albeit sometimes only briefly. Through this window, problem/potential solution combinations move forward to a new stage: development of legislation (see Exhibit 3.1). As we describe in Chapter 4, through the development of legislation, policymakers seek to convert some of their ideas, hopes, and hypotheses about addressing problems into concrete policies in the form of new public laws or amendments to existing ones.

Summary

The policy formulation phase involves agenda setting and the development of legislation, as Exhibit 3.1 shows. Agenda setting is the central topic of this chapter. We discuss the development of legislation in Chapter 4.

Following Kingdon's (1995) conceptualization, agenda setting in public policymaking is a function of the confluence of three streams of activity: problems, possible solutions to those problems, and political circumstances. When all three streams flow together in a favorable alignment, a window of opportunity opens (see Exhibit 3.1), allowing a problem/potential solution combination, which might be developed into a new public law or an amendment to an existing one, to advance to the next point in the policymaking process: development of legislation.

Review Questions

1. Discuss the formulation phase of policymaking in general terms.
2. Discuss agenda setting as the confluence of three streams of activities. Include the concept of a window of opportunity for legislation development in your answer.
3. Describe the nature of problems that drive policy formulation.
4. Discuss the role of research in health policy agenda setting.
5. Contrast decision making in the public and private sectors as it relates to selecting from among alternative solutions to problems.
6. Discuss the involvement of interest groups in the political circumstances that affect agenda setting. Incorporate the specific ways they influence agenda setting in your response.
7. Discuss the role of chief executives in agenda setting at the federal level.
8. Discuss the nature of the health policy agenda that results from agenda setting at the federal level.

POLICY FORMULATION: DEVELOPMENT OF LEGISLATION

As we noted in Chapter 3, the formulation phase of health policymaking is made up of two distinct and sequential parts: agenda setting and legislation development. Chapter 3 focused on agenda setting; in this chapter we turn our attention to the development of legislation. Policy formulation can be fully appreciated only through an understanding of the combination of activities associated with agenda setting and legislation development.

As with the discussion of agenda setting in Chapter 3, this discussion of legislation development is confined almost exclusively to its occurrence at the federal level of government. However, state and local governments develop their own legislation, and this is generally done using a similar approach. The problems legislation is developed to address differ at each level, as do many of the participants and the specific mechanisms and procedures used in developing legislation.

The result of the entire formulation phase of policymaking is public policy in the form of new public laws or amendments to existing laws. New health-related laws or amendments originate from the policy agenda. Recall that the health policy agenda is established through the interactions of a diverse array of problems, possible solutions to those problems, and the dynamic political circumstances that relate to the problems and to their potential solutions. Combinations of problems, potential solutions, and political circumstances that achieve priority on the policy agenda move on to the next component of the policy formulation phase: legislation development (see the shaded portion of Exhibit 4.1).

The laws and amendments to existing laws that result from the formulation phase of policymaking are quite tangible, and purposely so. They can be seen and read in a number of places. The U.S. Constitution prohibits the enactment of laws that are not specifically and directly made known to the people who are to be bound by them. In practice, federal laws are published for the citizenry immediately upon enactment. Of course, it is incumbent on persons who might be affected by laws to know of them and to be certain that they understand the effects of those laws. Health professionals must devote a great deal of attention to the potential and real impact of laws.

At the federal level, enacted laws are first printed in pamphlet form called *slip law*. Later, laws are published in the *U.S. Statutes at Large* and eventually

EXHIBIT 4.1 A Model of the Public Policymaking Process in the United States: Policy Formulation Phase

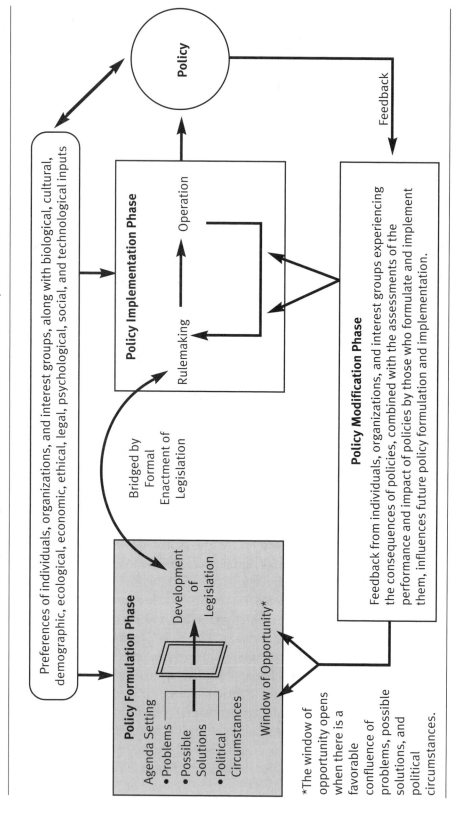

incorporated into the *U.S. Code*. The *Statutes at Large*, published annually, contains the laws enacted during each session of Congress. In effect, they are compilations of all laws enacted in a particular year. The *U.S. Code* is a complete compilation of all of the nation's laws. A new edition of the code is published every six years, with cumulative supplements published annually. Federal public laws can be read at thomas.loc.gov.

The Choreography of Legislation Development

Development of legislation is the point in policy formulation at which specific legislative proposals, which are characterized in Chapter 3 as hypothetical or unproved potential solutions to the problems they are intended to address, advance through a series of steps that can end in new or amended public laws. These steps, not unlike those of a dance, are specified or choreographed. The steps followed at the federal level are shown schematically in Exhibit 4.2. Only when all of the steps are completed does a change in policy result, either in the form of a new public law or, far more typically, an amendment to a previously enacted law. The steps that make up legislation development provide the framework for most of the discussion in this chapter.

Legislation development begins with the origination of ideas for legislation and extends through the enactment of some of those ideas into law or the amendment of existing laws. The steps of this process apply equally whether the resulting legislation is a new law or an amendment. Johnson (2003) provides an extensive description of the steps through which federal legislation is developed. Similarly, most states include descriptions of their legislative processes on their websites. For example, Pennsylvania publishes *Making Law in Pennsylvania: Legislation in the PA House of Representatives* (Pennsylvania House of Representatives 2009). Exhibit 4.3 illustrates the steps in the State of Washington's legislative process, a process typical of the states.

At the federal level, the path through which legislation is developed begins with ideas for proposed legislation or bills in the agenda-setting stage, extends through formal drafting of legislative proposals and then several other steps, and culminates in the enactment of laws derived from some of the proposals. In practice, only a fraction of the legislative proposals that are formally introduced in a Congress—the two annual sessions spanning the terms of office of members of the House of Representatives—are actually enacted into law. Proposals that are not enacted by the end of the congressional session in which they were introduced die and must be reintroduced in the next Congress to be considered further.

As the bridge between policy formulation and implementation (shown in Exhibit 4.1), formal enactment of proposed legislation into law represents

EXHIBIT 4.2 The Choreography of Legislation Development

Bill is originated and drafted.	Bill is originated and drafted.
Representative introduces bill in the House.	Senator introduces bill in the Senate.
Bill is read in the House and assigned to a committee by the Speaker.	Bill is read in the Senate and assigned to a committee by the Majority Leader.
Bill leaves committee, is scheduled for floor consideration and debate, and may be amended.	Bill leaves committee, is scheduled for floor consideration and debate, and may be amended.
House passes bill.	Senate passes bill.
Bill is sent to Senate.	Bill is sent to House.

A conference committee is created to resolve differences if both chambers do not pass an identical bill.

Identical bill is passed by both House and Senate OR one branch agrees to the other branch's version OR bill is amended and both branches vote again and pass amended version.

Bill is presented to the President, who has four options.

Option 1:	*Option 2:*	*Option 3:*	*Option 4:*
President signs bill into law.	During congressional session, bill becomes law after 10 days without presidential signature.	When Congress is not in session, bill does not become law without presidential signature.	President vetoes bill. Two-thirds vote in House and Senate can override veto.

SOURCE: Adapted from Teitelbaum, J. B., and S. E. Wilensky, *Essentials of Health Policy and Law,* 2007: Jones and Bartlett Publishers, Sudbury, MA. www.jbpub.com. Reprinted with permission.

EXHIBIT 4.3
Steps in the
Legislative
Process
in the State
of Washington

1. A bill (a proposed law presented to the Legislature for consideration) may be introduced in either the Senate or House of Representatives by a member.
2. It is referred to a committee for a hearing. The committee studies the bill and may hold public hearings on it. It can then pass, reject, or take no action on the bill.
3. The committee report on the passed bill is read in open session of the House or Senate, and the bill is then referred to the Rules Committee.
4. The Rules Committee can either place the bill on the second reading of the calendar for debate before the entire body or take no action.
5. At the second reading, a bill is subject to debate and amendment before being placed on the third reading calendar for final passage.
6. After passing one house, the bill goes through the same procedure in the other house.
7. If amendments are made, the other house must approve the changes.
8. When the bill is accepted in both houses, it is signed by the respective leaders and sent to the governor.
9. The governor signs the bill into law or may veto all or part of it. If the governor fails to act on the bill, it may become law without a signature.

SOURCE: Washington State Legislature (2009).

a significant transition between these two phases of the overall public policy-making process. The focus in this chapter is on ways in which public laws are developed and enacted in the policymaking process; their implementation is discussed in chapters 5 and 6.

It is important to remember, as we described in Chapter 3, that individuals, health-related organizations, and especially the interest groups to which they belong are instrumental in the agenda setting that precedes legislation development. They also actively participate in the development itself: Once a health policy issue achieves a prominent place on the policy agenda and moves to the next stage of policy formulation—development of legislation—those with concerns and preferences often continue to seek to influence its formulation.

Individuals and health-related organizations and interest groups can participate directly in originating ideas for legislation, helping with the actual drafting of legislative proposals, and participating in the hearings sponsored by legislative committees. When competing bills seek to address a problem, those with interests in the problems align themselves with favored legislative solutions and oppose those they do not favor. The following sections present a detailed discussion of the steps in legislation development at the federal level, although much of this information also applies to legislative processes in the states.

Originating and Drafting Legislative Proposals

The development of legislation begins with the conversion of ideas, hopes, and hypotheses about how problems might be addressed through changes in policy—ideas that emerge from agenda setting—into concrete legislative proposals or bills (see Exhibit 4.2). Proposed legislation can also be introduced as a resolution. There is little practical difference between a bill and a resolution, and they are not differentiated operationally here.

Origins of Ideas for Public Policy

Ideas for public policy originate in many places. They obviously come from members of the House of Representatives and the Senate. In fact, many Congress members are elected, at least in part, on the basis of the legislative ideas they expressed in their campaigns. Promises to introduce certain proposals, made specifically to the constituents candidates seek to represent, are core aspects of the American form of government and frequent sources of eventual legislative proposals. Once in office, legislators become more aware of and knowledgeable about the need to amend or repeal existing laws or enact new laws as their understanding of the problems and potential solutions that face their constituents or the larger society evolves.

But legislators are not the only source of ideas for laws. Individual citizens, health-related organizations, and interest groups representing many individuals or organizations may petition the government—a right guaranteed by the First Amendment—and propose ideas for the development of legislation. In effect, this process results directly from the participation of individuals, organizations, and groups in agenda setting as described in Chapter 3. Many of the nation's public laws originate in this way, because certain individuals, organizations, and interest groups have considerable knowledge of the problem/potential solution combinations that affect them or their members.

Interest groups tend to be influential in legislation development, as they are in agenda setting, because of their pooled resources. Well-staffed interest groups, for example, can draw on the services of legislative draftspersons to transform ideas and concepts into appropriate legislative language.

An increasingly important source of ideas for legislative proposals is "executive communication" from members of the executive branch to members of the legislative branch. Such communications, which also play a role in agenda setting, usually take the form of a letter from a senior member of the executive branch (such as a member of the president's cabinet), the head of an independent agency, or even the president. These communications typically include comprehensive drafts of proposed bills. They are sent simultaneously to the speaker of the House of Representatives and the president of the

Senate, who can insert them into the legislation development procedures at appropriate places.

The executive branch's role as a source of policy ideas is based in the U.S. Constitution. Although the Constitution establishes a government characterized by the separation of powers, Article II, Section 3, imposes an obligation on the president to report to Congress from time to time on the state of the union and to recommend such policies in the form of laws as the president considers necessary, useful, or expedient. Many of the executive communications to Congress follow up on ideas first aired in the president's annual State of the Union address to Congress.

Executive communications that pertain to proposed legislation are referred by the legislative leaders who receive them to the appropriate standing committee or committees that have jurisdiction in the relevant areas. The chairperson of the standing committee involved promptly introduces the bill either in the form in which it was received or with whatever changes the chairperson considers necessary or desirable. Only members of Congress can actually introduce proposed legislation, no matter who originates the idea or drafts the proposal.

The practice of having committee chairpersons introduce legislative proposals that arise through executive communication is followed even when the majority of the House or Senate and the president are not of the same political party, although there is no constitutional or statutory requirement that a bill be introduced to put the executive branch's recommendations into effect. When the chairperson of the committee with jurisdiction does not introduce a bill that is based on executive communication, the committee or one of its subcommittees considers the proposed legislation to determine whether the bill should be introduced.

The most important regular executive communication is the proposed federal budget the president transmits annually to Congress (Oleszek 2007). Recently prepared budgets and related supporting documents are available from the Office of Management and Budget (2008). More is said about the budget process later in this chapter; here, suffice it to say that the president's budget proposal, together with supportive testimony by officials of the various executive branch departments and agencies, individuals, organizations, and interest groups concerned about the budget—before one of the 13 subcommittees of the Appropriations Committees of the House and Senate—is the basis of the appropriation bills that these committees eventually draft.

Drafting Legislative Proposals

Drafting legislative proposals is an art in itself, one requiring considerable skill, knowledge, and experience. Any member of the Senate or House of Representatives can draft bills, and these legislators' staffs are usually instrumental

Information on how the Office of the Legislative Counsel in the House of Representatives supports legislation development is available at www.house.gov/legcoun. Information on how the Senate's Office of the Legislative Counsel supports legislation development is available at slc.senate.gov.

in this, often with assistance from the Office of Legislative Counsel in the Senate or House of Representatives.

Sandra Strokoff (2005), senior counsel in the Office of the Legislative Counsel, U.S. House of Representatives, describes the work of the attorneys who work in the counsel's office as follows:

> Frequently, on the floor of the House of Representatives, one will hear a Member refer to another as the "author" of a bill who has "carefully crafted" the language of the proposed legislation. Statements like these make me smile, because if the Members are the authors, then I and my colleagues in the Office of the Legislative Counsel of the House of Representatives are the ghost writers.
>
> The Office of the Legislative Counsel, created by statute originally in 1918, is currently composed of 30-plus attorneys who generally toil in anonymity, at least as far as those outside the legislative process are concerned. Attorneys are charged with taking the idea of any Member or committee of the House of Representatives requesting the services of the Office and transforming it into legislative language or, as one of my clients used to say, "the magic words." We participate in all stages of the legislative process, be it preparing a bill for introduction, drafting amendments, participating in any conference of the two Houses of Congress to resolve differences between the two versions of the bill, or incorporating changes in the bill at each stage for publication and ultimately for presentation to the President. Frequently, we draft while debate is going on—both during committee consideration and on the House Floor, and may be asked to explain the meaning or effect of legislative language.

When bills are drafted in the executive branch, trained legislative counsels are typically involved. These counsels work in several executive branch departments, and their work includes drafting bills to be forwarded to Congress. Similarly, proposed legislation that arises in the private sector, typically from interest groups, is drafted by people with expertise in this intricate task.

On occasion, as was the case in the Clinton health reform proposal in 1993, legislation drafting is undertaken as a public/private partnership (Hacker 1996, 1997). In late 1993, after many months of feverish drafting by a team including some of the nation's foremost health policy experts,

President Clinton presented his proposal for legislation that would fundamentally reform the American healthcare system. The document, 1,431 pages in length, outlined the president's vision of the way health services should be provided and financed in the United States. The proposal was in the form of a comprehensive draft of a bill (to be called the Health Security Act) that could be enacted into law. However, the proposal faced a long and difficult path from legislation development to possible enactment. Hacker and Skocpol (1997, 315–16) note that "President Clinton sought to enact comprehensive federal rules that would, in theory, simultaneously control medical costs and ensure universal insurance coverage. The bold Health Security initiative was meant to give everyone what they wanted, delicately balancing competing ideas and claimants, deftly maneuvering between major factions in Congress, and helping to revive the political prospects of the Democratic Party in the process." However, the bill failed miserably (Skocpol 1996; Johnson and Broder 1996).

Peterson (1997, 291) characterized the failure of this proposal to make it successfully through the remaining steps to enactment into law as a matter in which "the bold gambit of comprehensive reform had once again succumbed to the power of antagonistic stakeholders, a public paralyzed by the fears of disrupting what it already had, and the challenge of coalition building engendered by the highly decentralized character of American government."

No matter who drafts legislation, however, only members of Congress can officially sponsor a proposal, and the legislative sponsors are ultimately responsible for the language in their bills. It is common for a bill to have multiple sponsors and many cosponsors. Once ideas for solving problems through policy are drafted in legislative language, they are ready for the next step: introduction for formal consideration by Congress. Although the Health Security proposal the Clinton administration drafted was not enacted into law, it did make it through the formal introduction step.

Introducing and Referring Proposed Legislation to Committees

Members of the Senate and the House of Representatives who have chosen to sponsor or cosponsor legislation introduce their proposals in the form of bills (see Exhibit 4.2). On occasion, identical bills are introduced in the Senate and House for simultaneous consideration. When bills are introduced in either chamber of Congress, they are assigned a sequential number (e.g., H.R. 1, H.R. 2, H.R. 3, etc.; S. 1, S. 2, S. 3, etc.) based on the order of introduction by the presiding officer, and are referred to the appropriate standing committee or committees for further study and consideration.

Legislative Committees and Subcommittees

The Senate and the House of Representatives are organized into committees and subcommittees. The committee structure of Congress is crucial to the development of legislation. Committee and subcommittee deliberations provide the settings for intensive and thorough consideration of legislative proposals and issues. Appendix 16 provides more information on how the Senate organizes its committees.

At present, there are 20 standing committees in the House and 20 in the Senate. Both the Senate and the House also participate in several joint committees and select committees. Each standing committee has jurisdiction over a certain area of legislation, and all bills that pertain to a particular area are referred to its committee. Information about the committees is available on their websites, which can be accessed through thomas.loc.gov. Committees are divided into subcommittees to facilitate work. For example, the Ways and Means Committee of the House of Representatives has six subcommittees: Trade, Oversight, Health, Social Security, Income Security and Family Support, and Select Revenue Measures.

Sometimes the content of a bill calls for assignment to more than one committee. In this case, the bill is assigned to multiple committees either jointly or, more commonly, sequentially. For example, the Clinton administration's Health Security plan was introduced simultaneously in the House and the Senate as H.R. 3600 and S. 1757. Because of its scope and complexity, the bill was then referred jointly to ten House committees and two Senate committees for consideration and debate.

Membership on the various congressional committees is divided between the two major political parties. The proportion of members from each party is determined by the majority party. Legislators typically seek membership on committees that have jurisdiction in their particular areas of interest and expertise. The interests of their constituencies typically influence the interests of policymakers. For example, members of the House of Representatives from agricultural districts or financial centers often prefer to join committees that deal with these areas. The same is true of senators in terms of whether they hail from primarily rural or highly urbanized states or from the industrialized northeast or the more agrarian west. The seniority of committee members follows the order of their appointment to the committee.

The majority party in each chamber also controls the appointment of committee and subcommittee chairpersons. These chairpersons exert great power in the development of legislation, because they determine the order and the pace in which the committees or subcommittees they lead consider legislative proposals.

Each committee has a professional staff to assist with administrative details involved in its consideration of bills. Under certain conditions, a standing committee may also appoint consultants on a temporary or intermittent basis to assist the committee in its work. By virtue of expert knowledge, the professional staff members who serve committees and subcommittees are key participants in legislation development.

Committees with Health Policy Jurisdiction

Although no congressional committee is devoted exclusively to the health policy domain, several committees and subcommittees have jurisdiction in health-related legislation development. In an analysis of the period from 1980 to 1991, Baumgartner and Talbert (1995) show that congressional committee hearings on health-related issues were divided among more committees than hearings in any other policy domain.

There is some overlap in the jurisdictions of committees with health-related legislative responsibilities. Most general health bills are referred to the House Committee on Energy and Commerce and the Senate Committee on Health, Education, Labor, and Pensions. However, any bills involving taxes and revenues must be referred to the House Committee on Ways and Means and the Senate Committee on Finance. These two committees have substantial health policy jurisdiction because so much health policy involves taxes as a source of funding. The main health policy interests of these committees are outlined here.

- *Committee on Finance* (finance.senate.gov), *with its Subcommittee on Health Care*. This Senate committee has jurisdiction over health programs under the Social Security Act and health programs financed by a specific tax or trust fund. This gives the committee jurisdiction over matters related to Medicare and Medicaid.
- *Committee on Health, Education, Labor, and Pensions* (help.senate.gov), *also known as the HELP Committee, with its Subcommittees on Children and Families, Employment and Workplace Safety, and Retirement and Aging*. This Senate committee's jurisdiction encompasses most of the agencies, institutes, and programs of the Department of Health and Human Services, including the Food and Drug Administration, the Centers for Disease Control and Prevention, the National Institutes of Health, the Administration on Aging, the Substance Abuse and Mental Health Services Administration, and the Agency for Healthcare Research and Quality. The committee also oversees public health and health insurance policy.
- *Committee on Ways and Means* (waysandmeans.house.gov) *with its Subcommittee on Health*. This House committee has jurisdiction over bills and matters that pertain to providing payments from any source for healthcare, health delivery systems, or health research. The jurisdiction of the Subcommittee on Health includes bills and matters related to the healthcare programs of the Social Security Act (including Titles XVIII and XIX, which are the Medicare and Medicaid programs); and tax

credit and deduction provisions of the Internal Revenue Code dealing with health insurance premiums and healthcare costs.

- *Committee on Energy and Commerce* (energycommerce.house.gov), *with its Subcommittees including those on Health and on Energy and Environment.* This House committee has jurisdiction over all bills and matters related to Medicaid and national health insurance; public health and quarantine; hospital construction; mental health and research; biomedical research and development programs; food and drugs; drug abuse; the Clean Air Act; and environmental protection in general, including the Safe Drinking Water Act.

Committee and Subcommittee Operations

Depending on whether the chairperson of a committee has assigned a bill to a subcommittee, either the full committee or the subcommittee can, if it chooses, hold hearings on the bill. At these public hearings, members of the executive branch, representatives of health-related organizations and interest groups, and other individuals can present their views and recommendations on the legislation under consideration. For example, H.R. 1014, a bill to amend the Federal Food, Drug, and Cosmetic Act and the Public Health Service Act to improve the prevention, diagnosis, and treatment of heart disease, stroke, and cardiovascular diseases in women, was introduced in the House of Representatives on February 13, 2007. An identical bill, S. 573, was simultaneously introduced in the Senate. The bills followed very different courses. In the House, H.R. 1014 was referred to the House Committee on Energy and Commerce on the day it was introduced, and it was sent to the Subcommittee on Health the following day. Hearings on the bill were held on May 1, 2007. Following further discussion and consideration, the bill, with some modification, passed the House on September 23, 2008. In the Senate, S. 573 was introduced on September 13, 2007. The bill was immediately referred to the Senate Committee on Health, Education, Labor, and Pensions, where it received no further action. Appendix 17 provides an example of testimony at a hearing before the House Subcommittee on Health of the Committee on Energy and Commerce.

Following such hearings, members of committees or subcommittees "mark up" the bills they are considering. This term refers to going through the original bill line by line and making changes. Sometimes, when similar bills or bills addressing the same issue have been introduced, they are combined in the markup process. In cases of subcommittee involvement, when the subcommittee has completed its markup and voted to approve the bill, it reports out the bill to the full committee with jurisdiction. When no subcommittee is involved, or when a full committee has reviewed the work of a subcommittee and voted to approve the bill, the full committee reports out the bill for a vote, this time to the floor of the Senate or House. At this point, the administration can formally weigh in with support for or opposition to a bill. This input is issued through a Statement of Administration Policy (SAP), examples of which are available at www.whitehouse.gov/omb/legislative/sap/index.html.

If a committee votes to report a bill favorably, a member of the committee staff writes a report in the name of a committee member. This is an extremely important document. The committee report describes the purposes and scope of the bill and the reasons the committee recommends its approval by the entire Senate or House. As an example, the report for H.R. 1014 can be read at frwebgate.access.gpo.gov/cgi-bin/getdoc.cgi?dbname=110_cong_reports&docid=f:hr874.110.pdf.

Committee reports are useful and informative documents in the legislative history of a public law. They are used by courts in considering matters related to particular laws that have been enacted and by executive branch departments and agencies as guidance for implementing enacted laws. They provide information regarding legislative proposals for those who are interested in the history, purpose, and meaning of the enacted laws.

Generally, a committee report contains an analysis in which the purpose of each section of a bill is described. All changes to existing law that the bill would require are indicated in the report, and the text of laws the bill would repeal are set out. The report begins by describing and explaining committee amendments to the bill as it was originally referred to the committee. Executive communications pertaining to the bill are usually quoted in full in the report.

House or Senate Floor Action on Proposed Legislation

Following approval of a bill by the full committee with jurisdiction, the bill and its report are discharged from the committee. The House or Senate receives it from the committee and places it on the legislative calendar for floor action (see Exhibit 4.2).

Bills can be further amended in debate on the House or Senate floor. However, because great reliance is placed on the committee process in both chambers, amendments to bills proposed from the floor require considerable support.

Once a bill passes in either the House or the Senate, it is sent to the other chamber. The step of referral to a committee with jurisdiction, and perhaps then to a subcommittee, is repeated, and another round of hearings, markup, and eventual action may or may not take place. If the bill is again reported out of committee, it goes to the involved chamber's floor for a final vote. If it is passed in the second chamber, any differences in the House and Senate versions of a bill must be resolved before the bill is sent to the White House for action by the president.

Conference Committee Actions on Proposed Legislation

To resolve differences in a bill that both chambers of Congress have passed, a conference committee (see Exhibit 4.2) may be established (U.S. Senate 2008). Conferees are usually the ranking members of the committees that reported out the bill in each chamber. If they can resolve the differences, a conference report is written, and both houses of Congress vote on it. If the conferees cannot reach agreement, or if either chamber does not accept the report, the bill dies. However, if both chambers accept the conference report, the bill is sent to the president for action. This process is described more fully in Appendix 18.

Presidential Action on Proposed Legislation

The president has several options regarding proposed legislation that has been approved by both the House and the Senate (see Exhibit 4.2). The president can sign the bill, in which case it immediately becomes law. The president can veto the bill, in which case it must be returned to Congress along with an explanation for the rejection. A two-thirds vote in both houses of Congress can override a presidential veto. The president's third option is neither to veto the bill nor to sign it. In this case, the bill becomes law in ten days, but the president has made a political statement of disfavor regarding the legislation. A fourth option may apply when the president receives proposed legislation near the close of a Congressional session; the bill can be pocket vetoed if the president does nothing about it until the Congress is adjourned. In this case, the bill dies.

Legislation Development for the Federal Budget

Because enactment of legislation related to the federal government's annual budget is so crucial to the government's performance and the well-being of the American people, special procedures have been developed to guide this process. The Congressional Budget and Impoundment Control Act of 1974 (P.L. 93-344) and its subsequent amendments provide Congress with the process through which it establishes target levels for revenues, expenditures, and the overall deficit for the coming fiscal year. The budget process is designed to coordinate decisions on sources and levels of federal revenues and on the objectives and levels of federal expenditures. Such decisions affect other policy decisions, including those that pertain to health. Exhibit 4.4 shows, step by step, the process through which the annual federal budget is developed. The schedule begins when the president submits a proposed

EXHIBIT 4.4 Steps in the Federal Budget Process

President's Budget Proposal

▼

House & Senate Budget Committees
- Hearings and markup
- Report conclusions to full House & Senate

▼

House of Representatives & Senate
- Consider amendments
- Pass individual budget resolutions

▼

House/Senate Conference Committee
- House & Senate agree to identical budget numbers
- Each chamber passes an identical conference report, which includes spending allocations for appropriations committees and also includes reconciliation instructions for authorizing

▼   ▼

House & Senate Appropriations Committees	**House & Senate Authorizing Committees**
• 13 separate Appropriations Subcommittees (10 in the House) hold hearings & markups to fund federal programs, limited by the overall allocation passed in the budget. • Report appropriations bills to the House & Senate.	• Hearings & markups to change existing law to meet reconciliation instructions for the purpose of decreasing spending or increasing revenue by a certain date. • Report out authorization legislation.

▼   ▼

(continued)

budget to Congress (see the first box in Exhibit 4.4). Appendix 19 describes these steps in greater detail.

The development of legislation for the federal budget differs in several important ways from the process through which all legislation is developed. First, because the Constitution requires that any bill raising revenue must originate in the House of Representatives, the House traditionally takes the lead in the budget process.

The second distinctive feature of the budget process is that the president's role in developing budget legislation is more formalized. The president is required by statute to submit a budget to Congress each year. By doing so,

EXHIBIT 4.4 (continued)

House & Senate • Consider amendments. • Vote to adopt individual appropriations bills and send to House/Senate conference.	**House & Senate Budget Committees** • Package reconciliation language from the authorizing committees into one bill. • Report Reconciliation Bill to House and Senate.
Appropriations Bill Conference Reports • House & Senate adopt identical conference reports and send to the President. • Failure to pass all appropriations bills requires a "Continuing Resolution" to continue funding government programs. Otherwise, the government shuts down.	**House & Senate** • Consider amendments. • Pass individual reconciliation bills and send to House/Senate Conference.
White House • President signs or vetoes the individual appropriations bills.	**Reconciliation Bill Conference Report** • House & Senate adopt conference report and send to the President.
	White House • President signs or vetoes the Reconciliation Bill.

SOURCE: Reprinted with permission from American Public Health Association. The Budget and Appropriations Process: How the Congress Funds Public Health Programs. http://www.apha.org/NR/rdonlyres/E68C75BA-F173-4C48-BF96-6844FBAEB35A/0/budget_101.pdf. Published March 2, 2005. (Table on p. 1.)

the president establishes the starting point and the framework for the annual process of legislation development for the federal budget.

The third difference between the budget process and the normal legislative process is that federal budget making has three distinct stages. First, Congress drafts and approves a budget resolution that provides the framework for overall federal government taxation and spending for various programs and purposes for the upcoming year. Second, the programs and purposes are authorized by way of establishment, extension, or modification. This must take place before any money can be appropriated for a particular program or purpose, which is the third stage of federal budget making. The amount of money authorized for a program or purpose is generally less than the actual amount appropriated for it. The appropriations process is a key element in the development of annual federal budget legislation. *The Congressional Appropriations Process: An Introduction, 2008* (appropriations.house.gov/pdf/appfacts1.pdf), produced by the Appropriations Committee of the U.S. House of Representatives, provides information about this process.

Legislation Development for State Budgets

The states also develop budget legislation, although the process varies considerably from state to state. In all states, however, the budget is among the most—if not the most—important mechanisms for establishing policy priorities. Pennsylvania uses a process that includes the following four key stages (Office of the Budget 2009):

1. *Budget preparation.* The budget is developed and submitted to the General Assembly.
2. *Legislative review and enactment.* The budget is reviewed by Appropriations Committees of the House and the Senate. The General Assembly enacts its decisions about the budget in the form of the General Appropriation Bill and several individual appropriation bills.
3. *Budget execution.* The Governor assumes responsibility for implementing the budget, although the various state agencies share this responsibility and the Office of the Budget is heavily involved.
4. *Audit.* There is an ongoing audit of financial performance and monitoring and evaluating performance of the state's various programs.

The activities in each of the four stages are described more fully below.

Stage 1: Budget Preparation

The preparation stage of the budget process for a fiscal year that begins July 1 is initiated nearly 12 months prior to that date. The governor controls the first phase of building the budget. The governor establishes initial direction for the budget in August, and state agencies are guided by these priorities as they develop funding requests. The agency heads seek to balance the wants and needs of their constituencies with the administration's priorities and guidelines on total spending.

The Office of the Budget, whose director reports directly to the governor, exerts considerable influence as the office evaluates the agencies' requests and begins to help them formulate preliminary spending and revenue recommendations. Agency heads meet with the governor to express their views on desired changes to those recommendations. This input influences the governor's final recommendations. The governor's Executive Budget, the result of the preparation stage, is finalized in January and submitted to a joint session of the General Assembly through the governor's budget address in early February.

Stage 2: Legislative Review and Enactment

Upon receiving the Executive Budget, the House and Senate appropriations committees hold hearings to review agency requests for funds. Cabinet secretaries and others participate in these hearings, which provide legislators with an opportunity to review the specific programmatic, financial, and policy aspects of each agency's programs and requests. At the same time, legislative staff members analyze the details of the proposals. These review activities provide interest groups with their greatest opportunities to influence the outcome in specific areas by interacting with the legislature. The General Assembly makes its decisions on the budget in the form of the General Appropriation Bill and individual appropriation bills.

Pennsylvania's governor has the power of "line-item veto," which means the governor can reduce or eliminate, but not increase, specific items in the budget legislation. This allows the governor to insist on certain items in the budget and exert additional influence over the legislative process before the budget legislation reaches the governor's desk. Pennsylvania's Constitution requires a balanced budget, which means the governor must veto spending that exceeds the estimated available revenues.

Stage 3: Budget Execution

The governor's signing of the General Appropriation Bill signals the beginning of the execution stage of the budget cycle. With the signing, the Office of the Budget issues detailed "rebudget," or spending plan, instructions. The agencies rebudget the funds appropriated in the legislation. The governor assumes responsibility for implementing the budget, although the various state agencies share this responsibility and the Office of the Budget is highly involved in these activities. The Office of the Budget has the authority to establish the authorized salaried complement for agencies and to request and approve agency spending plans or rebudgets. The executive branch must periodically report the progress of spending to the General Assembly.

Stage 4: Audit

The final stage of the budget cycle for a particular year encompasses an audit and a review of financial and program performance. The Office of the Budget monitors and reviews performance and may conduct program audits or evaluations of selected programs. In addition, the state's Auditor General performs a financial post audit. Audits may be administrative reviews or more official performance audits with published results available to other government officials and the public. Agency officials or the General Assembly act on significant audit findings and recommendations.

Pennsylvania's budget process authorizes the Office of the Budget to evaluate the effectiveness and management efficiency of programs supported by any agency under the governor's jurisdiction. The process also requires the secretary of the budget to prepare reports detailing the results of program evaluations for distribution to the governor, the General Assembly, interested agencies, stakeholders and interest groups, and the public. A more complete description of another state's budget process is presented in Appendix 20.

Most states include descriptions of their budget process on state websites. For example, California's process can be seen at www.dof.ca.gov/fisa/bag/process.htm; New York's at www.budget.state.ny.us/citizen/process/process.html; North Carolina's at www.osbm.state.nc.us/files/pdf_files/2003_budget_manual.pdf; and Texas's at www.senate.state.tx.us/SRC/pdf/Budget101_2005.pdf.

From Formulation to Implementation

When a legislature, whether the U.S. Congress or a state legislature, approves proposed legislation, and the chief executive, whether the president or a governor, signs it, the policymaking process crosses an important threshold. The point at which proposed legislation is formally enacted into law is the point of transition from policy formulation to policy implementation. As shown in Exhibit 4.1, the formal enactment of legislation bridges the formulation and implementation phases of the policymaking process and triggers the implementation phase. Policy implementation is considered in the next chapter.

Summary

The policy formulation phase of policymaking involves agenda setting and the development of legislation. Agenda setting, which we discussed in Chapter 3, entails the confluence of problems, possible solutions to those problems, and political circumstances that permit certain problem/possible solution combinations to progress to the development of legislation.

Legislation development, the other component of policy formulation and the central topic of this chapter, follows carefully choreographed steps that include the drafting and introduction of legislative proposals, their referral to appropriate committees and subcommittees, House and Senate floor action on proposed legislation, conference committee action when necessary, and presidential action on legislation voted on favorably by the legislature. These steps apply whether the legislation is new or, as is often the case, an amendment of prior legislation.

The tangible final products of legislation development are new public laws, amendments to existing ones, or budgets, in the case of legislation development in the budget process. At the federal level, laws are first printed in pamphlet form called *slip law*. Subsequently, laws are published in the *Statutes at Large* and then incorporated into the *U.S. Code*.

Review Questions

1. Discuss the link between agenda setting and the development of legislation.
2. Describe the steps in legislation development.
3. Discuss the various sources of ideas for legislative proposals.
4. What congressional committees are most important to health policy? Briefly describe their roles.
5. Describe the federal budget process. Include the relationship between the federal budget and health policy in your response.

POLICY IMPLEMENTATION: RULEMAKING

5

A s chapters 3 and 4 describe, the policy formulation phase of the public policymaking process is made up of two sets of interrelated activities— agenda setting and legislation development. Sometimes these formulation activities lead to policies in the form of new or amended public laws, such as the enactment of P.L. 108-173 (the Medicare Prescription Drug, Improvement, and Modernization Act of 2003), which amends Title XVIII of the Social Security Act to provide for a voluntary prescription drug coverage program under Medicare. Enactment of laws marks the transition from policy formulation to policy implementation, although the boundary between the two phases is porous. The bridge connecting policy formulation and policy implementation in the center of Exhibit 5.1 is intentionally shown as a two-way connector.

Implementing organizations, primarily the departments and agencies in the executive branch, are established and maintained and the people within them employed to carry out the intent of public laws as enacted by the legislative branch. Legislators rely on implementers to bring their legislation to life. Thus, the relationship between those who formulate policies and those who implement them is symbiotic.

In short, health policies must be implemented effectively if they are to affect the determinants of health. Otherwise, policies are only so much paper and rhetoric. An implemented law can change the physical or social environment in which people live and work, affect their behavior and even their biology, and influence the availability and accessibility of health services.

This chapter focuses on the rulemaking stage of the implementation phase. As the shaded portion of Exhibit 5.1 shows, policy implementation begins with *rulemaking*, which is the establishment of the formal rules ("regulations" is used interchangeably with "rules" in this context) necessary to fully effect the intent embedded in public laws. The second set of activities in policy implementation, covered in Chapter 6, is associated with the *operation* of public laws. If a policy in the form of a public law is intended to protect people from exposure to toxic substances in their environments, for example, its operation entails the activities involved in providing that protection. Such activities might include measuring and assessing dangers from substances in the environment or imposing fines to prevent or restrict environmental pollution.

The implementation phase of public policymaking involves managing human resources, financial resources, and other resources in ways that facilitate achievement of the goals and objectives embodied in enacted legislation.

EXHIBIT 5.1 A Model of the Public Policymaking Process in the United States: Policy Implementation Phase

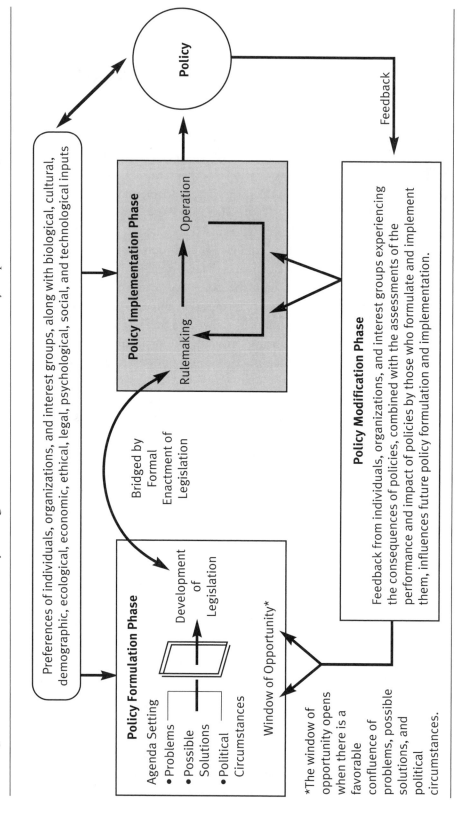

Policy implementation is primarily a *management* undertaking. That is, policy implementation in its essence is the use of resources to pursue the objectives inherent in public laws.

Depending on the scope of policies being implemented, the managerial tasks involved can be simple and straightforward, or they can require massive effort. President Lyndon Johnson once observed that preparations for implementing the Medicare program represented "the largest managerial effort the nation [had] undertaken since the Normandy invasion" (Iglehart 1992, 1468). No matter the scale, however, the implementation of public laws always includes two separate but interrelated sets of activities: rulemaking and operation.

The relationship between rulemaking and the operational activities involved with the implementation of a law is cyclical. As shown in the shaded portion of Exhibit 5.1, rulemaking precedes operation, but the operational activities feed back into rulemaking. This means that experience gained in the operation of policies can influence the modification of rules or regulations used in implementation. The rules promulgated to implement policies can undergo revision—sometimes extensive and continual revision—and new rules can be adopted as experience dictates. This characteristic of policymaking tends to make the process more dynamic than it would be otherwise.

Authoritative decisions made within the executive branch to implement public laws are themselves policies. Recall from Chapter 1 that authoritative decisions refer to those made anywhere within the three branches of government that are under the legitimate purview (i.e., within the official roles, responsibilities, and authorities) of those making the decisions. For example, rules promulgated to implement a law are as much policies as are the laws they support. Similarly, operational decisions made by implementing organizations, to the extent that they require or influence particular behaviors, actions, or decisions by others, are policies. Furthermore, decisions made in the judicial branch regarding the applicability of laws to specific situations or the appropriateness of the actions of implementing organizations are policies. Recall the definition of public policy, given in Chapter 1, as authoritative decisions made in the legislative, executive, or judicial branches of government that are intended to direct or influence the actions, behaviors, or decisions of others. By definition, policies are established in the formulation and implementation phases of the policymaking process.

Responsibility for Policy Implementation

In the implementation phase, responsibility for policymaking shifts from the legislative branch to the executive branch. However, the legislative branch oversees implementation, and the judicial branch also plays a role. Each branch's responsibility is described in the following sections, beginning with the executive branch agencies.

Executive Agencies' Implementation Responsibilities

Agencies such as the DHHS and the DOJ (and subdivisions of those departments); independent federal agencies such as the EPA, the CPSC, and the FDA; and many other executive branch organizations exist primarily to implement the laws formulated by the legislative branch.

CMS is one example of an implementing organization. CMS is a federal agency located organizationally within DHHS, as shown in Exhibit 5.2. It was created in 1977 specifically to administer the Medicare and Medicaid programs and is the primary federal implementing agent for the public laws that established and now continue these programs. Exhibit 5.3 is an organization chart of CMS. The agency is organized around three centers to support its key functions.

The Center for Drug and Health Plan Choice has the following stated responsibilities (Centers for Medicare & Medicaid Services 2009a):

- Responsible for all national policies and operations necessary for the purchasing of Medicare Prescription Drug (Part D) and Medicare Advantage (Part C) health plan benefits. Designs, implements, and manages the procurement of prescription drug plans (PDPs) and Medicare Advantage plans (MA and MA-PD plans), including the solicitation and approval of applications, review of benefits and negotiation of competitive bids, the implementation of quality improvement and performance measures, review of fiscal solvency and contractor management activities.
- Develops and improves all bidding and payment policies related to the Medicare Prescription Drug Benefit and the Medicare Advantage (MA) program.
- Validates payments to the Part D prescription drug and MA plans, including routine annual risk adjustment data validation based on medical record review.
- Coordinates the development and management of business requirements for the national systems for enrollment, payment, and contractor management for the Prescription Drug Benefit and the Medicare Advantage (MA) programs.
- Develops and implements the national policy and oversees operational implementation for all issues related to the Retiree Drug Subsidy Program.
- Develops national policy for eligibility, enrollment and entitlement for Medicare Parts A, B, C, and D, including oversight of activities related to Part D auto-enrollment, low income subsidy, and creditable coverage.

EXHIBIT 5.2 Organization Chart of the Department of Health and Human Services

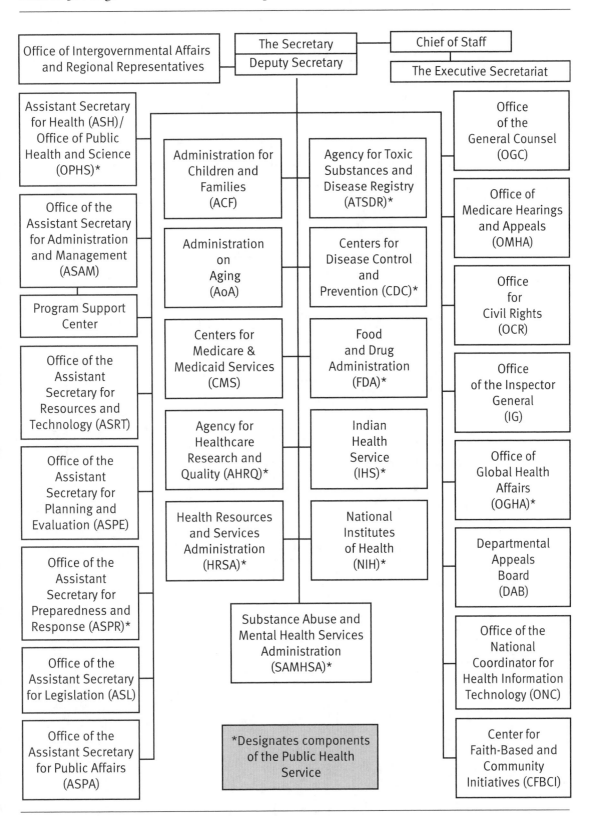

EXHIBIT 5.3 Organization Chart of the Centers for Medicare & Medicaid Services

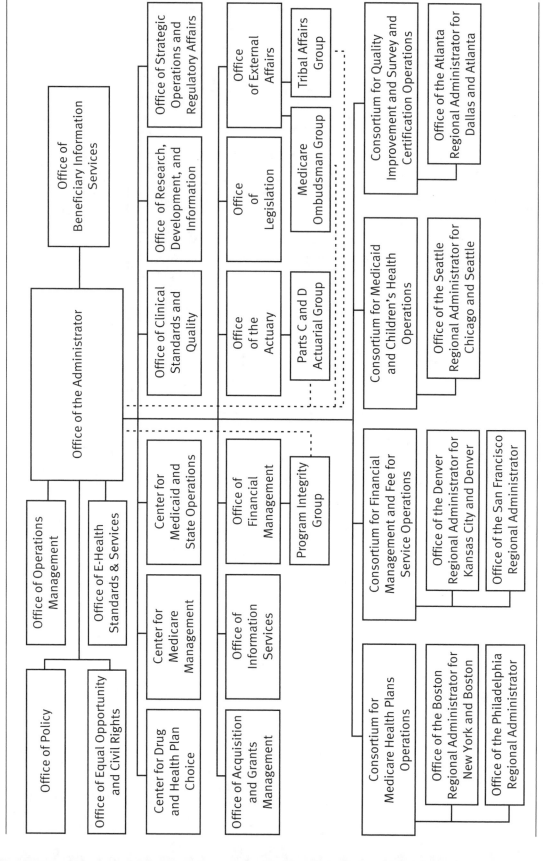

- Develops national policy and oversees operational activities related to Medicare Part A, B, C, and D claims-related hearings, appeals, grievances and other beneficiary-centered dispute resolution processes.
- Serves as the focal point for issues related to a variety of Federal standards affecting private health insurance coverage, including those pertaining to its administration of the Medigap program, Title I of the Health Insurance Portability and Accountability Act and the Consolidated Omnibus Budget Reconciliation Act.
- Works closely with the regional Consortium for Medicare Health Plans Operations (CMHPO) on all operational aspects of the Part C and Part D programs.
- Develops and implements Part C and Part D contractor performance monitoring programs and Part C and Part D compliance and oversight programs and carries out these programs collaboratively with CMHPO.
- Develops surveys to measure consumer experiences with their health plans and healthcare providers; manages the Consumer Assessment of Health Care Provider and Systems (CAHPS) survey; develops and prepares performance measures for Part C sponsors; analyzes and reports Health Plan Employers Data and Information Set data for Part C performance measures and consumer reports; and assesses the effectiveness of CMS's quality reporting activities.
- Effectively communicates program policies related to the Prescription Drug and Medicare Advantage (MA) programs to heath plans and drug plan contractors, employer group sponsors, beneficiary advocates and other stakeholders in the healthcare field.
- Develops new policies (e.g., health plan access, benefits, special needs plans) and programs to reflect changes in program objectives, the healthcare delivery system, beneficiary healthcare needs, and new plan types to support an appropriate range of choices for beneficiaries.
- Collaborates with our partners, such as industry, other government entities and advocacy groups, to understand their perspectives on Prescription Drug and Medicare Managed Care policies and procedures and to drive best practices in the healthcare industry.
- Develops and implements a comprehensive strategic plan, objectives and measures for overseeing an effective compliance and oversight program for all Part C (Medicare Advantage) and Part D (Medicare Prescription Drug) contractors in close collaboration with CMHPO, the Medicare Drug Benefit and C & D Data Group, the Medicare Drug and Health Plan Contract Administration Group and other Center for Drug and Health Plan Choice components.
- Develops and implements a comprehensive and effective audit program for all Part C (Medicare Advantage) and Part D (Medicare Prescription Drug) contractors.

The Center for Medicare Management has the following stated responsibilities (Centers for Medicare & Medicaid Services 2009c):

- Serves as the focal point for all Agency interactions with healthcare providers, intermediaries, carriers, and Medicare Administrative Contractors (MACs) for issues relating to Agency fee-for-service (FFS) policies and operations.
- Responsible for policies related to scope of benefits; and other statutory, regulatory, and contractual provisions.
- Based on program data, develops payment mechanisms, administrative mechanisms, and regulations to ensure that CMS is purchasing medically necessary items and services under Medicare FFS.
- Develops, evaluates and maintains policies, regulations, and instructions that define the scope of benefits and payment amounts for

    1. hospitals for inpatient services under the inpatient prospective payment system and the long-term care hospital prospective payment system;
    2. inpatient services in hospitals and units excluded from the prospective payment systems;
    3. physicians and non-physician practitioners;
    4. hospital outpatient departments, comprehensive outpatient rehabilitation facilities and ambulatory surgical centers;
    5. clinical laboratory services;
    6. ambulance services;
    7. prescription drugs and blood, blood products, and hemophilia clotting factor; and
    8. telemedicine services, rural health clinics, and federally qualified health centers.

- Formulates CMS policy for development, analysis, and maintenance of new and revised medical codes and medical classification systems (including ICD-9-CM, Healthcare Common Procedure Coding System, Diagnosis Related Groups, and Ambulatory Payment Classifications) and develops common medical coding standards and policy.
- Participates in the development and evaluation of proposed legislation pertaining to assigned subject areas.
- Coordinates with the Office of Clinical Standards and Quality on coverage issues in assigned areas.
- Develops, evaluates, and reviews regulations, manuals, program guidelines, and instructions required for the dissemination of program policies to program contractors and the healthcare field.

- Identifies, studies, and makes recommendations for modifying Medicare policies to reflect changes in beneficiary healthcare needs, program objectives, and the healthcare delivery system.
- Develops, evaluates, and maintains policies, regulations, and instructions that define the scope of benefits and payment amounts for skilled nursing facilities, home health agencies, hospice, durable medical equipment, orthotics, prosthetics, and supplies.
- Develops and evaluates national Medicare policies and principles for applying limitations to the costs of skilled nursing facilities and home health agencies.
- Develops criteria for exceptions to the cost limitations for skilled nursing facilities and exceptions to the cost limitations for skilled nursing facilities. Reviews and makes decisions on requests for such exceptions.
- Analyzes payment data; develops, maintains, and updates payment rates for End Stage Renal Disease (ESRD) services and PACE sites.
- Manages designation process for Medicare organ transplant centers, organ procurement organizations, and hospitals seeking out-of-service-area waivers.
- Develops, issues, and administers the specifications, requirements, methods, standards, policies, procedures, and budget guidelines for Medicare claims processing related activities, including detailed definitions of the relative responsibilities of providers, contractors, CMS, other third-party payers, and the beneficiaries of the Medicare program.
- Develops and releases the coding and pricing databases and software for physician, laboratory, SNF, Home Health, Inpatient, Outpatient, and supplier services in the Medicare claims processing standard systems.
- Develops policies related to the integration of healthcare services, including policies on ownership and referral arrangements, business relationships, and conflict of interest.
- Serves as the CMS lead for management, oversight, budget, and performance issues relating to Medicare carriers, fiscal intermediaries, and MACs.
- Functions as CMS liaison for all Medicare carrier, fiscal intermediary, and MAC program issues and, in close collaboration with the regional offices and other CMS components, coordinates the agency-wide contractor activities.
- Manages contractor instructions, workload, and change management process.
- Manages and oversees Medicare contractor provider inquiry, outreach and education activities including specifying Budget Performance Requirements (BPRs), allocation and management of budget dollars

across contractors, evaluating supplemental budget requests, issuing program instructions, and participating in contractor performance evaluation activities.

- In conjunction with CMS program area experts, develops training programs and materials and training tools to educate providers, physicians, suppliers, and Medicare contractor provider education staff on new initiatives and changes to the Medicare program.
- Develops national provider/supplier education products and training tools for Medicare contractors as well as for provider education provided directly by CMS.
- Supports communication between CMS and the provider/supplier community through facilitation of "open door" and Participating Physician Advisory Committee (PPAC) meetings and other listening sessions and promotes awareness of Agency initiatives by sponsoring exhibit programs at industry conferences.
- Develops system requirements and computer software for select portions of Medicare FFS claims processing systems.
- Develops and implements Medicare FFS program requirements for provider billing and for claims processing systems.
- Implements the Medicare Health Support Program.

The Center for Medicaid and State Operations has the following stated responsibilities (Centers for Medicare & Medicaid Services 2009b):

- Serves as the focal point for all Centers for Medicare & Medicaid Services activities relating to Medicaid, the State Children's Health Insurance Program, the Clinical Laboratory Improvement Act (CLIA), the survey and certification of health facilities, and all interactions with States and local governments (including the Territories).
- Develops national Medicaid policies and procedures which support and ensure effective State program administration and beneficiary protection. In partnership with States, evaluates the success of State agencies in carrying out their responsibilities and, as necessary, assists States in correcting problems and improving the quality of their operations.
- Develops, interprets, and applies specific laws, regulations, and policies that directly govern the financial operation and management of the Medicaid program and the related interactions with States and regional offices.
- In coordination with other components, develops, implements, evaluates and refines standardized provider performance measures used within provider certification programs. Supports States in their use of standardized measures for provider feedback and quality improvement activities. Develops, implements, and supports the data collection and analysis systems needed by States to administer the certification program.

- Reviews, approves, and conducts oversight of Medicaid managed care waiver programs. Provides assistance to States and external customers on all Medicaid managed care issues.
- Develops national policies and procedures on Medicaid automated claims/encounter processing and information retrieval systems such as the Medicaid Management Information System and integrated eligibility determination systems.
- In coordination with the Office of Financial Management (OFM), directs, coordinates, and monitors program integrity efforts and activities by States and regions. Works with OFM to provide input in the development of program integrity policy.
- Through administration of the home and community-based services program and policy collaboration with other Agency components and the States, promotes the appropriate choice and continuity of quality services available to frail elderly, disabled, and chronically ill beneficiaries.
- Develops and tests new and innovative methods to improve the Medicaid program through demonstrations and best practices including managing review, approval, and oversight of the Section 1115 demonstrations.
- Directs the planning, coordination, and implementation of the survey, certification, and enforcement programs for all Medicare and Medicaid providers and suppliers and for laboratories under the auspices of CLIA. Reviews and approves applications by States for "exemption" from CLIA and applications from private accreditation organizations for deeming authority. Develops assessment techniques and protocols for periodically evaluating the performance of these entities. Monitors the performance of proficiency testing programs under the auspices of CLIA.
- Provides leadership to the Medicaid Integrity Program (MIP). Develops strategies to prevent and earlier detect improper payments, including fraud and abuse by providers and others, from Medicaid and SCHIP. Offers support and assistance to the States to combat provider fraud, waste, and abuse. Provides guidance and direction to State Medicaid programs based on the insights gained through MIP's efforts.

CMS staff works in the organization's Baltimore headquarters and in ten regional offices (ROs) organized in a consortia structure based on the agency's key lines of business: Medicare health plans, Medicare financial management and fee for service operations, Medicaid and children's health, and quality improvement and survey and certification (see Exhibit 5.3). Each of the four consortia is led by a "Consortium Administrator (CA) who serves as the agency's national focal point in the field for his or her business line(s) and as such is responsible for consistent implementation of CMS programs, policy, and guidance across all ten regions for matters pertaining to his or her business line. In addition to responsibility for a business line, each CA also serves as the agency's senior management official for two or three ROs, representing the CMS Administrator in external affairs matters and overseeing administrative operations" (Centers for Medicare & Medicaid Services 2009d).

Legislative Oversight of Implementation

Although organizations in the executive branch bear most of the responsibility for implementing policies, the legislative branch maintains oversight responsibility in the implementation phase, as mandated by the Legislative Reorganization Act of 1946. Generally, legislative oversight is intended to accomplish the following:

- ensure that implementing organizations adhere to congressional intent
- improve the efficiency, effectiveness, and economy of government's operations
- assess the ability of implementing organizations and individuals to manage and accomplish implementation, including investigation of alleged instances of inadequate management, waste, fraud, dishonesty, or arbitrary action
- ensure that implementation of policies reflects the public interest

Effective legislative oversight is accomplished through several means. One powerful technique involves the funding appropriations that Congress must make to continue implementation of many of the laws it enacts. Although some health policies, such as the Medicare program, are entitlements, others require annual funding through appropriations acts. Examples include the research programs of the NIH, health activities of the Department of Veterans Affairs (VA; www.va.gov), and the activities of the U.S. Public Health Service (USPHS; www.usphs.gov) and the FDA. The House and Senate appropriations committees review the performance of these and similar organizations in carrying out their implementation responsibilities. Implementation inadequacies—real or perceived—may be reflected in the budgets appropriated by Congress for implementing organizations.

Other means of oversight include direct contact between members of Congress and their staffs and executive branch personnel who are involved in implementing policies and using implementation oversight agencies (Congressional Research Service 2007; Nadel 1995), including the CBO and the Government Accountability Office (GAO; www.gao.gov).

Legislative oversight responsibility goes beyond the appropriations procedure. Each standing committee of the House and Senate has certain oversight responsibilities. Those for the House standing committees are spelled out in Clause 2(d)(1) of Rule X of the Rules of the House for the 111th Congress (www.rules.house.gov/ruleprec/111th.pdf); a parallel rule exists in the Senate. Rule X requires that "not later than February 15 of the first session of a Congress, each standing committee shall, in a meeting that is open to the public and with a quorum present, adopt its oversight plan for that Congress. Such plan shall be submitted simultaneously to the Committee on Oversight and Government Reform and to the Committee on House Administration" (U.S. House of Representatives 2009, 9). Clause 2(b)(1) of Rule X states,

> In order to determine whether laws and programs addressing subjects within the jurisdiction of a committee are being implemented and carried out in accordance with the intent of Congress and whether they should be continued, curtailed, or eliminated, each standing committee (other than the Committee on Appropriations) shall review and study on a continuing basis:

- the application, administration, execution, and effectiveness of laws and programs addressing subjects within its jurisdiction;
- the organization and operation of Federal agencies and entities having responsibilities for the administration and execution of laws and programs addressing subjects within its jurisdiction;
- any conditions or circumstances that may indicate the necessity or desirability of enacting new or additional legislation addressing subjects within its jurisdiction (whether or not a bill or resolution has been introduced with respect thereto); and
- future research and forecasting on subjects within its jurisdiction.

Appendix 21 shows relevant parts of a typical oversight plan, in this instance of a committee with important oversight responsibilities for health policy.

Judicial Dimension of Implementation

Legislation and the rules for its implementation can be challenged in the courts. Administrative law judges in the implementing agencies hear the appeals of people or organizations who are dissatisfied with the way the implementation of a policy affects them. For example, the Office of Administrative Law Judges (OALJ; www.epa.gov/oalj) is an independent office in the Office of the Administrator of EPA. These judges conduct hearings and render decisions in proceedings between EPA and people, businesses, government entities, and other organizations that are regulated under environmental laws. Administrative law judges preside over enforcement and permit proceedings under the Administrative Procedure Act, and they conduct other proceedings involving alleged violations of environmental laws, including the following:

- Clean Air Act (CAA)
- Clean Water Act (CWA)
- Comprehensive Environmental Response, Compensation, and Liability Act (CERCLA)
- Emergency Planning and Community Right-to-Know Act (EPCRA)
- Federal Insecticide, Fungicide, and Rodenticide Act (FIFRA)
- Marine Protection, Research, and Sanctuaries Act (MPRSA)

- Safe Drinking Water Act (SDWA)
- Solid Waste Disposal Act, as amended by the Resource Conservation and Recovery Act (RCRA)
- Toxic Substances Control Act (TSCA)
- Subchapter II of TSCA, known as the Asbestos Hazard Emergency Response Act (AHERA)

Federal administrative law judges are certified by the Office of Personnel Management and ensured decisional independence. Decisions issued by administrative law judges at EPA are subject to review by the Environmental Appeals Board (EAB). The initial decision of these judges—unless a party appeals to EAB, or EAB on its own initiative elects to review the initial decision—becomes EPA's final order.

Rulemaking: The Beginning of Implementation

The Administrative Procedure Act of 1946 defines a *rule* as "the whole or part of an agency statement of general or particular applicability and future effect designed to implement, interpret, or prescribe law or policy." Enacted laws are seldom explicit enough to guide their implementation completely. Rather, they tend to be vague, leaving it to the implementing organizations to specify, publish, and circulate the rules or regulations (remember, these terms have the same meaning in the policy context) that will guide the law's actual operation. For this reason, implementation typically begins with rulemaking, the process through which federal agencies develop, amend, or repeal rules. Exhibit 5.4 is an outline of the process most federal agencies are required to follow in writing or revising a rule. Federal agencies issue approximately 4,000 final rules annually on topics ranging from bank operations, to lock operation on the nation's rivers, to the permissible levels of lead in drinking water.

Diver (1989, 199) suggests that rulemaking is "the climactic act of the policy making process." As we will discuss in Chapter 7, this description might be better applied to the modification of previously made policies. Nevertheless, as Kerwin (2003, ix) notes, the rulemaking process is "absolutely central to the definition and implementation of public policy in the United States," and "no significant attempt to alter the direction of a public program can succeed without effective management of the rulemaking process."

Key Features of the Rulemaking Process

Rulemaking is typically a timely process, allowing implementation to proceed smoothly, but this is not always the case. Laws are formulated in the legislative branch and implemented primarily in the executive branch, and sometimes this separation of roles creates significant delays. For example, in 1946,

EXHIBIT 5.4 Federal Rulemaking Process

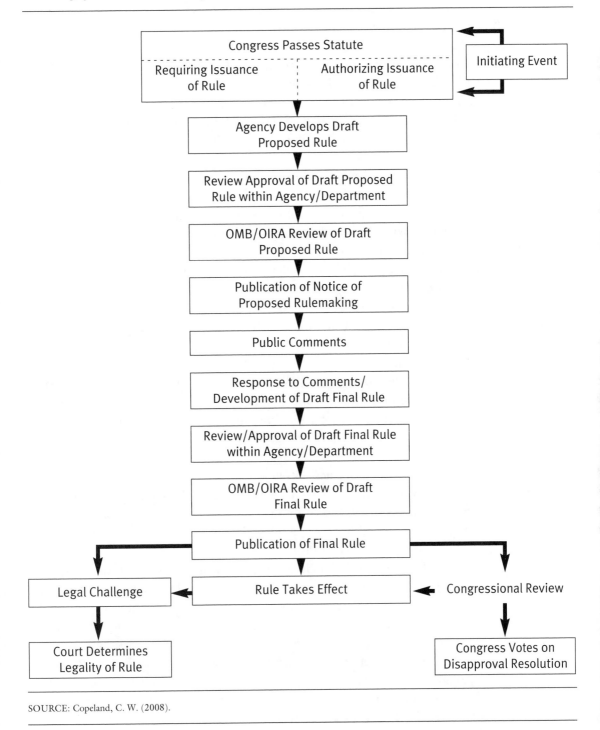

SOURCE: Copeland, C. W. (2008).

Congress enacted the Hospital Survey and Construction Act (P.L. 79-725), also known as the Hill-Burton Act, after its sponsors, Senators Lester Hill and Harold Burton. This law provided grants to build, expand, or modernize hospitals and contained provisions that required grantees to provide "a reasonable volume of services to those unable to pay" and to make their facilities "available to all persons residing in their service areas." However, it was not until significant court action took place in the 1970s that the Department of Health, Education, and Welfare (now DHHS) issued effective rules governing these free-care obligations. For 30 years, those responsible for implementing the law avoided issuing final rules that required hospitals to meet these obligations, probably to avoid anticipated conflict with the hospital industry.

Granting of Rulemaking Authority

As shown at the top of Exhibit 5.4, the rulemaking process begins when Congress takes an action (usually the enactment of a new or amended law) that either requires or authorizes an executive branch agency to write and issue rules. The delegation of rulemaking authority to implementing agencies is an essential feature of rulemaking, but Congress does not relinquish involvement in the process once this authority is shifted. As shown at the bottom of Exhibit 5.4, Congress and the courts can determine that a rule must be returned to an earlier point in the process for further action or even that a rule be vacated.

Usually, however, the link between the enactment of a new or amended law and the promulgation of the rules necessary for its full implementation is fairly direct, and the process goes smoothly. In large part, this is because the development of rules follows the highly prescribed process shown in Exhibit 5.4.

Rules of Rulemaking

The promulgation of rules is itself guided by certain rules and protocols, primarily set forth in the Federal Register Act of 1935 and the Administrative Procedure Act of 1946. Key among these is the requirement that implementing agencies publish *proposed* rules. This step is shown in Exhibit 5.4 as "Publication of Notice of Proposed Rulemaking."

The purpose of publishing proposed rules is to give those with interests in the issue an opportunity to participate in the rulemaking prior to the adoption of a *final* rule. Proposed and final rules are published in the *FR* (www.gpoaccess.gov/fr/index.html), a daily publication that provides a uniform system for publishing presidential and federal agency documents. It includes the following major sections: Presidential Documents, Rules and Regulations, Proposed Rules, and Notices. The *FR*, along with other documents, can be read on a website maintained by the Government Printing Office (GPO) called GPO Access (www.gpoaccess.gov/index.html).

A proposed rule is effectively a *draft* of a rule or set of rules that will guide the implementation of a law while the final rules are under development. Rules can be added, deleted, or modified; thus, rulemaking is an ongoing component in the life of any public law. Publication of a proposed rule is an open invitation for all parties with an interest in the rule to react before it becomes final. For example, in 1989, Congress amended the Medicare policy to change the way physicians who treat Medicare patients are paid for their services. This procedure—which used resource-based relative value scales (RBRVS)—sought to base payment on the actual demands of professional work involved in various physician-provided services and to capture for each service the relevant physician practice expenses, liability insurance costs, and regional norms.

This policy change would decrease the amount of payment for many procedure-based services, such as surgery, and increase payment for many primary care services. Publication in the *FR* of the proposed rules to implement this change literally served as an invitation to physicians and their interest groups to bargain and negotiate the new levels of payment for their services (Moon 1993). As might be expected, many accepted the invitation.

Changes to proposed rules often result from the interactions between implementing officials and those the rules will affect directly. In fact, these interactions, triggered by the publication of a proposed rule, are among the most active points of involvement in the policymaking process for individuals, health-related organizations, and interest groups with a stake in how a particular public law is implemented. The role of interest groups is especially potent at this point in the process, as the next section will demonstrate.

Appendix 5 contains examples of a proposed rule and a final rule—in this instance, the rules to implement the Medicare Prescription Drug Benefit enacted as Title I of the Medicare Prescription Drug, Improvement, and Modernization Act of 2003 (P.L. 108-173). As these examples show, proposed rules begin with a heading that includes the name of the issuing agency, the *Code of Federal Regulations (CFR)* title and part(s) affected, a brief description of the specific subject of the document, and, in some cases, an agency docket number, which identifies the document within the agency's internal filing system. A regulation identifier number (RIN) may also be included. Instructions for filing comments and the date by which comments must be filed are provided as well. Naughton and colleagues (2009) have demonstrated that early commenters can influence the content of emerging rules and may even thwart unwanted regulations.

The Proposed Rules section of the *FR* also contains documents related to previously published proposed rules, extending comment periods, announcing public hearings, making available supplemental information, withdrawing proposed rules, or correcting previously published proposed rules. This section also includes advance notices of proposed rulemaking. An advance notice describes a problem or situation and the agency's anticipated regulatory action and seeks public response concerning the necessity of regulation and the adequacy of the agency's anticipated regulatory action.

In addition to new or amended laws, other factors can trigger rule-making. These include congressional hearings/reports, executive orders, court orders, agencies acting on their own initiative to carry out their mission, petitions for rulemaking from affected parties, and advisory committee recommendations. An example of such an advisory committee is the National Advisory Committee on Occupational Safety and Health (NACOSH), established under the Occupational Safety and Health Act of 1970 to advise the secretaries of labor and health and human services on occupational safety and health programs and policies. Members of the 12-person advisory committee are chosen on the basis of their knowledge and experience in occupational safety and health.

No matter what triggers the rulemaking, any rules formally established by executive departments and agencies have legal effect. As authoritative decisions made within government for the purpose of guiding the decisions, actions, and behaviors of others, rules or regulations are, by definition, policies. These policies are codified in *CFR*, which can be read at www.gpoaccess.gov/cfr.

The Role of Interest Groups in Rulemaking

Implementation of any complex health-related law involves what Thompson (1997) calls the "strategic interaction" that occurs between implementing organizations and affected interest groups. For example, some of the rules proposed in implementing the 1974 National Health Planning and Resources Development Act (P.L. 93-641) sought to reduce obstetrical capacity in the nation's hospitals. One 1977 proposal called for hospitals to perform at least 500 deliveries annually or close their obstetrical units. Notice of this proposed rule elicited immediate objections, especially from hospitals in rural areas where compliance would be difficult, if not impossible. The implementing organization (DHEW, now DHHS) received more than 55,000 written reactions to the proposed rule, almost all of them negative (Zwick 1978). As a result, the final rule was far less restrictive and did not specify a required number of deliveries to keep rural obstetrics units open.

Every policy affects one or more interest groups. Because rules established to implement health-related public laws often target members of interest groups, these groups routinely seek to influence rulemaking. Regulatory policies are implemented to prescribe and control the actions, behaviors, and decisions of certain individuals or organizations. Allocative policies provide income, services, or other benefits to certain individuals or organizations at the expense of others. Interest groups that represent the individuals and organizations directly affected by such policies are actively interested in all aspects of policymaking, including rulemaking. As the discussion in Chapter 2 of interest groups in the political marketplace shows, these groups tend to be well organized and aggressive in pursuit of their preferences, seeking to influence the formulation and implementation of policies that affect them.

EXHIBIT 5.5 Typical Policy Preferences of Selected Health-Related
Individuals and Organizations

Federal Government
- Deficit reduction/increased surpluses
- Control over growth of Medicare and Medicaid expenditures
- Fewer uninsured citizens
- Slower growth in healthcare costs

Employers
- Slower growth in healthcare costs
- Simplified benefit administration
- Elimination of cost shifting
- No mandates

Insurers
- Administrative simplification
- Elimination of cost shifting
- Slower growth in healthcare costs
- No mandates

Individual Practitioners
- Income maintenance/growth
- Professional autonomy
- Malpractice reform

Suppliers
- Continued demand
- Sustained profitability
- Favorable tax treatment

State Government
- Medicaid funding relief
- More Medicaid flexibility
- Fewer uninsured citizens
- More federal funds and slower growth in healthcare costs

Consumers
- Insurance availability
- Access to care (with choices)
- Lower deductibles and copayments

Technology Producers
- Continued demand
- Sustained research funding
- Favorable tax treatment

Provider Organizations
- Improved financial condition
- Administrative simplification
- Less uncompensated care

Professional Schools
- Continued demand
- Student subsidies

Lobbying and other forms of influence become especially intense when
some interest groups strongly support the formulation of a particular law or
the manner in which it is to be implemented, and other groups oppose it.
Policymakers almost always face this dilemma in the formulation and implementation of policies. As we noted in Chapter 2, legislators in such situations
will seek to maximize their net political support through their decisions and
actions. Those responsible for the management of implementing agencies and
organizations are likely to do the same. The result is that rulemaking is often
influenced by interest group preferences, with the more politically powerful
groups exerting the greatest influence.

The potential for conflicting interests among groups concerned with
health policy can be seen in Exhibit 5.5. Although some similarities exist

among the preferences of the various categories, there are also important differences. Policymakers can anticipate that these individuals and organizations, largely working through their interest groups, will seek to ensure that any policies that are enacted reflect their preferences and that their preferences influence the subsequent implementation of such policies.

Health policy is replete with examples of the influence of interest groups on rulemaking. One such example can be seen in the rulemaking that stemmed from enactment of the Medicare program. In part to improve its chances for passage, the Medicare legislation (P.L. 89-97) was written so that the Social Security Administration (www.ssa.gov; the original implementing agency, later replaced by the Health Care Financing Administration, which became the Centers for Medicare & Medicaid Services) would reimburse hospitals and physicians in their customary manner. This meant that they would be paid on a fee-for-service basis, with the fees established by the providers. Each time providers gave services to Medicare program beneficiaries, they were paid their "usual and customary" fees for doing so.

However, unlike the physicians and hospitals, some prepaid providers, such as health maintenance organizations (HMOs), had a different method for charging for their services. Their approach was to charge an annual fee per patient no matter how many times the patient might see a physician or use a hospital. In this situation, hospitals and fee-for-service physicians had obviously preferred to have the Social Security Administration reimburse them according to their customary payment pattern. But they could also see an advantage in making the competing prepaid organizations subject to the fee-for-service payment rules. Their preferences, which they vigorously made known to the Social Security Administration through the powerful AMA and to a somewhat lesser extent through the AHA, forced the prepaid organizations to operate under fee-for-service payment rules until the rules were finally changed in 1985 (Feldstein 2006).

The Medicare Prescription Drug, Improvement, and Modernization Act (MMA) was signed into law in December 2003. Title I of MMA established Part D of Medicare to provide an outpatient prescription drug benefit beginning in 2006. On August 3, 2004, CMS published a proposed rule in *FR* to implement this benefit. Comments about the proposed rule were due by October 4, 2004. More than 7,000 comments were received, including many from health-related interest groups. The comments helped shape the final rule, which was published on January 28, 2005. (See Appendix 5.)

Other Interactions Between Rulemakers and Those Affected by the Rules

In certain instances, especially when rule development is anticipated to be unusually difficult, when such development seems likely to attract severe disagreement and conflict, or when continual revision is expected, special provisions may be made. For example, after passage of the Health Maintenance Organization Act (P.L. 93-222) in 1973, DHEW (now DHHS) organized a series of task forces, with some members drawn from outside the implementing organization, to help develop the proposed rules for implementing the law. This strategy produced rules that were more acceptable to those who would be affected by them.

Another strategy used to support rulemaking is the creation of advisory commissions. For example, following enactment of the 1983 Amendments to the Social Security Act (P.L. 98-21), which established the prospective payment system (PPS) for Medicare reimbursement, Congress established the Prospective Payment Assessment Commission (ProPAC) to provide nonbinding advice to the Health Care Financing Administration (now CMS) in implementing the reimbursement system. A second commission, the Physician Payment Review Commission (PPRC), was established later to advise Congress and CMS regarding payment for physicians' services under the Medicare program. The Balanced Budget Act of 1997 (P.L. 105-33) replaced both commissions with a new commission—the Medicare Payment Advisory Commission (MedPAC; www.medpac.gov)—which incorporates and expands the roles of ProPAC and PPRC. Appendix 22 briefly describes MedPAC's role.

After laws have been enacted and initial rules necessary for implementing them have been promulgated, the implementation phase enters an operational stage (see Exhibit 5.1), which we discuss in Chapter 6. At the point of operation, those who implement policies are required to follow the rules promulgated to guide that implementation according to the mandates inherent in the laws. Ideally, this is exactly what happens. However, implementation does not always go smoothly. Some individuals with implementing responsibilities may disagree with the purposes of the enacted laws and may seek to stall, alter, or even subvert the laws in their implementation phases.

The power of those with implementation responsibilities to affect the final outcomes and consequences of policies should not be underestimated. It is a power equivalent to that of executives in private-sector organizations with operational responsibilities for the achievement of organizational missions, goals, and objectives.

Summary

The implementation phase of the policymaking process includes rulemaking in support of implementation, which is the focus of this chapter, and the operation of policies, which is the focus of Chapter 6. Rulemaking is a necessary part of policymaking, because enacted laws are seldom explicit enough concerning the steps necessary to guide their implementation adequately.

Implementing organizations routinely promulgate rules to guide the operation of enacted laws. The drafting and issuing of rules are themselves guided by certain rules and established procedures. These underlying rules and procedures ensure that those affected by a policy will have ample opportunity to participate in the rulemaking associated with its implementation.

Review Questions

1. Describe in general terms the implementation phase of the public policymaking process.
2. Who is responsible for policy implementation?
3. Discuss legislative oversight of policy implementation.
4. Discuss rulemaking. Include the role of interest groups in rulemaking in your response.

6

POLICY IMPLEMENTATION: OPERATION

This chapter continues our focus on the implementation phase of public policymaking—a phase that involves two interrelated sets of activities. The shaded portion of Exhibit 5.1 shows that policy implementation begins with *rulemaking*, which was the focus of Chapter 5. The second stage in policy implementation, also shown in the shaded portion of Exhibit 5.1, is the *operation* of public laws, and that stage is our focus in this chapter. If a policy in the form of a public law is intended to protect people from exposure to toxic substances in their environments, for example, its operation entails the activities involved in actually providing such protection. Operational activities in this situation might include measuring and assessing dangers from substances in the environment or imposing fines as a means to prevent or restrict environmental pollution.

As we noted in Chapter 5, implementation involves the management of human, financial, and other resources to attain the goals and objectives embodied in enacted legislation. The key to understanding the implementation phase is that policy implementation is primarily a *management* undertaking. The operation stage of implementation involves the actual conduct or running of the programs and processes embedded in enacted public laws. This stage is the domain—although not exclusively—of the appointees and civil servants who staff the government. Government's conduct of the policy operation stage in the past two decades is characterized by increased attention to the importance of management and its practice in various agencies. Appendix 23 illustrates the continuing interest in improving the management of government agencies.

An examination of an agency with implementation duties and responsibilities will provide a background for our discussion of management in the implementation phase and an example of the setting in which operation takes place. As Exhibit 5.2, the organization chart of HSS, shows, this large department contains numerous implementing organizations, such as the FDA, CMS, CDC, and so on. In the following section, we examine the Administration on Aging (AoA; www.aoa.gov) to provide a sense of the origin, mission, organizational structure, and budget of a typical federal implementing agency or organization. AoA is the type of organization that requires extensive management to run the various programs for which it bears operational responsibility.

Example of an Implementing Organization: Administration on Aging

The Older Americans Act of 1965 (OAA; P.L. 89-73) created AoA as its primary implementation agency. The original law was significantly amended in 2006 (P.L. 109-365). Older individuals receive services under many Federal programs. However, the OAA is the major vehicle for the organization and delivery of social and nutrition services to this group and their caregivers. OAA authorizes a wide array of service programs through the National Aging Network of 56 state agencies on aging, 629 area agencies on aging, nearly 20,000 service providers, 244 Tribal organizations, and 2 Native Hawaiian organizations (Administration on Aging 2009c).

AoA Mission

The mission of AoA is to help elderly individuals maintain their dignity and independence in their homes and communities through comprehensive, coordinated, and cost effective systems of long-term care, and livable communities across the United States (Administration on Aging 2009b). In fulfilling its mission, the agency provides a number of services and programs, including, but not limited to (Administration on Aging 2009e):

Supportive Services and Senior Centers Program Home and Community-Based Supportive Services provides grants to states and territories using a formula based primarily on their share of the national population aged 60 and over. The grants fund a broad array of services that enable seniors to remain in their homes for as long as possible. These services include but are not limited to

- access services such as transportation, case management, and information and assistance;
- in-home services such as personal care, chore, and homemaker assistance; and
- community services such as legal services, mental health services, and adult day care.

This program also funds multi-purpose senior centers that coordinate and integrate services for older adults, such as congregate meals, community education, health screening, exercise/health promotion programs, and transportation.

Nutrition Program Since its creation, the OAA Nutrition Program has sought to

- reduce hunger and food insecurity,
- promote socialization of older individuals, and
- promote the health and well-being of older individuals and delay adverse health conditions through access to nutrition and other disease prevention and health promotion services.

Each day in communities across America, senior citizens come together in senior centers or other group settings to share a meal, camaraderie, and friendship. Nutrition services also provide nutrition education, health screenings, and counseling at senior centers. Homebound seniors are able to remain in their homes largely because of the daily delivery of a hot meal, sometimes by a senior volunteer who is their only visitor.

Health, Prevention, and Wellness Program

Services provided through this program enable older persons to make healthy lifestyle choices. Every year, illness and disability that result from chronic disease affects the quality of life for millions of older adults and their caregivers. Through collaboration with Health and Human Services agencies, the National Council on Aging (NCOA), and philanthropic organizations, AoA has created national partnerships that have addressed the need for community-based health, prevention, and wellness programs. These evidence-based programs have been proven to increase self-efficacy, decrease health service utilization, and enable participants to adopt healthy self-management behaviors. AoA's Health, Prevention, and Wellness Program

- focuses on the utilization of evidence-based self-management programs;
- implements and maintains self-management classes within the comfort of participants' communities, using traditional nonclinical settings such as area agencies on aging or senior centers; and
- enables participants to modify existing health self-management behaviors through group interaction and reinforcement.

The National Family Caregiver Support Program (NFCSP)

This program, funded initially in 2000, is a significant addition to the OAA. It was created to help the millions of people who provide the primary care for spouses, parents, older relatives, and friends. The program includes information to caregivers about available services; assistance to caregivers in gaining access to services; individual counseling; organization of support groups; caregiver training to assist caregivers in making decisions and solving problems relating to their caregiving roles; and supplemental services to complement care provided by caregivers. The program also recognizes the needs of grandparents caring for grandchildren, the needs of caregivers of those 18 and under with mental retardation or developmental difficulties, and the diverse needs of Native Americans.

Elder Rights Protection Programs

Services provided through these programs are designed to empower older persons and their family members to detect and prevent elder abuse and consumer fraud as well as to enhance the physical, mental, emotional and financial well-being of America's elderly. The services include, for example, pension counseling programs that help older Americans access their pensions and make informed insurance and healthcare choices; and long-term care ombudsman programs that serve to investigate and resolve complaints made by or for residents of nursing, board and care, and similar adult homes. AoA supports the training of thousands of paid and volunteer long-term care ombudsmen, insurance counselors, and other professionals who assist with reporting waste, fraud, and abuse in nursing homes and other settings; and senior Medicare patrol projects, which operate in 47 states plus the District of Columbia and Puerto Rico. AoA awards grants to state units on aging, area agencies on aging, and community organizations to train senior volunteers how to educate older Americans to take a more active role in monitoring and understanding their healthcare.

AoA Organizational Structure

AoA, as the federal focal point and advocate agency for older persons, is organized as shown in Exhibit 6.1. The assistant secretary for aging at DHHS, who is a presidential appointee, manages AoA. The organizational structure features a pair of centers and a number of offices. The Center for Policy and Management advises and supports the assistant secretary for aging in developing effective policies, programs, and budgets to address the aging of the population and provides leadership related to AoA's administrative, financial, grants, information resources, and strategic planning activities. The Center for Program Operations advises the assistant secretary for aging on and provides leadership related to programs under the Older Americans Act (Administration on Aging 2009d).

AoA Budget (FY2010 Request)

The fiscal year (FY) 2010 president's budget request for the AoA is $1,491,343,000—the same level of funding as was appropriated for FY 2009. This means that the majority of AoA programs will remain funded at the same level as in FY 2009 (Administration on Aging 2009a). However, the FY 2010 request included additional funding in two areas (Administration on Aging 2009a):

- *Health and Long Term Care Programs (+$2,589,000):* The AoA intends to use this additional funding to build on the evaluation that began in FY 2009 of AoA's health and long-term care programs—Aging and Disability Resource Centers, Evidence-Based Disease and Disability Prevention Programs, and Community Living. Congress has directed AoA to expand these programs nationally.
- *Program Administration (+$2,534,000):* The request also provides additional funding for administrative resources. According to AoA, these resources are necessary to allow it to begin to make needed investments in human capital development, information technology, and other activities that are needed to effectively reach out to citizens,

EXHIBIT 6.1 Organization Chart of the Administration on Aging

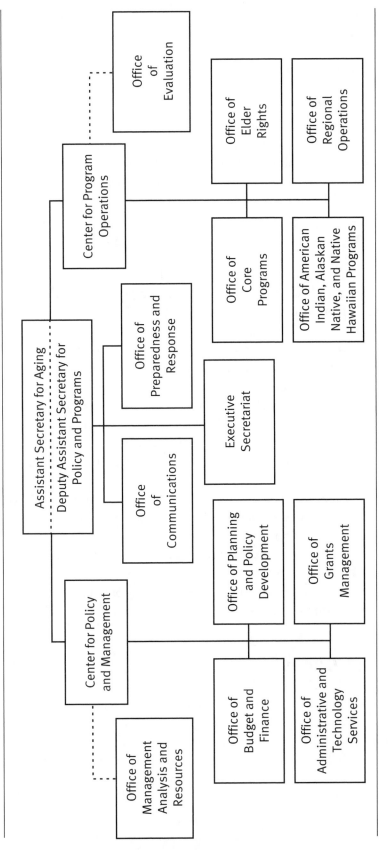

SOURCE: Administration on Aging (2009d).

promote efficiency and innovation, and provide transparency and accountability. This will begin to enable AoA to meet the challenges posed by an increasing aging population in an environment of reforming health and long-term care.

AoA Strategic Plan

AoA developed a Strategic Action Plan for the period 2003–2008 that provided a framework for modernizing the role of the Aging Services Network in long-term care. This modernization strategy was designed to strengthen the network's role in advancing systemic changes in long-term care at the state and community levels to improve consumer access to information and services, enhance consumer choice and control, and empower seniors to live healthier and more active lives.

AoA advanced this strategy by partnering with other federal agencies and national organizations, including private foundations, on grant programs and technical assistance efforts. This included support for the network's role in helping millions of seniors learn about and enroll in the prescription drug benefit available under Medicare.

In 2006, Congress incorporated the key elements of AoA's modernization strategy into the core components of the Older Americans Act and authorized AoA and the network to advance the strategy nationwide.

The most recent AoA Strategic Action Plan, covering 2007–2012, continues the focus on modernizing the Aging Services Network's role in long-term care and gives particular attention to implementing the new provisions contained in the Older Americans Act Amendments of 2006 (Administration on Aging 2009f).

The current Strategic Action Plan establishes five goals and 13 objectives. The plan does not encompass all the agency's activities. Instead, it describes the agency's priorities and provides an overall strategic framework to guide its fiscal and human capital investments. Exhibit 6.2 outlines the five goals and 13 objectives in the plan.

Now that we have examined an implementing organization in some detail, we can turn our attention to the operation of policies within this context.

Operating Policies

The success of any policy's operational stage depends on two variables: (1) how the policy is designed or constructed and (2) certain characteristics of the organization(s) charged with implementation, including the capability of the managers. Exhibit 6.3 summarizes the variables that affect the operational phase. Each of these variables is examined in the sections that follow.

EXHIBIT 6.2 AoA Strategic Goals and Objectives for 2007–2012

Goal 1: Empower older people, their families, and other consumers to make informed decisions about, and to be able to easily access, existing health and long-term care options.
- Provide streamlined access to health and long-term care through Aging and Disability Resource Center programs.
- Empower individuals, including middle-aged individuals, to plan for future long-term care needs.

Goal 2: Enable seniors to remain in their own homes with high quality of life for as long as possible through the provision of home and community-based services, including supports for family caregivers.
- Enable seniors to remain in their homes and communities through flexible service models and consumer-directed approaches.
- Continue to use Older Americans Act programs and services to advance long-term care systems change.
- Continue to improve the planning and assessment efforts of the National Aging Service Network.

Goal 3: Empower older people to stay active and healthy through Older Americans Act services and the new prevention benefits under Medicare.
- Increase the use of Evidence-Based Disease and Disability Prevention Programs for older people at the community level.
- Promote the use of the prevention benefits available under Medicare.

Goal 4: Ensure the rights of older people and prevent their abuse, neglect, and exploitation.
- Facilitate the integration of Older Americans Act elder rights programs into Aging Services Network systems change efforts.
- Improve the identification and utilization of measurable consumer outcomes for elder rights programs.
- Foster quality implementation of new Older Americans Act provisions supporting elder rights.

Goal 5: Maintain effective and responsive management.
- Promote state-of-the-art management practices, including the use of performance-based standards and outcomes, within AoA and the National Aging Services Network.
- Implement the President's Management Agenda.
- Support the Department of Health and Human Services and the National Aging Services Network in administering emergency preparedness and response for older people.

SOURCE: Administration on Aging (2009f).

The Effect of a Policy's Design or Construction on Operation

As with any writing intended to influence the actions, behaviors, or decisions of others (e.g., legal contracts, procedure manuals), the language and construction of a policy—especially in the form of a public law—are crucial to the course and success of its operation. The way laws are written affects how they are subsequently implemented. The effect can be seen in rulemaking and in

- The impact of a policy's design or construction on operation
  - ◆ Objectives of the policy
  - ◆ Hypothesis of the policy
  - ◆ Degree of flexibility in operating the policy
- The impact of implementing organizations and their managers on operation
  - ◆ The fit between implementing organizations and the goals and objectives of the policy
  - ◆ The capability of managers to contribute to operation
  - ◆ Managerial competencies underpinning operating performance

operation. For example, the Older Americans Act of 1965 (P.L. 89-73) not only created AoA as the agency with primary responsibility to implement the law, but the law was also written in such a way that the agency knew what was expected of it in the implementation phase. The design or construction of a policy includes its goals and objectives, the hypotheses or causal relationships embedded in it, and the degree of flexibility allowed those responsible for implementation. As with laws, the design of other policies heavily influences their implementation. Appendix 24 is an example of an executive order issued by a president. The example gives specific guidance as to who is authorized to do what in implementing the order.

Objectives of the Policy

Well-written laws always include clearly articulated objectives, although these are only one element of a good policy. When those who are responsible for implementation know what the law is really intended to accomplish—what its objectives are—they can more easily operate the programs and procedures embedded in it. For example, the Older Americans Act contained the following ambitious set of objectives (Older Americans Act of 2006, Section 101):

> The Congress hereby finds and declares that, in keeping with the traditional American concept of the inherent dignity of the individual in our democratic society, the older people of our Nation are entitled to, and it is the joint and several duty and responsibility of the governments of the U.S., of the several States and their political subdivisions, and of Indian tribes to assist our older people to secure equal opportunity to the full and free enjoyment of the following objectives:
>
> 1. An adequate income in retirement in accordance with the American standard of living.
> 2. The best possible physical and mental health which science can make available and without regard to economic status.

3. Obtaining and maintaining suitable housing, independently selected, designed, and located with reference to special needs and available at costs which older citizens can afford.

4. Full restorative services for those who require institutional care and a comprehensive array of community-based, long-term care services adequate to appropriately sustain older people in their communities and in their homes, including support to family members and other persons providing voluntary care to older individuals needing long-term care services.

5. Opportunity for employment with no discriminatory personnel practices because of age.

6. Retirement in health, honor, dignity—after years of contribution to the economy.

7. Participating in and contributing to meaningful activity within the widest range of civic, cultural, educational, and training and recreational opportunities.

8. Efficient community services, including access to low cost transportation, which provide a choice in supported living arrangements and social assistance in a coordinated manner and which are readily available when needed, with emphasis on maintaining a continuum of care for vulnerable older individuals.

9. Immediate benefit from proven research knowledge which can sustain and improve health and happiness.

10. Freedom, independence, and the free exercise of individual initiative in planning and managing their own lives, full participation in the planning and operation of community based services and programs provided for their benefit, and protection against abuse, neglect, and exploitation.

When the objectives of a policy are unclear, multiple, or conflicting, successful operation is difficult, if not impossible.

An example of the problem of multiple, conflicting objectives can be found in the National Health Planning and Resources Development Act of 1974 (P.L. 93-641). Congress hoped this massive policy would fulfill many of the goals it had previously attempted to attain through a wide variety of more focused policies. As outlined in Section 1513 of P.L. 93-641, its multiple objectives included

- improving the health of people;
- increasing the accessibility (including overcoming geographic, architectural, and transportation barriers), acceptability, continuity, and quality of health services; and
- restraining increases in the cost of providing health services.

As Morone (1990, 272) notes regarding P.L. 93-641, "the legislation proposed every health system desideratum its authors could imagine." These inherently contradictory objectives eventually doomed the policy; Congress repealed it in 1986.

Multiple objectives embedded in a single policy can make implementation extremely difficult, especially if the objectives conflict or are not mutually supportive. In one study, managers of the Medicare program report that they are often torn by the competing demands imposed by the multiple objectives established for the program (Gluck and Sorian 2004). This study notes that these managers are simultaneously required under Medicare policy to

- serve Medicare beneficiaries' healthcare needs;
- protect the financial integrity of the program and preserve the solvency of the Medicare trust funds;
- make sure payments to providers are adequate to ensure their participation in the program;
- ensure the quality of services provided to program beneficiaries;
- guard against fraud and abuse in the program's operation;
- work with numerous private contractors, ensuring their quality and keeping them satisfied with the relationship; and
- work with states, respond to congressional oversight, and serve the political and policy priorities of the executive branch.

This means, for example, that "Medicare managers must ensure adequate participation in Medicare by healthcare providers, but also see to it that providers meet performance and quality standards" (Gluck and Sorian 2004, 65).

Hypothesis of the Policy

Vague or conflicting objectives are not the only problem that can hinder a policy's operational stage. The procedural paradigm set forth in a public law can also be flawed. Embedded in every policy is a theory, or *hypothesis*, about the effect of operationalizing the policy: if someone does A, then B will result. As Thompson (1997, 158) notes, however, only in a perfect world would policymakers always base their laws on entirely plausible hypotheses, as "limits to their knowledge and the political dynamics of policy formulation often impede this development."

Because an underlying rationale—flawed though it may be—is implicit in any policy, we can think of the policy as a *logic model* (Knowlton and Phillips 2008). Policies are not written as logic models, but there is a logic model inherent in any policy in the form of a public law. The logic model can be expressed in terms of how resources are supposed to be processed to achieve the policy's goals and objectives. We elaborate on the utility of thinking of policies as logic models in Chapter 8.

If the hypothesis underpinning a policy is wrong, the operational stage will not solve the problem the policy is intended to address, which means the policy cannot be successfully implemented. It will not matter that its objectives are appropriate, or even that they are noble. In formulating the National Health Planning and Resources Development Act (P.L. 93-641), for example, Congress combined an oddly matched pair of strategies: voluntary, community-based planning on the one hand and heavy-handed regulation, at least of capital expansion in the health sector, on the other. To no one's surprise (at least in hindsight), the combination did not work well. The core hypothesis of the policy was seriously flawed.

By contrast, when the Older Americans Act was introduced in 1965, it had a clear underlying hypothesis. The OAA "was intended to provide resources necessary for public and private social service providers to meet the social service needs of the elderly" (U.S. Senate 2006). The original act received wide bipartisan support and has endured, with amendments, to the present day. When President Johnson signed the legislation in 1965, he noted that the new law would provide "an orderly, intelligent, and constructive program to help us meet the new dimensions of responsibilities which lie ahead in the remaining years of this century. Under this program every State and every community can now move toward a coordinated program of services and opportunities for our older citizens" (Johnson 1965, 744). The logic in a policy that established AoA and continues to provide resources to support services and the provision and consumption of those services is clear. If the policy does A (establishes AoA and provides it with resources), then B will result (services will be provided and consumed).

Degree of Flexibility in Operating the Policy

Another aspect of policy construction that can significantly affect implementation is the nature and extent of any decisions left to the implementing organizations. These decisions may be necessitated by directive language in the law, by what the law does not say, or by confusing or vague language in the law. Although some flexibility in developing policy implementation rules can be advantageous, vague policy directives can create problems for those with implementation responsibilities.

The Occupational Safety and Health Act of 1970 (P.L. 91-596), for example, contained vague directives and phrases that created significant problems for its implementers. Section 2 of the law stressed the importance of fostering healthful working conditions "in so far as possible" rather than specifying objectives or targets for achieving reductions in occupational injuries or diseases. In Section 6, the statute authorized the secretary of labor, in implementing the law, to issue standards dealing with toxic substances in the workplace "to the extent feasible." Considerable time and energy were expended in deciding if this phrase meant that implementers could take the economic costs of their actions to employers into account in establishing standards dealing with workplace toxic substances. In these instances, effective implementation was impeded by the policy's vague and imprecise language.

Language that is too restrictive can also impede the implementation of a policy. In contrast with the imprecise language in the Occupational Safety and Health Act, Congress wrote into the law a precise and extremely restrictive range of fines that could be assessed against firms that violated standards. For less serious violations, the fine would be $1,000. For serious, willful violations, the fine could be up to $10,000. Most analysts considered the limits of these fines far too low to be effective deterrents, especially for large, profitable enterprises. In this instance, effective operation of the law was impeded by very specific language.

The Older Americans Act Amendments of 2006, which reauthorized the Older Americans Act of 1965, provides extensive implementation guidance. However, considerable flexibility is left to the implementing organization, AoA. Much of the language in the law, while providing detailed information about *what* is to be accomplished in implementation, leaves to the AoA's managers a great deal of flexibility as to *how* to accomplish these responsibilities. For example, the 2006 policy adds provisions on elder justice, which is defined in the law as "effort to prevent, detect, treat, intervene in, and respond to elder abuse, neglect, and exploitation and to protect elders with diminished capacity while maximizing their autonomy" (Congressional Research Service 2006). The law provides guidance for addressing elder justice. Specifically, Section 201, Elder Abuse Prevention and Services (Congressional Research Service 2006),

> authorizes the Assistant Secretary for Aging to designate within the Administration on Aging responsibility for elder abuse prevention and services. Assigns to the Assistant Secretary the duty of developing objectives, priorities, policy, and a plan for: (1) facilitating the implementation of an elder justice system in the U. S.; (2) supporting states' efforts in carrying out elder justice programs; (3) establishing federal guidelines and disseminating best practices for uniform data collection and reporting by states; (4) collecting and disseminating data relating to the abuse, neglect, and exploitation of older individuals (abuse); (5) establishing an information clearinghouse; (6) researching such abuse; (7) providing technical assistance to states and other entities; (8) conducting a study concerning the degree of abuse; and (9) promoting collaborative efforts and diminishing duplicative efforts in elder justice programs in all levels of government.

This wording gives AoA explicit direction for what is to be done, leaving the organization and its managers to decide how it is to be done, for the most part. This flexibility will facilitate the operation of these new provisions.

Congress has tended in recent decades to enact longer and more detailed laws to enhance their implementation. For example, the Medicare Prescription Drug, Improvement, and Modernization Act of 2003 is 416 pages long. But no matter how a law is written, its implementation is also directly affected by the organization or agency charged with the task, including the abilities and competence of its managers.

The Effect of Implementing Organizations and Their Managers on Operation

The essence of the implementation phase of policymaking is that one or more organizations or agencies undertake the operation of enacted legislation, ideally in a manner that realizes the intent behind the legislation. This involves promulgating the rules under which implementation will proceed and actually putting the laws into operation.

As we noted earlier, the bulk of these implementation responsibilities rests with executive branch organizations. For example, CMS is primarily responsible for implementing the Medicare program, the FDA is primarily responsible for implementing many of the nation's food and drug policies, and, as we have seen, the AoA is responsible for implementing the Older Americans Act. State insurance departments are responsible for implementing the states' policies regarding health insurance, and so on. The characteristics and attributes of implementing organizations that contribute to their organizational success at policy implementation, including the roles of their managers in successful implementation, must be considered in policy operation (Trattner and McGinnis 2004).

The Fit Between Implementing Organizations and Policy Objectives

No characteristic of an implementing organization is more essential to success than a close fit between the organization and the objectives of the policies it must implement. Fit is determined by whether (1) the organization is sympathetic to the policy's goals and objectives and (2) the organization has the necessary resources—authority, money, personnel, status or prestige, information and expertise, technology, and physical facilities and equipment—to implement the policy effectively.

Whether a policy-implementing organization is sympathetic to the goals and objectives of the policy depends on the attitudes and perspectives of its senior leaders and managers. They are the people who ensure that the necessary support for implementation is garnered. In the case of AoA, for example, attitudes and commitments critical to the organization's success include those of the assistant secretary for aging, who manages this organization, and the managers of AoA's centers and offices (see Exhibit 6.1). If an implementing organization's leaders are not sympathetic to the policies they must implement, they are unlikely to protect those policies from unwarranted amendments or intrusions by nonsupporters. Legislators who are hostile to the policy and those who seek to influence those legislators pose a particular threat. Strong allies in the legislative branch and among interest groups can assist with this protective task, but much of the responsibility rests with the leaders of the implementing organization.

The connection between any organization's resources and its capacity to fulfill its purposes is straightforward. AoA's budget and staff must be adequate matches for the implementation challenges facing the organization. Another factor in the fit between an implementing organization and the policies it is supposed to implement is technology. Implementing organizations rely on a variety of methods and technologies to implement policies. Just as policies differ in substantial ways (recall the distinction made in Chapter 1 between allocative and regulatory policies), the technologies needed to implement them also differ (Dye 2008).

Regulatory policies require implementation technologies that prescribe and control the behaviors of whoever is being regulated. Such technologies include capacity for rule promulgation, investigatory capacity, and ability to impose sanctions. Allocative policies, on the other hand, require technologies through which implementing organizations deliver income, goods, or services. Such technologies include targeting recipients or beneficiaries, determining eligibility for benefits, and managing the supply and quality of goods or services provided through the policy. OSHA, for example, relies heavily on regulatory technologies as it seeks to protect workers from hazards in the workplace. In contrast, AoA relies heavily, although not exclusively, on allocative technologies in the operation of its programs and activities.

Only when the leaders of an implementing organization are fully sympathetic to a policy's objectives and have adequate operational resources, including the appropriate technologies to get the job done, can they effectively carry out their implementation duties. Even then, however, other factors affect the degree of success achieved, including the contributions of the organization's managers.

The Capability of Managers to Contribute to Operation

The performance of the managers of implementing organizations, especially those at senior levels, directly affects organizational performance (White and Newcomer 2005). Appendix 25 illustrates the attention government pays to appropriately training its managers to fulfill their roles. Appendix 23 provides another perspective on this.

The type, quality, and extent of the contributions managers make depend on their managerial capability—that is, how adeptly they strategize, design, and lead (Longest 2005). Although we discuss these activities in sequence in the following sections, in reality all three are undertaken continuously and more or less simultaneously by managers. The relationship among these core management activities is depicted in Exhibit 6.4.

Strategizing This activity involves efforts to establish suitable organizational missions, goals, and objectives and to develop and carry out plans or strategies to accomplish the purposes of the organization. When managers think strategically, they consider how to adapt their organizational domains to the challenges and opportunities in their environment. Implementing organizations are dynamic, open systems. Their external environments and organizational histories are often remarkably complex.

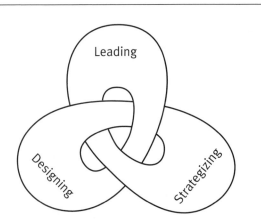

EXHIBIT 6.4
The Core
Activities
in Managing

The managers of an implementing organization are influenced, sometimes dramatically, by what goes on in the external environment. Imagine, for example, the significance for an implementing organization of being assigned major new responsibilities or having some of its core responsibilities curtailed. Or consider the operational effect of a decisive shift in control of Congress, such as the one that occurred in the 1992 congressional election or the midterm defection of Senator James Jeffords in 2001 from the Republican Party, which shifted the control of the U.S. Senate from the Republicans to the Democrats overnight.

When managers think and act strategically, they acknowledge that their organization is affected by what goes on outside it, and their decisions and actions reflect this relationship. Thus, expertise in discerning the significant information in one's environment is crucial to effective strategizing.

Effective managers engage in situational analysis to identify and assess pertinent environmental information. Managers of implementing organizations must analyze enormous amounts of information that could affect their organizations, including information about the plans of executive branch administration and the activities occurring in the legislative branch. In addition, external biological, cultural, demographic, ecological, economic, ethical, legal, psychological, social, and technological information must be analyzed for its potential effect on the organization.

In conducting comprehensive situational analyses, managers are required to follow four interrelated steps: (1) scanning the environment to identify strategic issues (i.e., trends, developments, opportunities, threats, or possible events) that could affect the organization, (2) monitoring the strategic issues identified, (3) forecasting or projecting the future directions of strategic issues, and (4) assessing the implications of the strategic issues for the organization.

Good situational analysis, however, goes beyond external discernment. It also involves a comprehensive assessment of the internal strengths and weaknesses of the organization and the values held by individuals in the organization.

Armed with this information, managers can formulate or refine organizational goals and develop suitable strategic plans for achieving them. The importance of effective strategizing is determined by the relationship between an organization and its external environment and the volatility of its external and internal environments. Most implementation organizations are highly dependent on their external environments, and their internal and external environments tend to be dynamic and fluid.

Designing   In designing, managers establish relationships among people and other resources in their organization. They designate individual positions and aggregate these positions into work groups such as teams, departments, and divisions. In short, they design the organizational structure.

The designing responsibilities of managers in implementing organizations are a constant challenge. In these volatile environments, managers cannot simply design the organization once and then turn their attention elsewhere. Instead, this task is ongoing and involves not only initial design but also routine redesign. Some of the circumstances under which public-sector managers are likely to be involved in changing organization design include the following:

- A significant change occurs in an implementing organization's external environment that directly influences its operations. This could be a new or amended public law for the organization to implement or a change in the rules that affect the operationalization of public laws. Environmental changes might also include a major reduction in the organization's budget or a reorganization initiative undertaken in the executive branch.
- An organization adopts new technologies for carrying out its work or is given new implementation responsibilities. An organizational design change may be required to channel necessary resources into the new activities. Conversely, when old technologies are abandoned or when previous responsibilities are shifted elsewhere, new structural arrangements may be necessary.
- An organization experiences a change in management personnel. Leadership changes are routine in the executive branch organizations that carry out policy implementation. People move in and out of public service. Administrations change. Changes at or near the top level of organizations stimulate organizational redesigns. New leadership provides an opportunity to rethink the way the organization is designed and how it conducts its work. New managers typically view their organization's design from a fresh perspective and may wish to have its design reflect their own ideas and preferences.
- Often, large-scale design changes that involve substantial reorganization or restructuring occur in the context of larger change programs.

Changes in the environments of many implementing organizations have stimulated organizational change, making the designer role of their managers more important and more challenging. But the designer role is only one of the three roles played by these managers. How they perform in the others also affects the performance of their organizations.

Leadership is essential in any purposeful organization. Someone must determine, initiate, integrate, and oversee the work of others. As leaders, the senior-level managers in implementing organizations are responsible for

Leading

- molding internal and external agreement on the organization's purposes and priorities;
- building support for the organization's purposes and priorities among internal and external stakeholders, especially among administrative branch superiors, legislators with oversight responsibility for the organization, and relevant interest groups;
- striking a workable balance among the economic and professional interests of the organization's members, the demands and preferences of its external stakeholders, and the public interest the organization is required to serve; and
- negotiating and maintaining effective relationships with people and organizations, regulated by or otherwise affected by the implementing organization, who supply resources to the implementing organization or with whom the implementing organization must work closely in carrying out its policy implementation responsibilities.

Effective implementation organizations require *transformational leadership*. This is accomplished through decisions about organizational mission and structure, resources, priorities, quality and other performance standards, and acquisition of new technologies. It differs from *transactional leadership*, through which leaders help meet certain needs of the followers if they perform to the leader's expectations (Burns 1978). Such transactions are not the main determinants of success in leading policy-implementing organizations. In this role, the focus must be on leadership of the entire organization, which calls for transformational leadership.

The essence of transformational leadership is the ability to develop and instill a common vision of what the organization is to accomplish and how it is to be accomplished and to stimulate determined and widespread adherence to that vision. Successful leaders at the organizational level must focus on decisions and activities that affect the entire organization, including those intended to ensure its survival and overall well-being. They must establish missions, goals, and objectives; inculcate appropriate values in the individuals who make up the organization; manage the organizational culture; build intra- and interorganizational coalitions; and interpret and respond to challenges and opportunities presented by the external environment.

As in any organization, the leaders of implementing agencies and organizations can benefit from knowing the histories and experiences of their organization. Organizational leadership improves where

- long-standing shared values and commonly accepted principles and norms help shape the organization's mission and operating practices and resolve conflicts among competing views,
- a history of success in implementing policies helps legitimize the organization's claims for support from internal and external stakeholders, and
- a history of effective relationships with oversight actors and relevant interest groups and the availability of adequate financial resources provide a sense of organizational pride, stability, self-determination, and autonomy.

Basic management skills—especially in communication, conflict resolution, and motivation—also facilitate organizational leadership. Leaders who can effectively communicate their views and preferences have a distinct advantage in guiding the behaviors of their followers. Similarly, successful organizational leaders are able to minimize conflict, mobilize widespread commitment to their preferences regarding the organization, and motivate stakeholders to realize these preferences.

Appendix 26 illustrates the magnitude of the challenges facing managers in implementing organizations. Meeting such challenges will depend on how well the agency's managers strategize, design, and lead. Success also depends on managers' possession of specific competencies.

Managerial Competencies Underpinning Operation

Successfully strategizing, designing, and leading requires that managers possess certain competencies, which are defined as clusters of "related knowledge, skills, and ability (sometimes referred to by the acronym SKA) that (1) affect a major part of one's job (a role or responsibility), (2) correlate with performance on the job, (3) can be measured against well accepted standards, and (4) can be improved by training and development" (Lucia and Lepsinger 1999).

The competencies required of managers in the organizations and agencies that implement policy begin with *policy competence*. The other necessary competencies parallel Katz's (1974) classification of the competencies appropriate for work in the private sector: *conceptual, technical,* and *interpersonal.* Katz's concept of interpersonal skill is expanded in this context to include collaboration between and among organizations, yielding an *interpersonal/ collaborative* competency. We discuss each of these competencies in the following sections.

For managers in policy implementing organizations, policy competence can be thought of as the knowledge, skills, and abilities that permit one to successfully analyze the public policymaking process, accurately assess its impact on the organization's domain of interest or responsibility, and successfully influence the public policymaking process. Managers working within implementing organizations need a higher level of policy competence than do those who are outside implementing organizations but are affected by policy and its implementation.

Policy Competence

Managers of implementing organizations need to understand the policymaking process in its entirety so that, through analysis, they can predict the effects of various decisions on their domains of responsibility. For example, policies that determine an organization's budget and the scope of its implementation responsibilities obviously affect the organization. Similarly, managers in an implementing organization must be able to influence the policymaking process from the inside.

In any organizational setting, adequate conceptual knowledge and skills permit managers to envision the organization's place and roles in the larger context in which it exists. This competency also allows managers to visualize the complex interrelationships within their workplace—relationships among staff and other resources and departments or other units. Conceptual competence allows managers to identify, understand, and interact with external and internal stakeholders—that is, with the individuals, groups, organizations, and agencies that have an interest or stake in the decisions and actions of the organization or agency.

Conceptual Competence

Conceptual competence also enhances managers' abilities to comprehend organizational cultures and historically developed values, beliefs, and norms and to visualize the future of their organization or agency.

The knowledge and associated skills that make up technical competence pertain to management competence—knowing how to effectively strategize, design, and lead—*and* to the actual work of a particular agency or organization. For example, managers in FDA must know about managing *and* at least some aspects of food or drug safety and efficacy. CDC managers must know about managing *and* some aspects of developing and applying disease prevention and control, environmental health, or health promotion and education activities designed to help in the pursuit of health.

Technical Competence

Another factor in managerial success in any setting is the cluster of knowledge and skills related to the human interactions by which managers direct or lead others in pursuit of objectives. *Interpersonal* competence permits managers to develop and instill a common vision and stimulate determination to pursue that vision. The essence of interpersonal competence is knowledge of and skill

Interpersonal/ Collaborative Competence

in motivating people, communicating visions and preferences, handling negotiations, and managing conflicts.

The core elements of traditional interpersonal competence expand considerably when organizations or agencies collaborate or cooperate with one another. Interpersonal relationships within organizations differ from those among or between collaborating organizations, agencies, or different levels of government. *Collaborative* competence is the ability to partner with other entities. This requires the abilities to create and maintain multiparty organizational arrangements; to negotiate complex agreements, perhaps even contracts, that sustain these arrangements; and to produce mutually beneficial outcomes through such arrangements.

The ability to develop shared cultures, or at least to minimize the differences that exist in the cultures of collaborating entities, is crucial to establishing and maintaining effective interorganizational or interagency collaborations. In this context, culture is the pattern of shared values and beliefs ingrained in an organization or agency over time that influences the behaviors and decisions of the people in it. Collaborating organizations and agencies frequently have different cultures, which complicates relationships between or among them.

Within organizations or agencies, conflict management responsibilities primarily involve intrapersonal conflict (within a person), interpersonal conflict (between or among individuals), intragroup conflict (within a group), or intergroup conflict (between or among groups). In interorganizational or interagency collaborations, managers become involved in conflicts between and among the participating organizations or agencies.

When more than one organization or agency is involved in the implementation of a policy, as is frequently the case, the capability of the implementing organizations to collaborate in a coordinated manner is important to success. Laws often require an implementing agency to coordinate or collaborate with other agencies. For example, the Older Americans Amendments of 2006 requires the assistant secretary for aging "to coordinate with other federal agencies responsible for formulating and implementing programs, benefits, and services related to providing long-term care" and to "facilitate, in coordination with the Administrator of the Centers for Medicare and Medicaid Services and other federal entities, the provision of long-term care in home and community-based settings." This legislation also requires the secretary of HHS "to establish an Interagency Coordinating Committee on Aging that meets at least once a year," and further requires this committee to "establish a system to improve coordination of federal agencies" (Congressional Research Service 2006).

Rarely does a single organization implement a health policy, and never when the scope of the policy is large. The responsibility for implementing the Medicaid program, for example, does not rest entirely with a single organization. It involves CMS working with the Medicaid agencies in each state and with such private-sector organizations as hospitals, nursing homes, and health plans. Successful implementation of the Medicaid program depends heavily on interactions among these and other organizations.

Even more likely to call collaborative capabilities into play are situations in which several implementing organizations are required to coordinate and integrate their implementation responsibilities for a variety of policies intended to address a particular problem. It is not unusual for a chief executive (president or governor) to issue an executive order directing two or more agencies to collaborate or to establish a mechanism such as a joint task force to facilitate collaboration.

For example, Pennsylvania's Governor Rendell issued an executive order establishing the Office of Health Care Reform for the purpose of coordinating key elements of the state government's healthcare resources (Executive Order #2003-1, Commonwealth's Health Care Reform Agenda 2003). Excerpts from the order are shown in italics below, beginning with the rationale for the new office, which was stated as follows:

WHEREAS, the citizens of the Commonwealth are entitled to an accessible and affordable health care system of the highest quality; and

WHEREAS, the Commonwealth agencies responsible for administering and delivering health care services have over time been delegated overlapping responsibilities; and

WHEREAS, due to redundant responsibilities, the current health care system is subject to unnecessary duplication, inefficiency, and added costs; and

WHEREAS, it is the responsibility of the Commonwealth to determine how best to reform Pennsylvania's health care system and to develop sound fiscal policy so as to resolve the concerns of the Commonwealth's patients, health care providers, and insurance carriers; and

WHEREAS, the establishment of an Office of Health Care Reform and the establishment of the Governor's Health Care Reform Cabinet will coordinate and implement the Commonwealth's Health Care Reform Agenda.

NOW, THEREFORE, I, Edward G. Rendell, Governor of the Commonwealth of Pennsylvania, by virtue of the authority vested in me by the Constitution of the Commonwealth of Pennsylvania and other laws of the Commonwealth, do hereby establish the Office of Health Care Reform and the Governor's Health Care Reform Cabinet.

The executive order provided for appointment of the following members of the Health Care Reform Cabinet:

- Director of the Office of Health Care Reform
- Secretary of Aging
- Adjutant General

- Secretary of Health
- Commissioner of Insurance
- Secretary of Public Welfare
- Director of the Governor's Policy Office

The order states that the purpose of the Office of Health Care Reform is to "coordinate the Commonwealth's Health Care Reform Agenda." It also states that the purpose of the Health Care Reform Cabinet is to "advise the director and the governor on matters related to healthcare reform and (to) direct government resources in the implementation of the Health Care Reform Agenda." Finally, the order specifies that "all agencies under the Governor's jurisdiction shall cooperate with and provide assistance and support to the Office of Health Care Reform and the Governor's Health Care Reform Cabinet."

The language of this executive order clearly reflects the governor's intent for this administrative apparatus to link and coordinate many of the state's resources in pursuit of the state's health reform agenda. The establishment of the office alone does not guarantee a coordinated effort, but it supports the likelihood of achieving coordination through the clarity and specificity of the governor's directives to managers of various state agencies.

Summary

The implementation phase of the policymaking process includes rulemaking in support of implementation, the focus of Chapter 5, and the actual operation of policies, the focus of this chapter. The operation stage of implementation involves running the programs embedded in enacted legislation. Operational activities are largely the domain of the appointees and civil servants who staff the executive branch of government.

We examine two variables that affect implementation and are important to successful operation. First is the clarity of the policy's objectives and the embedded hypothesis for how the policy should work. Related to this variable, the flexibility a policy gives the implementing organizations directly affects the course of implementation and the outcome. The second important variable in the implementation of any policy consists of the characteristics and attributes of the organizations with implementation responsibilities and the capabilities and competencies of the managers of these organizations.

Review Questions

1. What does it mean to characterize policy implementation as public management?
2. Describe, in general terms, the operation stage of policy implementation.

3. Discuss the effect of a policy on its own implementation.
4. Discuss the effect of implementing organizations on policy implementation.
5. Discuss managing an implementation organization. What competencies underpin successful management in implementing organizations?

POLICY MODIFICATION

Policymaking is not a perfect process. Mistakes of omission and commission are routinely made in the formulation and implementation phases. The policymaking process model used throughout this book is brought full circle by the third phase of the process, modification. This phase is necessary because perfection eludes policymakers in the formulation and implementation phases. Even policy decisions that are correct when they are made must adjust to accommodate changing circumstances.

In a hypothetical policymaking process without a modification phase, policies would be formulated in their original version and then implemented, and that would be the end of the process—except, of course, for the policies' consequences. In practice, however, policymaking does not work this way. The consequences of policies—including consequences for those who formulate and implement the policies and for the individuals, organizations, and interest groups outside the process but affected by policies—cause people to seek modification. This occurs continually throughout the life of the policy.

At a minimum, individuals, organizations, or interest groups who benefit from a particular policy may seek modifications that increase or maintain these benefits over time. Similarly, those who are negatively affected by a policy will seek to modify it to minimize the negative consequences. In addition, when the policymakers who formulate and implement a public policy observe it in operation, they will evaluate it against their objectives for that policy. When preferences and reality do not match, efforts to modify the policy typically ensue.

Almost every policy has a history. An initial version is formulated which then evolves as it is implemented, either through amendments to the original legislation or through new or revised rules and changes in operation. Some policies eventually die—they are repealed by the legislative branch—but most have long and dynamic lives during which they are continually modified in various ways. This chapter addresses the policy modification phase of public policymaking (see the shaded portion of Exhibit 7.1). We begin by drawing a distinction between policy initiation and policy modification.

EXHIBIT 7.1 A Model of the Public Policymaking Process in the United States: Policy Modification Phase

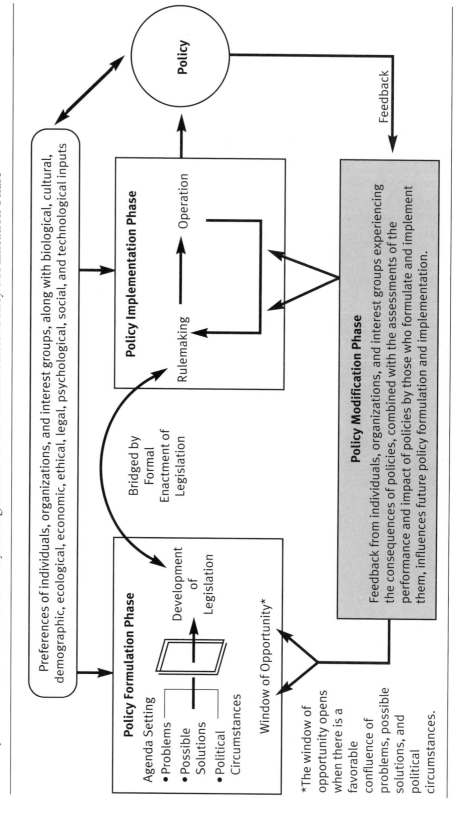

Distinguishing Policy Modification from Policy Initiation

Conceptually, we can differentiate policy *modification* and policy *initiation*, although in reality the two are closely intertwined. Policy initiation—the establishment of an original public law—results when the confluence of problems, possible solutions, and political circumstances leads to the initial development of legislation in the formulation phase and then to rulemaking and operation as the law is implemented. By contrast, policy modification results when the consequences of existing policies feed back into the agenda-setting and legislation-development stages of the formulation phase and the rulemaking and operational stages of the implementation phase and stimulate changes in legislation, rules, or operations. This is shown as the feedback loop in Exhibit 7.1. Examine the loop closely, noting that it feeds back into the overall process in several places.

The history of American health policy demonstrates that policymakers can, and on occasion do, initiate entirely new policies. For example, in 1798, Congress established the U.S. Marine Hospital Service to provide medical care for sick and disabled seamen. This was the initial policy from which the U.S. Public Health Service eventually grew. In 1921, Congress enacted the Maternity and Infancy Act (P.L. 67-97), through which grants were made to states to encourage the development of health services for mothers and children. This new policy became the prototype for federal grants in aid to the states. In 1935, Congress enacted the Social Security Act (P.L. 74-271), which initiated the major entrance of the federal government into the area of social insurance. This policy, which has been modified many times, now encompasses, among other things, the Medicare and Medicaid programs. The American Recovery and Reinvestment Act of 2009 (P.L. 111-5), which contains extensive health policy provisions, is a recent example of a new policy.

As these examples illustrate, some health policies are indeed formulated and implemented *de novo*. But the vast majority of contemporary health policies spring from existing policies. In other words, most health policies are the result of modifying prior policies. This is why understanding the modification phase is so important.

A review of important American health policies, such as those presented in Appendix 3, readily illustrates just how many contemporary health policies are amendments to previously enacted public laws or the result of changes—often, a string of changes—in the rules and practices that determine how laws are implemented. In fact, no policy is permanent. Modification of prior policies—whether in the form of decisions representing public laws, implementation rules or regulations, rulings of a court, or operational practices—pervades the entire policymaking process. The likelihood that prior decisions will be revisited and changed distinguishes public policymaking in the United States. It is the feature that makes policymaking a distinctly cyclical process.

The Policymaking Cycle

Careful consideration of the modification phase of policymaking is fundamental to understanding the process as a continual cycle of interrelated activities. Negative consequences of an existing policy will trigger modification efforts. If the consequences of an existing policy are positive for individuals, organizations, or groups, they may seek modifications that give them more benefits or protect existing ones.

In addition to such efforts, those who formulate and implement policies may seek modifications based on the performance and consequences of existing policies. Although such people—and many of those affected by the policies—typically prefer incremental policy changes, which we discuss further in the next section, pressure for policy modification is relentless.

As this chapter describes, pressure to modify is exerted at many points in the policymaking process. The modification phase makes the public policymaking process dynamic. Decisions are always subject to further review and revision. Policy modifications—large and small—emphasize that the separate components of the policymaking process are, in reality, highly interactive and interdependent.

Incrementalism in Policymaking

Not only are most public policies modifications of previously established policies, but also, historically, most modifications reflect only modest changes (Hinckley 1983). The combination of a process that is characterized by continual modification with the fact that these changes tend to be modest has led to the apt characterization of U.S. public policymaking as a process of *incrementalism* (Lindblom 1969; 1992). Of course, some policy modifications are large scale, but these are exceptions to the general trend. The enactment of Medicare was certainly a large modification. The Obama administration's efforts to reform healthcare could result in major modifications to current health policy as well. However, the pattern of incrementalism is likely to continue in the area of healthcare reform, as Gruber (2008, 51) notes: "The latest wave of healthcare proposals and laws in the United States has been marked by what I call 'incremental universalism'; that is, getting to universal health insurance coverage by filling the gaps in the existing system, rather than ripping up the system and starting over."

The affinity for modest, incremental policy change is not restricted to the health arena. The operation of the nation's overall political, social, and economic systems reflects preferences for modest rather than fundamental change. As we noted in Chapter 2, members of the U.S. power elite have a strong preference for incremental changes in public policies. They believe that incrementalism—building on existing policies via modification in small, incremental steps—allows the economic and social systems to adjust without being unduly threatened by change. Incremental policymaking limits economic dislocation or disruption and causes minimal alteration in the social system's status quo. These strong preferences for stability ran headlong into the financial crisis that began in late 2008. They didn't disappear, but they have been supplanted by the urgent need to stabilize the economy, in part through certain health reforms that may result in additional large-scale policy modifications. However, when the economy eventually stabilizes, the historical preference for incrementalism in policymaking may well reemerge.

The Basis for the Incrementalism Preference

In policymaking that is characterized by incrementalism, significant departures from the existing patterns of policies occur only rarely. Most of the time, the effects and consequences of policies play out slowly and somewhat predictably. This supports the idea that policymakers in all three branches of government, leaders in health-related organizations and interest groups, and many individuals who benefit from such policies as the Medicare and Medicaid programs typically have a strong preference for incrementalism in health policymaking.

The results and consequences of incremental decisions are more predictable and stable than are those of decisions not made incrementally. Unless a person—whether a policymaker or someone affected by policies—is unhappy with a situation and wishes an immediate and drastic change, the preference for incrementalism will almost always prevail.

Incrementalism in policymaking increases the likelihood of reaching compromises among the diverse interests in the political marketplace. The potential for compromise is an important feature of a smooth policymaking process. Words like "incrementalism" and "compromise" used in the context of public policymaking may bring to mind compromised principles, inappropriate influence peddling, and corrupt deals made behind closed doors. However, "in a democracy compromise is not merely unavoidable; it is a source of creative invention, sometimes generating solutions that unexpectedly combine seemingly opposed ideas" (Starr and Zelman 1993, 8).

The health policy domain is replete with incrementally developed policies. For instance, the history of NIH reflects incremental policymaking over more than 100 years. Ranging from 1887, when the federal government's expenditures on biomedical research totaled about $300, and through the 1930s, when a small federal laboratory conducting biomedical research was initiated, NIH has experienced extensive elaboration (the addition of new institutes as biomedical science evolved), growth (its annual budget is more than $30 billion in 2010), and shifts in the emphases of its research agenda (cancer, AIDS, women's health, health disparities, schizophrenia, and pediatric diseases). Every step in NIH's continuing and incremental evolution has been guided by specific policy changes, each an incremental modification intending carefully measured adjustments in NIH's actions, decisions, and behaviors.

Consistent with our earlier discussion that crises (war, collapse of major financial institutions, major economic instability) can alter the incremental nature of most policymaking, the American Recovery and Reinvestment Act of 2009 (P.L. 111-5) included provisions for a one-time infusion of $10 billion into the NIH budget ($8.5 billion for research grants and $1.5 billion for upgrading and renovating university laboratories and science infrastructure). A budgetary increase of this magnitude is certainly not consistent with NIH's history of incremental increases, but this modification resulted from an unprecedented—or nearly so—financial crisis. The general preference for incremental policy changes didn't disappear, but it was ignored in favor of infusing new money into the NIH budget to stimulate economic activity in the nation. When the economy stabilizes, the historical preference for incrementalism in policymaking, including in the pattern of growth in the NIH budget, will likely reassert itself.

Mechanics of the Modification Phase

The policymaking process provides abundant opportunities for the consequences of public laws to influence future iterations and change the rules and operational practices that guide their implementation. As the feedback arrows in Exhibit 7.1 illustrate, policies can be modified at four points in the policymaking process: in the agenda setting and legislation development stages that occur in the formulation phase and in the rulemaking and operation stages that occur in the implementation phase. Modification at each of these points in the overall process is discussed in the following sections.

Modification in the Policy Formulation Phase
Modification of policies in the formulation phase—the reformulation of existing policies—occurs in agenda setting and legislation development. Recall from chapters 3 and 4 that policy formulation—making the decisions that result in public laws—entails two distinct and sequential sets of activities: agenda setting and legislation development. The result of the formulation phase of policymaking is new public laws or amendments to existing laws.

Initial public laws that pertain to health and subsequent amendments to them stem from the interactions of (1) a diverse array of health-related problems, (2) possible solutions to those problems, and (3) dynamic political circumstances that relate to both. The creation of an entirely new legislative proposal and amendment of previously enacted public laws occur through legislation development. The only significant difference is that previously enacted legislation already has a developmental history and an implementation experience, both of which can influence its amendment.

Policy modification routinely begins at agenda setting, because problems already receiving attention become more sharply defined and better understood in light of the ongoing implementation of existing policies. Possible solutions to problems can be assessed and clarified in the same context, especially when operational experience and the results of demonstrations and evaluations provide concrete evidence of the performance of potential solutions. In addition, interactions among the branches of government and health-related organizations and interest groups involved with and affected by ongoing policies become important components of the political circumstances surrounding their reformulation and the initial formulation of future policies. People learn from their experiences with policies, and those in a position to do so may act on what they learn.

Modification at Agenda Setting

Leaders in health-related organizations and interest groups, by virtue of their keen interest in certain health policies—interest driven by the fact that they, and their organizations and groups, are directly affected by these policies—may be among the first to observe the need to modify a policy. They can use their experience to help policymakers better define or document problems that led to the original policy. These leaders can gather, catalog, and correlate facts that more accurately depict the actual state of a problem and can then share this information with policymakers.

Similarly, these leaders are well positioned to observe the actual consequences of a policy. Leaders can devise and assess possible new solutions or alterations to existing ones through the operational experience of the organizations and groups they lead. Finally, their experiences with ongoing policies may become a basis for their attempts to change the political circumstances involved in a particular situation. When the confluence of problems, possible solutions, and political circumstances that led to an original policy is altered, a new window of opportunity may open, this time permitting the amendment of previously enacted legislation.

Health policies in the form of public laws are routinely amended, some of them repeatedly and over many years. Such amendments reflect, among other occurrences, the emergence of new medical technologies, change in federal budgetary conditions, and evolution of beneficiary demands. These and other stimuli for change often gain the attention of policymakers through routine activities and reporting mechanisms in implementation. Pressure to modify policy through changes in existing public laws may also come from the leaders of health-related organizations and interest groups—including those that represent individual memberships—who feel the policy consequences. When modifications occur at the point of legislation development, they follow the

Modification at Legislation Development

same procedures as the original legislative proposals or bills (discussed fully in Chapter 4).

In some instances, the impetus to modify an existing law arises from changes in another law. For example, policies intended to reduce the federal budget deficit have typically impinged on other policies, which often results in their modification. Implementation of the Deficit Reduction Act of 1984 (P.L. 98-369) required a temporary freeze on physicians' fees paid under the Medicare program, and implementation of the Emergency Deficit Reduction and Balanced Budget Act of 1985 (P.L. 99-177), also known as the Gramm-Rudman-Hollins Act, required budget cuts in defense and certain domestic programs, including a number of health programs.

Modification in the Policy Implementation Phase

Modification of policies in the implementation phase can occur in rulemaking or in the operational stage. Feedback from the consequences of formulated and implemented policies can also stimulate modification at either stage in the implementation phase, and often at both points concurrently.

Modification at Rulemaking

As we noted in Chapter 5, rulemaking is a necessary precursor to the operation and full implementation of new public laws, because enacted legislation is rarely explicit enough to completely guide implementation. Newly enacted policies are often vague on implementation details, usually intentionally so, and implementing organizations are left to promulgate the rules needed to guide operation of the policies. Beyond this initial modification, existing policies are modified most frequently through changes in the rules or regulations used to guide their implementation.

The practice of modifying policies by updating or changing the rules for their implementation pervades policymaking. As we discussed in Chapter 5, rules that are promulgated by executive branch agencies and departments to guide policy implementation possess the force of law. The rules themselves are policies. As implementation occurs, rulemaking becomes a means to modify policies and their implementation over time. In the process, rulemaking creates new policies. Changed rules are modified policies.

Modification in Operation

Policy operation, as we discussed in Chapter 6, involves the actual running of the programs embedded in public laws. The appointees and civil servants who staff the government, particularly those who manage the implementing departments and agencies, are primarily responsible for the operational stage of policymaking. The managers responsible for operating a public law have significant opportunities to modify the policy—especially in terms of its effect on and consequences for those affected by the law—through the management of its operation.

Policies implemented by managers who are committed to the objectives of those policies and who have the talent and resources available to vigorously implement them are qualitatively different from policies operated by managers who are not committed or who lack adequate talent and resources. Modification of policies through changes in implementation is a routine occurrence in the ongoing policymaking process.

Stimulus for modification in the operation of policies comes from two principal sources, one internal and the other external. Internally, the managers responsible for operating policies approach the task as a manager in any setting approaches a task: They seek to *control* the results of their operations. To accomplish this, they establish standards or operating objectives (e.g., to serve so many clients per day, to process so many reports in a quarter, to distribute benefits to certain categories of beneficiaries, to assess compliance with certain regulations by so many firms). Operations ensue, results are monitored, and when results do not measure up to the predetermined standards, changes are made in operations, objectives, or both (Longest 2005). Such routine operational modifications are part of the daily work that occurs within organizations that implement health policies.

In addition to the internal pressures to modify policy operation, there are external pressures. These pressures come from individuals and especially health-related organizations and interest groups that experience the consequences of implemented policies. As we have noted, anyone who feels the consequences of policies may seek to modify them. One avenue open to them is the opportunity to influence the modification of policies through influencing those who manage their operation.

These opportunities for policy modification arise within the (sometimes close) working relationships that can develop between those responsible for implementing public policies and those directly affected by their decisions and activities. Opportunities to build these relationships are enhanced by a prominent feature of the careers of bureaucrats: longevity (Kingdon 1995). Elected policymakers come and go, but the bureaucracy endures. Leaders of health-related organizations and interest groups can and do build long-standing working relationships with some of the people responsible for implementing the public policies that are of strategic importance to them.

The most solid base for these relationships is the exchange of useful information and expertise. The leader of a health-related organization or interest group, speaking from an authoritative position and imparting relevant information based on actual operational experience with the implementation of a policy, can influence the policy's further implementation. If the information supports change, especially if it is buttressed by similar information from others who are experiencing the effect of a particular policy, it may influence reasonable implementers to make needed changes. This is especially likely if there is a well-established working relationship based on mutual respect for the roles of each party and the challenges they face.

Sometimes the relationships among those who experience the consequences of policies, usually operating through their interest groups, and those responsible for implementing policies that are important to them include members of the legislative committees or subcommittees with jurisdiction over the policies. This triad of mutual interests forms an "iron triangle," so called because the interests of the three parts of the triangle "dovetail nicely and because they are alleged to be impenetrable from the outside and uncontrollable by president, political appointees, or legislators not on the committees in question" (Kingdon 1995, 33). As we discussed in Chapter 2, however, the widely divergent interests of so many organizations and groups, coupled with their increasing presence in the policymaking arena, have made the formation of iron triangles more difficult and rarer in the health policy domain.

An obvious and limiting problem for those who wish to modify health policies through influencing their operation and the rulemaking that precedes it is the sheer enormity of the bureaucracy with which they might need to interact. Consider the number of components of the federal government involved in health policy rulemaking and operation. The number increases when relevant units of state and local government are added. The challenge of simply keeping track of where working relationships might be useful—to say nothing of actually developing and maintaining the relationships—begins to come into focus. Obviously, selectivity is necessary in determining which of these relationships are most strategically important.

Modification Through the Cyclical Relationship Between Rulemaking and Operation

An important aspect of the implementation phase is represented by the feedback loop between rulemaking and operation in Exhibit 7.1. As we discussed in chapters 5 and 6, there is a cyclical relationship between rulemaking and the operational activities involved in a public law's implementation. Although rulemaking precedes operation, the experiences gained in operation feed back into rulemaking.

This cyclical relationship means that experience gained with the operation of policies can influence the modification of rules or regulations subsequently used in their operation. Appendix 27 illustrates this situation. OSHA proposed a rule on occupational exposure to tuberculosis (TB) only to subsequently withdraw it based on the fact that the occupational risk of acquiring TB declined as the incidence of TB in the population as a whole declined. Practically, the cyclical relationship between rulemaking and operation means that rules promulgated to implement policies undergo revision—which is sometimes extensive and continual—and that new rules can be adopted or existing ones changed or dropped as experience dictates.

The Medicare Program: A Long History of Policy Modification in Practice

As we described in the foregoing sections, modification of previous decisions is possible at many points in the policymaking process. In fact, modification characterizes the process. The role of policy modification can be seen vividly, for example, in the legislative history of the Medicare program. Much of this history is chronicled in Appendix 3.

Many examples of how the modification phase plays out are embedded in the history of Medicare-related legislation. A review of this history begins with the enactment of a new policy, the 1935 Social Security Act (P.L. 74-271); from that point forward, however, the establishment and continuation of the Medicare program is largely a matter of modifying previous policies.

The Medicare program emerged on the nation's policy agenda in large part through the operation of the Social Security program over a span of three decades, from the mid-1930s to the mid-1960s. President Franklin D. Roosevelt formed the Committee on Economic Security in 1934 and charged its members to develop a program that could ensure the "economic security" of the nation's citizens. The committee considered the inclusion of health insurance in the Social Security program from the outset. In fact, sentiment for its inclusion was strong among members of the committee (Starr 1982). But in the end, they decided against recommending the inclusion of health insurance because of the tremendous political burdens associated with such a proposal. AMA in particular strongly opposed the concept (Peterson 1993).

As stated in the original legislation, the objective of the Social Security Act of 1935 was

> to provide for the general welfare by establishing a system of federal old age benefits, and by enabling the several States to make more adequate provision for aged persons, blind persons, dependent and crippled children, maternal and child welfare, public health, and the administration of their unemployment compensation laws.

Although health insurance was not included among the program's original provisions, its addition was considered from time to time in the ensuing years. President Harry S. Truman considered national health insurance a key part of his legislative agenda (Altmeyer 1968). But AMA's continued powerful opposition and the Truman administration's need to divert its attention to Korea in 1950 meant that the president was unable to stimulate the development and enactment of any sort of universal health insurance policy. Faced with dim political prospects for universal health insurance, proponents turned to a much more limited idea—hospital insurance for the aged.

Following a number of modest proposals for such insurance, none of which could muster the necessary political support for enactment, two powerful members of Congress, Senator Robert Kerr (D-OK) and Representative Wilbur Mills (D-AR), were able to pass a bill that provided federal support for state programs in welfare medicine. The Amendments to the Social Security Act of 1960 (P.L. 86-778) provided health benefits to the aged poor. Not until the Democratic margin in Congress was significantly increased in President Lyndon B. Johnson's landslide election in 1964 did a more expansive initiative have much chance of passage.

With Medicare's prospects significantly improved by the 1964 election, it reached a high priority among President Johnson's Great Society programs and was enacted as part of the Social Security Amendments of 1965 (P.L. 89-97). Medicare emerged on the nation's policy agenda through a series of attempts to modify the original Social Security Act by expanding the benefits provided to include health insurance. Although these attempts at modifying the original Social Security Act failed more often than not, they set the stage for the eventual modification that resulted in the Medicare program. As Peterson (1997, 292) notes, "The (policy) choices of one period are intimately linked to the choices grasped or missed in a previous era."

Following the enactment of the original legislation that established the Medicare program, the chronology of related legislation shows a remarkable pattern of evolutionary, incremental modification of a single, although massive, public policy. In a progression of modifications that continues today, among other changes, Medicare benefits have been added and deleted, who is covered by the program has been adjusted, premiums and copayment provisions have been changed, reimbursement rates and payment mechanisms for service providers have shifted, and features to ensure quality and medical necessity of services have been added, changed, and deleted. A history of these changes by Hoffman, Klees, and Curtis (2008) divides the list into changes pertaining to who Medicare covers (insured status), to benefits offered by Medicare, and to Medicare financing.

The list reproduced in the following section is limited to changes in Medicare benefits, excluding the changes in insured status and Medicare financing. Even so, this chronology reflects significant legislative change from year to year, a pattern likely to continue as long as this complex and expensive program exists. Indeed, considering the current challenges in financing the Medicare program and the larger debates about health reform, Medicare faces one of the most volatile periods in its history, and many more modifications are likely in the next several years.

The pattern of modifications to Medicare benefits has been heavily influenced by ongoing experience with the implementation of the original legislation and its subsequent modifications. This list illustrates how Medicare policy has been modified extensively over the course of the program's life and emphasizes the role modification plays in the overall policymaking process. The authors of the list caution that it should be used only as a broad overview of the history of the provisions of the Medicare program. The list does not render any legal, accounting, or other professional advice and is not intended to explain fully all the provisions and exclusions of the relevant laws, regulations, and rulings of the Medicare program (Hoffman, Klees, and Curtis 2008).

Medicare Benefits Provided Under Part A

1965. In each benefit period, inpatient hospital services, 90 days. Includes semiprivate accommodations, operating room, hospital equipment (including renal dialysis), laboratory tests and X-ray, drugs, dressings, general nursing services, and services of interns and residents in medical osteopathic or dentistry training. Inpatient psychiatric hospital care limited to 190-day lifetime maximum. Outpatient hospital diagnostic services. Post-hospital extended-care services, 100 days (including physical, occupational, and speech therapy). Post-hospital home health services, 100 visits.

1967. Lifetime reserve of 60 additional days of inpatient hospital services. Outpatient hospital diagnostic services transferred to Supplementary Medical Insurance (SMI).

1972. Services of interns and residents in podiatry training.

1980. Unlimited home health visits in a year. Requirement for prior hospitalization eliminated. Home health services provided for up to 4 days a week and up to 21 consecutive days.
    Alcohol detoxification facility services added.

1981. Part A coinsurance is based on the deductible for the calendar year in which services are received rather than the deductible in effect at the time the beneficiary's spell of illness began, starting in 1982.
    Alcohol detoxification facility services eliminated.

1982. Beneficiaries expected to live 6 months or less may elect to receive hospice care benefits instead of other Medicare benefits. May elect maximum of two 90-day and one 30-day hospice care periods, effective November 1, 1983, to October 1, 1986.

1984. For durable medical equipment provided by home health agencies, the payment amount is reduced from 100 percent of costs to 80 percent of reasonable charges.

1986. Set the Part A deductible for 1987 at $520 with resulting increases in cost sharing. Increased the Part A deductible annually by the applicable percentage increase in the hospital prospective payment rates.

Hospice care benefit (enacted in 1982) made permanent.

1987. Specifies in law that to be eligible for home healthcare, a Medicare beneficiary must have a restricted ability to leave the home, requiring the assistance of another or the aid of a supportive device (such as crutches, a cane, a wheelchair, or a walker).

1988. Enrollee pays annual hospital deductible (set at $560 for 1989) and Medicare pays balance of covered charges, regardless of the number of days of hospitalization (except for psychiatric hospital care, which is still limited by 190-day lifetime maximum).

The number of days in a skilled nursing facility changed to 150 per year. Deletes the requirement for a prior hospital stay of 3 or more consecutive days.

Expands home healthcare to provide care for less than 7 days per week and up to 38 consecutive days.

Hospice care extended beyond 210 days when beneficiary is certified as terminally ill.

1989. The spell of illness and benefit period coverage of laws before 1988 return to the determination of inpatient hospital benefits in 1990 and later. After the deductible is paid in the benefit period, Medicare pays 100 percent of covered costs for the first 60 days of inpatient hospital care. Coinsurance applies for the next 30 days in a benefit period.

The requirement for a prior hospital stay of 3 or more consecutive days is reinstated for skilled nursing facility services. Coverage returns to 100 days post-hospital care per spell of illness with a daily coinsurance rate in effect for days 21 through 100.

Home health services return to a limit of 21 consecutive days of care. Provision providing for home healthcare for fewer than 7 days per week continued due to a court decision.

Hospice care is returned to a lifetime limit of 210 days.

1990. Hospice care is extended beyond 210 days when beneficiary is certified as terminally ill.

1997. Home health services not associated with a hospital or skilled nursing facility stay for individuals enrolled in both Hospital Insurance (HI) and SMI are transferred from the HI program to the SMI program, effective January 1998. The HI program will continue to cover the first 100 visits following a hospital stay of at least 3 consecutive days or a skilled nursing facility stay. The cost to the SMI trust fund of the transferred services will phase in over a six-year period (that is, the HI trust fund will transfer funds to the SMI trust fund during that period).

Limits on the number of hours and days that home healthcare can be provided have been clarified. *Part-time* now defined as skilled nursing and home health aide services (combined) furnished any number of days per week, for less than 8 hours per day and 28 or fewer hours per week. *Intermittent* now defined as skilled nursing care provided for fewer than 7 days each week, or less than 8 hours each day (combined) for 21 days or less.

Hospice benefit periods are restructured to include two 90-day periods, followed by an unlimited number of 60-day periods.

Medicare coverage provided for a number of prevention initiatives, most of which are covered under SMI program. HI program affected mainly by two of the initiatives: (1) annual prostate cancer screening for male beneficiaries aged 50 or older, effective January 1, 2000, and (2) colorectal screening procedures, including fecal-occult blood tests and flexible sigmoidoscopies, for beneficiaries aged 50 or older, colonoscopy for beneficiaries at high risk for colorectal cancer, and other procedures, including screening barium enemas under certain circumstances.

2000. The homebound criterion for home health services is clarified to specify that beneficiaries who require home health services may attend adult day care for therapeutic, psychosocial, or medical treatment and still remain eligible for the home health benefit. Homebound beneficiaries may also attend religious services without being disqualified from receiving home health benefits.

Screening colonoscopies are covered for all beneficiaries, not just for those at high risk, beginning July 1, 2001. For persons not at high risk, a screening colonoscopy is covered ten years after a previous one, or four years after a screening flexible sigmoidoscopy. (See 1997.)

Medicare Benefits Provided Under Part B

1965. Physician and surgeon services. In-hospital services of anesthesiologists, pathologists, radiologists, and psychiatrists. Limited dental services. Home health services, 100 visits in calendar year. Other medical services including various diagnostic tests, limited ambulance services, prosthetic devices, rental of durable medical equipment (DME) used at home (including equipment for dialysis), and supplies used for fractures.

Beginning in 1966, the beneficiary pays a $50 deductible, with a three-month carryover provision.

1967. Outpatient hospital diagnostic services transferred from HI. Includes physical therapy services in a facility. Purchase of DME.

1972. Physical therapy services furnished by a therapist in his or her office or individual's home (calendar year limit of $100). Chiropractor services (limited to manual manipulation of the spine). Outpatient services include speech pathology services furnished in, or under arrangements with, a facility or agency. Services of a doctor of optometry in furnishing prosthetic lenses.

Beginning in 1973, the beneficiary pays a $60 deductible.

1977. Services in rural health clinics.

1980. Home health services. Deductible applicable to home health services is eliminated, effective July 1, 1981.

Facility costs of certain surgical procedures performed in freestanding ambulatory surgical centers.

Increase in annual limit for outpatient therapy from $100 to $500.

Recognizes comprehensive outpatient rehabilitation facilities as Medicare providers.

1981. Beginning in 1982, the beneficiary pays a $75 deductible, with the carryover provision eliminated.

1984. Hepatitis B and pneumococcal vaccines and blood clotting factors and necessary supplies are included as Part B benefits. Debridement of mycotic toenails is limited.

For outpatient physical therapy services, includes services of a podiatrist. For outpatient ambulatory surgery, includes services of a dentist or podiatrist furnished in his or her office.

1986. Includes vision care services furnished by an optometrist.

For occupational therapy services, includes services furnished in a skilled nursing facility (when Part A coverage has been exhausted), in a clinic, rehabilitation agency, public health agency, or by an independently practicing therapist.

Includes outpatient (in addition to previously covered inpatient) immunosuppressive drugs for 1 year after covered transplant.

Includes occupational therapy services provided in certain delivery settings.

For ambulatory surgical procedures performed in ambulatory surgical centers, hospital outpatient departments, and certain physician offices, the Part B coinsurance and deductible are no longer waived.

1987. Increases the maximum payment for mental health services and includes outpatient mental health services provided by ambulatory hospital-based or hospital-affiliated programs under the supervision of a physician.

Services provided by clinical social workers when furnished by risk-sharing HMOs and competitive medical plans, physician assistants in rural health manpower shortage areas, clinical psychologists in rural health clinics and community mental health centers, and certified nurse midwives.

Coverage of outpatient immunosuppressive drugs (see 1986) is broadened and clarified to include prescription drugs used in immunosuppressive therapy.

Specifies in law that to be eligible for home healthcare, a Medicare beneficiary must have a restricted ability to leave the home, requiring the assistance of another or the aid of a supportive device (such as crutches, a cane, a wheelchair, or a walker).

1988. Beginning January 1, 1990, the beneficiary pays a $75 deductible and 20 percent coinsurance, but once out-of-pocket expenses for the deductible and coinsurance exceed $1,370, Medicare pays 100 percent of allowable charges for remainder of year.

Beginning in 1991, Medicare pays 50 percent of the cost of outpatient prescription drugs above $600. When fully implemented in 1993, Medicare will pay 80 percent of prescription drug costs above a deductible that assumes that 16.8 percent of Part B enrollees will exceed the deductible.

Certain prescription drugs administered in an outpatient or home setting, including immunosuppressive drugs (previously covered for 1 year after a covered transplant), home intravenous drugs, and certain others, will be covered in 1990 under a new prescription drug provision.

1989. Provisions enacted in 1988 and to begin in 1990 and 1991 are repealed, and benefits are restored to levels in effect before January 1, 1989.

Limits on mental health benefits eliminated in 1990. Coverage extended to services of clinical psychologists and social workers.

The annual payment limits of $500 per beneficiary for outpatient physical therapy services and outpatient occupational therapy services, each, are raised to $750 for 1990 and later. (See 1980.)

1990. Beginning in 1991, routine mammography screenings are covered.

The Part B deductible is set at $100 in 1991 and subsequent years.

Beginning in 1992, physicians' services are reimbursed on a fee-schedule basis.

1993. Includes coverage of oral, self-administered anticancer drugs.

Lengthens the coverage period for immunosuppressive drugs after a transplant to 18 months in 1995, 24 months in 1996, 30 months in 1997, and 36 months thereafter. (See 1986.)

The annual payment limits of $750 per beneficiary for outpatient physical therapy services and outpatient occupational therapy services, each, are raised to $900 for 1994 and later. (See 1989.)

1997. Home health services not associated with a hospital or skilled nursing facility stay for individuals enrolled in both HI and SMI are transferred from the HI program to the SMI program, effective January 1998. The HI program will continue to cover the first 100 visits following a hospital stay of at least 3 consecutive days or a skilled nursing facility stay. The cost to the SMI trust fund of the transferred services will phase in over a 6-year period, while the cost of the home health services will phase into the SMI premium over 7 years.

Coverage provided for a number of prevention initiatives, including (1) annual screening mammograms for female beneficiaries aged 40 or older, with SMI deductible waived; (2) screening Pap smear and pelvic exam (including clinical breast exam) every 3 years or annually for beneficiaries at higher risk, with SMI deductible waived; (3) annual prostate cancer screening for male beneficiaries aged 50 or older, effective January 1, 2000; (4) colorectal screening procedures, including fecal occult blood tests and flexible sigmoidoscopies, for beneficiaries aged 50 or older, colonoscopy for beneficiaries at high risk for colorectal cancer, and other procedures, including screening barium enemas under certain circumstances; (5) diabetes outpatient self-management training in nonhospital-based programs (previously covered in hospital-based programs only) and blood glucose monitors and testing strips for all diabetics (previously provided for insulin-dependent diabetics only), effective July 1, 1998; (6) procedures to identify bone mass, detect bone loss, or determine bone quality for certain qualified beneficiaries, at frequencies determined by the secretary of Health and Human Services, effective July 1, 1998.

Beginning January 1999, an annual beneficiary limit of $1,500 will apply to all outpatient physical therapy services, except for services furnished by a hospital outpatient department. A separate $1,500 limit will also apply to outpatient occupational therapy services, except for services furnished by hospital outpatient departments. Beginning with 2002, these caps will be increased by the percentage increase in the Medical Economic Index. (See 1993.)

1999. The coverage period for immunosuppressive drugs after a transplant is lengthened to 44 months for individuals who exhaust their 36 months of coverage in 2000. For those exhausting their 36 months of coverage in 2001, at least 8 more months will be covered. (The secretary of Health and Human Services will specify the increase, if any, beyond 8 months.) For those exhausting their 36 months of coverage in 2002, 2003, or 2004, the number of additional months may be more or fewer than 8. (The secretary will specify the increase for each of these years.) (See 1993.)

The annual payment limits of $1,500 per beneficiary for outpatient physical therapy services and outpatient occupational therapy services, each, for services furnished by independent practitioners (that is, not by a hospital outpatient department) are suspended for 2000 and 2001. (See 1997.)

2000. Coverage for screening Pap smears and pelvic exams (including a clinical breast exam) is provided every 2 years (increased from every 3 years) beginning July 1, 2001. (Annual coverage continues for beneficiaries at higher risk, and SMI deductible continues to be waived; see 1997.)

Annual coverage of glaucoma screenings is provided for certain high-risk beneficiaries, effective January 1, 2002.

Screening colonoscopies are covered for all beneficiaries, not just for those at high risk, beginning July 1, 2001. For persons not at high risk, a screening colonoscopy is covered 10 years after a previous one, or 4 years after a screening flexible sigmoidoscopy. (See 1997.)

Coverage is provided for medical nutrition therapy services under certain circumstances for beneficiaries who have diabetes or a renal disease, effective January 1, 2002.

The amount of a beneficiary's copayment for a procedure in a hospital outpatient department is limited, beginning April 1, 2001, to the hospital inpatient deductible applicable for that year. Also, the secretary of Health and Human Services must reduce the effective copayment rate for outpatient services to a maximum rate of 57 percent in 2001 (for services received after April 1), 55 percent in 2002 and 2003, 50 percent in 2004, 45 percent in 2005, and 40 percent in 2006 and later.

Time and budget limitations are removed on the coverage of immunosuppressive drugs, making coverage of these drugs a permanent benefit for beneficiaries who have received a covered organ transplant. (See 1999.)

The annual payment limits of $1,500 per beneficiary for outpatient physical therapy services and outpatient occupational therapy services, each, for services provided by independent practitioners (that is, not by a hospital outpatient department), which were suspended for 2000 and 2001, are also suspended for 2002. (See 1999.)

The homebound criterion for home health services is clarified to specify that beneficiaries who require home health services may attend adult day care for therapeutic, psychosocial, or medical treatment and still remain eligible for the home health benefit. Homebound beneficiaries may also attend religious services without being disqualified from receiving home health benefits.

2003. The Part B deductible remains at $100 through 2004 and increases to $110 in 2005. Beginning in 2006, it will be increased each year by the annual percentage increase in the Part B aged actuarial rate.

A one-time, initial preventive physical exam is covered within 6 months of a beneficiary's first coverage under Part B, beginning January 1, 2005, for beneficiaries whose Part B coverage begins on or after that date.

Certain screening blood tests are covered for the early detection of cardiovascular disease and abnormalities associated with elevated risk for such disease, including certain tests for cholesterol and other lipid or triglyceride levels, effective January 1, 2005, under frequency standards to be established (but not to exceed once every 2 years).

Diabetes screening tests, including a fasting plasma glucose test and other such tests determined appropriate by the secretary of Health and

Human Services, are covered for beneficiaries at risk for diabetes, beginning January 1, 2005, under frequency standards to be established (but not to exceed two times per year).

2005. The colorectal screening benefit (see 1997 and 2000) is exempt from the Part B deductible, effective January 2007.

Exceptions to the financial limits on therapy services not provided by a hospital outpatient department are allowed for services furnished in 2006, if such services are determined to be medically necessary. (See 1997, 1999, and 2000.)

2006. Exceptions to the financial limits on nonhospital therapy services when deemed medically appropriate are extended through December 31, 2007. (See 2005.)

2007. Exceptions to the financial limits on nonhospital therapy services when deemed medically appropriate are extended through July 1, 2008. (See 2005 and 2006).

2008. For outpatient mental health services, the percentage of approved charges for which the beneficiary is liable phases down from 50 percent to 20 percent, over the five-year period 2010–2014.

For the one-time, initial preventive examination (see 2003), the Part B deductible is waived, the eligibility period is extended from 6 months to 1 year after enrollment in Part B, measurement of body mass index is covered, and, upon agreement with the beneficiary, end-of-life planning is covered. Effective January 1, 2009.

Exceptions to the financial limits on nonhospital therapy services when deemed medically appropriate are extended through December 31, 2009. (See 2005, 2006, and 2007.)

Medicare Benefits Provided Under Parts A and B

1965. Requires that Medicare be secondary payer to benefits provided by liability insurance policies or under no-fault insurance.

1981. Requires that Medicare be secondary payer to employer-based group health plans for beneficiaries entitled to Medicare solely on the basis of end-stage renal disease (ESRD) for up to 12 months.

1982. For workers and their spouses aged 65 to 69, Medicare is the secondary payer when benefits are provided under an employer-based group health plan (applicable to employers with 20 or more employees who sponsor or contribute to the group plan).

HMOs will be authorized as providers of benefits. The secretary of Health and Human Services must certify the prospective payment mechanism for HMOs before implementation.

1984. Medicare secondary-payer provisions are extended to spouses aged 65 to 69 of workers under the age of 65 whose employer-based group health plan covers such spouses.

For HMOs, includes medical and other health services furnished by clinical psychologists.

1985. Provides payment for liver transplant services.

1986. Extends the working-age, secondary-payer provision to cover workers and their spouses beyond age 69.

For HMOs that offered organ transplants as a basic health service on April 15, 1985, such services may be offered from October 1, 1985, through April 1, 1988.

For disabled individuals who are covered by employer-based health plans (with at least 100 employees), Medicare is the secondary payer, effective for the period from 1987 to 1991.

1987. Requires HMOs and competitive medical plans that cease to contract with Medicare to provide or arrange supplemental coverage of benefits related to preexisting conditions for the lesser of 6 months or the duration of an exclusion period.

Specifies in law that to be eligible for home healthcare, a Medicare beneficiary must have a restricted ability to leave the home, requiring the assistance of another or the aid of a supportive device (such as crutches, a cane, a wheelchair, or a walker).

Clarifies that the secondary-payer provision for disabled individuals covered under employer-based health plans for employers with at least 500 employees applies to employers who are government entities.

1990. Requires that Medicare be the secondary payer to employer-based group health plans for beneficiaries entitled to Medicare solely on the basis of ESRD for up to 18 months (extended from 12 months), effective February 1, 1991, to January 1, 1996.

The secondary-payer provision for disabled beneficiaries covered under large employer plans (see 1986) is effective through September 30, 1995.

1993. The secondary-payer provision for disabled beneficiaries covered under large employer plans is effective through September 30, 1998.

The secondary-payer provision for beneficiaries with ESRD applies to all beneficiaries with ESRD, not only those entitled to Medicare solely on the basis of ESRD. The extension to include the first 18 months of an individual's entitlement on the basis of ESRD is effective through September 30, 1998.

1996. The Medicare Integrity Program (MIP) is created, providing dedicated funds to identify and combat improper payments, including those caused by fraud and abuse, and, for the first time, allowing for contracts to be awarded competitively to entities other than carriers and intermediaries to conduct these activities.

1997. Established an expanded set of options for the delivery of healthcare under Medicare, referred to as "Medicare+Choice" (and also known as "Medicare Part C"). All Medicare beneficiaries can receive their Medicare benefits through the original fee-for-service program. In addition, most beneficiaries can choose instead to receive their Medicare benefits through one of the following Medicare+Choice plans: (1) coordinated care plans (such as HMOs, provider-sponsored organizations, and preferred provider organizations), (2) Medical Savings Account (MSA)/High Deductible plans (through a demonstration available for up to 390,000 beneficiaries), or (3) private fee-for-service plans. Except for MSA plans, all Medicare+Choice plans are required to provide the current Medicare benefit package (excluding hospice services) and any additional health services required under the adjusted community rate (ACR) process. MSA plans provide Medicare benefits after a single high deductible is met, and enrollees receive an annual deposit in their MSA. Transition rules for current Medicare HMO program also provided. (See also HMO provision of 1982.)

The provision making Medicare the secondary payer for disabled beneficiaries covered under large employer plans, previously scheduled to expire September 30, 1998, made permanent.

The provision making Medicare the secondary payer for the first 12 months of entitlement because of ESRD, which had been extended on a temporary basis (through September 30, 1998) to include the first 18 months of entitlement, has been extended, permanently, to include the first 30 months of entitlement on the basis of ESRD.

2003. Medicare+Choice is renamed Medicare Advantage. (It is still sometimes referred to as "Medicare Part C.") As before, beneficiaries enrolled in both Part A and Part B can receive their Medicare benefits through the original fee-for-service program; most can opt instead to use a Medicare Advantage plan in their area. Medicare Advantage plans include (1) Medicare Managed Care plans (like HMOs), (2) Medicare Preferred Provider Organization plans (PPOs), (3) Private Fee-for-Service plans, and (4) Medicare Specialty plans (available in some areas to provide Medicare benefits for certain people with special needs, such as beneficiaries in institutions). Beginning in 2006, Medicare Advantage plan choices will be expanded to include regional PPOs. Participating regional PPOs will be required to serve an entire region (10 to 50 regions are to be established), and there are provisions to encourage plan participation. Regional PPOs must have a single deductible for benefits under parts A and B, and they must include catastrophic limits for out-of-pocket expenditures. Beginning in 2006, the ACR process for determining plan payments is replaced by a competitive bidding process.

(Historical reference points to this item include the Medicare+Choice provision of 1997 and the HMO provision of 1982, both of which are displayed in this section.)

2007. Group health plans are required to provide information identifying situations in which the plan is, or has been, primary to Medicare, effective January 2009. Effective June 2009, liability insurance, no-fault insurance, and workers' compensation plans must submit specific information to enable appropriate determinations concerning coordination of benefits and any applicable recovery claims.

Medicare Benefits Provided Under Part D

2003. Under temporary Medicare-endorsed prescription drug discount card program, eligible beneficiaries voluntarily enrolling and paying up to $30 annually, receive discounts on certain prescription drugs, as specified by card sponsors. Under Transitional Assistance (TA) provision, eligible beneficiaries whose incomes do not exceed 135 percent of the federal poverty level and do not have third-party prescription drug coverage are eligible for (1) financial assistance of up to $600 per year for purchasing prescription drugs and (2) a subsidized enrollment fee under the temporary Medicare-endorsed prescription drug discount card program. Enrollment begins in May 2004, access to discounts begins in June 2004, and program phases out as drug benefit becomes available in 2006 (see next entry).

Beginning January 1, 2006, upon voluntary enrollment in either a stand-alone prescription drug plan (PDP) or an integrated Medicare Advantage plan that offers Part D coverage in its benefit, subsidized prescription drug coverage. Most FDA-approved drugs and biologicals are covered. However, plans may set up formularies for their drug coverage, subject to certain statutory standards. (Drugs currently covered in Parts A and B remain covered there.) Part D coverage can consist of either standard coverage or an alternative design that provides the same actuarial value. (For an additional premium, plans may also offer supplemental coverage exceeding the value of basic coverage.) Standard Part D coverage is defined for 2006 as having a $250 deductible, with 25 percent coinsurance (or other actuarially equivalent amounts) for drug costs above the deductible and below the initial coverage limit of $2,250. The beneficiary is then responsible for all costs until the $3,600 out-of-pocket limit (which is equivalent to total drug costs of $5,100) is reached. For higher costs, there is catastrophic coverage; it requires enrollees to pay the greater of 5 percent coinsurance or a small copay ($2 for generic or preferred multisource brand and $5 for other drugs). After 2006, these benefit parameters are indexed to the growth in per capita Part D spending. In determining out-of-pocket costs, only those amounts actually paid by the enrollee or another individual (and not reimbursed through insurance) are counted; the exception is cost-sharing assistance from Medicare's low-income subsidies (certain beneficiaries with low incomes and modest assets will be eligible for certain subsidies that eliminate or reduce their Part D premiums, cost-sharing, or both) and from State Pharmacy Assistance Programs. A beneficiary premium, representing 25.5 percent of the cost of basic coverage on average, is required (except for certain low-income beneficiaries, as previously mentioned, who may pay a reduced premium or no premium). For PDPs and the drug portion of Medicare Advantage plans, the premium will be determined by a bid process; each plan's premium will be 25.5 percent of the national weighted average plus or minus the difference between the plan's bid and the average. To help them gain experience with the Medicare population, plans will be protected by a system of risk corridors, which allow Part D to assist with unexpected costs and to share in unexpected savings; after 2007, the risk corridors became less protective. To encourage employer and union plans to continue prescription drug coverage to Medicare retirees, subsidies to these plans are authorized; the plan must meet or exceed the value of standard Part D coverage, and the subsidy pays 28 percent of the allowable costs associated with enrollee prescription drug costs between a specified cost threshold ($250 in 2006, indexed thereafter) and a specified cost limit ($5,000 in 2006, indexed thereafter).

2008. Part D plans are required to include two classes of drugs in their formularies: (1) benzodiazepines and (2) for the treatment of epilepsy, cancer, or chronic mental disorder, barbiturates. Effective January 1, 2013.

Modification is a ubiquitous component of the overall policymaking process, as the chronology of modification of Medicare benefits policy clearly illustrates. With this as our background, we turn our attention in the next section to two structural aspects of the modification phase.

Key Structural Features of Policy Modification

Two structural features drive much of the activity in the modification phase of the policymaking process: oversight actors and the results of formal analyses (also called assessments or evaluations) of policy performance. The important roles these two structural features play are considered in the next sections.

The Role of Oversight Actors in Policy Modification

Oversight actors in the public policymaking process include participants from each branch of government. Their roles differ, but each has important implications for policy modification. In the legislative branch, oversight responsibilities are assigned to committees and subcommittees, which can stimulate modification during policy formulation and implementation. Chief executives (presidents, governors, or mayors, depending on the level of government) and their top appointees monitor implementation and can point out when adjustments and modifications are needed. Courts can also determine when modifications are needed, such as when the results of one policy infringe on or conflict with the desired results of other policies.

Legislative Branch

In the case of Congress, and with parallel arrangements in many state legislatures, committees and subcommittees have specific oversight responsibilities. The purpose of oversight in a legislative context "is to analyze and evaluate both the execution and effectiveness of laws administered by the executive branch, and to determine if there are areas in which additional legislation (including amendment of existing legislation) is necessary or desirable" (National Health Council, Inc. 1993, 10).

While any committee with jurisdiction can hold oversight hearings, the House and Senate appropriations committees (appropriations.house.gov and appropriations.senate.gov, respectively) have especially important oversight responsibilities in their annual reviews of the budgets of implementing organizations and agencies. Legislators seeking to influence implementation decisions routinely use the budget review mechanism.

In addition, the first or clarifying indications that existing legislation needs to be amended or that new legislation may be needed in a particular area often emerge from oversight hearings. For example, Appendix 28 contains information on an oversight hearing by the Subcommittee on Health of the House Committee on Ways and Means.

Executive Branch

Chief executives (presidents, governors, or mayors) exert oversight and control of the implementation phase of policymaking. This provides them with unique power to initiate policy modification. Chief executives are supported in oversight activity by staff in the executive office and the appointees in various departments and agencies who are responsible to the chief executive.

In particular, the federal Office of Management and Budget (OMB; www.whitehouse.gov/omb) plays a powerful role in policy modification. The predominant mission of OMB (n.d.) is

> to assist the President in overseeing the preparation of the federal budget and to supervise its administration in Executive Branch agencies. In helping to formulate the President's spending plans, OMB evaluates the effectiveness of agency programs, policies, and procedures, assesses competing funding demands among agencies, and sets funding priorities. OMB ensures that agency reports, rules, testimony, and proposed legislation are consistent with the President's Budget and with Administration policies.

> In addition, OMB oversees and coordinates the Administration's procurement, financial management, information, and regulatory policies. In each of these areas, OMB's role is to help improve administrative management, to develop better

performance measures and coordinating mechanisms, and to reduce any unnecessary burdens on the public.

OMB plays a crucial analytical role: In helping to formulate the president's spending plans, OMB evaluates the effectiveness of agency programs, policies, and procedures; assesses competing funding demands among agencies; and sets funding priorities. These assessments help establish the administration's funding priorities, which then guide the development of the budget.

In supervising the various executive branch organizations through its administration of the federal budget, OMB ensures that the organizations' reports, rules, testimony, and proposed legislation are consistent with the administration's preferences. In addition, OMB oversees and coordinates the administration's procurement, financial management, and information practices and procedures. In each of these areas, OMB's role is to improve the management of policy implementation, which, as we discussed in chapters 5 and 6, is largely the responsibility of executive branch organizations.

Judicial Branch

The courts also play a role in modifying health policy. The federal courts have oversight responsibility regarding how laws are interpreted and enforced. (Information on the U.S. federal court system is available at www.uscourts.gov/about.html.) State courts are involved in interpreting and enforcing state laws and other policies within their jurisdictions. Anderson (1992) notes the courts' health policy modification roles in areas such as (1) coverage decisions made by public and private health insurers, (2) states' payment rates for hospitals and nursing homes, and (3) antitrust rulings relating to mergers between healthcare organizations.

Teitelbaum and Wilensky (2007, 5) see the healthcare domain as concerned with individuals' access to care, the quality of that care, and the financing of the care. In their view, the court's focus in the public health domain "is on why and how the government regulates private individuals and corporations in the name of protecting the health, safety, and welfare of the general public."

One of the more important ways courts have modified policy is through their involvement in the implementation of the nation's environmental protection laws and other policies. The Occupational Safety and Health Act (P.L. 91-596) set into motion a massive federal program of standard setting and enforcement that sought to improve safety and health conditions in the nation's workplaces. As Thompson (1981, 24) notes, "Business and labor leaders ... have repeatedly appealed decisions by the Occupational Safety and Health Administration (OSHA) to the courts. The development of this program in some respects reads like a legal history."

Although enough adverse judicial decisions growing out of a particular policy can lead to its amendment or even stimulate new legislation, the courts' most direct modifying effect is on policy implementation, especially in ensuring the appropriate application of laws and supporting rules and provisions. In a widely followed example, in 1999 California enacted a nurse staffing ratio law that required a ratio of one registered nurse (RN) per five patients by January 1, 2001. Subsequent legislation moved the deadline to January 1, 2002; eventually, the deadline was set for January 1, 2005. In November 2004, California's governor, Arnold Schwarzenegger, issued an emergency order delaying implementation of the ratio until 2008. This elicited a lawsuit by the California Nurses Association. A Superior Court judge ruled that the governor acted illegally by delaying implementation of the state law.

The aspect of the courts' role that most complicates policy modification arises from the fact that the U.S. court system is highly decentralized. Although court autonomy is an important element in the American system of government, one consequence of this autonomy is the possibility of inconsistent treatment of policy-relevant issues. As Anderson (1992, 106) notes, "The structure of the judicial system has made it difficult for the courts to provide consistent guidance about what constitutes acceptable behavior." Limitations of the courts aside, the judicial branch is a vital and integral structural feature of the policymaking process and is especially significant in the modification phase.

The Role of Analysis in Policy Modification

A second key structural feature of policy modification is formal analysis (also called assessments or evaluations) of policy performance. The results of these efforts can trigger and guide modification in policies (Moran, Rein, and Goodin 2008). Good policy analysis increases the likelihood of appropriate modifications. The most efficacious modification of policies is generally based on solid information, including that obtained through formal analysis.

Analysis that occurs *after* a policy has been implemented is less valuable in guiding modification. Effective policy analysis is a continuum of analytical activities that can begin in agenda setting and pervade and support the entire policymaking process. This continuum can be organized as ex-ante policy analysis, policy maintenance, policy monitoring, and ex-post policy analysis (Patton and Sawicki 1993).

- *Ex-ante policy analysis.* This type of analysis, also called "anticipatory" or "prospective" policy analysis, mainly influences agenda setting, whether in the original formulation of a policy or in its subsequent modification. Ex-ante policy analysis helps decision makers clarify the problems they face and identify and assess potential solutions to those problems. It may also include analyses of the relative benefits and costs of the various alternatives, thereby providing quantitative information that can help decision makers assess the potential consequences and political implications of their decisions.

- *Policy maintenance.* This type of analysis is typically undertaken to help ensure that policies are implemented as their formulators designed them and intended them to be implemented. Policy maintenance involves analysis that is part of the exercise of legislative oversight and managerial control in implementation. As such, it can play a powerful role in identifying when and how to modify a policy, either by reformulating it or by making changes in its implementation.
- *Policy monitoring.* This type of analysis is the relatively straightforward measuring and recording of the ongoing operation of a policy's implementation. Such monitoring frequently provides valuable information for subsequent ex-post analysis. Policy monitoring can play a useful role in the exercise of appropriate managerial control and legislative oversight in the implementation phase, pointing out when and where modifications in rules and in operations might be needed.
- *Ex-post policy analysis.* This type of retrospective analysis is a way to determine the real value of a policy. This determination depends on an assessment of the degree to which a policy's objectives are achieved through its implementation.

Policy Analysis as a Basis for Modification

Analyzing policies, especially in terms of their effects and consequences, is a highly technical procedure that can be approached in a variety of ways. These include before-and-after comparisons, with-and-without comparisons, actual-versus-planned performance comparisons, experimental and quasi-experimental designs, and cost-oriented analytical approaches (Patton and Sawicki 1993).

Analyses based on *before-and-after comparisons*, as the name suggests, involve comparing conditions or situations before a policy is implemented with conditions or situations after it has had an opportunity to affect individuals, organizations, and groups. This is the most widely used approach to policy analysis. A variation on this approach, known as *with-and-without comparisons*, involves assessing the consequences of the policy for individuals, organizations, or groups and comparing them to situations in which the policy does not exist.

Analyses based on with-and-without comparisons prevail in the health policy domain, because variation in the nation's states provides a natural laboratory in which such comparisons are possible. For example, studies have compared variations in states' use of managed care options for Medicaid populations (Kaiser Family Foundation 2009a). In some situations, states do try policies first, and the results inform consideration of these policies by other states and at the national level.

However, Oliver and Paul-Shaheen (1997) studied policy innovation in states by examining states' enactment of major health-related legislation in the late 1980s and early 1990s. Their findings cast considerable doubt on the popular proposition that a state can invent policies for substantial health system reforms for subsequent use by other states or by the federal government.

The authors argue that it is more appropriate to think of states as "specialized political markets" in which, under certain circumstances, unique solutions to unique problems can be addressed through public policy.

Another useful approach to assessing policy performance, *actual-versus-planned performance comparisons*, involves comparing policy objectives (e.g., health status improvements, dollars saved, people inoculated, tons of solid waste removed) with actual postimplementation results. Neither this nor the other two approaches to ex-post analysis, however, supports the unassailable assignment of causation to the policies being assessed or evaluated. This limitation is a significant weakness of all three approaches. Nevertheless, these approaches are widely used, because they tend to be easily implemented and cost relatively little. The results of any of these comparison approaches, however, must be interpreted carefully.

To offset some of the technical limitations and weaknesses of the comparison approaches, two alternative approaches have been developed. These *experimental* and *quasi-experimental* analytical designs can permit more meaningful conclusions. In policy analyses that use experimental designs, individuals are randomly assigned to control groups. An excellent example of the power of experimental designs to evaluate policies can be found in the health insurance experiment conducted by the RAND Corporation in the 1970s (Newhouse 1974).

At the time, randomized controlled trials were the standard in clinical research, but this approach was rare in policy analysis. The now famous analysis by RAND clearly demonstrated the usefulness of the approach for assessing policy performance. However, experimental analysis is so expensive and difficult to conduct that its effect on modifying policy remains limited.

Quasi-experimental designs can be useful in the conduct of policy analyses. This approach maintains the logic of full experimentation but without some of its restrictions and expenses (Shadish, Cook, and Campbell 2001). Quasi-experimental designs can provide the ability to ascribe causality to a particular policy, although typically this is extremely difficult. This approach is frequently used when it is not feasible or ethical to randomly assign subjects in a study or evaluation.

A final approach to policy analysis is one based on cost-oriented assessments or evaluations. This approach can be especially important in the search for policies that provide value for public dollars. *Cost-benefit analysis* (CBA) and *cost-effectiveness analysis* (CEA) are the two most widely used forms of cost-oriented policy evaluation. In CBA, the evaluation is based on the relationship between the benefits and costs of a particular policy, where all costs and benefits are expressed in monetary terms. Such analyses can help answer the fundamental question of whether a policy's benefits are worth its costs. Typically, these analyses result in a measure of net benefits, which is "the difference between the total monetary input costs of an intervention and the consequences of that intervention, also valued in monetary terms" (Elixhauser et al. 1993, JS2).

In CEA, performance assessment is based on the desire to achieve certain policy objectives in the least costly way. This form of analysis compares alternative policies that might be used to achieve the same or very similar objectives. Typically, the results of CEA determinations are expressed as "the net costs required to produce a certain unit of output measured in terms of health, e.g., lives saved, years of life saved, or quality-adjusted life years" (Elixhauser et al. 1993, JS2–JS3). The use of these health-related policy analysis techniques has centered on variations in utilization and the relative effectiveness of various medical practices and surgical interventions.

Responsibility for Policy Analyses

The legislative and executive branches of the federal government are involved in policy analyses because they are interested in the performance of the policies they enact and implement. Key federal policy analysis organizations are briefly described in the following sections.

Government Accountability Office

GAO is the investigative arm of Congress. It is often called the "congressional watchdog," because it investigates how the federal government spends taxpayer dollars. The agency advises Congress and the heads of executive branch agencies on making government more efficient, effective, ethical, equitable, and responsive. The stated mission of GAO is "to support the Congress in meeting its constitutional responsibilities and to help improve the performance and ensure the accountability of the federal government for the benefit of the American people" (GAO n.d.). The agency seeks to provide Congress with timely information that is objective, fact-based, nonpartisan, nonideological, fair, and balanced.

In carrying out its mission, GAO audits and analyzes a host of programs and activities that arise from the implementation of federal policies. Organizationally, GAO is under the direction of the comptroller general of the United States, who is appointed by the president, with the advice and consent of the Senate, to a 15-year term. This gives GAO a level of independence and continuity of leadership that is rare in government. The Budget and Accounting Act of 1921 established the organization for the limited purpose of independently auditing federal agencies. Over the years, however, Congress has expanded GAO's audit authority, added extensive new responsibilities and duties, and strengthened the organization's ability to perform its work independently.

GAO does its work largely at the request of congressional committees or subcommittees or by mandate of public laws or committee reports. In fact, GAO is required to perform work requested by committee chairpersons and assigns equal status to requests from ranking minority members of congressional committees. When possible, GAO also responds to requests for analyses and audits from individual members of Congress. The agency supports congressional oversight by (GAO n.d.)

- auditing agency operations to determine whether federal funds are being spent efficiently and effectively,

- investigating allegations of illegal and improper activities,
- reporting on how well government programs and policies are meeting their objectives,
- performing policy analyses and outlining options for congressional consideration, and
- issuing legal decisions and opinions, such as bid protest rulings and reports on agency rules.

Appendix 28 is a GAO-prepared summary of a report that provides an example of the agency's work.

Because GAO conducts a wide range of policy analyses, its staff is drawn from a variety of disciplines, including accounting, law, public and business administration, economics, and the social and physical sciences. Their work is organized so each staff member concentrates on a specific subject area, facilitating the development of expertise and in-depth knowledge. When an analytical assignment requires specialized experience not available within GAO, outside experts assist the permanent staff. Reflecting the organization's need to attract and maintain a highly capable professional staff, the GAO Human Capital Reform Act of 2004 (P. L. 108-271) made a number of significant changes to how GAO operates (www.gao.gov/about/namechange.html), including

- decoupling GAO from the federal employee pay system,
- establishing a compensation system that places greater emphasis on job performance while protecting the purchasing power of employees who are performing acceptably,
- giving GAO permanent authority to offer voluntary early retirement opportunities and voluntary separation payments (buy-outs),
- providing greater flexibility in reimbursing employees for relocation benefits,
- allowing certain employees and officers with fewer than three years of federal service to earn increased amounts of annual leave, and
- authorizing an exchange program with private-sector organizations.

Congressional Budget Office

CBO was created by the Congressional Budget and Impoundment Control Act of 1974. The agency's mission is to provide Congress with the objective, timely, and nonpartisan analyses needed for economic and budget decisions and with the information and estimates required for the congressional budget process. Compared with the missions of Congress's other support agencies—the Congressional Research Service and the GAO—CBO's mission is narrow and focused. Even so, because the federal budget covers a wide array of activities, the agency is involved in wide-ranging health policy activity.

The Budget Act requires CBO to produce a cost estimate for every bill "reported out" (approved) by a congressional committee. CBO's cost estimates show how the legislation would affect spending or revenues over the subsequent five years or more. They also provide information about the proposal and explain how CBO prepared the estimate. Appendix 29 is an example of the work CBO does in estimating the cost of a policy. Like many of CBO's estimates, this example is straightforward. However, on occasion, the estimates become extremely complicated, as they did in projecting the costs of adding a prescription drug benefit to the Medicare program or of the American Recovery and Reinvestment Act of 2009.

CBO's primary responsibility is to assist the congressional budget committees with the matters under their jurisdiction—principally the congressional budget resolution and its enforcement. To help the budget committees enforce the budget resolution, CBO provides estimates of the budgetary costs of legislation approved by the various congressional committees and tracks the progress of spending and revenue legislation.

Overall, CBO's services can be grouped into four categories: helping Congress formulate budget plans, helping it stay within these plans, helping it assess the impact of federal mandates, and helping it consider the impact of policies on the federal budget. In the last role, for example, the analyses examine current and proposed policies, sometimes suggesting alternative approaches and projecting how the alternatives would affect current programs, the federal budget, and the economy. In line with its nonpartisan mandate, CBO does not offer specific policy recommendations.

Congressional Research Service

The Congressional Research Service (CRS; www.loc.gov/crsinfo) is another analytical resource available to members of Congress. Born in 1914 through legislation establishing a separate department within the Library of Congress called the Legislative Reference Service, the agency was established to provide Congress with information and analysis that would allow it to make more informed decisions. The Legislative Reorganization Act of 1970 renamed the agency the Congressional Research Service and significantly expanded its responsibilities. Today, the agency's mission is to serve "the Congress throughout the legislative process by providing comprehensive and reliable legislative research and analysis that are timely, objective, authoritative, and confidential, thereby contributing to an informed national legislature" (CRS 2009).

As a legislative branch organization, CRS serves as shared staff to congressional committees and members, assisting at every stage of the legislative process—from the early considerations in agenda setting that precede bill drafting, through committee hearings and floor debate, to the oversight and modification of enacted laws and various agency activities. CRS operates in many ways as an extension of, or supplement to, the members' own office staff.

The agency's staff includes more than 450 policy analysts, attorneys, information professionals, and experts in a variety of disciplines: law, economics, foreign affairs, defense and homeland security, public administration, education, healthcare, immigration, energy, environmental protection, science, and technology.

CRS is organized into five interdisciplinary research divisions, which are clustered around American law; domestic social policy; foreign affairs, defense, and trade; government and finance; and resources, science, and industry. Within each division, CRS analysts and specialists are organized into smaller sections that focus on specific areas of public policy such as education, labor, taxes, and health.

CRS provides its services in many forms, including (CRS 2009):

- tailored confidential memoranda, briefings, and consultations
- expert congressional testimony
- reports on current legislative issues available 24/7 via a website
- the Legislative Information System (LIS)
- seminars and workshops, including the twice yearly Federal Law Update
- training for congressional staff in legislative and budget procedures
- a premier work in constitutional law, entitled *The Constitution of the United States of America, Analysis and Interpretation*

As we noted at the beginning of this chapter, and as we have seen throughout this book, policymaking is not a perfect process. The decisions made within this process must be reviewed and changed as necessary. Behind this need for policy modification lies the fact that policies have huge consequences for individuals, populations, and health-related organizations and interest groups. Because they are affected so directly by health policy, the leaders of these entities typically devote considerable attention and resources to analyzing this process and the larger public policy environments. They also seek to exert influence in these environments; one pervasive result of this is the ongoing participation of the leaders of health-related organizations and interest groups in the modification phase of the public policymaking process.

When policies have positive consequences, such as more services, higher incomes, less pollution, or more money for biomedical research, those enjoying the benefits will likely seek to maintain or increase them through modification of the existing policies that affect these benefits. Similarly, those who are negatively affected by a policy will likely seek to remedy this through modification. The constant modification of existing policies is an important hallmark of policymaking in the United States. This aspect of policymaking permits the results of the process to be corrected or improved over time—an important attribute, given the complexity of the world in which the policymaking process plays out and the human fallibility of the participants in the process.

Summary

The modification phase of the public policymaking process involves the consequences of policies feeding back into the policymaking cycle and stimulating further policymaking. As the feedback loop depicted in Exhibit 7.1 shows, policy modification occurs in the agenda setting and legislation development stages of policy formulation and in the rulemaking and operations stages of policy implementation.

The modification phase is extremely important to the health policymaking process, because it provides continuing opportunities for the performance of policies and their consequences to stimulate modifications. Changes occur through the influence of policy outcomes on agenda setting or through the amendment of previously enacted public laws. In addition, the results of policy implementation routinely lead to modifications in the rulemaking and operation of policies.

As we pointed out in Chapter 2 and reemphasized in this chapter, the modification phase of policymaking exists because perfection cannot be achieved in the other phases and because policies are established and exist in a dynamic world. Suitable policies made today may become inadequate with biological, cultural, demographic, ecological, economic, ethical, legal, psychological, social, and technological changes in the future.

Review Questions

1. Discuss the distinction between policy initiation and policy modification.
2. Discuss the concept of incrementalism in public policymaking.
3. Describe modification in the agenda setting that precedes policy formulation.
4. Discuss how modification occurs in legislation development.
5. Discuss how modification occurs in rulemaking.
6. Discuss how modification occurs at the operational stage of implementing policies.
7. Discuss the cyclical relationship between rulemaking and operation and how this affects modification.
8. Discuss the role of oversight actors in policy modification.
9. Discuss the role of policy analysis in policy modification. Include brief descriptions of three federal agencies that support policymaking through policy analysis.

DEVELOPING COMPETENCE
IN THE POLICYMAKING PROCESS

As we have discussed throughout this book, health policies—the author-itative decisions made within government—affect people, communi-ties, populations, organizations, and interest groups. All those affected share two related areas of interest about policies and the process that produces them.

1. They want to know how policies will affect them and the people and things they care about or for which they are responsible. In other words, they have an analytical interest in policymaking and its results. People normally want information about anything that will affect them, and they prefer to have this information in advance so they can prepare.

2. They want to be able to influence the policies that affect them and the people and things they care about or for which they are responsible. These effects, after all, can have significant consequences. As a result of specific policies, for instance, certain people gain or lose access to a particular medical procedure or obtain or fail to obtain grants to support research projects. Certain organizations see demand for their services increase or decrease or see their revenues and expenses rise or fall.

We labeled the capability to successfully *analyze* and *influence* the pub-lic policymaking process *policy competence* in Chapter 1. This chapter explores in greater depth how the demanders of health policies can more effectively an-alyze and influence the policymaking process—that is, how they can increase their policy competence. First, however, we provide additional information about the concerns people, organizations, and interest groups have about health policy.

Health Policy and People, Organizations, and Interest Groups

In previous chapters, we considered how health policy affects the determi-nants of health: the physical environment, human behavior and biology, social factors, and health services. It is also useful to consider the effect of policies on people, organizations, and interest groups. Health is a state that exists in every person, community, and population, and health policy can affect the pursuit of this state. However, policies can affect people in different ways, under different circumstances, to different degrees, at different times. Therefore, their levels of interest vary.

Many organizations actively participate in the nation's pursuit of health. People who are employed in these organizations, who govern them, or who independently practice their professions within them have an interest in health policies that affect them. Health policies also directly affect the mission and purpose of these organizations, their day-to-day operations, and, ultimately, their successes and failures.

The people and organizations that have the greatest or most concentrated interest in the policymaking process are most likely to become involved with formal interest groups to more effectively address their concerns and interests. Remember, interest groups are groups of people with similar policy goals who band together to pursue those goals. Thus, it is useful to consider the effect of health policies on people, on organizations that participate in the pursuit of health, and on health-related interest groups to which individuals and organizations can belong.

Health Policy and People

The consequences of health policies at the level of individuals, communities, or populations can be enormous. Government engages in health policymaking primarily to support citizens in their quest for health, although secondary purposes, such as the economic interests of certain participants, may also be served. As we discussed in Chapter 1, government supports the pursuit of health through the effect of health policy on the determinants of human health: the physical and social environments in which people live and work; their behaviors and biology; and the type, quality, and timing of the health services they receive.

Extensive studies show that the uninsured have less access to health services, and reduced access to healthcare is associated with poorer health (Committee on the Consequences of Uninsurance 2004). Lack of coverage negatively affects not only the uninsured individual, but also that person's entire family and the community in which he or she lives. Economic costs to society are another consequence (Institute of Medicine 2001; 2002a; 2002b; 2003a; 2003b). The five reports just cited clearly show that

- the number of uninsured individuals under age 65 is large and increasing, and high rates of uninsurance have persisted even during periods of strong economic growth;
- uninsured children and adults do not receive the care they need, suffer from poorer health and development, and are more likely to die early than are those with coverage;

- even one uninsured person in a family can put the financial stability and health of the whole family at risk; and
- a high uninsured rate can adversely affect the overall health status of the community, its healthcare institutions and providers, and the access of its residents to certain services.

Although the determinants of health are important to people, the relationship between health policy and the hundreds of millions of affected individuals is highly idiosyncratic. The relationship between policies and collectives or groups of individuals—organizations and interest groups—is easier to understand. Even so, all health policy eventually affects individuals. People breathe cleaner or dirtier air, eat more or less healthful food, have more or less access to health services, and benefit from more or fewer technological advances as a direct result of health policies.

Health Policy and Health-Related Organizations

The accomplishments of many organizations are affected by health policies. Certainly, the missions, objectives, and internal structures and resources of these organizations influence their accomplishments. However, the performance levels they achieve—whether measured in terms of contribution to health outcomes for customers, financial strength, reputation, growth, competitive position, scope of services provided, or some other parameter—are also influenced by the opportunities and threats posed by their external environments.

The external environments that health-related organizations face have biological, cultural, demographic, ecological, economic, ethical, legal, psychological, social, technological, and policy dimensions. Policies that affect an organization are only part of its external environment, although they may be critical. As Exhibit 8.1 illustrates, policies, along with the other variables in the external environment, present an organization with a set of opportunities and threats to which it must respond.

The organization responds to these threats and opportunities with strategies and organizational structures created to carry them out. The ability of the strategies and structures to respond appropriately results in organizational performance. But these opportunities and threats are the direct result of conditions in the external environment, including the public policies that affect the organization. Thus, we must consider the specific nature of the health policy concerns and interests of health-related organizations.

The organizations that populate the health sector defy easy categorization, but they are all affected by and have interests in health policies. Hospitals, state or county health departments, HMOs, hospices, and nursing homes are examples of health services providers. While the future is unclear, abundant evidence indicates that, for the most part, provider organizations in the United States have developed under extraordinarily favorable public policies. For example, enactment in 1946 of the Hospital Survey and

EXHIBIT 8.1 The Relationship Between an Organization's External Environment and Its Performance

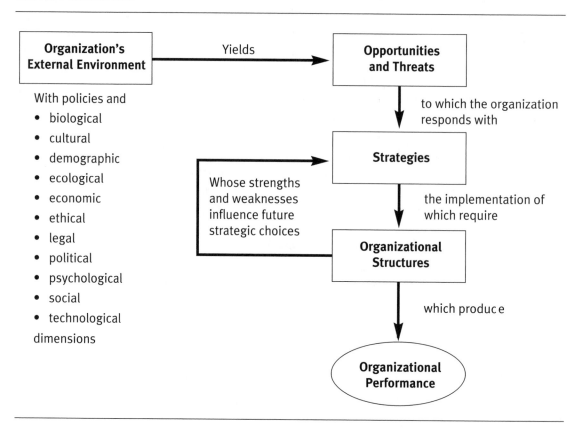

Construction Act (P.L. 79-725) placed Congress squarely in support of expanded availability of health services and improved facilities. Called the Hill-Burton Act after its authors, this legislation provided funds for hospital construction and marked the beginning of a decades-long program of extensive federal developmental subsidies aimed at increasing the availability of health services.

Public policy has also supported and facilitated the expansion of health insurance coverage. During World War II, when wages were frozen for many workers, health insurance and other benefits in lieu of wages became attractive features of the American workplace. Encouraged by policies that excluded these fringe benefits from income taxes and by a U.S. Supreme Court ruling that employee benefits, including health insurance, could be legitimately included in the collective bargaining process, employer-provided health insurance benefits grew rapidly in the mid-twentieth century (Murray 2007).

Outside the private sector, Medicare and Medicaid legislation was enacted in 1965, providing greater access to mainstream health services through publicly subsidized health insurance for the aged and many poor. With enactment of these programs, 85 percent of the American population had some form of health insurance.

Although public policies have been extremely important in the development of health-related organizations, the vast majority of them have emerged in the context of a market economy. Thus, the U.S. healthcare system has largely been shaped by supply and demand and the decisions and actions of buyers and sellers. The combination of market forces and public policies has shaped a complex and dynamic healthcare system.

Types of Organizations in the Healthcare System

Although they sometimes defy easy categorization, there are three main types of organizations in the healthcare system. Organizations that that provide health services can be categorized as *primary health service providers*. A second category can be classified as *secondary provider organizations*; these organizations provide resources for the primary providers to use in conducting their work. The third category of organizations is *health-related interest groups*.

Primary Health Services Providers

One way to envision the variety and diversity of health service provider organizations is to consider a continuum of health services that people might use over the course of their lives and to think of the organizational settings that provide them (Longest and Darr 2008). The continuum could begin before birth with organizations (or programs) that minimize negative environmental impact on human fetuses or that provide genetic counseling, family planning services, prenatal counseling, prenatal ambulatory care services, and birthing services. This would be followed early in life by pediatric ambulatory services; pediatric inpatient hospital services, including neonatal and pediatric intensive care units (ICUs); and ambulatory and inpatient psychiatric services for children.

Health services organizations for adults include those providing adult ambulatory services, including ambulatory surgery centers and emergency and trauma services; adult inpatient hospital services, including routine medical, surgical, and obstetrical services, as well as specialized cardiac care units (CCUs), medical ICUs, surgical ICUs, and monitored units; stand-alone cancer units with radiotherapy capability and short-stay recovery beds; ambulatory and inpatient rehabilitation services, including specific subprograms for orthopedic, neurological, cardiac, arthritis, speech, otologic, and other services; ambulatory and inpatient psychiatric services, including specific subprograms for psychotics, day programs, counseling services, and detoxification; and home healthcare services.

In their later years, people might add to the list of relevant health services organizations those providing skilled and intermediate nursing services;

adult day care services; respite services for caregivers of homebound patients, including such services as providing meals, visiting nurse and home health aides, electronic emergency call capability, cleaning, and simple home maintenance; and hospice care, palliative care, and associated family services, including bereavement, legal, and financial counseling.

Health services were traditionally provided by autonomous organizations, with little attention to coordination of the continuum of services. In recent decades, however, most health services organizations have significantly changed how they relate to one another (Shortell et al. 2000). Mergers, consolidations, acquisitions, and affiliations are now commonplace. At the extreme end of this activity is vertical integration, in which multiple organizations unify in organizational arrangements or systems. Vertically integrated systems capable of providing a largely seamless continuum of health services—including primary, acute, rehabilitation, long-term, and hospice care—increasingly characterize healthcare.

Health services in the future may be organized and delivered through even more extensively integrated systems and networks in which providers, spanning the full continuum of health services, are integrated with health plans or insurers and perhaps with suppliers. Some of these more fully integrated systems have already formed. Whether the integration of insurers and health plans with delivery systems will be successful is unclear, but these networks can provide an extensive and coordinated continuum of health services and may be the future of the nation's decreasingly fragmented approach to its pursuit of health.

Policy Interests of Primary Health Service Providers

The policy interests of service provider organizations vary, but their leaders share certain generic interests. Those in charge of provider organizations tend to focus, for example, on policies that might affect access to their services, the costs of those services, or their revenues from them. These executives and governing board members also are typically concerned about policies that relate to the structure of the healthcare system, including antitrust issues involved in mergers and consolidations, policies that relate to meeting the needs of special populations that they may serve, policies pertaining to quality assurance, and a number of ethical and legal issues related to providing access to affordable health services of an appropriate quality to all who need them.

Secondary Provider Organizations

Related to the organizations that provide health services directly are those that produce resources for providers to use in conducting their work or that facilitate this work in some way. Such organizations are called *secondary provider organizations*. This category includes educational institutions that produce the healthcare system's workforce; insurance companies and health plans that organize and facilitate payment for health services (at least those insurers and plans that are not integrated into provider systems); and organizations, such as pharmaceutical, medical supply, and biomedical technology companies, whose products are used in providing health services.

Secondary provider organizations have health policy interests of their own. Educational organizations and programs involved in producing the health workforce are interested in policies that affect the resources used in their educational missions, such as faculty, buildings, and equipment. Interest is also keen in policies that relate to licensure and practice guidelines and those that may influence the demand for their programs' graduates, including policies that affect coverage under public insurance programs. They are also interested in policies that affect people's ability to pay for education.

Policy Interests of Secondary Provider Organizations

Health plans and insurance organizations are vitally interested in policies that affect their operations and decisions. Because these organizations are licensed by the states, they are affected by federal and state policies. Similarly, pharmaceutical and biotechnology firms and medical supply companies have wide-ranging health policy interests, including specific interests in policies that affect their markets, products, and profits.

Indeed, all primary service provider organizations and secondary provider organizations are interested in health policy, if only because policy affects their performance levels. Mesch (1984) constructed a list of questions that senior-level managers can use to determine their relative interest in public policies. The questions, in an adapted form, are as follows:

- Do public policies influence your organization's capital allocation decisions or its strategic plans for services and markets?
- Have previous strategic plans been scrapped or substantially altered because of changes in public policy?
- Is your organization's industry becoming more competitive? More marketing oriented? More technology dependent?
- Does the interplay of public policies and the other variables in your organization's external environment seem to be influencing strategic decisions?
- Are you and other senior-level managers in your organization displeased with the results of past strategic planning because of surprises resulting from changes in public policies that affected your organization's performance?

If the managers of a health-related organization, whether a primary service provider or a secondary provider of resources, can answer yes to even one of these questions, they are likely to be interested in the public policymaking process and in relevant policies. If the answer to most or all of the questions is yes, as is typical for contemporary health-related organizations, they will consider interest in their public policy environment to be absolutely imperative and will make strong operational commitments to understanding and effectively responding to the threats and opportunities public policy presents to their organization or system (Longest 2003).

Health Policy and Health-Related Interest Groups

Primary health service provider organizations and secondary provider organizations, as we discussed in the previous sections, are not the only entities with health policy concerns and interests. A wide variety of health-related interest groups, including some that are consumer based or organized around individual health practitioner memberships, exist because of the collective interests of their members in health policymaking and the resulting policies.

As we discussed in Chapter 2, a significant feature of the U.S. policymaking process and its political environment is the presence of interest groups that exist to serve the collective interests of their members. These groups analyze the policymaking process to discern policy changes that might affect their members and inform them about such changes. They also seek to influence the process to provide the group's members with some advantage. The interests of their constituent members define the health policy interests of these groups.

Interest Groups of Primary Service Provider Organizations and Individual Health Practitioners

Some interest groups have primary service provider organizations as their members. Hospitals can join the American Hospital Association (AHA; www.aha.org), long-term-care organizations can join the American Health Care Association (AHCA; www.ahca.org) or the American Association of Homes and Services for the Aging (AAHSA; www.aahsa.org), and health insurers and health plans can join America's Health Insurance Plans (AHIP; www.ahip.org).

Other interest groups represent individual health practitioners. Physicians can join the American Medical Association (AMA; www.ama-assn.org). African American physicians may also choose to join the National Medical Association (NMA; www.natmed.org), and female physicians may also choose to join the American Medical Women's Association (AMWA; www.amwa-doc.org). In addition, physicians have the opportunity to affiliate with groups, usually termed "colleges" or "academies," where membership is based on medical specialty. Prominent examples are the American College of Surgeons (ACS; www.facs.org) and the American Academy of Pediatrics (AAP; www.aap.org). Other personal membership groups include the American College of Healthcare Executives (ACHE; www.ache.org), the American Nurses Association (ANA; www.ana.org), and the American Dental Association (ADA; www.ada.org), to name a few.

Often, in addition to national interest groups, provider organizations and individual practitioners can join state and local groups—usually affiliates or chapters of national groups—that also represent their interests. For example, states have state hospital associations and state medical societies. Many urban centers and densely populated areas even have groups at the regional, county, or city level.

Secondary provider organizations have their own interest groups. Examples include the following:

Interest Groups of Secondary Provider Organizations

- Association of American Medical Colleges (AAMC; www.aamc.org)
- Association of University Programs in Health Administration (AUPHA; www.aupha.org)
- Biotechnology Industry Organization (BIO; www.bio.org)
- Blue Cross and Blue Shield Association (BCBSA; www.bluecares.com)
- Pharmaceutical Research and Manufacturers of America (PhRMA; www.phrma.org)

Like groups whose members are primary service providers, these groups focus particularly on policies that affect their members directly.

There are a number of interest groups that individuals—as private individuals or consumers rather than as executives or health practitioners—can join. Reflecting the populations from which their members are drawn, groups with individual member constituencies are diverse. Some are based in part on a shared characteristic such as race, gender, age, or connection to a specific disease or condition. Examples include the following:

Interest Groups with Individual Member Constituencies

- American Association of Retired Persons (AARP; www.aarp.org)
- American Heart Association (AHA; www.americanheart.org)
- National Association for the Advancement of Colored People (NAACP; www.naacp.org)
- National Organization for Women (NOW; www.now.org)

Interest groups such as NAACP and NOW serve the health interests of their members as part of agendas focused broadly on racial and gender equality. Although the Fourteenth Amendment to the U.S. Constitution guarantees equal protection under the law, American history clearly shows how difficult this equality has been to achieve. Interest groups such as NAACP and NOW have made their central public policy goal equality at the polls, in the workplace, and in education, housing, health services, and other facets of life in the United States.

The specific health policy interests of groups representing African Americans include adequately addressing this population segment's unique health problems: widespread disparities in health status and access to health services, higher infant mortality, higher exposure to violence among adolescents, higher levels of substance abuse among adults, and, compared to other segments of the population, earlier deaths from cardiovascular disease and other causes. Similarly, groups representing the interests of women seek to address their unique health problems. In particular, they focus on such interests as breast cancer, childbearing, osteoporosis, family health, and funding for biomedical research on women's health problems.

A growing proportion of the American population is older than 65. The elderly have specific health interests related to their stage of life; as people age, they consume relatively more healthcare services, and their healthcare needs differ from those of younger people. They also become more likely to consume long-term-care services and community-based services intended to help them cope with limitations in the activities of daily living.

In addition to their health needs, older citizens have a unique health policy history and, therefore, a unique set of expectations and preferences regarding the nation's health policy. The Medicare program, a key feature of this history, includes extensive provisions for health benefits for older citizens. Building on the specific interests of older people and their preferences to preserve and extend their healthcare benefits through public policies, organizations such as AARP and the National Council of Senior Citizens (www.ncscinc.org) play an important role in addressing the health policy interests of their members.

Other interest groups with individual constituencies reflect member interests based primarily on specific diseases or conditions, such as the American Cancer Society (ACS; www.cancer.org) or the Consortium for Citizens with Disabilities (CCD; www.c-c-d.org). AHA, for example, has 22.5 million volunteers and supporters pursuing the organization's mission of building healthier lives, free of cardiovascular diseases and stroke.

AHA pursues its mission through such avenues as direct funding of research, public and professional education programs, and community programs designed to prevent heart disease. It also seeks to serve its members' interests through influencing public policy related to heart disease. As AHA (2009) notes on its web page, its public policy agenda is organized into the following categories:

- heart disease and stroke research
- heart disease and stroke prevention
- tobacco control
- obesity prevention
- quality and availability of care
- chain of survival
- stroke treatment and systems of care
- health disparities
- nonprofit issues

As is typical of these categories, the association has specific goals listed under the category Heart Disease and Stroke Research, including one related to federal funding for research related to its interest as follows (AHA 2009):

> To reduce disability and death from cardiovascular diseases and stroke, the Association seeks to increase funding for the National Institutes of Health, including for congenital and acquired heart disease, stroke, cardiac and respiratory arrest, and other cardiovascular diseases. This includes significant real growth in federal funding of medical research programs of the National Heart, Lung, and Blood Institute (NHLBI) and the National Institute of Neurological Disorders and Stroke (NINDS).
>
> Attention should also be given to other institutes conducting heart and stroke research, such as the National Institute on Aging (NIA), the National Institute of Diabetes and Digestive and Kidney Diseases (NIDDK), and the National Institute of Nursing Research (NINR). The Association also advocates for identifying additional federal funding sources to supplement, not reduce, monies awarded through the appropriations process.

AHA's federal policy agenda is typical of many interest groups—it seeks to serve its membership by outlining and pursuing clear-cut public policy agendas on behalf of its members.

The people, organizations, and interest groups noted above, and many more beyond these, have extensive policy interests. Policy really matters to them in highly tangible ways. Thus, these people, organizations, and groups have vested interests in developing competence in the policy arena. The remainder of this chapter is focused on how this can be done, beginning with a discussion of the concepts of competence and, specifically, of policy competence.

Concepts of Competence

"Definitions and terminology surrounding the concept of competence are replete with imprecise and inconsistent meanings, resulting in a certain level of bewilderment among those seeking to identify the concept" (Shewchuck, O'Connor, and Fine 2005, 33). For purposes of this discussion, we will use Lucia and Lepsinger's (1999) definition of competence:

> a cluster of related knowledge, skills, and ability (sometimes referred to by the acronym SKA) that: (1) affect a major part of one's job (a role or responsibility), (2) correlate with performance on the job, (3) can be measured against well accepted standards, and (4) can be improved by training and development.

Thus, *policy competence* is the knowledge, skills, and abilities that permit one to successfully (1) analyze the public policymaking process to the point of accurately assessing its effect on his or her domain of interest or responsibility and (2) influence the process. Obviously, policy competence comes in degrees, and the policy competence of demanders certainly is not the only factor that affects suppliers' decisions. However, demanders' policy competence can and often does play a role in policymaking and its results.

Remember from the brief introductory discussion of policy competence in Chapter 1 that the single most important factor in policy competence is seeing the public policymaking process as a *decision-making* process. Public policies, including health policies, are decisions. Policy competence requires an understanding of the context, participants, and processes of this particular type of decision making. In short, it requires an understanding of the *public policy environment* of a particular entity. This environment is formed by the policymaking process, its results, and the forces that can affect the process and are relevant to the entity.

Organization Design to Support Policy Competence

The people, organizations, and interest groups we discussed in the preceding sections can possess various levels of policy competence. The resources of organizations and interest groups can enhance the policy competence of their individual members beyond that of individuals acting alone.

Managers in these organizations and groups must establish the patterns of relationships among human and other resources within their domains of responsibility. These patterns are called *organization designs*. Intentional patterns of relationships established by managers are *formal* organization designs. This distinction is important; coexisting within formal organization designs are *informal* structures that exist because people working together within formal designs invariably establish relationships and interactions that lie outside the boundaries of the formal structure. All organization designs have formal aspects, which are developed by managers, and informal aspects, which reflect the wishes and preferences of other participants (Longest 2004).

Examples of Organization Designs

Entities with policy interests and sufficient resources can build formal structures for effectively analyzing their public policy environments and influencing those environments. Any organization's or interest group's approach to organization design is likely to be unique to its situation, as the following examples suggest. In each example, responsibility for analyzing public policy environment and seeking to influence events and outcomes rests predominantly with senior-level managers and governing board members. These leaders, especially in large entities, may be assisted by specialized staff organized to fulfill these responsibilities.

1. *American Academy of Pediatrics.* The academy's Department of Federal Affairs is its link to federal policymaking. Pediatricians who wish to

make a difference in child and adolescent health through Congress or federal agencies receive the information and tools they need to become effective child advocates. This office prepares them to offer testimony in legislation development or meet with representatives or senators. AAP's policy agenda includes access to healthcare for all children, immunizations, disaster preparedness, and childhood obesity and injury prevention. Its other interests include legislation and regulations involving the education of new physicians, the ethics of medical practice, biomedical research, and clinical laboratory testing.

2. *Wisconsin Medical Society* (www.wismed.org). The society's mission is to "improve the health of the people of Wisconsin by supporting and strengthening physicians' ability to practice high-quality patient care in a changing environment."

   The society's Government Relations Department is responsible for legislative affairs (lobbying), policy research and development, and WISMedPAC, the society's political action committee. Members of the lobbying team represent the society before the state and federal governments. At the state level, this includes the legislature and a variety of government agencies. The policy staff assists the lobbyists in seeking to affect legislation and rule changes. The society regularly submits testimony to the state legislature. The department staff collaborates with a variety of patient advocacy organizations to strengthen mutual political agendas. In addition, staff communicates with other medical societies, including the American Medical Association and state and national specialty societies, to learn from related legislative activities in other states.

3. *Council on Governmental Relations* (COGR; www.cogr.edu). The council is an association of 150 leading research-intensive universities that receive a significant share of the federal funds available to higher education through contracts and grants for research and scholarship. COGR concerns itself with the influence of government regulations, policies, and practices on research conducted at colleges and universities. COGR's primary function is to help develop policies and practices that fairly reflect the mutual interest and separate obligations of federal agencies and universities in federal research and training. COGR deals mainly with policies and technical issues involved in the administration of federally sponsored programs at universities. COGR provides advice and information to its membership and makes certain that federal agencies understand academic operations and the burden their proposed regulations might impose on colleges and universities.

4. *University of Pittsburgh Medical Center* (UPMC, www.upmc.com). The organizational structure of this academic health center includes a vice president for government relations and community health services, who

analyzes and influences the center's public policy environment at the local, state, and federal levels. The vice president oversees all of UPMC's government relations programs and keeps the senior managers informed about relevant federal and state policies, including legislative and regulatory matters. This vice president

- identifies and analyzes relevant legislative and regulatory matters;
- recommends appropriate responses to matters of legislative and regulatory interest;
- carries out the responses, including facilitating the participation of others; and
- advocates proactively in specific policy areas, including Medicare reimbursement, biomedical research funding, and transplantation issues.

Best Practices in Creating Designs for Policy Competence

Management literature is replete with recommendations for creating specialized administrative units to analyze and influence public policy environments (Swayne, Duncan, and Ginter 2007). When a health-related organization or interest group makes analyzing and influencing its public policy environment a high priority, its leaders typically establish a specialized department or unit, usually called the public affairs department or government (sometimes called governmental) affairs (or relations) department to perform the actual work.

Some large organizations and many interest groups divide government relations into separate departments or units within a department, one for the federal government and another for state government. The directors of such departments often report to the CEO, because CEOs have vital interests in the public policy environments of the entities they lead. Departments or units devoted to government affairs mainly serve to enhance the policy competence of an entity's senior-level managers, especially its CEO. If these units are well designed and staffed with policy-competent people, they can give an entity and its leaders the enormous advantage of lead time in dealing with its public policy environment. When the leaders of organizations or groups are able to anticipate policy changes months—or better still, years—in advance, their responses can be more effective and more appropriate.

Beyond giving themselves more lead time, those who understand emerging policies or modifications in existing policies can better influence emerging policies to the advantage of their entities. They foresee the emergence of relevant public policies and the consequences on their domains of responsibility. This foresight—derived from policy competence—serves as a basis for efforts to participate in shaping policies that will affect their organizations or groups (Longest 1997).

But how is such prescience achieved? The answer lies in the approach to policy analysis. People who look beyond specific policies to the larger public policy environments have a great advantage over those who merely wait until a policy is determined and then react to it. Former hockey player Wayne Gretzky is commonly known to have said, "Most players skate to the puck. I skate to where the puck will be. This has made all the difference in my success." People benefit when they focus on the policies that affect their domains, but they gain much greater advantage when they consider why and how these policies emerge. Those who focus broadly on the public policy environment of their domain increase their chances of anticipating policy changes.

This anticipatory focus—thinking about where the puck is going, not simply where it is now—provides an opportunity to influence policies in their emergent states. Leaders of entities who understand public policy environments, with all their complex interplay of actors, actions, inactions, and other variables, are better equipped to anticipate and influence policies than their less policy-competent counterparts. They are prepared to ask more anticipatory, "what if" questions.

Leading an entity based on solid predictions of *future* policies differs significantly from reacting to announced changes, or even to soon-to-be-announced changes. Proactive preparation and the opportunity to influence the ultimate shape of policies are possible with enough foreknowledge. After policy changes occur, only reaction is possible, typically with inadequate time for thoughtful responses. In subsequent sections, we look at how to effectively analyze and influence public policy environments.

Analyzing Public Policy Environments

The leaders of an organization or group must be able to accurately analyze the public policy environment of their entity. Such analyses lead to an understanding of the strategic consequences of events and forces in that environment. Policy-competent leaders are able to assess the effects, in terms of opportunities and threats, of public policies on their domains and make strategic adjustments that reflect their planned responses.

Consider as an example significant potential changes to a state's Medicaid program. Such changes could affect many policy demanders, including acute and long-term-care service providers and their interest groups, county governments, and the state's Medicaid population. The policy competence of parties who may be affected by eventual changes will affect their ability to influence the ultimate outcome and prepare for the consequences.

Benefits and Limitations

The effective analysis by its leaders of an organization's or interest group's public policy environment leads to a number of concrete benefits. Such analysis permits an entity's leaders to

- classify and organize complex information about the public policymaking process and the forces and pressures that affect the process;
- identify and assess current public policies that do or will affect the entity;
- identify and assess the formulation of emerging public policies— including new laws, amendments, and changes in rules—that might eventually affect their entity;
- speculate in a systematic way about potential future relevant public policies; and
- link information about public policies to the entity's objectives and strategies, and thus to its performance.

These potential benefits can be offset by several limitations inherent in any attempt to analyze a complex public policy environment. These limitations in the ability of individuals, no matter how talented they are or how well supported their endeavors may be, include some of the following truths:

- No one can foretell the future through analyses of public policy environments; at best, one can devise informed opinions and guesses about the future.
- People cannot possibly see every aspect of the policymaking process, nor can they be aware of every detail of public policies that will affect their organization or interest group.
- Leaders may effectively discern relevant public policies or emergent ones but be unable to correctly interpret the effect of the policies on their organization or group.
- Leaders may effectively discern and interpret the effect of relevant or emergent policies but find that their organization or group is unable to respond appropriately.

Efforts to analyze the public policy environments of health-related organizations and interest groups face limitations, but the benefits leaders of these entities derive from doing so justify the use of substantial resources. The most important of these resources is the commitment of senior-level leaders to ensuring that effective analysis occurs.

If effective environmental analyses are to be carried out, senior leaders must bear responsibility, although they typically rely on others to carry out the functions and specific activities involved. These functions extend beyond discerning the important information to include organizing and evaluating that information to determine how it affects the entity.

Procedural Steps in Analyzing Public Policy Environments

Analysis of the public policy environment is part of the larger external environmental analysis through which an entity's leaders determine the externally imposed opportunities and threats facing their organization or, in the case of interest groups, their members. Their external environments include, but are not limited to, the public policy environment. In fact, the external environments of entities include *all* factors outside their boundaries that can influence their performance. Public policies are certainly among the factors, but biological, cultural, demographic, ecological, economic, ethical, legal, psychological, social, and technological factors are also relevant and must be routinely analyzed.

Effective analysis of a public policy environment requires a variety of tools and techniques. Among the more common are trend identification and extrapolation, expert opinion gathered through the Delphi technique (a means of eliciting opinions and judgments from experts through structured exchange of email, mail, or facsimile that permits successive rounds of interactions) or focus groups, and scenario development. Any of these techniques is most productively applied within the framework of a five-step process.

Four of the steps are routinely considered in the general strategic management literature (David 2009) and have been adapted for use in health-related organizations by Swayne, Duncan, and Ginter (2007). A fifth step is added to their list below. The interrelated steps are

1. *scanning* the environment to identify strategic public policy issues—specific public policies or problems, possible solutions to the problems, and political circumstances that might eventually lead to policies—that are relevant and important to the organization or interest group;
2. *monitoring* the strategic public policy issues identified;
3. *forecasting* or projecting the future direction of strategic public policy issues;
4. *assessing* the importance of the strategic public policy issues for the entity; and
5. *diffusing* the results among those in the organization or interest group who can help formulate and implement its response.

Each of these steps is examined in turn in the following sections.

Scanning the Environment to Identify Strategic Public Policy Issues

Scanning involves acquiring and strategically organizing important information from an entity's external environment. This step properly begins with careful consideration by the leaders of what they believe to be strategic public policy issues. In guiding the focus of scanning, it is useful to remember that public policies are authoritative decisions intended to direct or influence the actions, behaviors, or decisions of others. Authoritative decisions that influence the strategic actions, behaviors, or decisions of an entity's leaders are strategically important.

The set of strategic public policies for any entity constitutes a large set of decisions. Some of these decisions are codified in the statutory language of specific public laws. Others are the rules or regulations established to implement public laws or to operate government and its various programs. Still others are the judicial branch's relevant decisions.

Strategically important public policies, however, represent only part of an entity's strategic public policy *issues*. Problems, potential solutions, and political circumstances that might lead to strategic policies must also be considered important issues. Thus, effective scanning of the public policy environment involves identifying specific strategic policies *and* emerging problems, possible solutions, and the political circumstances that surround them, which could eventually lead to policies of strategic importance. Together, these form the set of strategic *public policy issues* that should be scanned.

Consideration about what issues are of strategic importance is largely judgmental, speculative, or conjectural (Klein and Linneman 1984). Obviously, the quality of the judgments, speculations, and conjectures is important. It is useful to have more than one person decide which of the scanned issues are strategically significant. One widely used approach is to rely on an ad hoc task force or a committee of people from within the organization or interest group to render their collective opinion.

Another popular approach is to use outside consultants who can provide expert opinions and judgments. It is also possible to use any of several more formal expert-based techniques. The most useful among these are the Delphi technique, the nominal group technique (NGT), brainstorming, and focus groups, each of which is an interactive group problem-identification and problem-solving technique (Swayne, Duncan, and Ginter 2007; Fogler and LeBlanc 2008). The starting point in scanning, no matter who is doing it or which techniques might be employed, is the question of who or what to scan.

The appropriate foci of scanning activities are the policymakers in federal, state, and local governments and those who can influence their decisions. Those who can influence policymakers' decisions may do so through helping shape conceptualizations of problems and their potential solutions or through the political circumstances that help drive the policymaking process. The focus can be limited to strategically important policies and the problems, potential solutions, and political circumstances that might eventually lead to policies that affect the entity doing the scanning.

Another focus is made up of the suppliers of relevant public policies and those who can influence them. As we discussed in Chapter 1, members of each branch of government supply policies in the political market, although the role of each branch is different. Each should receive attention in scanning. Because policies are made in all three branches of government, the list of potential policymakers is lengthy, and adding those who can influence them makes it even longer.

Effectively scanning an entity's public policy environment identifies specific policies that are of strategic importance. *Very* effective scanning also identifies the emerging problems, possible solutions to them, and the political circumstances that surround them that could eventually lead to strategically important policies. But scanning is only the first step in analyzing a public policy environment.

Monitoring Strategic Public Policy Issues

Monitoring is tracking, or following, strategically important public policy issues over time. The leaders or support staff of organizations, systems, or interest groups monitor public policy issues they believe are of strategic importance. Monitoring, especially when the issues are poorly structured or ambiguous, permits the entity to assemble more information so that issues can be clarified and their strategic importance can be determined (Heath and Palenchar 2009).

Monitoring takes a much narrower focus than does scanning (Swayne, Duncan, and Ginter 2007). The purpose of monitoring is to build a base of information around the strategically important public policy issues that are identified through scanning or are verified through earlier monitoring. Fewer—usually far fewer—issues will be monitored than will be scanned in the analysis of public policy environments.

The strategic importance of public policy issues is difficult to determine. If this were not the case, leaders analyzing their entities' environments would fully understand strategic issues and all consequential implications for their decisions and actions. However, uncertainty characterizes the external environments of most health-related organizations and groups. Monitoring will not remove uncertainty, but it will likely reduce it significantly as more detailed and sustained information is acquired. As with scanning, multiple perspectives and expert opinions can help leaders determine what should be monitored; experts in the form of consultants can also be used for the actual monitoring if this is beyond the ability of the entity's regular staff.

For most organizations and interest groups in the health domain, monitoring strategic public policy issues will affirm for their leaders that the vast majority of contemporary policies spring from a relatively few earlier policies. Monitoring reveals that public policies have histories. Many of them continually, although incrementally, evolve through modification. As people monitor these changes, they tend to become intimately familiar with the policies' evolutionary paths. Such familiarity can serve as a background for the next step in analyzing public policy environments: forecasting changes.

Forecasting Changes in Strategic Public Policy Issues

Effective scanning and monitoring cannot, by themselves, provide all the information about the strategic public policy issues in an entity's environment that its leaders require. An effective response to strategic issues depends on reliable forecasts of future conditions or states. This may give leaders time to formulate and implement their response.

Scanning and monitoring the public policy environment involves searching for signals, sometimes distant and faint, that may be the forerunners of strategically important issues. Forecasting involves extending the issues and their impacts beyond their current state. For some public policy issues (e.g., the impact on patient demand of a change in eligibility requirements for the Medicaid program), adequate forecasts can be made by extending past trends or applying a formula. In other situations, forecasting must rely on conjecture and speculation, or on the interactive group problem-identification and problem-solving techniques noted earlier. Sometimes, sophisticated simulations are conducted to forecast the future.

However, strategically important public policy issues never exist in a vacuum and typically involve many issues simultaneously. Existing forecasting techniques and models do not fully address this condition.

Trend Extrapolation   The most widely used technique for forecasting changes in public policy issues is trend extrapolation (Hanke and Wichern 2008). When properly used, this technique is relatively simple and can be remarkably effective. Trend extrapolation is simply tracking a particular issue and then using the information to predict future changes. Public policies do not emerge de novo. Instead, they result from chains of activities that can and typically do span many years. Understanding the history of policies and related policy issues makes the results of the policymaking process easier to predict.

Even so, trend extrapolation must be handled carefully. It works best under highly stable conditions; under other conditions it has significant limitations. When used to forecast changes in public policy, it usually predicts some general trend—such as a directional trend in the number of people served by a program or in a funding stream—rather than quantifies the trend with great specificity.

Significant policy changes and changes in technology, demographics, or other variables can render the extrapolation of a trend meaningless or misleading. In spite of this, predictions based on extrapolation can be useful to the leaders of organizations, systems, and interest groups as they seek to predict the paths of strategically important policy issues. For those who exercise caution in its use and who factor in the effect of changes such as the introduction of a new or modified policy, trend extrapolation can be useful in forecasting certain aspects of the public policy environments of their health-related organizations, systems, or interest groups.

Scenario Development   Another technique for forecasting the public policy environment is the development, usually in writing, of scenarios of the future (Ramirez, Selsky, and Van der Heijden 2008). A scenario is simply a plausible story about the future. This technique is especially appropriate for analyzing environments, such as health-related organizations and interest groups, that include many uncertainties and imponderables.

The essence of scenario development is to define several alternative scenarios, or states of affairs. These can be used as the basis for developing contingent responses; alternatively, the organization, system, or interest group leaders can select the most likely from among the scenarios and prepare appropriately.

Scenarios of the future can pertain to a single policy issue (e.g., the federal government's policy regarding approval procedures for new medical technology) or to broader-based sets of policy issues (e.g., the federal government's policies on regulation of health plans, funding for medical education or research, or a preventive approach to improved health). Scenarios can, and in practice do, vary considerably in scope and depth (Lindgren and Bandhold 2009).

As a general rule, it is useful to develop several scenarios. Multiple scenarios permit the breadth of future possibilities to be explored. After the full range of possibilities has been reflected in a set of scenarios, one can be chosen as the most likely. However, the most common mistake in scenario development is envisioning one particular scenario too early in the process and basing a response on it. Leaders who think they know which scenario will prevail and who prepare only for the one they select may find that the price of guessing incorrectly can be high indeed.

Assessing the Strategic Importance of Public Policy Issues

Scanning and monitoring strategic public policy issues and forecasting future changes in them are important steps in environmental analysis. However, the leaders of organizations and interest groups must also concern themselves with the specific and relative strategic importance of the issues they are analyzing. That is, they must assess or interpret the strategic importance and implications of public policy issues for their entities.

Frequently, this assessment involves characterizing issues as opportunities or threats (see Exhibit 8.1). However, such assessments are far from exact. Sound human judgment may well be the best technique for making these determinations, although the strategic importance of public policy issues can be considered on several bases.

Experience with similar issues is frequently a useful basis for assessing the strategic importance of a public policy issue. The experience may have been acquired firsthand within the organization or interest group where an assessment is being made, or it may come from contact with colleagues in other organizations or groups that have experienced similar public policy issues and who are willing to share their experiences. Public policies that affect the pursuit of health vary among the states; this variety can be instructive. Similarly, leaders can draw insight from experiences in other countries. Other bases for assessments include intuition or best guesses about what particular public policy issues might mean to an entity and advice from well-informed and experienced others. When possible, quantification, modeling, and simulation of the potential effects of the issues being assessed can be useful.

Making the appropriate determination is rarely simple, even when all the bases we have suggested are considered. Aside from the difficulties in collecting and properly analyzing enough information to inform the assessment fully, problems sometimes derive from the personal prejudices and biases of those conducting the assessment. Such problems can force assessments that fit some preconceived notions about what is strategically important rather than reflect a particular situation (Lindgren and Bandhold 2009).

Diffusing the Results of Environmental Analysis into Organizations and Interest Groups

The final step in analyzing public policy environments is diffusing or spreading the results of the effort to those who need the information to carry out their own responsibilities. For example, the identification of a shift in a funding stream for certain services may be of strategic importance to several managers in an organization. This information should be diffused in such a way that it reaches all of them. This step is frequently undervalued and may even be overlooked. Unless information is effectively diffused, it does not matter how well the other steps in environmental analysis are performed.

Leaders can diffuse relevant information about the public policy environment by

1. using their *power* to dictate diffusion and use of the information (this approach works best in entities whose leaders can, if they choose, use coercion or sanctions to see that the information is diffused and used in all the appropriate places),
2. using *reason* to persuade all who are affected by the information to use it (this works as well as or better than relying on power, if the leaders are persuasive), or
3. perhaps best of all in most situations, using *education* of participants in the entity to emphasize and convince those who need to be convinced of the importance and usefulness of the information as a way of improving the chances that the information will be properly used.

However it is done, diffusion of strategically important information about public policy issues among the relevant participants in organizations or interest groups brings the environmental analysis process to completion.

In the next section, we explore the potential value of viewing policies as logic models to facilitate their analysis. As we noted in Chapter 6, policies contain, at least implicitly, an underlying rationale or logic. They are not written as logic models, but a logic model is inherent in most policies, whether they take the form of public laws, rules or regulations, judicial decisions, or operational decisions. Essentially, a policy's logic model is an expression of how resources are meant to be utilized or processed to achieve the policy's goals and objectives.

Logic Models in Analyzing Policies

Any mechanism that can help better analyze policies has utility. Logic models were developed in the context of program evaluation (CDC Evaluation

Working Group 2009) and were subsequently found to be useful in managing programs more effectively. Regarding programs, logic models depict what inputs will be used in various processes to yield results. They can be used in the same manner to depict the relationships among the desired results of a policy and the inputs and processes necessary to attain those results. In fact, such models can help policymakers more carefully conceptualize policies as they are being formulated. Similarly, a policy based on a logic model can be more readily analyzed or evaluated, primarily because its intended results and the means of achieving those results will have been specified.

The Logic Model Concept

One way to visualize the purpose of a public policy is to think of it as a theory. A policy's theory is a plausible model of how the policy is supposed to work. A good policy theory is based on an underlying rationale or logic. For example, one can theorize about a proposed policy as follows: If resources a, b, and c are assembled and then processed by doing m, n, and o with the resources, the results will be x, y, and z.

The relationships among resources, processes, and desired results form the policy's underlying theory, which can be used to draw a logic model of how the policy is intended to operate. Exhibit 8.2 depicts a basic logic model template for a policy.

This model shows that *resources* are used in *processes* to accomplish the policy's *desired results*. The desired results are expressed in terms of desired *outputs*, *outcomes*, and ultimately the policy's *impact*. The model includes *feedback* in the form of a loop from desired results to resources and processes to indicate that policies can be adjusted as they are implemented. The logic model also shows that a policy exists in an *external environment*.

EXHIBIT 8.2 Logic Model Template for a Policy

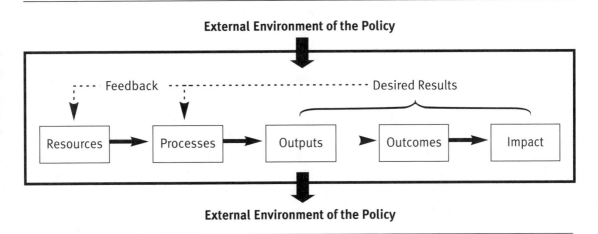

SOURCE: Adapted from Longest, B. B. (2004). Used with permission.

The external environment of a policy typically includes many factors that can influence operation and performance. These are illustrated in Exhibit 8.2 by the top arrow that flows from the environment into the policy's logic model. Relevant external factors include the preferences of affected individuals, organizations, and interest groups and biological, cultural, demographic, ecological, economic, ethical, legal, psychological, social, and technological factors that can influence formulation and implementation.

Public policies do not exist in isolation. All policies affect and are affected by their external environments. Resources needed for implementation flow from the external environment. A policy's results flow out into the external environment (see the bottom arrow in Exhibit 8.2). A policy's outputs, outcomes, and impact flow outward and affect individuals, groups, and organizations.

A useful way to express desired results—whether a new or amended law, rule, or judicial or operational decision—in a logic model is in terms of outputs, outcomes, and impact. These three forms of desired results move from the most tangible (outputs) to the broadest possible conceptualization of what a policy is intended to accomplish (impact). For example, some of the desired *outputs* of the Medicare Prescription Drug, Improvement, and Modernization Act (P.L. 108-173) intended to make prescription medication more readily available to Medicare beneficiaries can be expressed quantitatively, including:

- X prescriptions filled,
- Y beneficiaries served, and
- Z dollars expended.

The *outcomes* desired of a policy reflect changes in the attitudes, behaviors, and knowledge of those affected by the policy. For example, some of the outcomes desired for MMA could include

- X beneficiaries enroll in Medicare Part D,
- Y beneficiaries comply with their prescription protocols, and
- Z beneficiaries show improved hypertension control or diabetes control.

The desired *impact* of a policy represents the ultimate changes resulting from the policy. For the MMA policy, the desired impact includes improved health and quality of life among affected beneficiaries.

It is of course possible to specify desired results in different ways from those shown in Exhibit 8.2. Outputs and outcomes can be combined, for example. The differences between them are rather subtle. The use of outputs, outcomes, and impact permits finer detail in specifying desired results, which in turn leads to a more complete specification of the processes needed to achieve the results and the resources needed to carry out these processes. The more detailed the specifications, the better the logic model can support efforts to analyze a policy.

Given the vital link between entities and the public policies that affect them, no health-related organization or interest group can succeed without a reasonably effective set of activities through which its leaders discern and ultimately respond to strategically important public policy issues. However, this is only one component of the task facing these leaders regarding their public policy environments. They are also responsible for influencing these environments to the strategic advantage of their organization or interest group. We explore this complex activity, which is the other component of policy competence, in the next section.

Influencing Public Policy Environments

Leaders of health-related organizations and interest groups typically develop strong operational commitments to devising ways to influence their public policy environments. There is nothing innately wrong with a leader establishing an operational objective of influencing the public policy environment. However, activities directed to this objective can easily be tainted by self-serving purposes. Adherence to ethical principles is especially important in this area.

The Ethics of Influencing Policymaking

Humans control political markets. Thus, various mixes of altruism and egoism influence policymaking. The operation, outcomes, and consequences of the public policymaking process are directly affected by the ethics of those who participate in it.

Ethical considerations shape and guide the development of new policies by contributing to the definition of problems and the structure of policy solutions. The ethical behavior of all participants in the political markets where policymaking occurs should be guided by four philosophical principles: respect for the autonomy of other people, justice, beneficence, and nonmaleficence.

Respect for Autonomy

The ethical principle of respect for *autonomy* is based on the concept that individuals have the right to their own beliefs and values and to the decisions and choices that further these beliefs and values. This ethical principle undergirds much of the formal system of government that the nation's founders envisioned. Beauchamp and Childress (2008) point out that no fundamental inconsistency or incompatibility exists between the autonomy of individuals and the authority of government, so long as government's authority does not exceed the limits set by those who are governed.

In the context of seeking to influence policymaking, autonomy pertains to the rights inherent in U.S. citizenship. Specifically, autonomy relates to the rights of individuals to independent self-determination regarding how they live their lives and to their rights regarding the integrity of their bodies and minds. Respect for autonomy in seeking to influence health policymaking reflects issues that pertain to privacy and individual choice, including behavioral or lifestyle choices.

Respect for autonomy can sometimes be better understood in contrast to its opposite: paternalism. Paternalism implies that someone else determines what is best for people. Policies guided by a preference for autonomy limit paternalism. A vivid example of the influence of autonomy in health policymaking is the 1990 Patient Self-Determination Act (P.L. 101-508). This policy gives individuals the right to make decisions concerning their medical care, including the right to accept or refuse treatment and the right to formulate advance directives regarding their care.

Such directives allow competent individuals to give instructions about their healthcare, to be implemented at some later date should they then lack the capacity to make medical decisions. In concept, this policy gives people the right to exercise their autonomy in advance of a time when they might no longer be able to exercise that right actively. In the absence of such directives, decisions may fall to the courts. On occasion they have done so, generating national attention. Well-known cases include Karen Ann Quinlan (in 1976, a New Jersey court ruled in favor of the removal of a respirator from the brain-damaged woman); Nancy Cruzan (in 1990, the U.S. Supreme Court ruled that a feeding tube could be withdrawn); and Terri Schiavo (in 2005, a Florida court judge ruled that the feeding tube keeping her alive in a persistent vegetative state could be removed, and following unprecedented action by Congress, a federal judge refused to order the reinsertion of the feeding tube) (Goodnough and Hulse 2005; Findlaw.com 2005).

The principle of respect for autonomy includes several other elements that are important in guiding ethical policymaking behavior. One is telling the truth. Respect for people as autonomous beings implies honesty in relationships. Closely related to honesty is confidentiality. Confidences broken in policymaking can impair the process. A third element of the autonomy principle that is important to the policymaking process is fidelity. This means doing one's duty and keeping one's word. Fidelity is often equated with keeping promises. When participants in the policymaking process tell the truth, honor confidences, and keep promises, the process is more ethically sound.

Justice   Another ethical principle of importance to public policymaking is *justice*. The degree of adherence to this principle directly affects the policymaking process and policies themselves. In Rawls's (1971, 5) words, "One may think of a public conception of justice as constituting the fundamental charter of a well-ordered human association." Much of its effect on policies and policymaking hinges on defining justice as fairness (Rawls 1971). Justice also includes the concept of just deserts, which holds that justice is done when a person receives that which he or she deserves (Beauchamp and Childress 2008).

The principle of justice provides much of the underpinning for all health policies, whether allocative or regulatory. Just allocative policies distribute benefits and burdens according to the provisions of a morally defensible system rather than through arbitrary or capricious decisions. Just regulatory policies affect those to whom the regulations are targeted fairly and equitably. The nation's legal system exists in part to ensure that the principle of justice is respected in the formulation and implementation of public policies and to serve as an appeals mechanism for those who believe that the process has not adequately honored this principle.

The practical implications for health policymaking are felt largely in terms of distributive justice—that is, in terms of fairness in the distribution of health-related benefits and burdens in society. Gostin (2008, 69) argues that

> Public health policy conforms to the principle of social justice (it is fair) when, to the extent possible, it provides services to those in need and imposes burdens and costs on those who endanger the public health. Services provided to those without need are wasteful and, given scarce resources, may deny benefits to those with genuine need. Regulation aimed at persons or businesses where there is no danger imposes costs and burdens without a corresponding public benefit. Ideally, services should be allocated on the basis of need and burdens imposed only where necessary to prevent a serious health risk.

The most difficult policy question deriving from application of the ethical principle of justice is, of course, what is fair? The opinions of participants in political markets and in the health policymaking process vary on the issue of fair distribution of the benefits and burdens involved in the pursuit of health in American society. The three most prominent perspectives on justice provide useful insight into the range of possible views on this matter.

Egalitarian Perspective

The *egalitarian* perspective of justice holds that everyone should have equal access to the benefits and burdens arising from the pursuit of health and that fairness requires recognition of different levels of need. The influence of the egalitarian view is evident in, for example, policies intended to remove discrimination in the provision of health services and those intended to provide more resources to people who need them most (e.g., Medicare for the elderly, Medicaid for the poor, charging more for Medicare prescription coverage of higher-income people).

Libertarian Perspective

The *libertarian* perspective of fairness requires a maximum of social and economic liberty for individuals. Policies that favor unfettered markets as the means of distributing the benefits and burdens associated with the pursuit of health reflect the libertarian theory of justice.

Utilitarian Perspective

The *utilitarian* view of fairness is best served when public utility is maximized. This is sometimes expressed as the greatest good for the greatest number. Many health policies, including those pertaining to restricting pollution, ensuring safe workplaces, and controlling the spread of communicable diseases, have been heavily influenced by a utilitarian view.

Beneficence

Beneficence in policymaking means that participants in the process act with charity and kindness; that is, they overtly seek to do good. This principle is widely reflected in policies that provide tangible benefits. Thus, beneficence characterizes such allocative policies as the Medicare and Medicaid programs. But it also includes the complex concept of balancing benefits and burdens.

Participants in the political marketplace who seek to influence policymaking to produce policies that benefit them or their interests exclusively, while burdening others, violate the principle of beneficence. Those who seek to influence policymakers—and policymakers themselves—and who are guided by the principle of beneficence make decisions that maximize the net benefits to society as a whole and balance fairly the benefits and burdens of their decisions.

Nonmaleficence

A fourth principle with deep roots in medical ethics is *nonmaleficence*. This principle is exemplified in the dictum *primum non nocere*—first, do no harm. Policymakers who are guided by the principle of nonmaleficence make decisions that minimize harm. The principles of beneficence (do good) and nonmaleficence (do no harm) are clearly reflected in health policies that seek to ensure the quality of health services and products. Similarly, policies such as those the FDA uses to ensure the safety of pharmaceuticals and the policies that established and maintain the Agency for Healthcare Research and Quality (AHRQ) are also examples of policies that reflect the principles of beneficence and nonmaleficence.

Influence: A Matter of Power and Focus

Effective influence in the public policy environments of organizations and interest groups, either individually or in collaboration, depends on power and on knowing where and when to focus efforts.

The Power Part of the Influence Equation

As we discussed in detail in Chapter 2, power is the basis of influence in a public policy environment. Entities use power from three sources to influence their policy environments: positional power, reward or coercive power, and expert power.

Positional Power

Entities such as healthcare organizations or interest groups may possess power by virtue of their place or role in the larger society. Organizations and groups have positional power simply because they exist and are recognized as legitimate participants in the policy marketplace.

Policymakers entertain the opinions and consider the preferences of leaders of health-related organizations such as Baxter Worldwide, a global medical products and services company, and health-related interest groups such as America's Health Insurance Plans, a national association representing nearly 1,300 member companies providing health insurance to more than 200 million people, in part because they recognize these entities and their leaders as legitimate participants in the policymaking arena.

An important aspect of using positional power to influence policymaking is the ability of organizations and interest groups to bring legal actions as part of their efforts to exert influence. Positional power alone may gain a hearing for particular views or preferences. The exertion of influence, however, usually requires power of another kind.

Reward or Coercive Power

Some power is based on an entity's capacity to reward policymakers' compliance or punish their noncompliance with its preferred decisions, actions, and behaviors. Such rewards include campaign contributions, votes, and the organization and mobilization of grassroots activities designed to persuade other people on particular issues.

Expert Power

Another source of influence in policymaking is based on an entity's possession of expertise or information that is valued by others. In public policy environments, useful information and expertise may pertain to the definition or clarification of problems or to the development of solutions. Expertise in the intricacies of the public policymaking process is also valuable.

Organizations and interest groups that can marshal these bases of power, and especially those that can integrate the three, can be very influential. The degree of influence, of course, varies. Relative influence is determined by the amount of power each organization or interest group has, the reputation of each for exerting influence ethically and effectively, and the strength of ideological convictions held by those who seek to influence. Whatever its bases, however, power is only one part of the complex equation that determines influence.

The Focus Part of the Influence Equation

In addition to marshaling enough power to influence policymaking, leaders of organizations and interest groups must also consider the *focus* of their efforts to influence their public policy environments. Typically, focus is guided by the identification of policies that are of strategic importance and of problems, potential solutions, and political circumstances that might eventually lead to such policies. By focusing in this way, leaders will seek to influence strategically relevant policymakers in all three branches and all levels of government. Furthermore, they will extend their efforts to those who have influence with these policymakers.

In addition to influencing policymakers directly, leaders who wish to influence policymaking effectively must help shape the conceptualizations of problems, the development of potential solutions to the problems, and the political circumstances that help drive the policymaking process. The suppliers of relevant public policies and those who can influence them form the appropriate focus for organizations and groups seeking to influence their public policy environments.

A Map Can Sharpen Focus

The model of the policymaking process shown in Exhibit 2.3 can serve as a map to direct influencing efforts to where they can be most useful. Depending on the circumstances, the proper focus may be one or more of the component phases of the policymaking process, or the stages within them. Exhibit 8.3 offers another way to consider where in the process to exert influence and suggests some specific ways to do so.

Influencing Policy Formulation

Using the map to determine where to exert influence in their public policy environments, leaders of organizations and groups may focus on those areas where the health policy agenda is shaped by the interaction of problems,

---

EXHIBIT 8.3 Places to Influence Policymaking

Influencing Policy Formulation
   At agenda setting by
   - defining and documentating problems
   - developing and evaluating solutions
   - shaping political circumstances through lobbying and the courts
   At legislation development by
   - participating in drafting legislation
   - testifying at legislative hearings

Influencing Policy Implementation
   At rulemaking by
   - providing formal comments on draft rules
   - serving on and providing input to rulemaking advisory bodies
   At policy operation by
   - interactions with policy implementers

Influencing Policy Modification
   - by documenting the case for modification through operational experience and formal evaluations

---

possible solutions to the problems, and political circumstances. They can influence policymaking by helping to define the problems that eventually become the focus of public policymaking, by participating in the design of possible solutions to these problems, and by helping to create the political circumstances necessary to convert potential solutions into actual policies. In short, influencing the factors that establish the policy agenda itself can influence policies.

Once issues achieve a prominent place on the policy agenda, they can (but do not always) proceed to the next stage of the policy formulation phase, development of legislation. At this stage, specific legislative proposals go through a carefully prescribed set of steps that can, but do not always, lead to policies in the form of new legislation, or amendments to previously enacted legislation (see Chapter 4).

Although this path is long and arduous, it is replete with opportunities for leaders of organizations or groups to influence legislation development. Both as individuals and through the interest groups to which they belong, leaders of health-related organizations participate directly in the drafting of legislative proposals and the hearings associated with the development of legislation.

Influencing Policy Implementation

As we discussed in Chapter 5, enacted legislation is rarely explicit enough to fully guide its implementation. Rather, laws are often vague on implementation details, leaving to the implementing agencies and organizations the establishment of the rules needed to operationalize it.

Leaders of entities and others who have a stake in a particular policy can actively participate in policymaking at implementation, because this phase invites those affected by the rules to comment on proposals. The exertion of influence at this point can produce significant results.

Leaders can also exert influence indirectly. When the development of rules is anticipated to be unusually difficult or contentious or when continual revision is anticipated, special provisions may be made. In particular, advisory bodies or commissions may be established to help shape the development of rules.

MedPAC is one such body. Operationally, MedPAC meets publicly to discuss policy issues and formulate its recommendations to Congress. In the course of these meetings, commissioners consider the results of staff research, presentations by policy experts, and comments from interested parties, such as staff from congressional committees and CMS, health services researchers, health services providers, and beneficiary advocates.

Although opportunities for direct service on such commissions are limited to very few people, others can influence their thinking. Leaders of health-related organizations and interest groups can and do influence commission members, and thus the advice that commission members ultimately provide about formulating and implementing policy.

As we discussed in Chapter 6, influence can also be exerted in the operation of policies. The operation stage of implementing policies involves the actual running of programs and activities embedded in or stimulated by enacted legislation. Operation is the domain of the appointees and civil servants who staff the government. These people influence policies by their operational decisions and actions. Thus, policies can be influenced through interactions with those who have operational responsibility.

Building
Effective
Relationships
Between Policy
Demanders
and Policy
Implementers

Significant influence can arise from the sometimes close working relationships that may develop between those responsible for policy implementation and those their decisions and activities affect directly, including health-related organizations and groups.

Opportunities to build these relationships are supported by the longevity of bureaucrats' careers (Kingdon 1995). Elected policymakers come and go, but the bureaucracy endures. Leaders of entities can—and many do—build long-standing working relationships with people responsible for implementing the public policies that are of strategic importance to their organization or group.

The most solid base for these working relationships is the exchange of useful information and expertise. A leader, speaking from an authoritative position based on operational experience with the implementation of a policy, can influence the policy's further implementation. If the information that leader provides supports change, especially if it is buttressed by similar information from others who are experiencing the policy's effect, reasonable implementers may be influenced to make needed changes. This is especially likely in the context of a well-established working relationship based on mutual respect for the roles of each party and the challenges each faces.

An obvious—and limiting—problem for those wishing to influence the policymaking process though the rulemaking or operation stages of policy implementation is the enormity of the bureaucracy with which they might need to interact. Consider how many components of the federal government are involved in rulemaking and policy operation that is directly relevant to health-related organizations and groups. Add to this the relevant units of state and local government and the challenge of keeping track of where working relationships might be useful in influencing policymaking, to say nothing of the challenge of actually developing and maintaining the relationships. Obviously, selectivity is required in determining which of these relationships might have strategic value.

Influencing
Policy
Modification

The vast majority of health policies result from the modification of existing policies in modest, incremental steps. Policy modification occurs when the outcomes, perceptions, and consequences of existing policies feed back into the agenda-setting and legislation-development stages of the formulation phase and into the rulemaking and policy operation stages of the implementation phase and stimulate changes in legislation, rules, or operations (see the feedback loop running along the bottom of Exhibit 2.3).

Opportunities to influence policies continually arise as their outcomes and consequences trigger modification. Those who would influence policies have an opportunity to do so in the initial iteration of any particular policy, but additional opportunities arise during the subsequent modification of existing policies.

Following the feedback loop in Exhibit 2.3, we can see that because agenda setting involves the confluence of problems, possible solutions, and political circumstances, leaders of health-related entities can influence policy modification by making certain that problems become more sharply defined and better understood through the experiences of those affected by the policies. In fact, leaders of organizations or groups are often the best sources of feedback on a policy's consequences, including its effects on the people, communities, and populations they serve. Similarly, potential new solutions to problems can be conceived and assessed through the entities' operational experiences with particular policies, especially when demonstrations and evaluations provide concrete evidence of their performance and impact. Leaders—guided by their experiences and interactions with ongoing policies—become important components of the political circumstances surrounding the amendment of these policies.

Influencing Modification at Formulation: Agenda Setting

Experience with the consequences of their implementation helps leaders identify needed modifications in policies that affect their entities. The history of Medicare legislation is a good example of this phenomenon. Over the program's life, services have been added and deleted; premiums and copayment provisions have been changed; reimbursement mechanisms have been changed; features to ensure quality and medical necessity of services have been added, changed, and deleted; and so on. Feedback from directly affected entities played a role in each amendment to the original legislation, although other influences contributed.

Influencing Modification at Formulation: Legislation Development

Leaders of health-related organizations and interest groups can also influence modification at the implementation phase, in both the rulemaking and policy operation stages. Modification of rules and changes in operations often reflect the reported or documented experiences of those affected by the rules and operations. Leaders can provide this feedback directly to those with rulemaking or operational responsibilities. They can also take their views to the courts or to the legislative branch. Either action can lead to modifications.

Influencing Modification at Implementation

Appendix 30 provides an example of how the sources of power can be combined with the map to potential focus points in a broad strategy for influencing the public policy environment of an academic health center. The concepts presented there apply to most healthcare organizations and related interest groups.

The Human Element in Analyzing and Influencing Public Policy Environments

The fact that public policy environments are largely controlled by humans complicates efforts at analysis and influence, even for those with high levels of policy competence. The diverse preferences, objectives, priorities, levels of understanding of issues, and other variables among the people in an entity's public policy environment make accurate analysis or successful influence difficult. The widely divergent positions of policymakers in regard to funding and operating the Medicare program illustrate the nature of this challenge.

Medicare has from its inception been the focus of contention among policymakers, including legislators responsible for laws pertaining to the Medicare program and staff at CMS, which is responsible for implementing the program. Constant and sometimes intense pressure from organizations and groups with vested interests in the program fuel the policy battles over the program's funding and operation.

Policymakers' perspectives on Medicare are affected by the program's massive size. Current Medicare benefit payments total approximately $477 billion, accounting for 22 percent of total spending for personal health services in the United States (Kaiser Family Foundation 2009b). As they look to the retirement of the baby boomer generation, policymakers see a widening gap between program revenues and program expenditures. They know this creates a looming government financial crisis. Policymakers, especially those who stand for periodic reelection, detest difficult fiscal choices because of the political consequences such choices impose. They find themselves attempting to balance the preferences of hospitals and other providers for generous reimbursements against the understandable desires of beneficiaries for expanding benefits, all the while keeping a lid on escalating program costs and seeking new revenues. They have options in this balancing act, but none of them are politically palatable. The variety of opinions among policy suppliers and demanders makes it more difficult to effectively analyze and anticipate the results of the policymaking process regarding this policy, or to influence the outcome.

Summary

Health policies, once formulated and implemented, have consequences for individuals, communities, populations, and health-related organizations and interest groups. The ability of health-related organizations to fulfill their missions is heavily influenced by such factors as the relative generosity or parsimony of reimbursement policies. Interest groups exist to serve the interests of their members, and these interests often involve influencing the development of health policy.

Those who are affected by policies share two fundamental concerns about the public policymaking process. They are concerned with analyzing their public policy environments so that they can discern in advance how policies might affect them, and they are concerned with influencing the formulation and implementation of these policies. To successfully address these concerns requires a degree of *policy competence*, defined in this chapter as the knowledge, skills, and abilities that permit one to successfully analyze the public policymaking process, and accurately assess its effect on his or her domain of interest or responsibility, and successfully influence the policymaking process.

The capacity to effectively analyze public policy environments and exert influence in these environments is enhanced by pooling resources that can be devoted to the tasks. The leaders of interest groups and organizations can best analyze their public policy environments through five steps: scanning, monitoring, forecasting, assessing, and diffusing information about their public policy environments into the entity.

Health-related organizations and interest groups seek to influence their public policy environments so that the consequences for them will be more favorable—or at least less unfavorable. Success at influencing these environments is a function of *power* bases on which to mount the efforts and the *focus* of the efforts.

Review Questions

1. Discuss the concept of policy competence.
2. Discuss the effect of health policies on individuals, health-related organizations, and interest groups.
3. What two major areas of concern do individuals share with health-related organizations and interest groups regarding policies and the process through which they are produced? Why are these concerns more easily addressed by organizations and groups than by individuals?

4. Discuss the benefits and limitations facing organizations and interest groups that undertake analysis of their public policy environments.
5. Who is responsible for the analysis of the public policy environment of an organization or interest group? Who helps in the process?
6. Discuss the recommended steps in effectively analyzing the public policy environment of an organization or group.
7. Who is responsible for efforts to influence an organization's or interest group's public policy environment on behalf of the entity? Who helps in the process?
8. Discuss the fact that influence in public policy environments is a matter of power and focus.

OVERVIEW OF MEDICARE

Title XVIII of the Social Security Act, designated "Health Insurance for the Aged and Disabled," is commonly known as Medicare. As part of the Social Security Amendments of 1965, the Medicare legislation established a health insurance program for aged persons to complement the retirement, survivors, and disability insurance benefits under Title II of the Social Security Act.

When first implemented in 1966, Medicare covered most persons aged 65 or older. In 1973, the following groups also became eligible for Medicare benefits: persons entitled to Social Security or Railroad Retirement disability cash benefits for at least 24 months, most persons with end-stage renal disease (ESRD), and certain otherwise noncovered aged persons who elect to pay a premium for Medicare coverage. Beginning in July 2001, persons with amyotrophic lateral sclerosis (Lou Gehrig's disease) are allowed to waive the 24-month waiting period. This very broad description of Medicare eligibility is expanded in the next section.

Medicare originally consisted of two parts: Hospital Insurance (HI), also known as Part A, and Supplementary Medical Insurance (SMI), which in the past was also known simply as Part B. Part A helps pay for inpatient hospital, home health, skilled nursing facility, and hospice care. Part A is provided free of premiums to most eligible people; certain otherwise ineligible people may voluntarily pay a monthly premium for coverage. Part B helps pay for physician, outpatient hospital, home health, and other services. To be covered by Part B, all eligible people must pay a monthly premium.

A third part of Medicare, sometimes known as Part C, is the Medicare Advantage program, which was established as the Medicare+Choice program by the Balanced Budget Act (BBA) of 1997 (Public Law 105-33) and subsequently renamed and modified by the Medicare Prescription Drug, Improvement, and Modernization Act (MMA) of 2003 (Public Law 108-173). The Medicare Advantage program expands beneficiaries' options for participation in private-sector health care plans.

The MMA also established a fourth part of Medicare, known as Part D, to help pay for prescription drugs not otherwise covered by Part A or Part B. Part D initially provided access to prescription drug discount cards, on a voluntary basis and at limited cost, to all enrollees (except those entitled to Medicaid drug coverage), and, for low-income beneficiaries, transitional limited financial assistance for purchasing prescription drugs and a subsidized enrollment fee for the discount cards. This temporary plan began in mid-2004 and phased out during 2006. In 2006 and later, Part D provides subsidized access to prescription drug insurance coverage on a voluntary basis, upon payment of premium, for all beneficiaries, with premium and cost-sharing subsidies for low-income enrollees.

Part D activities are handled within the SMI trust fund but in an account separate from Part B. It should thus be noted that the traditional treatment of "SMI" and "Part B" as synonymous is no longer accurate, since SMI now consists of Parts B and D. The purpose of the two separate accounts within the SMI trust fund is to ensure that funds from one part are not used to finance the other.

When Medicare began on July 1, 1966, approximately 19 million people enrolled. In 2008, almost 45 million are enrolled in one or both of Parts A and B of the Medicare program, and over 9 million of them have chosen to participate in a Medicare Advantage plan.

Entitlement and Coverage

Part A is generally provided automatically and free of premiums to persons aged 65 or older who are eligible for Social Security or Railroad Retirement benefits, whether they have claimed these monthly cash benefits or not. Also, workers and their spouses with a sufficient period of Medicare-only coverage in federal, state, or local government employment are eligible beginning at age 65. Similarly, individuals who have been entitled to Social Security or Railroad Retirement disability benefits for at least 24 months, and government employees with Medicare-only coverage who have been disabled for more than 29 months, are entitled to Part A benefits. (As noted previously, the waiting period is waived for persons with Lou Gehrig's disease. It should also be noted that, over the years, there have been certain liberalizations made to both the waiting period requirement and the limit on earnings allowed for entitlement to Medicare coverage based on disability.) Part A coverage is also provided to insured workers with ESRD (and to insured workers' spouses and children with ESRD), as well as to some otherwise ineligible aged and disabled beneficiaries who voluntarily pay a monthly premium for their coverage. In 2007, Part A provided protection against the costs of hospital and specific other medical care to about 44 million people (37 million aged and 7 million disabled enrollees). Part A benefit payments totaled $200.2 billion in 2007.

The following healthcare services are covered under Part A:

- Inpatient hospital care. Coverage includes costs of a semiprivate room, meals, regular nursing services, operating and recovery rooms, intensive care, inpatient prescription drugs, laboratory tests, X-rays, psychiatric hospitals, inpatient rehabilitation, and long-term care hospitalization when medically necessary, as well as all other medically necessary services and supplies provided in the hospital. An initial deductible payment is required of beneficiaries who are admitted to a hospital, plus copayments for all hospital days following day 60 within a benefit period (described later).

- Skilled nursing facility (SNF) care. Coverage is provided by Part A only if it follows within 30 days (generally) a hospitalization of three days or more and is certified as medically necessary. Covered services are similar to those for inpatient hospital care, and include rehabilitation services and appliances. The number of SNF days provided under Medicare is limited to 100 days per benefit period (described later), with a copayment required for days 21 through 100. Part A does not cover nursing facility care if the patient does not require skilled nursing or skilled rehabilitation services.

- Home health agency (HHA) care (covered by Parts A and B). The Balanced Budget Act transferred from Part A to Part B those home health services furnished on or after January 1, 1998, that are unassociated with a hospital or SNF stay. Part A will continue to cover the first 100 visits following a three-day hospital stay or a SNF stay; Part B covers any visits thereafter. Home health care under Parts A and B has no copayment and no deductible.

  HHA care, including care provided by a home health aide, may be furnished part time by an HHA in the residence of a homebound beneficiary, if intermittent or part-time skilled nursing and/or certain other therapy or rehabilitation care is necessary. Certain medical supplies and durable medical equipment (DME) may also be provided, although beneficiaries must pay a 20 percent coinsurance for DME, as required under Part B of Medicare. There must be a plan of treatment and periodic review by a physician. Full-time nursing care, food, blood, and drugs are not provided as HHA services.

- Hospice care. Coverage is provided for services to terminally ill persons with life expectancies of 6 months or less who elect to forgo the standard Medicare benefits for treatment of their illness and to receive only hospice care for it. Such care includes pain relief, supportive medical and social services, physical therapy, nursing services, and symptom management. However, if a hospice patient requires treatment for a condition that is not related to the terminal illness, Medicare will pay for all covered services necessary for that condition. The Medicare beneficiary pays no deductible for the hospice program but does pay small coinsurance amounts for drugs and inpatient respite care.

An important Part A component is the benefit period, which starts when the beneficiary first enters a hospital and ends when there has been a break of at least 60 consecutive days since inpatient hospital or skilled nursing care was provided. There is no limit to the number of benefit periods covered by Part A during a beneficiary's lifetime; however, inpatient hospital care is normally limited to 90 days during a benefit period, and copayment requirements (detailed later) apply for days 61 through 90. If a beneficiary exhausts the 90 days of inpatient hospital care available in a benefit period, the beneficiary can elect to use days of Medicare coverage from a nonrenewable "lifetime reserve" of up to 60 (total) additional days of inpatient hospital care. Copayments are also required for such additional days.

All citizens (and certain legal aliens) aged 65 or older, and all disabled persons entitled to coverage under Part A, are eligible to enroll in Part B on a voluntary basis by payment of a monthly premium. Almost all persons entitled to Part A choose to enroll in Part B. In 2007, Part B provided protection against the costs of physician and other medical services to about 41 million people (35 million aged and 6 million disabled enrollees). Part B benefits totaled $176.4 billion in 2007.

Part B covers certain medical services and supplies, including the following:

- Physicians' and surgeons' services, including some covered services furnished by chiropractors, podiatrists, dentists, and optometrists
- Services provided by Medicare-approved practitioners who are not physicians, including certified registered nurse anesthetists, clinical psychologists, clinical social workers (other than in a hospital or SNF), physician assistants, and nurse practitioners and clinical nurse specialists in collaboration with a physician
- Services in an emergency room, outpatient clinic, or ambulatory surgical center, including same-day surgery
- Home health care not covered under Part A
- Laboratory tests, X-rays, and other diagnostic radiology services
- Certain preventive care services and screening tests
- Most physical and occupational therapy and speech pathology services
- Comprehensive outpatient rehabilitation facility services, and mental health care in a partial hospitalization psychiatric program, if a physician certifies that inpatient treatment would be required without it
- Radiation therapy; renal (kidney) dialysis and transplants; heart, lung, heart–lung, liver, pancreas, and bone marrow transplants; and, as of April 2001, intestinal transplants
- Approved DME for home use, such as oxygen equipment and wheelchairs, prosthetic devices, and surgical dressings, splints, casts, and braces
- Drugs and biologicals that are not usually self-administered, such as hepatitis B vaccines and immunosuppressive drugs (certain self-administered anticancer drugs are covered)

- Certain services specific to people with diabetes
- Ambulance services, when other methods of transportation are contraindicated
- Rural health clinic and federally qualified health center services, including some telemedicine services

To be covered, all services must be either medically necessary or one of several prescribed preventive benefits. Part B services are generally subject to a deductible and coinsurance (see next section). Certain medical services and related care are subject to special payment rules, including deductibles (for blood), maximum approved amounts (for Medicare-approved physical, speech, or occupational therapy services performed in settings other than hospitals), and higher cost-sharing requirements (such as those for certain outpatient hospital services). The preceding description of Part B-covered services should be used only as a general guide, due to the wide range of services covered under Part B and the quite specific rules and regulations that apply.

Medicare Parts A and B, as described above, constitute the original fee-for-service Medicare program. Medicare Part C, also known as Medicare Advantage, is an alternative to traditional Medicare. Although all Medicare beneficiaries can receive their benefits through the traditional fee-for-service program, most beneficiaries enrolled in Parts A and B can choose to participate in a Medicare Advantage plan instead. Medicare Advantage plans are offered by private companies and organizations and are required to provide at least those services covered by Parts A and B, except hospice services. These plans may (and in certain situations must) provide extra benefits (such as vision or hearing) or reduce cost sharing or premiums. The primary Medicare Advantage plans are as follows:

- Local coordinated care plans, including health maintenance organizations (HMOs), provider-sponsored organizations (PSOs), local preferred provider organizations (PPOs), and other certified coordinated care plans and entities that meet the standards set forth in the law. Generally, each plan has a network of participating providers. Enrollees may be required to use these providers or, alternatively, may be allowed to go outside the network but pay higher cost-sharing fees for doing so.
- Regional PPO (RPPO) plans, which began in 2006 and offer coverage to one of 26 defined regions. Like local PPOs, RPPOs have networks of participating providers, and enrollees must use these providers or pay higher cost-sharing fees. However, RPPOs are required to provide beneficiary financial protection in the form of limits on out-of-pocket cost sharing, and there are specific provisions to encourage RPPO plans to participate in Medicare.
- Private fee-for-service plans, which for the most part do not have provider networks. Rather, members of a plan may go to any Medicare provider willing to accept the plan's payment.

- Special Needs Plans (SNPs), which are restricted to beneficiaries who are dually eligible for Medicare and Medicaid, live in long-term care institutions, or have certain severe and disabling conditions.

For individuals entitled to Part A or enrolled in Part B (except those entitled to Medicaid drug coverage), the new Part D initially provided access to prescription drug discount cards, at a cost of no more than $30 annually, on a voluntary basis. For low-income beneficiaries, Part D initially provided transitional financial assistance (of up to $600 per year) for purchasing prescription drugs, plus a subsidized enrollment fee for the discount cards. This temporary plan began in mid-2004 and phased out in 2006.

Beginning in 2006, Part D provides subsidized access to prescription drug insurance coverage on a voluntary basis, upon payment of a premium, to individuals entitled to Part A or enrolled in Part B, with premium and cost-sharing subsidies for low-income enrollees. Beneficiaries may enroll in either a stand-alone prescription drug plan (PDP) or an integrated Medicare Advantage plan that offers Part D coverage. Enrollment began in late 2005. In 2007, Part D provided protection against the costs of prescription drugs to about 31 million people. Part D benefits totaled $48.6 billion in 2007.

Part D coverage includes most FDA-approved prescription drugs and biologicals. (The specific drugs currently covered in Parts A and B remain covered there.) However, plans may set up formularies for their prescription drug coverage, subject to certain statutory standards. Part D coverage can consist of either standard coverage (defined later) or an alternative design that provides the same actuarial value. For an additional premium, plans may also offer supplemental coverage exceeding the value of basic coverage.

It should be noted that some health care services are not covered by any portion of Medicare. Noncovered services include long-term nursing care, custodial care, and certain other health care needs, such as dentures and dental care, eyeglasses, and hearing aids. These services are not a part of the Medicare program, unless they are a part of a private health plan under the Medicare Advantage program.

Program Financing, Beneficiary Liabilities, and Payments to Providers

All financial operations for Medicare are handled through two trust funds, one for HI (Part A) and one for SMI (Parts B and D). These trust funds, which are special accounts in the U.S. Treasury, are credited with all receipts and charged with all expenditures for benefits and administrative costs. The trust funds cannot be used for any other purpose. Assets not needed for the payment of costs are invested in special Treasury securities. The following sections describe Medicare's financing provisions, beneficiary cost-sharing requirements, and the basis for determining Medicare reimbursements to health care providers.

Program Financing

The HI trust fund is financed primarily through a mandatory payroll tax. Almost all employees and self-employed workers in the United States work in employment covered by Part A and pay taxes to support the cost of benefits for aged and disabled beneficiaries. The Part A tax rate is 1.45 percent of earnings, to be paid by each employee and a matching amount by the employer for each employee, and 2.90 percent for self-employed persons. Beginning in 1994, this tax is paid on all covered wages and self-employment income without limit. (Prior to 1994, the tax applied only up to a specified maximum amount of earnings.) The Part A tax rate is specified in the Social Security Act and cannot be changed without legislation.

Part A also receives income from the following sources: (1) a portion of the income taxes levied on Social Security benefits paid to high-income beneficiaries, (2) premiums from certain persons who are not otherwise eligible and choose to enroll voluntarily, (3) reimbursements from the general fund of the U.S. Treasury for the cost of providing Part A coverage to certain aged persons who retired when Part A began and thus were unable to earn sufficient quarters of coverage (and those federal retirees similarly unable to earn sufficient quarters of Medicare-qualified federal employment), (4) interest earnings on its invested assets, and (5) other small miscellaneous income sources. The taxes paid each year are used mainly to pay benefits for current beneficiaries.

The SMI trust fund differs fundamentally from the HI trust fund with regard to the nature of its financing. As previously noted, SMI is now composed of two parts, Part B and Part D, each with its own separate account within the SMI trust fund. The nature of the financing for both parts of SMI is similar, in that both parts are primarily financed by contributions from the general fund of the U.S. Treasury and (to a much lesser degree) by beneficiary premiums.

For Part B, the contributions from the general fund of the U.S. Treasury are the largest source of income, since beneficiary premiums are generally set at a level that covers 25 percent of the average expenditures for aged beneficiaries. The standard Part B premium rate will be $96.40 per beneficiary per month in 2009. Although this will be the amount paid by most Part B beneficiaries, there are three provisions that can alter the premium rate for certain enrollees. First, penalties for late enrollment (that is, enrollment after an individual's initial enrollment period) may apply, subject to certain statutory criteria. Second, beginning in 2007, beneficiaries whose income is above certain thresholds are required to pay an income-related monthly adjustment amount, in addition to their standard monthly premium. The 2009 Part B income-related monthly adjustment amounts and total monthly premium amounts to be paid by beneficiaries, according to income level and filing status, are shown in the following table. Finally, a "hold-harmless" provision, which prohibits increases in the standard Part B premium from exceeding the dollar amount of an individual's Social Security cost-of-living adjustment, lowers the premium rate for certain individuals who have their premiums deducted from their Social Security checks.

2009 Part B income-related monthly adjustment amounts and total monthly premium amounts to be paid by beneficiaries, by filing status and income level

Income	Income-related monthly adjustment (dollars)	Total monthly premium (dollars)
Beneficiaries who file individual tax returns (single individuals, heads of households, qualifying widow(er)s with dependent children, and married individuals who lived apart from their spouse for the entire taxable year and file separately)		
Less than or equal to $85,000	0	96.40
Greater than $85,000 and less than or equal to $107,000	38.50	134.90
Greater than $107,000 and less than or equal to $160,000	96.30	192.70
Greater than $160,000 and less than or equal to $213,000	154.10	250.50
Greater than $213,000	211.90	308.30
Beneficiaries who file joint tax returns		
Less than or equal to $170,000	0	96.40
Greater than $170,000 and less than or equal to $214,000	38.50	134.90
Greater than $214,000 and less than or equal to $320,000	96.30	192.70
Greater than $320,000 and less than or equal to $426,000	154.10	250.50
Greater than $426,000	211.90	308.30
Beneficiaries who are married and lived with their spouse at any time during the year but file separate tax returns		
Less than or equal to $85,000	0	96.40
Greater than $85,000 and less than or equal to $128,000	154.10	250.50
Greater than $128,000	211.90	308.30

For Part D, as with Part B, general fund contributions account for the largest source of income, since Part D beneficiary premiums are to represent, on average, 25.5 percent of the cost of standard coverage. The Part D base beneficiary premium for 2009 will be $30.36. The actual Part D premiums paid by individual beneficiaries equal the base beneficiary premium adjusted by a number of factors. Premiums vary significantly from one Part D plan to another and seldom equal the base beneficiary premium. As of this writing, it is estimated that the average enrollee premium for basic Part D coverage, which reflects the specific plan-by-plan premiums and the actual number of beneficiaries in each plan, will be about $28 in 2009. Penalties for late enrollment may apply. (Late enrollment penalties do not apply to enrollees who have maintained creditable prescription drug coverage.) Beneficiaries meeting certain low-income and limited-resources requirements pay substantially reduced premiums or no premiums at all (and are not subject to late enrollment penalties).

In addition to contributions from the general fund of the U.S. Treasury and beneficiary premiums, Part D also receives payments from the states. With the availability of prescription drug coverage and low-income subsidies under Part D, Medicaid is no longer the primary payer for prescription drugs for Medicaid beneficiaries who also have Medicare, and states are required to defray a portion of Part D expenditures for those beneficiaries.

During the Part D transitional period that began in mid-2004 and was phased out during 2006, the general fund of the U.S. Treasury financed the transitional assistance benefit for low-income beneficiaries. Funds were transferred to, and paid from, a Transitional Assistance account within the SMI trust fund.

The SMI trust fund also receives income from interest earnings on its invested assets, as well as a small amount of miscellaneous income. It is important to note that beneficiary premiums and general fund payments for Parts B and D are redetermined annually and separately.

Payments to Medicare Advantage plans are financed from both the HI trust fund and the Part B account within the SMI trust fund in proportion to the relative weights of Part A and Part B benefits to the total benefits paid by the Medicare program.

Beneficiary Payment Liabilities

Fee-for-service beneficiaries are responsible for charges not covered by the Medicare program and for various cost-sharing aspects of Parts A and B. These liabilities may be paid (1) by the Medicare beneficiary; (2) by a third party, such as an employer-sponsored retiree health plan or private Medigap insurance; or (3) by Medicaid, if the person is eligible. The term "Medigap" is used to mean private health insurance that pays, within limits, most of the health care service charges not covered by Parts A or B of Medicare. These policies, which must meet federally imposed standards, are offered by Blue Cross and Blue Shield and various commercial health insurance companies.

For beneficiaries enrolled in Medicare Advantage plans, the beneficiary's payment share is based on the cost-sharing structure of the specific plan selected by the beneficiary, since each plan has its own requirements. Most plans have lower deductibles and coinsurance than are required of fee-for-service beneficiaries. Such beneficiaries, in general, pay the monthly Part B premium. However, some Medicare Advantage plans may pay part or all of the Part B premium for their enrollees as an added benefit. Depending on the plan, enrollees may also pay an additional premium for certain extra benefits provided (or, in a small number of cases, for certain Medicare-covered services).

For hospital care covered under Part A, a beneficiary's fee-for-service payment share includes a one-time deductible amount at the beginning of each benefit period ($1,068 in 2009). This deductible covers the beneficiary's part of the first 60 days of each spell of inpatient hospital care. If continued inpatient care is needed beyond the 60 days, additional coinsurance payments ($267 per day in 2009) are required through the 90th day of a benefit period. Each Part A beneficiary also has a "lifetime reserve" of 60 additional hospital days that may be used when the covered days within a benefit period have been exhausted. Lifetime reserve days may be used only once, and coinsurance payments ($534 per day in 2009) are required.

For skilled nursing care covered under Part A, Medicare fully covers the first 20 days of SNF care in a benefit period. But for days 21 through 100, a copayment ($133.50 per day in 2009) is required from the beneficiary. After 100 days per benefit period, Medicare pays nothing for SNF care. Home health care requires no deductible or coinsurance payment by the beneficiary. In any Part A service, the beneficiary is responsible for fees to cover the first 3 pints or units of nonreplaced blood per calendar year. The beneficiary has the option of paying the fee or of having the blood replaced.

There are no premiums for most people covered by Part A. Eligibility is generally earned through the work experience of the beneficiary or of the beneficiary's spouse. However, most aged people who are otherwise ineligible for premium-free Part A coverage can enroll voluntarily by paying a monthly premium, if they also enroll in Part B. For people with fewer than 30 quarters of coverage as defined by the Social Security Administration (SSA), the Part A monthly premium rate will be $443 in 2009; for those with 30 to 39 quarters of coverage, the rate will be reduced to $244. Penalties for late enrollment may apply. Voluntary coverage upon payment of the Part A premium, with or without enrolling in Part B, is also available to disabled individuals for whom coverage has ceased because earnings are in excess of those allowed.

For Part B, the beneficiary's payment share includes the following: one annual deductible ($135 in 2009), the monthly premiums, the coinsurance payments for Part B services (usually 20 percent of the remaining allowed charges with certain exceptions noted below), a deductible for blood, certain charges above the Medicare-allowed charge (for claims not on assignment), and payment for any services not covered by Medicare. For outpatient mental health services, the beneficiary is currently liable for 50 percent of the approved charges, but this percentage is to phase down to 20 percent over the 5-year period 2010–2014. For services reimbursed under the outpatient hospital prospective payment system, coinsurance percentages vary by service and currently fall in the range of 20 percent to 50 percent. For certain services, such as clinical lab tests, home health agency services, and some preventive care services, there are no deductibles or coinsurance.

For the standard Part D benefit design, there is an initial deductible ($295 in 2009). After meeting the deductible, the beneficiary pays 25 percent of the remaining costs, up to an initial coverage limit ($2,700 in 2009). The beneficiary is then responsible for all costs until an out-of-pocket threshold is reached. (The 2009 out-of-pocket threshold will be $4,350, which is equivalent to total covered drug costs of $6,153.75). For costs thereafter, catastrophic coverage is provided, which requires enrollees to pay the greater of 5 percent coinsurance or a small defined copayment amount ($2.40 in 2009 for generic or preferred multisource drugs, and $6.00 in 2009 for other drugs). The benefit parameters are indexed annually to the growth in average per capita Part D costs. Beneficiaries meeting certain low-income and limited-resources requirements pay substantially reduced cost-sharing amounts. In determining out-of-pocket costs, only those amounts actually paid by the enrollee or another individual (and not reimbursed through insurance) are counted; the exception to this "true out-of-pocket" provision is cost-sharing assistance from the low-income subsidies provided under Part D and from State Pharmacy Assistance programs. Many Part D plans offer alternative coverage that differs from the standard coverage described above. In fact, the majority of beneficiaries are not enrolled in the standard benefit design but rather in plans with low or no deductibles, flat payments for covered drugs, and, in some cases, partial coverage in the coverage gap. The monthly premiums required for Part D coverage are described in the previous section.

Payments to Providers

For Part A, before 1983, payments to providers were made on a reasonable cost basis. Medicare payments for most inpatient hospital services are now made under a reimbursement mechanism known as the prospective payment system (PPS). Under the PPS for acute inpatient hospitals, each stay is categorized into a diagnosis-related group (DRG). Each DRG has a specific predetermined amount associated with it, which serves as the basis for payment. A number of adjustments are applied to the DRG's specific predetermined amount to calculate the payment for each stay. In some cases the payment the hospital receives is less than the hospital's actual cost for providing Part A–covered inpatient hospital services for the stay; in other cases it is more. The hospital absorbs the loss or makes a profit. Certain payment adjustments exist for extraordinarily costly inpatient hospital stays and other situations. Payments for skilled nursing care, home health care, inpatient rehabilitation hospital care, long-term care hospitals, and hospice are made under separate prospective payment systems. A new prospective payment system for inpatient psychiatric hospitals has been implemented and is in a transition period; most facilities have fully transitioned to the new system, but some will still, for a short time, be paid based on a blend of the old reasonable cost basis payment system and the new prospective payment system.

For Part B, before 1992, physicians were paid on the basis of reasonable charge. This amount was initially defined as the lowest of (1) the physician's actual charge, (2) the physician's customary charge, or (3) the prevailing charge for similar services in that locality. Beginning January 1992, allowed charges were defined as the lesser of (1) the submitted charges or (2) the amount determined by a fee schedule based on a relative value scale (RVS). (In practice, most allowed charges are based on the fee schedule.) Payments for DME and clinical laboratory services are also based on a fee schedule. Most hospital outpatient services are reimbursed on a prospective payment system, and home health care is reimbursed under the same prospective payment system as Part A.

If a doctor or supplier agrees to accept the Medicare-approved rate as payment in full ("takes assignment"), then payments provided must be considered as payments in full for that service. The provider may not request any added payments (beyond the initial annual deductible and coinsurance) from the beneficiary or insurer. If the provider does not take assignment, the beneficiary will be charged for the excess (which may be paid by Medigap insurance). Limits now exist on the excess that doctors or suppliers can charge. Physicians are "participating physicians" if they agree before the beginning of the year to accept assignment for all Medicare services they furnish during the year. Since beneficiaries in the original Medicare fee-for-service program may select their doctors, they can choose participating physicians.

Medicare Advantage plans and their precursors have generally been paid on a capitation basis, meaning that a fixed, predetermined amount per month per member is paid to the plan, without regard to the actual number and nature of services used by the members. The specific mechanisms to determine the payment amounts have changed over the years. In 2006, Medicare began paying capitated payment rates to plans based on a competitive bidding process.

For Part D, each month for each plan member, Medicare pays stand-alone PDPs and the prescription drug portions of Medicare Advantage plans their risk-adjusted bid (net of estimated reinsurance), minus the enrollee premium. Plans also receive payments representing premiums and cost-sharing amounts for certain low-income beneficiaries for whom these items are reduced or waived. Under the reinsurance provision, plans receive payments for 80 percent of costs in the catastrophic coverage category.

To help them gain experience with the Medicare population, Part D plans are protected by a system of "risk corridors" that allow Medicare to assist with unexpected costs and to share in unexpected savings. The risk corridors became less protective after 2007.

Under Part D, Medicare provides certain subsidies to employer and union PDPs that continue to offer coverage to Medicare retirees and meet specific criteria in doing so.

Claims Processing

Medicare's Part A and Part B fee-for-service claims are processed by non-government organizations or agencies that contract to serve as the fiscal agent between providers and the federal government. These claims processors are known as intermediaries and carriers. They apply the Medicare coverage rules to determine the appropriateness of claims.

Medicare intermediaries process Part A claims for institutional services, including inpatient hospital claims, SNFs, HHAs, and hospice services. They also process outpatient hospital claims for Part B. Examples of intermediaries are Blue Cross and Blue Shield (which utilize their plans in various states) and other commercial insurance companies. Intermediaries' responsibilities include the following:

- Determining costs and reimbursement amounts
- Maintaining records
- Establishing controls
- Safeguarding against fraud and abuse or excess use
- Conducting reviews and audits
- Making the payments to providers for services
- Assisting both providers and beneficiaries as needed

Medicare carriers handle Part B claims for services by physicians and medical suppliers. Examples of carriers are the Blue Shield plans in a state and various commercial insurance companies. Carriers' responsibilities include the following:

- Determining charges allowed by Medicare
- Maintaining quality-of-performance records
- Assisting in fraud and abuse investigations
- Assisting both suppliers and beneficiaries as needed
- Making payments to physicians and suppliers for services that are covered under Part B

Claims for services provided by Medicare Advantage plans (that is, claims under Part C) are processed by the plans themselves.

Part D plans are responsible for processing their claims, akin to Part C. However, because of the "true out-of-pocket" provision discussed previously, the Centers for Medicare & Medicaid Services (CMS) has contracted the services of a facilitator, who works with CMS, Part D drug plans (stand-alone PDPs and the prescription drug portions of Medicare Advantage plans), and carriers of supplemental drug coverage to coordinate benefit payments and track the sources of cost-sharing payments. Claims under Part D also have to be submitted by the plans to CMS, so that certain payments based on actual experience (such as payments for low-income cost-sharing and premium subsidies, reinsurance, and risk corridors) can be determined.

Because of its size and complexity, Medicare is vulnerable to improper payments, ranging from inadvertent errors to outright fraud and abuse. Although providers are responsible for submitting accurate claims, and intermediaries and carriers are responsible for ensuring that only such claims are paid, there are additional groups whose duties include the prevention, reduction, and recovery of improper payments.

Quality improvement organizations (QIOs; formerly called peer review organizations, or PROs) are groups of practicing healthcare professionals who are paid by the federal government to improve the effectiveness, efficiency, economy, and quality of services delivered to Medicare beneficiaries. One function of QIOs is to ensure that Medicare pays only for services and goods that are reasonable and necessary and that are provided in the most appropriate setting.

The ongoing effort to address improper payments intensified after enactment of the Health Insurance Portability and Accountability Act (HIPAA) of 1996 (Public Law 104-191), which created the Medicare Integrity Program (MIP). The MIP provides CMS with dedicated funds to identify and combat improper payments, including those caused by fraud and abuse, and, for the first time, allows CMS to award contracts competitively with entities other than carriers and intermediaries to conduct these activities. MIP funds are used for (1) audits of cost reports, which are financial documents that hospitals and other institutions are required to submit annually to CMS; (2) medical reviews of claims to determine whether services provided are medically reasonable and necessary; (3) determinations of whether Medicare or other insurance sources have primary responsibility for payment; (4) identification and investigation of potential fraud cases; and (5) education to inform providers about appropriate billing procedures. In addition to creating the MIP, HIPAA established a fund to provide resources for the Department of Justice—including the Federal Bureau of Investigation—and the Office of Inspector General (OIG) within the Department of Health and Human Services (HHS) to investigate and prosecute healthcare fraud and abuse.

The Deficit Reduction Act (DRA) of 2005 (Public Law 109-171) established and funded the Medicare–Medicaid Data Match Program, which is designed to identify improper billing and utilization patterns by matching Medicare and Medicaid claims information. As is the case under the MIP, CMS can contract with third parties. The funds also can be used (1) to coordinate actions by CMS, the states, the Attorney General, and the HHS OIG to prevent improper Medicaid and Medicare expenditures and (2) to increase the effectiveness and efficiency of both Medicare and Medicaid through cost avoidance, savings, and the recoupment of fraudulent, wasteful, or abusive expenditures.

Administration

HHS has the overall responsibility for administration of the Medicare program. Within HHS, responsibility for administering Medicare rests with CMS. SSA assists, however, by initially determining an individual's Medicare entitlement, by withholding Part B premiums from the Social Security benefit checks of most beneficiaries, and by maintaining Medicare data on the Master Beneficiary Record, which is SSA's primary record of beneficiaries.

The MMA requires SSA to undertake a number of additional Medicare-related responsibilities, including making low-income subsidy determinations under Part D, notifying individuals of the availability of Part D subsidies, withholding Part D premiums from monthly Social Security cash benefits for beneficiaries who request such an arrangement, and, for 2007 and later, determining the individual's Part B premium if the income-related monthly adjustment applies. The Internal Revenue Service (IRS) in the Department of the Treasury collects the Part A payroll taxes from workers and their employers. IRS data, in the form of income tax returns, play a role in determining which Part D enrollees are eligible for low-income subsidies (and to what degree) and, for 2007 and later, which Part B enrollees are subject to the income-related monthly adjustment amount in their premiums (and to what degree).

A Board of Trustees, composed of two appointed members of the public and four members who serve by virtue of their positions in the federal government, oversees the financial operations of the HI and SMI trust funds. The Secretary of the Treasury is the managing trustee. Each year, around the first day of April, the Board of Trustees reports to Congress on the financial and actuarial status of the Medicare trust funds.

State agencies (usually state health departments under agreements with CMS) identify, survey, and inspect provider and supplier facilities and institutions wishing to participate in the Medicare program. In consultation with CMS, these agencies then certify the facilities that are qualified.

Data Summary

The Medicare program covers 95 percent of our nation's aged population, as well as many people who are on Social Security because of disability. In 2007, Part A covered almost 44 million enrollees with benefit payments of $200.2 billion, Part B covered almost 41 million enrollees with benefit payments of $176.4 billion, and Part D covered almost 31 million enrollees with benefit payments of $48.6 billion. Administrative costs in 2007 were under 1.4 percent, 1.4 percent, and 1.8 percent of expenditures for Part A, Part B, and Part D, respectively. Total expenditures for Medicare in 2007 were $431.5 billion.

SOURCE: Reprinted from Hoffman, E. D. Jr., B. S. Klees, and C. A. Curtis. 2008. *Medicare Program Description and Legislative History.* Office of the Actuary, Centers for Medicare & Medicaid Services (CMS), Department of Health and Human Services. [Online material; retrieved 3/14/09.] www.ssa.gov/policy/docs/statcomps/supplement/2008/medicare.html.

Additional information about the Medicare program can be found at research.aarp.org/health/fs103_medicare.html#pdf and at www.kff.org/medicare/index.cfm.

OVERVIEW OF MEDICAID

Title XIX of the Social Security Act is a federal and state entitlement program that pays for medical assistance for certain individuals and families with low incomes and resources. This program, known as Medicaid, became law in 1965 as a cooperative venture jointly funded by the federal and state governments (including the District of Columbia and the Territories) to assist states in furnishing medical assistance to eligible needy persons. Medicaid is the largest source of funding for medical and health-related services for America's poorest people.

Within broad national guidelines established by federal statutes, regulations, and policies, each state establishes its own eligibility standards; determines the type, amount, duration, and scope of services; sets the rate of payment for services; and administers its own program. Medicaid policies for eligibility, services, and payment are complex and vary considerably, even among states of similar size or geographic proximity. Thus, a person who is eligible for Medicaid in one state may not be eligible in another state, and the services provided by one state may differ considerably in amount, duration, or scope from services provided in a similar or neighboring state. In addition, state legislatures may change Medicaid eligibility, services, and/or reimbursement at any time.

Title XXI of the Social Security Act, known as the State Children's Health Insurance Program (SCHIP), is a program initiated by the Balanced Budget Act (BBA) of 1997 (Public Law 105-33). In addition to allowing states to craft or expand an existing state insurance program, SCHIP provides more federal funds for states to expand Medicaid eligibility to include a greater number of children who are currently uninsured. With certain exceptions, these are low-income children who would not qualify for Medicaid based on the plan that was in effect on April 15, 1997. Funds from SCHIP also may be used to provide medical assistance to children during a presumptive eligibility period for Medicaid. This is one of several options from which states may select to provide healthcare coverage for more children, as prescribed within the BBA's Title XXI program.

Medicaid Eligibility

Medicaid does not provide medical assistance for all poor persons. Under the broadest provisions of the federal statute, Medicaid does not provide health-care services even for very poor persons unless they are in one of the groups designated below. Low income is only one test for Medicaid eligibility for those within these groups; their financial resources also are tested against threshold levels (as determined by each state within federal guidelines).

States generally have broad discretion in determining which groups their Medicaid programs will cover and the financial criteria for Medicaid eligibility. To be eligible for federal funds, however, states are required to provide Medicaid coverage for certain individuals who receive federally assisted income-maintenance payments, as well as for related groups not receiving cash payments. In addition to their Medicaid programs, most states have additional "state-only" programs to provide medical assistance for specified poor persons who do not qualify for Medicaid. Federal funds are not provided for state-only programs. The following enumerates the mandatory Medicaid "categorically needy" eligibility groups for which federal matching funds are provided:

- Limited-income families with children, as described in section 1931 of the Social Security Act, are generally eligible for Medicaid if they meet the requirements for the Aid to Families with Dependent Children (AFDC) program that were in effect in their state on July 16, 1996.
- Children under age 6 whose family income is at or below 133 percent of the federal poverty level (FPL). (As of January 2007, 100 percent of the FPL has been set at $20,650 for a family of four in the continental U.S.; Alaska and Hawaii's FPLs are substantially higher.)
- Pregnant women whose family income is below 133 percent of the FPL. (Services to these women are limited to those related to pregnancy, complications of pregnancy, delivery, and postpartum care.)
- Infants born to Medicaid-eligible women, for the first year of life with certain restrictions.
- Supplemental Security Income (SSI) recipients in most states (or aged, blind, and disabled individuals in states using more restrictive Medicaid eligibility requirements that pre-date SSI).
- Recipients of adoption or foster care assistance under Title IV-E of the Social Security Act.
- Special protected groups (typically individuals who lose their cash assistance under Title IV-A or SSI because of earnings from work or from increased Social Security benefits, but who may keep Medicaid for a period of time).
- All children under age 19, in families with incomes at or below the FPL.
- Certain Medicare beneficiaries (described later).

States also have the option of providing Medicaid coverage for other "categorically related" groups. These optional groups share characteristics of the mandatory groups (that is, they fall within defined categories), but the eligibility criteria are somewhat more liberally defined. The broadest optional groups for which states can receive federal matching funds for coverage under the Medicaid program include the following:

- Infants up to age one and pregnant women not covered under the mandatory rules whose family income is no more than 185 percent of the FPL. (The percentage amount is set by each state.)
- Children under age 21 who meet criteria more liberal than the AFDC income and resources requirements that were in effect in their state on July 16, 1996.
- Institutionalized individuals eligible under a "special income level." (The amount is set by each state—up to 300 percent of the SSI federal benefit rate.)
- Individuals who would be eligible if institutionalized, but who are receiving care under home and community-based services (HCBS) waivers.
- Certain aged, blind, or disabled adults who have incomes above those requiring mandatory coverage, but below the FPL.
- Aged, blind, or disabled recipients of state supplementary income payments.
- Certain working-and-disabled persons with family income less than 250 percent of the FPL who would qualify for SSI if they did not work.
- Tuberculosis-infected persons who would be financially eligible for Medicaid at the SSI income level if they were within a Medicaid-covered category. (Coverage is limited to tuberculosis-related ambulatory services and tuberculosis drugs.)
- Certain uninsured or low-income women who are screened for breast or cervical cancer through a program administered by the Centers for Disease Control and Prevention. The Breast and Cervical Cancer Prevention and Treatment Act of 2000 (Public Law 106-354) provides these women with medical assistance and follow-up diagnostic services through Medicaid.
- "Optional targeted low-income children" included within the SCHIP program established by the BBA.
- "Medically needy" persons (description follows).

The medically needy (MN) option allows states to extend Medicaid eligibility to additional persons. These persons would be eligible for Medicaid under one of the mandatory or optional groups, except that their income and/or resources are above the eligibility level set by their state. Persons may qualify immediately or may "spend down" by incurring medical expenses greater than the amount by which their income exceeds their state's MN income level.

Medicaid eligibility and benefit provisions for the medically needy do not have to be as extensive as for the categorically needy, and may be quite restrictive. Federal matching funds are available for MN programs. However, if a state elects to have a MN program, there are federal requirements that certain groups and certain services must be included; for example, children under age 19 and pregnant women who are medically needy must be covered, and prenatal and delivery care for pregnant women, as well as ambulatory care for children, must be provided. A state may elect to provide MN eligibility to certain additional groups and may elect to provide certain additional services within its MN program. As of 2005, 34 states plus the District of Columbia have elected to have a MN program and are providing at least some MN services to at least some MN beneficiaries. All remaining states utilize the "special income level" option to extend Medicaid to the "near poor" in medical institutional settings.

The Personal Responsibility and Work Opportunity Reconciliation Act of 1996 (Public Law 104-193)—known as the "welfare reform" bill—made restrictive changes regarding eligibility for SSI coverage that affected the Medicaid program. For example, legal resident aliens and other qualified aliens who entered the United States on or after August 22, 1996 are ineligible for Medicaid for five years. States have the option of providing Medicaid coverage for most aliens entering before that date and coverage for those eligible after the five-year ban; emergency services, however, are mandatory for both of these alien coverage groups. For aliens who lose SSI benefits because of the new restrictions regarding SSI coverage, Medicaid coverage can continue only if these persons can be covered under some other eligibility status (again with the exception of emergency services, which are mandatory). Public Law 104-193 also affected a number of disabled children, who lost SSI as a result of the restrictive changes; however, their eligibility for Medicaid was reinstituted by Public Law 105-33, the BBA.

In addition, welfare reform repealed the open-ended federal entitlement program known as Aid to Families with Dependent Children (AFDC) and replaced it with Temporary Assistance for Needy Families (TANF), which provides states with grants to be spent on time-limited cash assistance. TANF generally limits a family's lifetime cash welfare benefits to a maximum of five years and permits states to impose a wide range of other requirements as well—in particular, those related to employment. However, the impact on Medicaid eligibility has not been significant. Under welfare reform, persons who would have been eligible for AFDC under the AFDC requirements in effect on July 16, 1996 are generally still eligible for Medicaid. Although most persons covered by TANF receive Medicaid, it is not required by law.

Medicaid coverage may begin as early as the third month prior to application—if the person would have been eligible for Medicaid had he or she applied during that time. Medicaid coverage generally stops at the end of the month in which a person no longer meets the criteria of any Medicaid eligibility group. The BBA allows states to provide 12 months of continuous Medicaid coverage (without reevaluation) for eligible children under age 19.

The Ticket to Work and Work Incentives Improvement Act of 1999 (Public Law 106-170) provides or continues Medicaid coverage to certain disabled beneficiaries who work despite their disability. Beneficiaries with higher incomes may pay a sliding scale premium based on income.

The Deficit Reduction Act (DRA) of 2005 (Public Law 109-171) refined eligibility requirements for Medicaid beneficiaries by tightening standards for citizenship and immigration documentation and by changing the rules concerning long-term care eligibility—specifically, the look-back period for determining community spouse income and assets has been lengthened from 36 months to 60 months, individuals whose homes exceed $500,000 in value are disqualified, and the states are required to impose partial months of ineligibility.

Scope of Medicaid Services

Title XIX of the Social Security Act allows considerable flexibility within the states' Medicaid plans. However, some federal requirements are mandatory if federal matching funds are to be received. A state's Medicaid program must offer medical assistance for certain basic services to most categorically needy populations. These services generally include the following:

- Inpatient hospital services
- Outpatient hospital services
- Pregnancy-related services, including prenatal care and 60 days postpartum pregnancy-related services
- Vaccines for children
- Physician services
- Nursing facility services for persons aged 21 or older
- Family planning services and supplies
- Rural health clinic services
- Home health care for persons eligible for skilled nursing services
- Laboratory and X-ray services
- Pediatric and family nurse practitioner services
- Nurse-midwife services
- Federally qualified health center (FQHC) services, and ambulatory services of an FQHC that would be available in other settings

- Early and periodic screening, diagnostic, and treatment (EPSDT) services for children under age 21

States may also receive federal matching funds to provide certain optional services. Some of the most common currently approved optional Medicaid services are

- diagnostic services,
- clinic services,
- intermediate care facilities for the mentally retarded (ICFs/MR),
- prescribed drugs and prosthetic devices,
- optometrist services and eyeglasses,
- nursing facility services for children under age 21,
- transportation services,
- rehabilitation and physical therapy services,
- hospice care,
- home and community-based care to certain persons with chronic impairments, and
- targeted case management services.

The BBA included a state option known as Programs of All-inclusive Care for the Elderly (PACE). PACE provides an alternative to institutional care for persons aged 55 and older who require a nursing-facility level of care. The PACE team offers and manages all health, medical, and social services and mobilizes other services as needed to provide preventive, rehabilitative, curative, and supportive care. This care, provided in day health centers, homes, hospitals, and nursing homes, helps the person maintain independence, dignity, and quality of life. PACE functions within the Medicare program as well. Regardless of source of payment, PACE providers receive payment only through the PACE agreement and must make available all items and services covered under both Titles XVIII and XIX, without amount, duration, or scope limitations and without application of any deductibles, copayments, or other cost sharing. The individuals enrolled in PACE receive benefits solely through the PACE program.

Amount and Duration of Medicaid Services

Within broad federal guidelines and certain limitations, states determine the amount and duration of services offered under their Medicaid programs. States may limit, for example, the number of days of hospital care or the number of physician visits covered. Two restrictions apply: (1) limits must result in a sufficient level of services to reasonably achieve the purpose of the benefits, and (2) limits on benefits may not discriminate among beneficiaries based on medical diagnosis or condition.

In general, states are required to provide comparable amounts, duration, and scope of services to all categorically needy and categorically related eligible persons. There are two important exceptions: (1) medically necessary health care services that are identified under the EPSDT program for eligible children, and that are within the scope of mandatory or optional services under federal law, must be covered even if those services are not included as part of the covered services in that state's plan, and (2) states may request "waivers" to pay for otherwise uncovered home and community-based services (HCBS) for Medicaid-eligible persons who might otherwise be institutionalized. As long as the services are cost effective, states have few limitations on the services that may be covered under these waivers (except that states may not provide room and board for the beneficiaries, other than as a part of respite care). With certain exceptions, a state's Medicaid program must allow beneficiaries to have some informed choices among participating providers of healthcare and to receive quality care that is appropriate and timely.

Payment for Medicaid Services

Medicaid operates as a vendor payment program. States may pay health care providers directly on a fee-for-service basis, or states may pay for Medicaid services through various prepayment arrangements, such as health maintenance organizations (HMOs). Within federally imposed upper limits and specific restrictions, each state for the most part has broad discretion in determining the payment methodology and payment rate for services. Generally, payment rates must be sufficient to enlist enough providers so that covered services are available at least to the extent that comparable care and services are available to the general population within that geographic area. Providers participating in Medicaid must accept Medicaid payment rates as payment in full. States must make additional payments to qualified hospitals that provide inpatient services to a disproportionate number of Medicaid beneficiaries and/or to other low-income or uninsured persons under what is known as the "disproportionate share hospital" (DSH) adjustment. From 1988 to 1991, excessive and inappropriate use of the DSH adjustment resulted in rapidly increasing federal expenditures for Medicaid. Legislation that was passed in 1991 and 1993, and again within the BBA of 1997, capped the federal share of payments to DSH hospitals. However, the Medicare, Medicaid, and SCHIP Benefits Improvement and Protection Act (BIPA) of 2000 (Public Law 106-554) increased DSH allotments for 2001 and 2002 and made other changes to DSH provisions that resulted in increased costs to the Medicaid program.

States may impose nominal deductibles, coinsurance, or copayments on some Medicaid beneficiaries for certain services. The following Medicaid beneficiaries, however, must be excluded from cost sharing: pregnant women, children under age 18, and hospital or nursing home patients who are expected to contribute most of their income to institutional care. In addition, all Medicaid beneficiaries must be exempt from copayments for emergency services and family planning services. Under the DRA, new cost sharing and benefit rules provide states the option of imposing new premiums and increased cost sharing on all Medicaid beneficiaries except for those mentioned above and for terminally ill patients in hospice care. The DRA also established special rules for cost sharing for prescription drugs and for nonemergency services furnished in emergency rooms.

The federal government pays a share of the medical assistance expenditures under each state's Medicaid program. That share, known as the Federal Medical Assistance Percentage (FMAP), is determined annually by a formula that compares the state's average per capita income level with the national income average. States with a higher per capita income level are reimbursed a smaller share of their costs. By law, the FMAP cannot be lower than 50 percent or higher than 83 percent. In fiscal year 2008, the FMAPs varied from 50 percent in 13 states to 76.29 percent in Mississippi and averaged 56.7 percent overall. The BBA permanently raised the FMAP for the District of Columbia from 50 percent to 70 percent. For children covered through the SCHIP program, the federal government pays states a higher share, or "enhanced" FMAP, which averages about 70 percent for all states.

The federal government also reimburses states for 100 percent of the cost of services provided through facilities of the Indian Health Service, for 100 percent of the cost of the Qualifying Individuals (QI) program (described later), and for 90 percent of the cost of family planning services, and shares in each state's expenditures for the administration of the Medicaid program. Most administrative costs are matched at 50 percent, although higher percentages are paid for certain activities and functions, such as development of mechanized claims processing systems.

Except for the SCHIP program, the QI program, and DSH payments, federal payments to states for medical assistance have no set limit (cap). Rather, the federal government matches (at FMAP rates) state expenditures for the mandatory services, as well as for the optional services that the individual state decides to cover for eligible beneficiaries, and matches (at the appropriate administrative rate) all necessary and proper administrative costs.

Summary and Trends

Medicaid was initially formulated as a medical care extension of federally funded programs providing cash income assistance for the poor, with an emphasis on dependent children and their mothers, the disabled, and the elderly.

Over the years, however, Medicaid eligibility has been incrementally expanded beyond its original ties with eligibility for cash programs. Legislation in the late 1980s extended Medicaid coverage to a larger number of low-income pregnant women and poor children and to some Medicare beneficiaries who are not eligible for any cash assistance program. Legislative changes also focused on increased access, better quality of care, specific benefits, enhanced outreach programs, and fewer limits on services.

In most years since its inception, Medicaid has had very rapid growth in expenditures. This rapid growth has been due primarily to the following factors:

- The increase in size of the Medicaid-covered populations as a result of federal mandates, population growth, and economic recessions
- The expanded coverage and utilization of services
- The DSH payment program, coupled with its inappropriate use to increase federal payments to states
- The increase in the number of very old and disabled persons requiring extensive acute and/or long-term health care and various related services
- The results of technological advances to keep a greater number of very low birth-weight babies and other critically ill or severely injured persons alive and in need of continued extensive and very costly care
- The increase in drug costs and the availability of new expensive drugs
- The increase in payment rates to providers of health care services, when compared with general inflation

As with all health insurance programs, most Medicaid beneficiaries incur relatively small average expenditures per person each year, and a relatively small proportion incurs very large costs. Moreover, the average cost varies substantially by type of beneficiary. National data for 2005, for example, indicate that Medicaid payments for services for 28.7 million children, who constituted 51 percent of all Medicaid beneficiaries, averaged about $1,667 per child. Similarly, for 13.7 million adults, who comprised 24 percent of beneficiaries, payments averaged about $2,475 per person. However, other groups had much larger per-person expenditures. Medicaid payments for services for 4.9 million aged, who constituted 9 percent of all Medicaid beneficiaries, averaged about $13,675 per person; for 9.1 million disabled, who comprised 16 percent of beneficiaries, payments averaged about $13,846 per person. When expenditures for these high- and lower-cost beneficiaries are combined, the 2005 payments to healthcare vendors for 56.3 million Medicaid beneficiaries averaged $4,859 per person.

Long-term care is an important provision of Medicaid that will be increasingly utilized as our nation's population ages. The Medicaid program paid for over 41 percent of the total cost of care for persons using nursing facility or home health services in 2005. National data for 2005 show that Medicaid payments for nursing facility services (excluding ICFs/MR) totaled $44.7 billion for more than 1.7 million beneficiaries of these services—an average expenditure of $26,234 per nursing home beneficiary. The national data also show that Medicaid payments for home health services totaled $5.4 billion for 1.2 million beneficiaries—an average expenditure of $4,510 per home health care beneficiary. With the percentage of our population who are elderly or disabled increasing faster than that of the younger groups, the need for long-term care is expected to increase.

Another significant development in Medicaid is the growth in managed care as an alternative service delivery concept different from the traditional fee-for-service system. Under managed care systems, HMOs, prepaid health plans (PHPs), or comparable entities agree to provide a specific set of services to Medicaid enrollees, usually in return for a predetermined periodic payment per enrollee. Managed care programs seek to enhance access to quality care in a cost-effective manner. Waivers may provide the states with greater flexibility in the design and implementation of their Medicaid managed care programs. Waiver authority under sections 1915(b) and 1115 of the Social Security Act is an important part of the Medicaid program. Section 1915(b) waivers allow states to develop innovative health care delivery or reimbursement systems. Section 1115 waivers allow experimental statewide health care reform demonstrations to cover uninsured populations and to test new delivery systems without increasing costs. Finally, the BBA provided states a new option to use managed care without a waiver. The number of Medicaid beneficiaries enrolled in some form of managed care program is growing rapidly, from 48 percent of enrollees in 1997 to 64 percent in 2007.

More than 56 million persons received health care services through the Medicaid program in fiscal year 2005 (the last year for which beneficiary data are available). In fiscal year 2007, total expenditures for the Medicaid program (federal and state) were $335.8 billion, including direct payment to providers of $232.6 billion, payments for various premiums (for HMOs, Medicare, etc.) of $67 billion, payments to disproportionate share hospitals of $16.1 billion, administrative costs of $17.3 billion, and $2.7 billion for the Vaccines for Children Program. Expenditures under the SCHIP program in fiscal year 2007 were $8.8 billion. With no changes to the program, spending under Medicaid is projected to reach $523 billion by fiscal year 2013.

The Medicaid–Medicare Relationship

Medicare beneficiaries who have low incomes and limited resources may also receive help from the Medicaid program. For such persons who are eligible for full Medicaid coverage, the Medicare health care coverage is supplemented by services that are available under their state's Medicaid program, according to eligibility category. These additional services may include, for example, nursing facility care beyond the 100-day limit covered by Medicare, prescription drugs, eyeglasses, and hearing aids. For persons enrolled in both programs, any services that are covered by Medicare are paid for by the Medicare program before any payments are made by the Medicaid program, since Medicaid is always the "payer of last resort."

Certain other Medicare beneficiaries may receive help with Medicare premium and cost-sharing payments through their state Medicaid program. Qualified Medicare Beneficiaries (QMBs) and Specified Low-Income Medicare Beneficiaries (SLMBs) are the best-known categories and the largest in numbers. QMBs are those Medicare beneficiaries who have financial resources at or below twice the standard allowed under the SSI program and incomes at or below 100 percent of the FPL. For QMBs, Medicaid pays the Hospital Insurance (HI, or Part A) and Supplementary Medical Insurance (SMI, or Part B) premiums and the Medicare coinsurance and deductibles, subject to limits that states may impose on payment rates. SLMBs are Medicare beneficiaries with resources like the QMBs but with incomes that are higher, though still less than 120 percent of the FPL. For SLMBs, the Medicaid program pays only the Part B premiums. A third category of Medicare beneficiaries who may receive help consists of disabled-and-working individuals. According to the Medicare law, disabled-and-working individuals who previously qualified for Medicare because of disability, but who lost entitlement because of their return to work (despite the disability), are allowed to purchase Medicare Part A and Part B coverage. If these persons have incomes below 200 percent of the FPL but do not meet any other Medicaid assistance category, they may qualify to have Medicaid pay their Part A premiums as Qualified Disabled and Working Individuals (QDWIs).

For Medicare beneficiaries with incomes above 120 percent and less than 135 percent of the FPL, states receive a capped allotment of federal funds for payment of Medicare Part B premiums. These beneficiaries are known as Qualifying Individuals (QIs). Unlike the QMBs and SLMBs, who may be eligible for other Medicaid benefits in addition to their QMB/SLMB benefits, the QIs cannot be otherwise eligible for medical assistance under a state plan. The QI benefit is 100 percent federally funded, up to the state's allotment. The QI program was established by the BBA for fiscal years 1998 through 2002 and has been extended several times. The most recent extension expired at the end of fiscal year 2007.

The Centers for Medicare & Medicaid Services (CMS) estimates that, in 2007, Medicaid provided some level of supplemental health coverage for about 8.1 million Medicare beneficiaries.

Starting January 2006, a new Medicare prescription drug benefit provides drug coverage for Medicare beneficiaries, including those who also receive coverage from Medicaid. In addition, individuals eligible for both Medicare and Medicaid receive the low-income subsidy for the Medicare drug plan premium and assistance with cost sharing for prescriptions. Medicaid no longer provides drug benefits for Medicare beneficiaries.

Since the Medicare drug benefit and low-income subsidy replace a portion of state Medicaid expenditures for drugs, states will see a reduction in Medicaid expenditures. To offset this reduction, the Medicare Prescription Drug, Improvement, and Modernization Act of 2003 (Public Law 108-173) requires each state to make a monthly payment to Medicare representing a percentage of the projected reduction. For 2006, this payment was 90 percent of the projected 2006 reduction in state spending. After 2006 the percentage will decrease by 1⅔ percent per year to 75 percent for 2015 and later.

SOURCE: Reprinted from Hoffman, E. D. Jr., B. S. Klees, and C. A. Curtis, 2008. *Medicaid Program Description and Legislative History.* Office of the Actuary, Centers for Medicare & Medicaid Services (CMS), Department of Health and Human Services. [Online material; retrieved 3/14/09.] www.ssa.gov/policy/docs/statcomps/supplement/2008/medicaid.html.

Additional material on the Medicaid program can be found at http://www.aarp.org/research/assistance/medicaid/and at www.kff.org/medicaid/index.cfm.

BRIEFLY ANNOTATED CHRONOLOGICAL LIST OF SELECTED U.S. FEDERAL LAWS PERTAINING TO HEALTH[1]

1798

An act of July 16, 1798, passed by the Fifth Congress of the United States, taxed the employers of merchant seamen to fund arrangements for their healthcare through the Marine Hospital Service. In the language of the act, "the master or owner of every ship or vessel of the United States arriving from a foreign port into any port in the United States shall...render to the collector a true account of the number of seamen that shall have been employed on board such vessel...and shall pay to the said collector, at the rate of twenty cents per month, for every seaman so employed...." The act stipulated in Section 2 that "the President of the United States is hereby authorized, out of the same, to provide for the temporary relief and maintenance of sick or disabled seamen in the hospitals, or other proper institutions now established in the several ports...."

1882

An act of August 3, 1882, was the nation's first general immigration law and included the first federal medical excludability provisions affecting those who wished to immigrate to the United States. The act authorized state officials to board arriving ships to examine the condition of passengers. In the language of the act, "if on such examination, there shall be found among such passengers any convict, lunatic, idiot, or any person unable to take care of himself or herself without becoming a public charge...such persons shall not be permitted to land."

1891

An act of March 3, 1891, added the phrase, "persons suffering from a loathsome or a contagious disease" to the list of medical excludability criteria for people seeking to immigrate to the United States.

1902

P.L. 57-244[2], the Biologics Control Act, was the first federal law regulating the interstate and foreign sale of biologics (viruses, serums, toxins, and analogous products). The law established a national board and gave its members authority to establish regulations for licensing producers of biologics.

1906

P.L. 59-384, the Pure Food and Drug Act (also known as the Wiley Act), defined adulterated and mislabeled foods and drugs and prohibited their transport in interstate commerce. Passage of this legislation followed several years of intense campaigning by reformers and extensive newspaper coverage of examples of unwholesome and adulterated foods and of the widespread use of ineffective patent medicines.

1920

P.L. 66-141, the Snyder Act, was the first federal legislation pertaining to healthcare for Native Americans. Prior to the passage of this legislation, there were some health-related provisions in treaties between the government and the Native Americans, but this was the first formal legislation on the subject. The act provided for general assistance, directing "the Bureau of Indian Affairs, under the supervision of the Secretary of the Interior to direct, supervise, and expend such monies as Congress may from time to time appropriate, for the benefit, care, and assistance of the Indians throughout the United States...."

1921

P.L. 67-97, the Maternity and Infancy Act (also known as the Sheppard-Towner Act), provided grants to states to help them develop health services for mothers and their children. The law was allowed to lapse in 1929, although it has served as a prototype for federal grants in aid to the states.

1935

P.L. 74-271, the Social Security Act, a landmark law developed and passed during the Great Depression, established the Social Security program of old-age benefits. The legislation also included provisions for other benefits such as federal financial assistance to the states for their public assistance programs for the needy elderly, dependent children, and the blind. This legislation also provided incentives for the establishment of state unemployment funds and provided financial assistance for maternal and child health and child welfare services and significantly increased federal assistance for state and local public health programs.

1936

P.L. 74-846, the Walsh-Healy Act, authorized federal regulation of industrial safety in companies doing business with the U.S. government.

1937

P.L. 75-244, the National Cancer Institute Act, established the first categorical institute within the National Institute of Health (NIH), which had been created in 1930 to serve as the administrative home for the research conducted by the U.S. Public Health Service.

1938

P.L. 75-540, the LaFollette-Bulwinkle Act, provided grants in aid to the states to support their investigation and control of venereal disease.

P.L. 75-717, the Food, Drug, and Cosmetic Act, extended federal authority to ban new drugs from the market until they were approved by the Food and Drug Administration (FDA). This law also gave the federal government more extensive power in dealing with adulterated or mislabeled food, drugs, and cosmetic products.

1939

P.L. 76-19, the Reorganization Act, transferred the Public Health Service from the Treasury Department to the new Federal Security Agency (FSA). In 1953 the FSA was transformed into the U.S. Department of Health, Education, and Welfare (DHEW), which, with the subsequent establishment of a new cabinet level Department of Education in 1980, was itself transformed into the U.S. Department of Health and Human Services (DHHS).

1941

P.L. 77-146, the Nurse Training Act, provided schools of nursing with support to permit them to increase enrollments and improve their physical facilities.

1944

P.L. 78-410, the *Public Health Service Act*, revised and consolidated in one place all existing legislation pertaining to the U.S. Public Health Service. The legislation provided for the organization, staffing, and functions and activities of the Public Health Service. This law has subsequently been used as a vehicle, through amendments to the legislation, for a number of important federal grant-in-aid programs.

1945

P.L. 79-15, the McCarran-Ferguson Act, expressly exempted the "business of insurance" from federal antitrust legislation (the Sherman Antitrust Act of 1890, the Clayton Act of 1914, and the Federal Trade Commission Act of 1914) to the extent that insurance was regulated by state law and did not involve "acts of boycott, coercion, or intimidation." A significant part of the underlying reasoning Congress used in exempting insurance, including health insurance, was the view that the determination of underwriting risks would require the cooperation and sharing of information among competing insurance companies.

1946

P.L. 79-487, the National Mental Health Act, authorized extensive federal support for mental health research and treatment programs and established grants in aid to the states for their mental health activities. The legislation also transformed the Public Health Services' Division of Mental Health into the National Institute of Mental Health.

P.L. 79-725, the *Hospital Survey and Construction Act* (also known as the Hill-Burton Act), was "an Act to amend the Public Health Service Act (see the 1944 P.L. 78-410 above) to authorize grants to the States for surveying their hospital and public health centers and for planning construction of additional facilities, and to authorize grants to assist in such construction." The legislation was enacted because Congress recognized a widespread shortage of hospital facilities (few were built during the Great Depression and World War II). Under provisions of the act, the states were required to submit a state plan for the construction of hospital facilities based on a survey of need to receive federal funds, which could be dispersed for projects within states.

1948

P.L. 80-655, the National Health Act, pluralized NIH by establishing a second categorical institute, the National Heart Institute. Hereafter, NIH became the National Institutes of Health.

P.L. 80-845, the Water Pollution Control Act, was enacted in part "in consequence of the benefits to the public health and welfare by the abatement of stream pollution...." The act left the primary responsibility for water pollution control with the states.

1952

P.L. 82-414, the Immigration and Nationality Act (also known as the McCarran-Walter Act), followed an extensive study by Congress of immigration policy and practice. Among the law's provisions were a number of modifications in the medical excludability scheme affecting people wishing to immigrate to the United States. The act contained extensive provisions for observation and examination of aliens for the purpose of determining if they should be excluded for any of a number of specified "diseases or mental or physical defects or disabilities."

1954

P.L. 83-482, the Medical Facilities Survey and Construction Act, amended the Hill-Burton Act (see the 1946 P.L. 79-725) to greatly expand the Hill-Burton program's scope. The legislation authorized grants for surveys and construction of diagnostic and treatment centers (including hospital outpatient departments), chronic disease hospitals, rehabilitation facilities, and nursing homes.

P.L. 83-703, the Atomic Energy Act, established the Atomic Energy Commission and authorized it to license the use of atomic material in medical care.

1955

P.L. 84-159, the Air Pollution Control Act, provided for a program of research and technical assistance related to air pollution control. The law was enacted in part "in recognition of the dangers to the public health and welfare...from air pollution...."

P.L. 84-377, the Polio Vaccination Assistance Act, provided for federal assistance to states for the operation of their polio vaccination programs.

1956

P.L. 84-569, the Dependents Medical Care Act, established the Civilian Health and Medical Program of the Uniformed Services (CHAMPUS) for the dependents of military personnel.

P.L. 84-652, the National Health Survey Act, provided for the first system of regularly collected health-related data by the Public Health Service. This continuing process is called the Health Interview Survey and provides a national U.S. household interview study of illness, disability, and health services utilization.

P.L. 84-660, the Water Pollution Control Act Amendments of 1956, amended the Water Pollution Control Act (see the 1948 P.L. 80-845) and provided for federal technical services and financial aid to the states and to municipalities in their efforts to prevent and control water pollution.

P.L. 84-911, the Health Amendments Act, amended the Public Health Service Act (see the 1944 P.L. 78-410) by initiating federal assistance for the education and training of health personnel. Specifically, the law authorized traineeships for public health personnel and for advanced training for nurses. This support has been gradually broadened and extended by subsequent legislation to many categories of health personnel.

1958

P.L. 85-544, Grants-in-Aid to Schools of Public Health, established a program of formula grants to the nation's schools of public health.

P.L. 85-929, the Food Additive Amendment, amended the Food, Drug, and Cosmetic Act (see the 1938 P.L. 75-717) to require premarketing clearance from FDA for new food additives. The so-called Delaney clause, after Representative James Delaney, who sponsored the provision, stated that "no additive shall be deemed to be safe if it is found to induce cancer when ingested by man or animal...."

1959

P.L. 86-121, the Indian Sanitation Facilities Act, provided for the surgeon general to "construct, improve, extend, or otherwise provide and maintain, by contract or otherwise, essential sanitation facilities for Indian homes, communities, and lands...."

P.L. 86-352, the Federal Employees Health Benefits Act, permitted Blue Cross to negotiate a contract with the Civil Service Commission to provide health insurance coverage for federal employees. The contract served as a prototype for Blue Cross's subsequent involvement in the Medicare and Medicaid programs as a fiscal intermediary.

1960

P.L. 86-778, the Social Security Amendments (also known as the Kerr-Mills Act), amended the Social Security Act (see the 1935 P.L. 74-271) to establish a new program of medical assistance for the aged. Through this program, the federal government provided aid to the states for payments for medical care for "medically indigent" persons who were 65 years of age or older. The Kerr-Mills program, as it was called, was the forerunner of the Medicaid program established in 1965 (see P.L. 89-97).

1962

P.L. 87-692, the Health Services for Agricultural Migratory Workers Act, authorized federal grants to clinics serving migrant farm workers and their families.

P.L. 87-781, the Drug Amendments (also known as the Kefauver-Harris amendments), amended the Food, Drug, and Cosmetic Act (see the 1938 P.L. 75-717) to significantly strengthen the provisions related to the regulation of therapeutic drugs. The changes required improved manufacturing practices and procedures and evidence that new drugs proposed for marketing be effective as well as safe. These amendments followed widespread adverse publicity about the serious negative side effects of the drug thalidomide.

1963

P.L. 88-129, the Health Professions Educational Assistance Act, inaugurated construction grants for teaching facilities that trained physicians, dentists, pharmacists, podiatrists, nurses, or professional public health personnel. The grants were made contingent on schools increasing their first-year enrollments. The legislation also provided for student loans and scholarships.

P.L. 88-156, the Maternal and Child Health and Mental Retardation Planning Amendments, amended the Social Security Act (see the 1935 P.L. 74-271). The changes were intended "to assist states and communities in preventing and combating mental retardation through expansion and improvement of the maternal and child health and crippled children's programs, through provision of prenatal, maternity, and infant care for individuals with conditions associated with childbearing that may lead to mental retardation, and through planning for comprehensive action to combat mental retardation."

P.L. 88-164, the Mental Retardation Facilities and Community Mental Health Centers Construction Act, was intended "to provide assistance in combating mental retardation through grants for construction of research centers and grants for facilities for the mentally retarded and assistance in improving mental health through grants for construction of community mental health centers, and for other purposes."

P.L. 88-206, the Clean Air Act, authorized direct grants to states and local governments to assist in their air pollution control efforts. The law also established federal enforcement of interstate air pollution restrictions.

1964

P.L. 88-443, the Hospital and Medical Facilities Amendments, amended the Hill-Burton Act (see the 1946 P.L. 79-725) to specifically earmark grants for modernizing or replacing existing hospitals.

P.L. 88-452, the Economic Opportunity Act, sometimes referred to as the Antipoverty Program, was intended to "mobilize the human and financial resources of the nation to combat poverty in the United States." This broad legislation affected health in a number of ways as it sought to improve the economic and social conditions under which many people lived.

P.L. 88-581, the Nurse Training Act, added a new title, Title VIII, to the Public Health Service Act (see the 1944 P.L. 78-410). The legislation authorized separate funding for construction grants to schools of nursing, including associate degree and diploma schools. The law also provided for project grants whereby schools of nursing could strengthen their academic programs and provided for the establishment of student loan funds at these schools.

1965

P.L. 89-4, the Appalachian Redevelopment Act, sought to promote the economic, physical, and social development of the Appalachian region. Provisions in the law facilitated a number of steps to achieve this purpose, including the establishment of community health centers and training programs for health personnel.

P.L. 89-73, the Older Americans Act, established an Administration on Aging to administer programs for the elderly through state agencies on aging. The agenda for the joint efforts of the federal agency and the state agencies was detailed in ten specific objectives for the nation's older citizens, including several that were related to their health.

P.L. 89-92, the Federal Cigarette Labeling and Advertising Act, required that all cigarette packages sold in the United States bear the label, "Caution: Cigarette Smoking May Be Hazardous to Your Health."

P.L. 89-97, the Social Security Amendments, a landmark in the nation's health policy, established two new titles to the Social Security Act (see the 1935 P.L. 74-271): (1) Title XVIII, Health Insurance for the Aged, or Medicare, and (2) Title XIX, Grants to the States for Medical Assistance Programs, or Medicaid. Enactment of these amendments followed many years of often acrimonious congressional debate about government's role and responsibility regarding ensuring access to health services for the citizenry. This legislation was made possible by the landslide dimensions of Lyndon B. Johnson's 1964 election to the presidency and by the accompanying largest Democratic majority in Congress since 1934.

In addition to establishing Titles XVIII and XIX, the Social Security Act Amendments of 1965 also amended Title V to authorize grant funds for maternal and child health and crippled children's services. These amendments also authorized grants for training professional personnel for the care of crippled children.

P.L. 89-239, the Heart Disease, Cancer and Stroke Amendments, amended the Public Health Act (see the 1944 P.L. 78-410) to establish a nationwide network of Regional Medical Programs. This legislation was intended to "assist in combating heart disease, cancer, stroke, and related diseases." Through its provisions, regional cooperative programs were established among medical schools, hospitals, and research institutions to foster research, training, continuing education, and demonstrations of patient care practices related to heart disease, cancer, and stroke.

P.L. 89-272, the Clean Air Act Amendments, amended the original Clean Air Act (see the 1963 P.L. 88-206) to provide for federal regulation of motor vehicle exhaust and to establish a program of federal research support and grants in aid in the area of solid waste disposal.

P.L. 89-290, the Health Professions Educational Assistance Amendments, amended the original act (see the 1963 P.L. 88-129) to provide further support "to improve the quality of schools of medicine, dentistry, osteopathy, optometry, and podiatry." The law expanded the availability of student loans and introduced a provision whereby 50 percent of a professional's student loan could be forgiven in exchange for practice in a designated shortage area.

1966

P.L. 89-564, the Highway Safety Act, sought to improve the nation's system of highways to make them safer for users.

P.L. 89-642, the Child Nutrition Act, established a federal program of support, including research, for child nutrition. A key component of the legislation was its authorization of the school breakfast program.

P.L. 89-749, the Comprehensive Health Planning Act (also known as the Partnership for Health Act), which amended the Public Health Service Act (see the 1944 P.L. 78-410), was intended "to promote and assist in the extension and improvement of comprehensive health planning and public health services, [and] to provide for a more effective use of available Federal funds for such planning and services...." This legislation sought to promote comprehensive planning for health facilities, services, and personnel within the framework of a federal/state/local partnership. It also gave states greater flexibility in the use of their grants in aid for public health services through block grants.

The law, in Section 314a, authorized grants to states for the development of comprehensive state health planning and, in Section 314b, authorized grants to public or not-for-profit organizations "for developing comprehensive regional, metropolitan area or other local area plans for coordination of existing and planned health services." State planning agencies created or designated under this legislation became known as "A" agencies or as "314a" agencies. Within states, the other planning agencies created or designated under this legislation became known as "B," "areawide," or "314b" agencies.

P.L. 89-751, the Allied Health Professions Personnel Training Act, provided grant support for the training of allied health professionals. The legislation was patterned after the 1963 Health Professions Education Assistance Act (see P.L. 88-129).

P.L. 89-794, the Economic Opportunity Act Amendments, amended the Economic Opportunity Act (see the 1964 P.L. 88-452) to establish Office of Economic Opportunity neighborhood health centers. Located especially in impoverished sections of cities and rural areas, these centers provided poor people with a comprehensive range of ambulatory health services. By the early 1970s, approximately 100 centers were to have been established under this program.

1967

P.L. 90-31, the Mental Health Amendments, amended the Mental Retardation Facilities and Community Mental Health Centers Construction Act (see the 1963 P.L. 88-164) to extend the program of construction grants for community mental health centers. The legislation also amended the term "construction" so that it covered acquisition of existing buildings.

P.L. 90-148, the Air Quality Act, amended the Clean Air Act (see the 1963 P.L. 88-206) "to authorize planning grants to air pollution control agencies; expand research provisions relating to fuels and vehicles; provide for interstate air pollution control agencies or commissions; authorize the establishment of air quality standards; and for other purposes." The act provided for each state to establish air quality standards depending on local conditions, but a minimum air quality was to be ensured through federal review of the states' standards.

P.L. 90-170, the Mental Retardation Amendments, amended the Mental Retardation Facilities and Community Mental Health Centers Construction Act (see the 1963 P.L. 88-164) to extend the program of construction grants for university-affiliated and community-based facilities for the mentally retarded. The legislation also authorized a new program of grants for the education of physical educators and recreation workers who work with mentally retarded and other handicapped children and for research in these areas.

P.L. 90-174, the Clinical Laboratory Improvement Act, amended the Public Health Service Act (see the 1944 P.L. 78-410) to provide for the regulation of laboratories in interstate commerce by the Centers for Disease Control through processes of licensure, standards setting, and proficiency testing.

P.L. 90-189, the Flammable Fabrics Act, was part of government's early efforts to rid the environment of hazards to human health. The legislation sought to regulate the manufacture and marketing of flammable fabrics.

P.L. 90-248, the Social Security Amendments, represented the first of many modifications to the Medicare and Medicaid programs, which were established by the Social Security Amendments of 1965 (see P.L. 89-97). Coming two years after their establishment, this legislation provided expanded coverage for such things as durable medical equipment for use in the home, podiatrist services for nonroutine foot care, outpatient physical therapy, and the addition of a lifetime reserve of 60 days of coverage for inpatient hospital care over and above the original coverage for up to 90 days during any spell of illness. In addition, certain payment rules were modified in favor of providers. For example, payment of full reasonable charges for radiologist and pathologist services provided to inpatients were authorized under one modification.

This law also sought to raise the quality of care provided in nursing homes by establishing a number of conditions that had to be met by nursing homes wanting to participate in the Medicare and Medicaid programs. There was also a provision for limiting the federal participation in medical assistance payments to families whose income did not exceed 133 percent of the income limit for Aid to Families with Dependent Children (AFDC) payments in any state.

1968

P.L. 90-490, the Health Manpower Act, extended previous programs of support for the training of health professionals (see the 1963 P.L. 88-129 and the

1964 P.L. 88-581), in effect authorizing formula institutional grants for training all health professionals.

1969

P.L. 91-173, the Federal Coal Mine Health and Safety Act, was intended to help secure and improve the health and safety of coal miners.

P.L. 91-190, the National Environmental Policy Act, was enacted "to declare a national policy which will encourage productive and enjoyable harmony between man and his environment; to promote efforts which will prevent or eliminate damage to the environment and biosphere and stimulate the health and welfare of man...." This law established the Council on Environmental Quality to advise the president on environmental matters. The legislation required that environmental impact statements be prepared prior to the initiation of major federal actions.

1970

P.L. 91-222, the Public Health Cigarette Smoking Act, banned cigarette advertising from radio and television.

P.L. 91-224, the Water Quality Improvement Act, a very comprehensive water pollution law, included among its numerous provisions those relating to oil pollution by vessels and on- and offshore oil wells, hazardous polluting substances other than oil, and pollution from sewage from vessels and provided for training people to work in the operation and maintenance of water treatment facilities. Perhaps its most important provisions pertain to the procedures whereby all federal agencies must deal with water pollution, including requirements for cooperation among the various agencies.

P.L. 91-296, the Medical Facilities Construction and Modernization Amendments, amended the Hill-Burton Act (see the 1946 P.L. 79-725) by extending the program and by initiating a new program of project grants for emergency rooms, communications networks, and medical transportation systems.

P.L. 91-464, the Communicable Disease Control Amendments, amended the Public Health Service Act (see the 1944 P.L. 78-410), which had established the Communicable Disease Center (CDC), by renaming the CDC the Centers for Disease Control. The legislation also broadened the functions of CDC beyond its traditional focus on communicable or infectious diseases (e.g., tuberculosis, venereal disease, rubella, measles, Rh disease, poliomyelitis, diphtheria, tetanus, whooping cough) to include other preventable conditions, including malnutrition.

P.L. 91-513, the Comprehensive Drug Abuse Prevention and Control Act, provided for special project grants for drug abuse and drug dependence treatment programs and grants for programs and activities related to drug education.

P.L. 91-572, the Family Planning Services and Population Research Act, established the Office of Population Affairs and added Title X, Population Research and Voluntary Family Planning Programs, to the Public Health Service Act (see the 1944 P.L. 78-410). The legislation authorized a range of projects, formulas, training, and research grants and contracts to support family planning programs and services, except for abortion.

P.L. 91-596, the Occupational Safety and Health Act, established an extensive federal program of standard-setting and enforcement activities that were intended to ensure healthful and safe workplaces.

P.L. 91-601, the Poison Prevention Packaging Act, required that most drugs be dispensed in containers designed to be difficult for children to open.

P.L. 91-604, the Clean Air Amendments, was enacted because Congress became dissatisfied with progress toward control and abatement of air pollution under the Air Quality Act of 1967 (see the 1967 P.L. 90-148). This law took away the power of the states to establish different air quality standards in different air quality control regions. Instead, this legislation required states to achieve national air quality standards within each of their regions.

P.L. 91-616, the Comprehensive Alcohol Abuse and Alcoholism Prevention, Treatment, and Rehabilitation Act, established the National Institute of Alcohol Abuse and Alcoholism. The law provided a separate statutory base for programs and activities related to alcohol abuse and alcoholism. The legislation also provided a comprehensive program of aid to states and localities in their efforts addressed to combating alcohol abuse and alcoholism.

P.L. 91-623, the Emergency Health Personnel Act, amended the Public Health Service Act (see the 1944 P.L. 78-410) to permit the secretary of DHEW (now DHHS) to assign commissioned officers and other health personnel of the U.S. Public Health Service to areas of the country experiencing critical shortages of health personnel. This legislation also established the National Health Service Corps.

P.L. 91-695, the Lead-Based Paint Poisoning Prevention Act, represented a specific attempt to address the problem of lead-based paint poisoning through a program of grants to the states to aid them in their efforts to combat this problem.

1971

P.L. 92-157, the Comprehensive Health Manpower Training Act, was, at the time of its enactment, the most comprehensive health personnel legislation yet enacted. The legislation replaced institutional formula grants with a new system of capitation grants through which health professions schools received fixed sums of money for each of their students (contingent on increasing first-year enrollments). Loan provisions were broadened so that health professionals who practiced in designated personnel shortage areas could cancel 85 percent of education loans. The legislation also established the National Health Manpower Clearinghouse, and the secretary of DHEW (now DHHS) was directed to make every effort to provide to counties without physicians at least one National Health Service Corps physician.

1972

P.L. 92-294, the National Sickle Cell Anemia Control Act, authorized grants and contracts to support screening, treatment, counseling, information and education programs, and research related to sickle-cell anemia.

P.L. 92-303, the Federal Coal Mine Health and Safety Amendments, amended the earlier Federal Coal Mine Health and Safety Act (see the 1969 P.L. 91-173) to provide financial benefits and other assistance to coal miners who were afflicted with black lung disease.

P.L. 92-426, the Uniformed Services Health Professions Revitalization Act, established the Uniformed Services University of the Health Sciences. The legislation provided for this educational institution to be operated under the auspices of the U.S. Department of Defense in Bethesda, Maryland. The legislation also created the Armed Forces Health Professions Scholarship Program.

P.L. 92-433, the National School Lunch and Child Nutrition Amendments, amended the Child Nutrition Act (see the 1966 P.L. 89-642) to add support for the provision of nutritious diets for pregnant and lactating women and for infants and children (the WIC program).

P.L. 92-573, the Consumer Product Safety Act, established the Consumer Product Safety Commission to develop safety standards and regulations for consumer products. Under provisions of the legislation, the administration of existing related legislation, including the Flammable Fabrics Act, the Hazardous Substances Act, and the Poison Prevention Packaging Act, was transferred to the commission.

P.L. 92-574, the Noise Control Act, much like the earlier Clean Air Act (see the 1963 P.L. 88-206) and the Flammable Fabrics Act (see the 1967 P.L. 90-189), continued government's efforts to rid the environment of harmful influences on human health.

P.L. 92-603, the Social Security Amendments, amended the Social Security Act (see the 1935 P.L. 74-271) to make several significant changes in the Medicare program. These amendments marked an important shift in the operation of the Medicare program as efforts were undertaken to help control its growing costs. Over the bitter opposition of organized medicine, the legislation established professional standards review organizations (PSROs) that were to monitor both the quality of services provided to Medicare beneficiaries and the medical necessity for the services.

One provision limited payments for capital expenditures by hospitals that had been disapproved by state or local planning agencies. Another provision authorized a program of grants and contracts to conduct experiments and demonstrations related to achieving increased economy and efficiency in the provision of health services. Some of the specifically targeted areas of these studies were to be prospective reimbursement, the requirement that patients spend three days in the hospital prior to admission to a skilled nursing home, the potential benefits of ambulatory surgery centers, payment for the services of physician assistants and nurse practitioners, and the use of clinical psychologists.

Coincident with these and other cost-containment amendments, several cost-increasing changes were also made in the Medicare program by this legislation. Notably, persons who were eligible for cash benefits under the disability provisions of the Social Security Act for at least 24 months were made eligible for medical benefits under the program. In addition, persons who were insured under Social Security, as well as their dependents, who required hemodialysis or renal transplantation for chronic renal disease were defined as disabled for the purpose of having them covered under the Medicare program for the costs of treating their end-stage renal disease (ESRD). The inclusion of coverage for the disabled and ESRD patients in 1972 was an extraordinarily expensive change in the Medicare program. In addition, certain less costly but still expensive additional coverages were extended, including chiropractic services and speech pathology services.

P.L. 92-714, the National Cooley's Anemia Control Act, authorized grants and contracts to support screening, treatment, counseling, information and education programs, and research related to Cooley's Anemia.

1973

P.L. 93-29, the Older Americans Act, established the National Clearinghouse for Information on Aging and created the Federal Council on Aging. The legislation also authorized funds to establish gerontology centers and provided grants for training and research related to the field of aging.

P.L. 93-154, the Emergency Medical Services Systems Act, provided aid to states and localities to assist them in developing coordinated emergency medical service (EMS) systems.

P.L. 93-222, the Health Maintenance Organization Act, amended the Public Health Service Act (see the 1944 P.L. 78-410) to "provide assistance and encouragement for the establishment and expansion of health mainte-nance organizations...." The legislation, which added a new title, Title XIII, Health Maintenance Organizations (HMOs), to the Public Health Service Act, authorized a program of grants, loans, and loan guarantees to support the conduct of feasibility and development studies and initial operations for new HMOs.

1974

P.L. 93-247, the Child Abuse Prevention and Treatment Act, created the National Center on Child Abuse and Neglect. The legislation authorized grants for research and demonstrations related to child abuse and neglect.

P.L. 93-270, the Sudden Infant Death Syndrome Act, added Part C, Sudden Infant Death Syndrome, to Title XI of the Public Health Service Act (see the 1944 P.L. 78-410). The legislation provided for the development of informational programs related to this syndrome for both public and profes-sional audiences.

P.L. 93-296, the Research in Aging Act, established the National Institute on Aging within the National Institutes of Health.

P.L. 93-344, the Congressional Budget and Impoundment Control Act, and its subsequent amendments, provided Congress with the procedures through which it establishes target levels for revenues, expenditures, and the overall deficit for the coming fiscal year (FY). The Congressional budget pro-cedures are designed to coordinate decisions on sources and levels of federal revenues and on the objectives and levels of federal expenditures. These deci-sions have substantial impact on health policy. The procedures formally begin each year with the initial decision as to the overall size of the budget pie for a given year, as well as the sizes of its various pieces. To accomplish this, each year Congress adopts a concurrent resolution that imposes overall constraints on spending, based in part on the size of the anticipated revenue budget for the year, and distributes the overall constraint on spending among groups of programs and activities. These constraints are implemented through the rec-onciliation process. The result of this process is the annual omnibus reconcil-iation bill, which is, in effect, a packaging together of all legislative changes made in the various standing committees necessitated by reconciling existing law with the budgetary targets established earlier in the concurrent resolution on the budget.

This act also established the U.S. Congressional Budget Office (CBO). The nonpartisan CBO conducts studies and analyses of the fiscal and budget im-plications of various decisions facing Congress, including those related to health.

P.L. 93-360, the Nonprofit Hospital Amendments, amended the 1947 Labor-Management Relations Act (or the Taft-Hartley Act) to end the exclusion of nongovernmental, nonprofit hospitals from the provisions of this act as well as from the earlier National Labor Relations Act of 1935 (or the Wagner Act). Both of these acts pertain to fair labor practices and collective bargaining.

P.L. 93-406, the Employee Retirement Income Security Act (also known as ERISA), provided for the regulation of almost all pension and benefit plans for employees, including pensions, medical or hospital benefits, disability, and death benefits. The legislation provides for the regulation of many features of these benefit plans.

P.L. 93-523, the Safe Drinking Water Act, required the Environmental Protection Agency (EPA) to establish national drinking water standards and to aid states and localities in the enforcement of these standards.

P.L. 93-641, the National Health Planning and Resources Development Act, amended the Public Health Service Act (see the 1944 P.L. 78-410) in an attempt "to assure the development of a national health policy and of effective state and area health planning and resource development programs, and for other purposes." The legislation added two new titles, XV and XVI, to the Public Health Service Act. These titles superseded and significantly modified the programs established under Sections 314a and 314b of Title III of the 1966 P.L. 89-749, the Comprehensive Health Planning Act (or the Partnership for Health Act) as well as the programs established under the Hill-Burton Act (see the 1946 P.L. 79-725).

The legislation essentially folded existing health planning activities into a new framework created by the legislation. The secretary of DHEW (now DHHS) was to enter into an agreement with each state's governor for the designation of a state health planning and development agency (SHPDA). The states were to also establish state health coordinating councils (SHCCs) to serve as advisors in setting overall state policy.

A network of local health systems agencies (HSAs) covering the entire nation was established by the legislation. The HSAs were to (1) improve the health of area residents; (2) increase the accessibility, acceptability, continuity, and quality of health services; and (3) restrain healthcare cost increases and prevent duplication of healthcare services and facilities. An important feature of the planning framework created by P.L. 93-641 was a provision that permitted the HSAs in states that had established certificate-of-need (CON) programs to conduct CON reviews and to make recommendations developed at the local level to the SHPDA.

Congress repealed this law in 1986 (effective January 1, 1987), leaving responsibility for the CON programs entirely in the hands of the states.

P.L. 93-647, the Social Security Amendments (also known as the Social Services Amendments), amended the Social Security Act (see the 1935 P.L. 74-271) to consolidate existing federal-state social service programs into a block grant program that would permit a ceiling on federal matching funds while providing more flexibility to the states in providing certain social services. The legislation added a new title, Title XX, Grants to the States for Services, to the Social Security Act.

The goals of the legislation pertained to the prevention and remedy of neglect, abuse, or exploitation of children or adults, the preservation of families, and the avoidance of inappropriate institutional care by substituting community-based programs and services. Social services covered under this law included child-care service; protective, foster, and day-care services for children and adults; counseling; family planning services; homemaker services; and home-delivered meals.

1976

P.L. 94-295, the Medical Devices Amendments, amended the Food, Drug and Cosmetic Act (see the 1938 P.L. 75-717) to strengthen the regulation of medical devices. This legislation was passed, after previous attempts had failed, amid growing public concern with the adverse effects of such medical devices as the Dalcon Shield intrauterine device.

P.L. 94-317, the National Consumer Health Information and Health Promotion Act, amended the Public Health Service Act (see the 1944 P.L. 78-410) to add Title XVII, Health Information and Promotion. The legislation authorized grants and contracts for research and community programs related to health information, health promotion, preventive health services, and education of the public in the appropriate use of healthcare services.

P.L. 94-437, the Indian Health Care Improvement Act, an extensive piece of legislation, was intended to fill existing gaps in the delivery of healthcare services to Native Americans.

P.L. 94-460, the Health Maintenance Organization Amendments, amended the Health Maintenance Organization Act (see the 1973 P.L. 93-222) to ease somewhat the requirements that had to be met for an HMO to become federally qualified. One provision, however, required that HMOs must be federally qualified if they were to receive reimbursement from the Medicare or Medicaid programs.

P.L. 94-469, the Toxic Substances Control Act (TSCA), sought to regulate chemical substances used in various production processes. The legislation defined chemical substances very broadly. The purpose of TSCA was to identify potentially harmful chemical substances before they were produced and entered the marketplace and, subsequently, the environment.

P.L. 94-484, the Health Professions Educational Assistance Act, extended the program of capitation grants to professional schools that had been established under the Comprehensive Health Manpower Training Act (see the 1971 P.L. 92-157). However, this legislation dropped the requirement that schools increase their first-year enrollments as a condition for receiving grants. Under this legislation, medical schools were required to have 50 percent of their graduates enter residency programs in primary care by 1980. They were also required to reserve positions in their third-year classes for U.S. citizens who were studying medicine in foreign medical schools. However, under intense protest from medical schools, this earlier provision was repealed in 1975.

1977

P.L. 95-142, the Medicare-Medicaid Antifraud and Abuse Amendments, amended the legislation governing the Medicare and Medicaid programs (see the 1965 P.L. 89-97) in an attempt to reduce fraud and abuse in the programs as a means to help contain their costs. Specific changes included strengthening criminal and civil penalties for fraud and abuse affecting the programs, modifying the operations of the PSROs, and promulgating uniform reporting systems and formats for hospitals and certain other healthcare organizations participating in the Medicare and Medicaid programs.

P.L. 95-210, the Rural Health Clinic Services Amendments, amended the legislation governing the Medicare and Medicaid programs (see the 1965 P.L. 89-97) to modify the categories of practitioners who could provide reimbursable services to Medicare and Medicaid beneficiaries, at least in rural settings. Under the provisions of this act, rural health clinics that did not routinely have physicians available on site could, if they met certain requirements regarding physician supervision of the clinic and review of services, be reimbursed for services provided by nurse practitioners and physician assistants through the Medicare and Medicaid programs. This act also authorized certain demonstration projects in underserved urban areas for reimbursement of these nonphysician practitioners.

1978

P.L. 95-292, the Medicare End-Stage Renal Disease Amendments, further amended the legislation governing the Medicare program (see the 1965 P.L. 89-97) in an attempt to help control the program's costs. Since the addition of coverage for ESRD under the Social Security Amendments of 1972 (P.L. 92-603), the costs to the Medicare program had risen steadily and quickly. This legislation added incentives to encourage the use of home dialysis and renal transplantation in ESRD.

The legislation also permitted the use of a variety of reimbursement methods for renal dialysis facilities, and it authorized funding for the conduct of studies of ESRD itself, especially studies incorporating possible cost reductions in treatment for this disease. It also directed the secretary of DHEW (now DHHS) to establish areawide network coordinating councils to help plan for and review ESRD programs.

P.L. 95-559, the Health Maintenance Organization Amendments, further amended the Health Maintenance Organization Act (see the 1973 P.L. 93-222) to add a new program of loans and loan guarantees to support the acquisition of ambulatory care facilities and related equipment. The legislation also provided for support for a program of training for HMO administrators and medical directors and for providing technical assistance to HMOs in their developmental efforts.

1979

P.L. 96-79, the Health Planning and Resources Development Amendments, amended the National Health Planning and Resources Development Act (see the 1974 P.L. 93-641) to add provisions intended to foster competition within the health sector, to address the need to integrate mental health and alcoholism and drug abuse resources into health system plans, and to make several revisions in the CON requirements.

1980

P.L. 96-398, the Mental Health Systems Act, extensively amended the Community Mental Health Centers program (see the 1970 P.L. 91-211) including provisions for the development and support of comprehensive state mental health systems. Subsequently, however, this legislation was almost completely superseded by the block grants to the states for mental health and alcohol and drug abuse that were provided under the Omnibus Budget Reconciliation Act of 1981 (see P.L. 97-35).

P.L. 96-499, the Omnibus Budget Reconciliation Act (OBRA '80), was contained in Title IX of the Medicare and Medicaid Amendments of 1980. These amendments made extensive modifications in the Medicare and Medicaid programs, with 57 separate sections pertaining to one or both of the programs. Many of the changes reflected continuing concern with the growing costs of the programs and were intended to help control these costs.

Examples of the changes that were specific to Medicare included removal of the 100 visits per year limitation on home health services and the requirement that patients pay a deductible for home care visits under Part B of the program. These changes were intended to encourage home care over more expensive institutional care. Another provision permitted small rural hospitals to use their beds as "swing beds" (alternating their use as acute or long-term-care beds as needed) and authorized swing-bed demonstration projects for large and urban hospitals. An important change in the Medicaid program required the programs to pay for the services that the states had authorized nurse-midwives to perform.

P.L. 96-510, the Comprehensive Environmental Response, Compensation and Liability Act (CERCLA), established the Superfund program that intended to provide resources for the cleanup of inactive hazardous waste dumps. The legislation assigned retroactive liability for the costs of cleaning up the dumps to their owners and operators as well as to the waste generators and transporters who had used the dump sites.

1981

P.L. 97-35, the Omnibus Budget Reconciliation Act (OBRA '81), in its Title XXI, Subtitles A, B, and C, contained further amendments to the Medicare and Medicaid programs. Just as in 1980, this legislation included extensive changes in the programs, with 46 sections pertaining to them. Enacted in the context of extensive efforts to reduce the federal budget, many of the provisions hit Medicare and Medicaid especially hard. For example, one provision eliminated the coverage of alcohol detoxification facility services, another removed the use of occupational therapy as a basis for initial entitlement to home health service, and yet another increased the Part B deductible.

In other provisions, OBRA '81 combined 20 existing categorical public health programs into four block grants. The block grants were (1) Preventive Health and Health Services, which combined such previously categorical programs as rodent control, fluoridation, hypertension control, and rape crisis centers among others into one block grant to be distributed among the states by a formula based on population and other factors; (2) Alcohol Abuse, Drug Abuse, and Mental Health Block Grant, which combined existing programs created under the Community Mental Health Centers Act, the Mental Health Systems Act, the Comprehensive Alcohol Abuse and Alcoholism Prevention, Treatment, and Rehabilitation Act, and the Drug Abuse, Prevention, Treatment, and Rehabilitation Act; (3) Primary Care Block Grant, which consisted of the Community Health Centers; and (4) Maternal and Child Health Block Grant, which consolidated seven previously categorical grant programs from Title V of the Social Security Act and from the Public Health Services Act, including the maternal and child health and crippled children's programs, genetic disease service, adolescent pregnancy services, sudden infant death syndrome, hemophilia treatment, Supplemental Security Income (SSI) payments to disabled children, and lead-based poisoning prevention.

1982

P.L. 97-248, the Tax Equity and Fiscal Responsibility Act (TEFRA), made a number of important changes in the Medicare program. One provision added coverage for hospice services provided to Medicare beneficiaries. These benefits were extended later and are now an integral part of the Medicare program. However, the most important provisions, in terms of impact on the Medicare program, were those that sought to control the program's costs by setting limits on how much Medicare would reimburse hospitals on a per-case basis and by limiting the annual rate of increase for Medicare's reasonable costs per discharge. These changes in reimbursement methodology represented fundamental changes in the Medicare program and reflected a dramatic shift in the nation's Medicare policy.

Another provision of TEFRA replaced PSROs, which had been established by the Social Security Amendments of 1972 (see P.L. 92-603), with a new utilization and quality control program called peer review organizations (PROs). The TEFRA changes regarding the operation of the Medicare program were extensive, but they were only the harbinger of the most sweeping legislative changes in the history of the Medicare program the following year.

P.L. 97-414, the Orphan Drug Act (ODA), provided financial incentives for the development and marketing of orphan drugs, defined by the legislation to be drugs for the treatment of diseases or conditions affecting so few people that revenues from sales of the drugs would not cover their development costs.

1983

P.L. 98-21, the Social Security Amendments, another landmark in the evolution of the Medicare program, amended the legislation governing the program (see the 1965 P.L. 89-97) to initiate the Medicare prospective payment system (PPS). The legislation included provisions to base payment for hospital inpatient services on predetermined rates per discharge for diagnosis-related groups (DRGs). PPS was a major departure from the cost-based system of reimbursement that had been used in the Medicare program since its inception in 1965. The legislation also directed the administration to study physician payment reform options, a feature that was to later have significant impact (see the 1989 P.L. 10-239).

1984

P.L. 98-369, the Deficit Reduction Act (DEFRA), among many provisions, temporarily froze increases in physicians' fees paid under the Medicare program. Another provision in the legislation placed a specific limitation on the rate of increase in the DRG payment rates that the secretary of DHHS could permit in the two subsequent years.

The legislation also established the Medicare Participating Physician and Supplier program and created two classes of physicians in regard to their relationships to the Medicare program and outlined different reimbursement approaches for them depending on whether they were classified as "participating" or "nonparticipating." As part of this legislation, Congress mandated that the Office of Technology Assessment study alternative methods of paying for physician services so that the information could guide the reform of the Medicare program.

P.L. 98-417, the Drug Price Competition and Patent Term Restoration Act, provided brand-name pharmaceutical manufacturers with patent term extensions. These extensions significantly increased manufacturers' opportunities for earning profits during the longer effective patent life (EPL) of their affected products.

P.L. 98-457, the Child Abuse Amendments, amended the Child Abuse Prevention and Treatment Act (see the 1974 P.L. 93-247) to involve Infant Care Review Committees in the medical decisions regarding the treatment of handicapped newborns, at least in hospitals with tertiary-level neonatal care units.

The legislation established treatment and reporting guidelines for severely disabled newborns, making it illegal to withhold "medically indicated treatment" from newborns except when "in the treating physician's reasonable medical judgment, (i) the infant is chronically and irreversibly comatose; (ii) the provision of such treatment would merely prolong dying, not be effective in ameliorating or correcting all of the infant's life-threatening conditions, or otherwise be futile in terms of survival of the infant; or (iii) the provision of such treatment would be virtually futile in terms of the survival of the infant and the treatment itself under such circumstances would be inhumane."

P.L. 98-507, the National Organ Transplant Act, made it illegal "to knowingly acquire, receive, or otherwise transfer any human organ for valuable consideration for use in human transplantation if the transfer affects interstate commerce."

1985

P.L. 99-177, the Emergency Deficit Reduction and Balanced Budget Act (also known as the Gramm-Rudman-Hollins Act), established mandatory deficit reduction targets for the five subsequent fiscal years. Under provisions of the legislation, the required budget cuts would come equally from defense spending and from domestic programs that were not exempted. The Gramm-Rudman-Hollins

Act had significant impact on the Medicare program throughout the last half of the 1980s, as well as on other health programs such as community and migrant health centers, veteran and Native American health, health professions education, and the National Institutes of Health. Among other things, this legislation led to substantial cuts in Medicare payments to hospitals and physicians.

P.L. 99-272, the Consolidated Omnibus Budget Reconciliation Act (COBRA '85), contained a number of provisions that affected the Medicare program. Hospitals that served a disproportionate share of poor patients received an adjustment in their PPS payments; hospice care was made a permanent part of the Medicare program, and states were given the ability to provide hospice services under the Medicaid program; FY 1986 PPS payment rates were frozen at 1985 levels through May 1, 1986, and increased 0.5 percent for the remainder of the year; payment to hospitals for the indirect costs of medical education was modified; and a schedule to phase out payment of a return on equity to proprietary hospitals was established.

This legislation established the Physician Payment Review Commission (PPRC) to advise Congress on physician payment policies for the Medicare program. The legislation also required that PPRC advise Congress and the secretary of DHHS regarding the development of a resource-based relative value scale for physician services.

Under another of COBRA's important provisions, employers were required to continue health insurance for employees and their dependents who would otherwise lose their eligibility for the coverage due to reduced hours of work or termination of their employment.

1986

P.L. 99-509, the Omnibus Budget Reconciliation Act (OBRA '86), altered the PPS payment rate for hospitals once again and reduced payment amounts for capital-related costs by 3.5 percent for part of FY 1987, by 7 percent for FY 1988, and by 10 percent for FY 1989. In addition, certain adjustments were made in the manner in which "outlier" or atypical cases were reimbursed.

The legislation established further limits to balance billing by physicians providing services to Medicare clients by setting "maximum allowable actual charges" (MAACs) for physicians who did not participate in the PAR program (see the Deficit Reduction Act of 1984, P.L. 98-369). In another provision intended to realize savings for the Medicare program, OBRA '86 directed DHHS to use the concept of "inherent reasonableness" to reduce payments for cataract surgery as well as for anesthesia during the surgery.

P.L. 99-660, the Omnibus Health Act, contained provisions to significantly liberalize coverage under the Medicaid program. Using family income up to the federal poverty line as a criterion, this change permitted states to offer coverage to all pregnant women, infants up to one year of age, and, by using a phase-in schedule, children up to five years of age.

One part of this omnibus health legislation was the National Childhood Vaccine Injury Act. This law established a federal vaccine injury compensation system. Under provisions of the legislation, parties injured by vaccines would be limited to awards of income losses plus $250,000 for pain and suffering or death.

Another important part of the omnibus health legislation of 1986 was the Health Care Quality Improvement Act. This law provided immunity from private damage lawsuits under federal or state law for "any professional review action" so long as that action followed standards set out in the legislation. This afforded members of peer review committees protection from most damage suits filed by physicians whom they disciplined. The law also mandated creation of a national data bank through which information on physician licensure actions, sanctions by boards of medical examiners, malpractice claims paid, and professional review actions that adversely affect the clinical privileges of physicians could be provided to authorized persons and organizations.

1987

P.L. 100-177, the National Health Service Corps Amendments, reauthorized the National Health Service Corps (NHSC), which had been created under a provision of the Emergency Health Personnel Act of 1970 (see P.L. 91-623).

P.L. 100-203, the Omnibus Budget Reconciliation Act (OBRA '87), contained a number of provisions that directly affected the Medicare program. It required the secretary of DHHS to update the wage index used in calculating hospital PPS payments by October 1, 1990, and to do so at least every three years thereafter. It also required the secretary to study and report to Congress on the criteria being used by the Medicare program to identify referral hospitals. Deepening the reductions established by OBRA '86, one provision of the act reduced payment amounts for capital-related costs by 12 percent for FY 1988 and by 15 percent for FY 1989.

Regarding payments to physicians for services provided to Medicare clients, the legislation reduced fees for 12 sets of "overvalued" procedures. It also allowed higher fee increases for primary care than for other physician services and increased the fee differential between participating and nonparticipating physicians (see the 1984 P.L. 98-369).

The legislation also contained a number of provisions that affected the Medicaid program. Key among these, the law provided additional options for children and pregnant women and required states to cover eligible children up to age six with an option for allowing coverage up to age eight. The distinction between skilled nursing facilities (SNFs) and intermediate care facilities (ICFs) was eliminated. The legislation contained a number of provisions intended to enhance the quality of services provided in nursing homes, including requirements that nursing homes enhance the quality of life of each resident and operate quality assurance programs.

1988

P.L. 100-360, the Medicare Catastrophic Coverage Act, provided the largest expansion of the benefits covered under the Medicare program since its establishment in 1965 (see P.L. 89-97). Among other things, provisions of this legislation added coverage for outpatient prescription drugs and respite care and placed a cap on out-of-pocket spending by the elderly for copayment costs for covered services.

The legislation included provisions that would have the new benefits phased in over a four-year period and paid for by premiums charged to Medicare program enrollees. Thirty-seven percent of the costs were to be covered by a fixed monthly premium paid by all enrollees, and the remainder of the costs were to be covered by an income-related supplemental premium that was, in effect, an income surtax that would apply to fewer than half of the enrollees. Under intense pressure from many of their elderly constituents and their interest groups who objected to having to pay additional premiums or the income surtax, Congress repealed P.L. 100-360 in 1989 without implementing most of its provisions.

P.L. 100-578, the Clinical Laboratory Improvement Amendments, amended the Clinical Laboratory Improvement Act (see the 1967 P.L. 90-174) to extend and modify government's ability to regulate clinical laboratories.

P.L. 100-582, the Medical Waste Tracking Act, was enacted in response to the highly publicized incidents of used and discarded syringes and needles washing up on the shores of a number of states in the eastern United States in the summer of 1988. The legislation itself was rather limited in that it focused on the tracking of medical wastes from their origin to their disposal rather than broader regulation of transportation and disposal of these wastes.

P.L. 100-607, the National Organ Transplant Amendments, amended the National Organ Transplant Act (see the 1986 P.L. 98-507) to extend the prohibition against the sale of human organs to the organs and other body parts of human fetuses.

P.L. 100-647, the Technical and Miscellaneous Revenue Act, directed the PPRC (see the 1985 P.L. 99-272) to consider policies for moderating the rate of increase in expenditures for physician services in the Medicare program and for reducing the utilization of these services.

1989

P.L. 101-239, the Omnibus Budget Reconciliation Act (OBRA '89), included provisions for minor, primarily technical, changes in PPS and a provision to extend coverage for mental health benefits and add coverage for Pap smears. Small adjustments were made in the disproportionate share regulations, and the 15 percent capital-related payment reduction established in OBRA '87 was continued in OBRA '89. Another provision required the secretary of DHHS to update the wage index annually in a budget-neutral manner beginning in FY 1993.

As part of the OBRA '89 legislation, the Health Care Financing Administration (HCFA) was directed to begin implementing a resource-based relative value scale (RBRVS) for reimbursing physicians under the Medicare program on January 1, 1992. The new system was to be phased in over a four-year period beginning in 1992.

Another important provision in this legislation initiated the establishment of the Agency for Health Care Policy and Research (AHCPR; now the Agency for Healthcare Research and Quality, or AHRQ). This agency succeeded the National Center for Health Services Research and Technology Assessment (NCHSR). The new agency was created to conduct or foster the conduct of studies of healthcare quality, effectiveness, and efficiency. In particular, the agency was to conduct or foster the conduct of studies on the outcomes of medical treatments and provide technical assistance to groups seeking to develop practice guidelines.

1990

P.L. 101-336, the Americans with Disabilities Act (ADA), provided a broad range of protections for the disabled, in effect combining protections contained in the Civil Rights Act of 1964, the Rehabilitation Act of 1973, and the Civil Rights Restoration Act of 1988. The central goal of the legislation was independence for the disabled, in effect to assist them in being self-supporting and able to lead independent lives.

P.L. 101-381, the Ryan White Comprehensive AIDS Resources Emergency Act (CARE), provided resources to 16 epicenters, including San Francisco and New York City, and to states hardest hit by AIDS to assist them in coping with the skyrocketing cost of care and treatment.

P.L. 101-508, the Omnibus Budget Reconciliation Act (OBRA '90), contained the Patient Self-Determination Act, which required healthcare institutions participating in the Medicare and Medicaid programs to provide all of their patients with written information on policies regarding self-determination and living wills. The institutions were also required under this legislation to inquire whether patients had advance medical directives and to document the replies in the patients' medical records.

The legislation made additional minor changes in PPS, including further adjustments in the wage index calculation and in the disproportionate share regulations. Regarding the wage index, one provision required the Prospective Payment Assessment Commission (ProPAC), which was established by the 1983 Social Security Amendments (see P.L. 98-21) to help guide Congress and the secretary of DHHS on implementing PPS to further study the available data on wages by occupational category and to develop recommendations on modifying the wage index to account for occupational mix.

The legislation also included a provision that continued the 15 percent capital-related payment reduction that was established in OBRA '87 and continued in OBRA '89 and another provision that made the reduced teaching adjustment payment established in OBRA '87 permanent. One of its more important provisions provided a five-year deficit reduction plan that was to reduce total Medicare outlays by more than $43 billion between FYs 1991 and 1995.

P.L. 101-629, the Safe Medical Devices Act, further amended the Federal Food, Drug and Cosmetic Act (see the 1938 P.L. 75-717) and the subsequent Medical Devices Amendments of 1976 (see P.L. 94-295) to require institutions that use medical devices to report device-related problems to the manufacturers and/or to FDA. Reportable problems include any incident in which any medical device may have caused or contributed to any person's death, serious illness, or serious injury.

P.L. 101-649, the Immigration and Nationality Act of 1990, restructured with minor modifications the medical exclusion scheme for screening people who desired to immigrate to the United States that had been in use since the enactment of the Immigration and Nationality Act of 1952 (see P.L. 82-414).

1992

P.L. 102-585, the Veterans Health Care Act, required the Department of Veterans Affairs to establish in each of its hospitals suitable indoor and outdoor smoking areas. This law ran counter to the department's 1991 internal policy of running its hospitals on a smoke-free basis and was out of step with the private-sector movement to establishing smoke-free hospitals.

1993

P.L. 103-43, the National Institutes of Health Revitalization Act, contained provisions for a number of structural and budgetary changes in the operation of NIH. It also set forth guidelines for the conduct of research on transplantation of human fetal tissue and added HIV infection to the list of excludable conditions covered by the Immigration and Nationality Act (see the 1990 P.L. 101-649).

P.L. 103-66, the Omnibus Budget Reconciliation Act (OBRA '93), established an all-time-record five-year cut in Medicare funding and included a number of other changes affecting the Medicare program. For example, the legislation included provisions to end return on equity (ROE) payments for capital to proprietary SNFs and reduced the previously established rate of increase in payment rates for care provided in hospices. In addition, the legislation cut laboratory fees drastically by changing the reimbursement formula and froze payments for durable medical equipment, parenteral and enteral services, and orthotics and prosthetics in FYs 1994 and 1995.

OBRA '93 contained the Comprehensive Childhood Immunization Act, which provided $585 million to support the provision of vaccines for children eligible for Medicaid, children who do not have health insurance, and Native American children.

Note on 1994 and 1995

Chronologies of American health policy will always show these years as a period in which health policymaking appeared dormant because almost no important new federal laws pertaining to health, nor amendments to existing laws, were enacted. This apparent dearth of health policy, however, is misleading. This was a period of extraordinary consideration of health legislation, although very little was enacted. President Clinton attempted a fundamental reform of the American healthcare system through introducing his Health Security proposal in late 1993. The proposed legislation died with the 1994 Congress. The debate consumed almost all of the health-related legislation development energy expended during 1994. Then, following this bill's demise, the 1995 attempt to enact unprecedented cutbacks in the Medicare and Medicaid programs as part of a far-reaching budget reconciliation bill that sought a balanced federal budget ended in veto by President Clinton. The political wrangling over the budget grew even worse in 1996. Proposed changes in the Medicare and Medicaid programs, changes that were linked to the development of a plan to balance the federal budget over a seven-year span, would have meant massive cuts in these programs. The differences over these plans between the Republican-controlled Congress and President Clinton, a Democrat, were so fundamental that they led to a complete impasse in the budget negotiations in 1996, including a brief shutdown of the federal government in the absence of budget authority to operate.

1995

P.L. 104-65, the Lobbying Disclosure Act, contained provisions requiring registration with the Secretary of the Senate and the Clerk of the House of Representatives by any individual lobbyist (or the individual's employer if it employs one or more lobbyists) within 45 days after the individual first makes, or is employed or retained to make, a lobbying contact with either the president, the vice president, a member of Congress, or any of a number of specified federal officers. This law defines a lobbyist as any individual employed or retained by a client for financial or other compensation for services that include more than one lobbying contact, unless the individual's lobbying activities constitute less than 20 percent of the time engaged in the services provided to that client over a six-month period.

1996

P.L. 104-134, the Departments of Veterans Affairs, Housing and Urban Development, and Independent Agencies Appropriations Act, contained several provisions that offered certain protections for enrollees in managed care plans. One provision prohibited plans from restricting hospital stays for mothers and newborns to less than 48 hours for vaginal deliveries and 96 hours following a cesarean section. Another provision required that group health plans that offer both medical and surgical benefits and mental health benefits not impose a more restrictive lifetime or annual limit on mental health benefits than is imposed on medical or surgical benefits.

P.L. 104-191, the Health Insurance Portability and Accountability Act (HIPAA) (also known as the Kassebaum-Kennedy Act), provided employees who work for companies that offer health insurance to their employees with guaranteed access to health insurance in the event that they change jobs or become unemployed. In addition, the legislation guaranteed renewability of health insurance coverage so long as premiums are paid. It also provided for increased tax deductions for the self-employed who purchase health insurance and allowed tax deductions for medical expenses related to long-term-care insurance coverage. The legislation also established a limited "medical savings accounts" demonstration project.

P.L. 104-193, the Personal Responsibility and Work Opportunity Reconciliation Act (also known as the Welfare Reform Act), made significant changes in the nation's welfare policy with implications for such health determinants as the social and economic environments faced by affected people and affected eligibility for the Medicaid program in a fundamental way. Since the establishment of the Medicaid program in 1965 (see P.L. 89-97), eligibility for a key welfare benefit, Aid to Families with Dependent Children (AFDC), and eligibility for Medicaid benefits have been linked. Families receiving AFDC have been automatically eligible for Medicaid and enrolled in the Medicaid program. The Personal Responsibility and Work Opportunity Reconciliation Act, however, replaced AFDC with the Temporary Assistance to Needy Families (TANF) block grant. Under the provisions of the TANF block grant, states are given broad flexibility to design income support and work programs for low-income families with children and are required to impose federally mandated restrictions, such as time limits, on federally funded assistance. The welfare reform law does provide that children and parents who would have qualified for Medicaid based on their eligibility for AFDC continue to be eligible for Medicaid, but, in the absence of AFDC, states must utilize different mechanisms to identify and enroll former AFDC recipients in their Medicaid programs.

1997

P.L. 105-33, the Balanced Budget Act of 1997 (BBA), contained the most significant changes in the Medicare program since the program's inception in 1965. Overall, this legislation required a five-year reduction of $115 billion in the Medicare program's expenditure growth and a $13 billion reduction in growth of the Medicaid program. A new "Medicare+Choice" program was created, which gives Medicare beneficiaries the opportunity to choose from a variety of health plan options the plan that best suits their needs and preferences. Significant changes were also made in the traditional Medicare program. Among them, hospital annual inflation updates were reduced, as were hospital payments for inpatient capital expenses and for bad debts. Other provisions established a cap on the number of medical residents supported by Medicare graduate medical education payments and provided incentives for reductions in the number of residents.

An important provision of this act established the State Children's Health Insurance Program (SCHIP) and provided states with $24 billion in federal funds for 1998 until 2002 to increase health insurance for children.

Other provisions established two new commissions. One of these, the Medicare Payment Review Commission (MedPAC), replaced the Physician Payment Review Commission and the Prospective Payment Review Commission. MedPAC was required to submit an annual report to Congress on the status of Medicare reforms and to make recommendations on Medicare payment issues. The second new commission, the National Bipartisan Commission on the Future of Medicare, established by this legislation was charged to develop recommendations for Congress on actions necessary to ensure the long-term fiscal health of the Medicare program. This commission was to consider several specific issues that were debated in the development of the BBA of 1997, but rejected. These issues included raising the eligibility age for Medicare, increasing the Part B premiums, and developing alternative approaches to financing graduate medical education.

P.L. 105-115, the Food and Drug Administration Modernization and Accountability Act, directs the secretary of DHHS, at the request of a new drug's sponsor, to identify the drug as a "fast track product" and to facilitate development and expedite review if the new drug is intended for serious conditions and demonstrates the potential to address unmet medical needs for those conditions. The law also mandates development, prioritization, publication, and annual updating of a list of approved drugs for which additional pediatric information may produce health benefits in the pediatric population. It also mandates development of guidance on the inclusion of women and minorities in clinical trials. Among numerous other provisions, the law also authorizes the secretary of DHHS to permit the shipment of investigational drugs or investigational devices for the diagnosis, monitoring, or treatment of a serious disease or condition in emergency situations. It permits any person through a licensed physician to request, and any manufacturer or distributor to provide to the physician, such a drug or device if specified requirements are met.

1998

P.L. 105-357, the Controlled Substances Trafficking Prohibition Act, amends the Controlled Substances Import and Export Act to prohibit U.S. residents from importing into the United States a non-Schedule I controlled substance exceeding 50 dosage units if they (1) enter the United States through an international land border and (2) do not possess a valid prescription or documentation verifying such a prescription. This law has a provision that declares that the federal requirements under the law not limit states from imposing additional requirements.

P.L. 105-369, the Ricky Ray Hemophilia Relief Fund Act, establishes in the U.S. Treasury the Ricky Ray Hemophilia Relief Fund. The law mandates a single payment of $100,000 from the fund to any individual infected with the human immunodeficiency virus (HIV) if the individual has any blood-clotting disorder and was treated with blood-clotting agents between July 1, 1982, and December 31, 1987; is the lawful current or former spouse of such an individual; or acquired the HIV infection from a parent who is such an individual. The law declares that it does not create or admit any claim of the individual against the United States or its agents regarding HIV and antihemophilic factor treatment and that acceptance of a payment under this act is in full satisfaction of all such claims of the individual.

1999

P.L. 106-113, the Medicare, Medicaid and SCHIP Balanced Budget Refinement Act of 1999 (BBRA), changed the provisions in the Balanced Budget Act of 1997 in a number of ways. One change, for example, pertained to the way that hospitals treating a disproportionate share (DSH) of low-income Medicare and Medicaid patients receive additional payments from Medicare. BBRA froze DSH adjustments at 3 percent (the FY 2000 level) through FY 2001 and reduced the formula to 4 percent from the BBA-established 5 percent in FY 2002 and then to 0 percent for subsequent years. The law increased hospice payment by 0.5 percent for FY 2001 and by 0.75 percent for FY 2002. Medicare reimburses teaching hospitals for their role in providing graduate medical education (GME). Prior to BBA, Medicare's indirect medical education adjustment (IME) payments increased 7.7 percent for each 10 percent increase in a hospital's ratio of interns and residents to beds. BBA decreased the adjustment to 6.5 percent in FY 1999, 6.0 percent in FY 2000, and 5.5 percent in FY 2001 and subsequent years. BBRA froze the IME adjustment at 6.5 percent through FY 2000, reduced it to 6.25 percent in FY 2001, and reduced it to 5.5 percent in FY 2002 and subsequent years.

P.L. 106-117, the Veterans Millennium Health Care and Benefits Act, directs the secretary of Veterans Affairs to provide nursing home care to any veteran in need of such care through December 31, 2003, (1) for a service-connected disability or (2) who has a service-connected disability rated at 70 percent or more. The law prohibits a veteran receiving such care from being transferred from the providing facility without the consent of the veteran or his or her representative. It also directs the secretary to operate and maintain a program to provide the following extended care services to eligible veterans: (1) geriatric evaluation; (2) nursing home care, either in facilities of the Department of Veterans Affairs or in community-based facilities; (3) domiciliary services; (4) adult day healthcare; (5) noninstitutional alternatives to nursing home care; and (6) respite care. The law has a provision that prohibits the secretary from furnishing such services for a nonservice-connected disability unless the veteran agrees to make a copayment for services of more than 21 days in a year and requires the secretary to establish a methodology for establishing the copayment amount.

2000

P.L. 106-354, the Breast and Cervical Cancer Prevention and Treatment Act, amends Title XIX (Medicaid) of the Social Security Act to give states the option of making medical assistance for breast and cervical cancer–related treatment services available during a presumptive eligibility period to certain low-income women who have already been screened for such cancers under the Centers for Disease Control and Prevention breast and cervical cancer early detection program. The law also provides for an enhanced match of federal funds to help states pay for these treatment services through their Medicaid programs.

P.L. 106-430, the Needlestick Safety and Prevention Act, revised the bloodborne pathogens standard in effect under the Occupational Safety and Health Act of 1970 to include safer medical devices, such as sharps with engineered sharps injury protections and needleless systems, as examples of engineering controls designed to eliminate or minimize occupational exposure to bloodborne pathogens through needlestick injuries. Other provisions require certain employers to (1) review and update exposure control plans to reflect changes in technology that eliminate or reduce such exposure and document their consideration and implementation of appropriate commercially available and effective safer medical devices for such purpose; (2) maintain a sharps injury log, noting the type and brand of device used, where the injury occurred, and an explanation of the incident (exempting employers who are not required to maintain specified OSHA logs); and (3) seek input on such engineering and work practice controls from the affected healthcare workers.

P.L. 106-525, the Minority Health and Health Disparities Research and Education Act, amends the Public Health Service Act to establish within the National Institutes of Health (NIH) the National Center on Minority and Health Disparities to conduct and support research, training, dissemination of information, and other programs with respect to minority health conditions and other populations with health disparities. This law requires the center director, in expending funds, to give priority to conducting and supporting minority health disparities research (research on minority health conditions, including research to prevent, diagnose, and treat such conditions). It also requires coordination of center research with other health disparities research conducted or supported by NIH and requires the center director, the NIH director, and the directors of all other agencies of NIH to, among other things, establish a comprehensive plan and budget for the conduct and support of all minority health and other health disparities research activities of the agencies of NIH. The law also has a provision requiring the directors to work together to carry out provisions of the act relating to participation by minority groups in clinical research.

P.L. 106-554, the Medicare, Medicaid, and SCHIP Benefits Improvement and Protection Act of 2000 (BIPA), changed numerous provisions previously enacted in BBA and BBRA. Among the important changes were the following:

- an increase of 3.4 percent for Medicare inpatient payments in FY 2001 and an estimated 3.5 percent in FY 2002

- an increase of 4.4 percent in Medicare outpatient payments in 2001
- indirect medical education (IME) payments at 6.5 percent in FY 2001 and FY 2002
- elimination of the additional 1 percent cut in Medicare disproportionate share (DSH) hospital payments in FY 2001 and 2002
- an increase from 55 to 70 percent in Medicare payments for bad debt
- an increase for the direct graduate medical education (GME) payment floor to 85 percent of the national average
- elimination of BBA's FY 2001 and 2002 Medicaid DSH cut
- removal of the 2 percent payment reduction for rehabilitation hospitals in FY 2001
- a 3.2 percent increase in skilled nursing service payments in FY 2001
- a one-year delay of the 15 percent reduction for home health and the full market basket in FY 2001
- an increase of 2 percent in incentive payments for psychiatric hospitals/units
- expansion of Medicare payment for telehealth services to rural areas

P.L. 106-580, the National Institute of Biomedical Imaging and Bioengineering Establishment Act, amends the Public Health Service Act to provide for the establishment of the National Institute of Biomedical Imaging and Bioengineering. The law requires the director of the institute to establish a national biomedical imaging and bioengineering program, which includes research and related technology assessments and development in biomedical imaging and bioengineering. It also requires the director to prepare and transmit to the secretary of DHHS and the director of the National Institutes of Health (NIH) a plan to initiate, expand, intensify, and coordinate institute biomedical imaging and bioengineering activities. It requires (1) the consolidation and coordination of institute biomedical imaging and bioengineering research and related activities with those of NIH and other federal agencies and (2) the establishment of an institute advisory council.

2001

P.L. 107-9, the Animal Disease Risk Assessment, Prevention, and Control Act, directs the Secretary of Agriculture to submit a preliminary report to specified congressional committees concerning (1) interagency measures to assess, prevent, and control the spread of foot and mouth disease and bovine spongiform encephalopathy ("mad cow disease") in the United States; (2) related federal information sources available to the public; and (3) the need for any additional legislative authority or product bans. The law directs the secretary, in consultation with governmental and private-sector parties, to submit a final report to such committees that discusses such diseases' economic impacts; public and animal health risks; and related legislative, federal agency, and product recommendations.

P.L. 107-38, the Emergency Supplemental Appropriations Act for Recovery from and Response to Terrorist Attacks on the United States, makes emergency supplemental appropriations for FY 2001 for emergency expenses to respond to the terrorist attacks on the United States on September 11, 2001, to provide assistance to the victims, and to deal with other consequences of the attacks. The law makes $40 billion available to the Executive Office of the President and Funds Appropriated to the President for the Emergency Response Fund for such expenses as (1) providing federal, state, and local preparedness for mitigating and responding to the attacks; (2) providing support to counter, investigate, or prosecute domestic or international terrorism; (3) providing increased transportation security; (4) repairing damaged public facilities and transportation systems; and (5) supporting national security.

P.L. 107-109, Best Pharmaceuticals for Children Act, amends the Public Health Service Act to direct the secretary of DHHS, through the National Institutes of Health (NIH), to develop an annual list of approved drugs for which (1) there is a referral, an approved or pending new drug application, or no patent or market exclusivity protection and (2) additional pediatric safety and effectiveness studies are needed. The act also directs the Secretary to award contracts to entities with appropriate experience for pediatric clinical trials of such drugs; requires the results of such trials to be reported to the Commissioner of Food and Drugs who shall then determine and request any necessary labeling changes; authorizes the Commissioner to deem a drug misbranded if the holder of an approved application refuses to make the requested change; requires the Secretary to send a nonbinding letter of recommendation to an approved application holder if such studies indicate a reformulation is necessary; and sets forth reporting, label change, and dispute resolution requirements.

P.L. 107-121, the Native American Breast and Cervical Cancer Treatment Technical Amendment Act of 2001, amends Title XIX of the Social Security Act to clarify that Indian women with breast or cervical cancer who are eligible for health services provided under a medical care program of the Indian Health Service or of a tribal organization are included in the optional Medicaid eligibility category of breast or cervical cancer patients added by the Breast and Cervical Prevention and Treatment Act of 2000.

P.L. 107-205, Nurse Reinvestment Act, amends the Public Health Service Act to direct the secretary of DHHS to promote the nursing profession through public service announcements and to make grants to support state and local advertising campaigns, excluding particular employment opportunities.

The legislation expands eligibility for the nursing loan repayment program to include service at any healthcare facility with a critical shortage of nurses. The legislation also authorizes the secretary to award grants or contracts to schools of nursing or healthcare facilities to expand nursing opportunities (1) in education, through increased enrollment in four-year degree programs, internship and residency programs, or new technologies such as distance learning and (2) in practice, through care to underserved populations, care in noninstitutional settings or organized healthcare systems, and through developing cultural competencies.

2002

P.L. 107-250, the Medical Device User Fee and Modernization Act, amends the Federal Food, Drug and Cosmetic Act to establish a new program that beginning on October 1, 2002, subjects each medical device manufacturer to a medical device fee for certain applications, reports, application supplements, and submissions sent to the FDA for evaluation. The legislation grants exceptions, including for humanitarian devices and certain devices sponsored by state governments or the federal government and directs the secretary of DHHS to waive one premarket application, or one premarket report where the applicant is a small business submitting its first premarket application or its first premarket report, respectively, for review.

P.L. 107-251, the Health Care Safety Net Amendments of 2002, amends the Public Health Service Act to reauthorize and strengthen the health centers program and the National Health Service Corps and to establish the Healthy Communities Access Program to help coordinate services for the uninsured and underinsured.

P.L. 107-280, the Rare Diseases Act, amends the Public Health Service Act to (1) establish the Office of Rare Diseases at the National Institutes of Health and (2) provide for rare disease regional centers of excellence. The legislation sets forth the duties of such an office and such regional centers, including research and educational duties. It also defines *rare disease* as any disease or condition affecting fewer than 200,000 persons in the United States.

P.L. 107-296, the Homeland Security Act, establishes the Department of Homeland Security (DHS) as an executive department of the United States, headed by the Secretary of Homeland Security (secretary) appointed by the president by and with the advice and consent of the Senate to (1) prevent terrorist attacks within the United States; (2) reduce the vulnerability of the United States to terrorism; (3) minimize the damage, and assist in the recovery, from terrorist attacks that occur within the United States; (4) carry out all functions of entities transferred to DHS; (5) ensure that the functions of the agencies and subdivisions within DHS that are not related directly to securing the homeland are not diminished or neglected except by a specific act of Congress; (6) ensure that the overall economic security of the United States is not diminished by efforts, activities, and programs aimed at securing the homeland; and (7) monitor connections between illegal drug trafficking and terrorism, coordinate efforts to sever such connections, and otherwise contribute to efforts to interdict illegal drug trafficking.

P.L. 107-313, the Mental Health Parity Reauthorization Act, amends the Employee Retirement Income Security Act of 1974 (ERISA) and the Public Health Service Act to extend the mental health benefits parity provisions through 2003.

2003

P.L. 108-74, the State Children's Health Insurance Program Allotments Extension, amends Title XXI (State Children's Health Insurance Program, or SCHIP) of the Social Security Act to revise the special rule for the redistribution and availability of unexpended FY 1998 and 1999 SCHIP allotments, including to (1) extend the availability of FY 1998 and 1999 reallocated funds through FY 2004 and (2) permit 50 percent of the total amount of unexpended FY 2000 and 2001 SCHIP allotments that remain available to a state through the end of FY 2002 and 2003 to remain available for expenditure by the state through the end of FY 2004 and 2005, respectively.

P.L. 108-155, the Pediatric Research Equity Act, amends the Federal Food, Drug and Cosmetic Act to authorize the Food and Drug Administration (FDA) to require license applications for new drugs and biological products to assess such drug's or product's safety and effectiveness for relevant pediatric subpopulations, including dosage. The legislation permits deferral of such assessments under specified circumstances, including if the secretary of DHHS finds that the drug or biological product is ready for approval for use in adults before pediatric studies are complete. It also permits full waiver of such assessments under certain conditions, including if (1) studies are highly impractical or impossible or (2) there is no meaningful therapeutic advantage or benefit in the pediatric population and the drug or biological product is not likely to be used in a substantial number of pediatric patients.

P.L. 108-170, the Veterans Health Care, Capital Asset, and Business Improvement Act, amends Title 38, United States Code, to improve and enhance provision of healthcare for veterans, to authorize major construction projects and other facilities matters for the Department of Veterans Affairs, to enhance and improve authorities relating to the administration of personnel of the Department of Veterans Affairs, and for other purposes.

P.L. 108-173, the Medicare Prescription Drug, Improvement, and Modernization Act (MMA), created a new drug benefit as Part D of Medicare. The new benefit is to begin in 2006, with an interim Medicare-endorsed drug discount card available to beneficiaries. In addition, this law adds certain preventive benefits including an initial routine physical examination for new beneficiaries, as well as cardiovascular blood screening tests and diabetes screening and services. MMA also renamed Medicare+Choice to Medicare Advantage (MA) and changed some of the enrollment and disenrollment rules for beneficiaries.

Another fundamental change in the Medicare program resulting from MMA is the Part B premium determination, which has been uniform for all beneficiaries since the program's inception. Beginning in 2007, this premium will be higher for those with incomes over $80,000 for a single beneficiary or $160,000 for a couple. In addition, the Part B deductible, set at $100 since 1991, is increased to $110 and thereafter will increase by the annual percentage increase in Part B expenditures.

2004

P.L. 108-216, the Organ Donation and Recovery Improvement Act, amends the Public Health Service Act to authorize the secretary of DHHS to award grants to states, transplant centers, qualified organ procurement organizations, or other public or private entities to reimburse travel, subsistence, and incidental nonmedical expenses incurred by individuals toward making living organ donations. The legislation also directs the secretary to establish a public education program to increase awareness about organ donation and the need to provide for an adequate rate of donations. It authorizes the secretary to (1) make peer-reviewed grants to or contracts with public and not-for-profit private entities for studies and demonstration projects to increase organ donation and recovery rates, including living donations; (2) make grants to states for organ donor awareness, public education, and outreach activities and programs designed to increase the number of organ donors within the state; and (3) support the development and dissemination of educational materials to inform healthcare professionals about organ, tissue, and eye donation issues.

P.L. 108-276, the Project BioShield Act, amends the Public Health Service Act to provide protections and countermeasures against chemical, radiological, or nuclear agents that may be used in a terrorist attack against the United States by giving the National Institutes of Health contracting flexibility to make infrastructure improvements and expedite the scientific peer review process and by streamlining the Food and Drug Administration approval process of countermeasures.

P.L. 108-355, the Garrett Lee Smith Memorial Act, amends the Public Health Service Act to support the planning, implementation, and evaluation of organized activities involving statewide youth suicide early intervention and prevention strategies and to authorize grants to institutions of higher education to reduce student mental and behavioral health problems.

P.L. 108-358, the Anabolic Steroid Control Act, amends the Controlled Substances Act to clarify the definition of anabolic steroids and to provide for research and education activities relating to steroids and steroid precursors. The legislation defines *anabolic steroid* as any drug or hormonal substance chemically and pharmacologically related to testosterone (other than estrogens, progestins, corticosteroids, and dehydroepiandrosterone).

2005

P.L. 109-18, Patient Navigator Outreach and Chronic Disease Prevention Act, amends the Public Health Service Act to authorize a demonstration grant program to provide patient navigator services to reduce barriers and improve healthcare outcomes. This act permits the secretary of DHHS, acting through the administrator of the Health Resources and Services Administration, to make grants to eligible entities for the development and operation of demonstration programs to provide patient navigator services to improve healthcare outcomes. The act requires the secretary to coordinate with and ensure the participation of the Indian Health Service, the National Cancer Institute, the Office of Rural Health Policy, and such other offices and agencies as deemed appropriate by the secretary regarding the design and evaluation of the demonstration programs.

P.L. 109-41, Patient Safety and Quality Improvement Act, amends the Public Health Service Act to designate patient safety data as privileged and confidential. The act defines a patient safety organization (PSO) as an organization certified by the secretary of DHHS that conducts efforts to improve patient safety and the quality of healthcare delivery through the collection and analysis of patient safety data. The act requires the secretary to (1) maintain a patient safety network of databases that has the capacity to accept, aggregate, and analyze nonidentifiable patient safety data voluntarily reported and that provides an interactive resource for providers and PSOs; (2) develop or adopt voluntary national standards to promote the electronic exchange of healthcare information; and (3) contract with a research organization to study the impact of medical technologies and therapies on healthcare.

P.L. 109-171, the Deficit Reduction Act (DRA) of 2005, established and funded the Medicare–Medicaid Data Match Program, which is designed to identify improper billing and utilization patterns by matching Medicare and Medicaid claims information. The funds also can be used (1) to coordinate actions by CMS, the states, the Attorney General, and the HHS OIG to prevent improper Medicaid and Medicare expenditures and (2) to increase the effectiveness and efficiency of both Medicare and Medicaid through cost avoidance, savings, and the recoupment of fraudulent, wasteful, or abusive expenditures.

2006

P.L. 109-307, the Children's Hospital GME Support Reauthorization Act of 2006, amends the Public Health Service Act to: (1) require the Secretary of Health and Human Services to make payments for FY2007–FY2011 to children's hospitals for expenses associated with operating approved graduate medical residency training programs; and (2) decrease from 26 to 12 the number of interim payments to hospitals per fiscal year. The Act also requires the Secretary, acting through the Administrator of the Health Resources and Services Administration (HRSA), to report to Congress on the residency training programs.

P. L. 109-415, the Ryan White HIV/AIDS Treatment Modernization Act of 2006, amends provisions of Title XXVI of the Public Health Service Act (popularly known as the Ryan White Care Act [RWCA]) concerning emergency relief grants for metropolitan areas to assist in delivering and enhancing HIV-related services. The Act reauthorizes for three years the RWCA, providing $2.1 billion annually for HIV/AIDS programs in the U.S. These amendments have the effect of shifting additional funds to rural areas and the South, where the disease is a newer phenomenon.

P.L. 109-417, the Pandemic and All-Hazards Preparedness Act, amends the Public Health Service Act with respect to public health security and all-hazards preparedness and response. This Act improves the public health and medical preparedness and response capabilities for emergencies, whether deliberate, accidental, or natural. The Act enhances the Nation's capacity to handle a major medical surge during an emergency by establishing a national infrastructure for registering health professional volunteers, improving core training, strengthening logistical support, and developing a clear organizational framework for health care providers.

The Act establishes overarching preparedness goals for essential federal, state, and local public health and medical capabilities to increase accountability and incentivize regional coordination, including

1. integrating public health and public and private medical capabilities with other first responder systems;

2. developing and maintaining Federal, State, local and tribal essential public health security capabilities;
3. increasing the preparedness and response capabilities, and the surge capacity of hospitals and health care facilities;
4. taking into account the needs of at-risk individuals during a public health emergency;
5. ensuring coordination of Federal, State, local and tribal planning, preparedness and response activities; and
6. maintaining continuity of operations of vital public health and medical services in the event of a public health emergency.

2007

P.L. 110-18, the National Breast and Cervical Cancer Early Detection Program Reauthorization Act of 2007 amends the Public Health Service Act to change from 2000 to 2020 the target year for achieving the objectives established by the Secretary of Health and Human Services for reductions in the rate of mortality from breast and cervical cancer in the United States for the committee coordinating Public Health Service activities. The Act also directs the Secretary to establish a demonstration project which allows the Secretary to waive certain requirements for awarding breast and cervical cancer grants for preventive health measures with respect to breast and cervical cancers.

P.L. 110-23, the Trauma Care Systems Planning and Development Act of 2007 amends the Public Health Service Act to direct the Secretary of Health and Human Services to: (1) collect, compile, and disseminate information on achievements and problems in providing trauma care and emergency medical services; and (2) promote the collection and categorization of trauma data in a consistent and standardized manner.

The Act authorizes the Secretary, acting through the Administrator of the Health Resources and Services Administration, to make grants to states, political subdivisions, or consortia thereof to improve access to and enhance the development of trauma care systems. Requires grant funds be used to: (1) integrate and broaden the reach of such a system; (2) strengthen, develop, and improve an existing system; (3) expand communications between the system and emergency medical services through improved equipment or a telemedicine system; (4) improve data collection and retention; or (5) increase education, training, and technical assistance opportunities. The Act requires the Secretary to give priority to applicants who will use the grants to focus on improving access to trauma care systems and to give special consideration to projects that demonstrate strong state or local support.

P.L. 110-26, the American National Red Cross Governance Modernization Act of 2007, amends the Congressional Charter of the American National Red Cross (ANRC) to modernize its governance structure, to enhance the ability of its board of governors to support the critical mission of ANRC in the 21st century. The Act requires the corporation to submit a report to the Secretary of Defense on the activities of the corporation during the preceding fiscal year, including a complete, itemized report of all receipts and expenditures.

P.L. 110-85, the Food and Drug Administration Amendments Act of 2007 amends the Federal Food, Drug, and Cosmetic Act (FFDCA) to revise and extend the user-fee programs for prescription drugs and for medical devices. The Act also amends FFDCA to include postmarket safety activities within the process for the review of human drug applications or supplements, including: (1) developing and using improved adverse event data collection systems and improved analytical tools to assess potential safety problems; (2) implementing and enforcing provisions relating to post approval studies, clinical trials, labeling changes, and risk evaluation and mitigation strategies; and (3) conducting screenings of the Adverse Event Reporting System database and reporting on new safety concerns.

P.L. 110-173, the Medicare, Medicaid, and SCHIP Extension Act of 2007, prevented a 10.1 percent reduction in Medicare payments to physicians that was scheduled to take effect in 2008 and, instead, gave physicians a 0.5 increase through June 30, 2008.

2008

P.L. 110-233, the Genetic Information Nondiscrimination Act of 2008, amends the Employee Retirement Income Security Act of 1974 (ERISA), the Public Health Service Act, and the Internal Revenue Code to prohibit a group health plan from adjusting premium or contribution amounts for a group on the basis of genetic information. The Act also prohibits a group health plan from requesting or requiring an individual or family member of an individual from undergoing a genetic test and requires the plan to request only the minimum amount of information necessary to accomplish the intended purpose. The Act prohibits an issuer of a Medicare supplemental policy from: (1) requesting or requiring an individual or a family member to undergo a genetic test; or (2) requesting, requiring, or purchasing genetic information for underwriting purposes or for any individual prior to enrollment.

P.L. 110-275, the Medicare Improvements for Patients and Providers Act of 2008 (MIPPA), extended the planned reduction in Medicare payments to physicians through the end of 2008, and increased payment of their fees for all of 2009 by 1.1 percent. Benefit improvements for Medicare beneficiaries included reduced coinsurance payments for mental health visits and elimination of the deductibles for Welcome to Medicare physical examinations.

P.L. 110-314, the Consumer Product Safety Improvement Act of 2008, treats as a banned hazardous substance under the Federal Hazardous Substances Act (FHSA) any children's product (a consumer product designed or intended primarily for children 12 years of age or younger) containing more than specified amounts of lead. The Act establishes a more stringent limit on the amount of lead allowed in paint. It also requires the Consumer Product Safety Commission (CPSC) to: (1) evaluate the effectiveness, precision, and reliability of X-ray fluorescence technology and other alternative methods for measuring lead in paint or other surface coatings when used on a children's product or furniture article in order to determine compliance with specified regulations; and (2) conduct an ongoing effort to study and encourage the further development of alternative methods for measuring lead in paint and other surface coatings.

The Act requires a manufacturer of a children's product, before importing any children's product that is subject to a safety rule, to have the product tested by an accredited third party for compliance with such rule and to certify that such product complies.

P.L. 110-335, the Health Care Safety Net Act of 2008, amends the Public Health Service Act to reauthorize appropriations for FY2008–FY2012 for health centers to meet the healthcare needs of medically underserved populations. The Act requires the Comptroller General to study the economic costs and benefits of school-based health centers and their impact on the health of students, including an analysis of: (1) the impact that federal funding could have on the operation of such centers; (2) any cost savings to other federal programs derived from providing health services in such centers; and (3) the impact of such centers in rural or underserved areas.

The Act also requires the Secretary of Health and Human Services, acting through the Administrator of the Health Resources and Services Administration (HRSA), to submit a report to the relevant congressional committees that describes efforts to expand and accelerate quality improvement activities in community health centers. It also requires the Administrator to establish a mechanism for the dissemination of initiatives, best practices, and other information that may assist health care quality improvement efforts in community health centers.

P.L. 110-354, the Breast Cancer and Environmental Research Act of 2008, amends the Public Health Service Act to require the Secretary of Health and Human Services to establish the Interagency Breast Cancer and Environmental Research Coordinating Committee to: (1) share and coordinate information on existing breast cancer research activities and make recommendations for improvement of research programs; (2) develop a comprehensive strategy and advise the National Institutes of Health (NIH) and other federal agencies in the solicitation of proposals for collaborative, multidisciplinary research, including proposals to evaluate environmental and genomic factors that may be related to the etiology of breast cancer; (3) develop a summary of advances in federal breast cancer research relevant to the diagnosis, prevention, and treatment of cancer and other diseases and disorders; and (4) make recommendations to the Secretary regarding changes to research activities, avoiding unnecessary duplication of effort among federal agencies, public participation in decisions relating to breast cancer research, how best to disseminate information on breast cancer research progress, and how to expand partnerships between public and private entities to expand collaborative, crosscutting research. The Act authorizes appropriations for FY2009–FY2012.

P.L. 110-374, the Emergency Economic Stabilization Act of 2008, contains in Title V, Subtitle B, the Paul Wellstone and Pete Domenici Mental Health Parity and Addiction Equity Act of 2008, which amends the Employee Retirement Income Security Act of 1974 (ERISA), the Public Health Service Act, and the Internal Revenue Code to require a group health plan that provides both medical and surgical benefits and mental health or substance use disorder benefits to ensure that: (1) the financial requirements, such as deductibles and copayments, applicable to such mental health or substance use disorder benefits are no more restrictive than the predominant financial requirements applied to substantially all medical and surgical benefits covered by the plan; (2) there are no separate cost sharing requirements that are applicable only with respect to mental health or substance use disorder benefits; (3) the treatment limitations applicable to such mental health or substance use disorder benefits are no more restrictive than the predominant treatment limitations applied to substantially all medical and surgical benefits covered by the plan; and (4) there are no separate treatment limitations that are applicable only with respect to mental health or substance use disorder benefits.

P.L. 110-377, the Poison Center Support, Enhancement, and Awareness Act of 2008 amends the Public Health Service Act to require the Secretary of Health and Human Services to provide coordination and assistance for the maintenance of the nationwide toll-free phone number to access poison control centers.

The Act requires the Secretary to carry out and expand upon a national media campaign to educate the public and healthcare providers about poison prevention and the availability of poison control center resources in local communities. The Secretary is authorized to enter into contracts with nationally recognized organizations in the field of poison control and national media firms for the development and implementation of a nationwide poison prevention and poison control center awareness campaign.

This Act also expands the poison control center grant program to allow the Secretary to award grants for poison control centers to comply with the operational requirements needed to sustain certification. The Act authorizes appropriations for FY2009–FY2014.

2009

P.L. 111-3, the Children's Health Insurance Program Reauthorization Act of 2009, amends Title XXI of the Social Security Act to extend and improve the Children's Health Insurance Program (CHIP). The Act reauthorizes CHIP through 2013 at increased levels of funding by providing an additional $35 billion over five years. Among other things, the Act lowers the rate of uninsured low-income children, in part by providing states with incentives and tools for outreach and enrollment to accomplish this. Other provisions improve the quality of care for low-income children and reduce racial and ethnic disparities in coverage and quality. The legislation also reduces administrative barriers, maintains state flexibility, and enhances premium assistance options for low-income families.

P.L. 111-5, the American Recovery and Reinvestment Act of 2009, was enacted in response to the global financial crisis that emerged in 2008. The purposes of the act are

- to preserve and create jobs and promote economic recovery;
- to assist those most impacted by the recession;
- to provide investments needed to increase economic efficiency by spurring technological advances in science and health;
- to invest in transportation, environmental protection, and other infrastructure that will provide long-term economic benefits; and
- to stabilize State and local government budgets, in order to minimize and avoid reductions in essential services and counterproductive state and local tax increases.

Within this massive economic stimulus package ($787 billion), a significant amount of the resources (about $150 billion in new funds) are directed to healthcare. The specific allocations to healthcare are as follows:

Program or Investment Area	Amount and Purpose of Funding
Comparative effectiveness research	$1.1 billion, of which $300 million will be administered by the Agency for Healthcare Research and Quality, $400 million by the NIH, and $400 million by the secretary of health and human services.
Continuation of health insurance coverage for unemployed workers	$24.7 billion to provide a 65% federal subsidy for up to 9 months of premiums under the Consolidated Omnibus Budget Reconciliation Act. The subsidy will help workers who lose their jobs to continue coverage for themselves and their families.
Departments of Defense and Veterans Affairs	More than $1.4 billion for the construction and renovation of health care facilities.
Health information technology	$19.2 billion, including $17.2 billion for financial incentives to physicians and hospitals through Medicare and Medicaid to promote the use of electronic health records and other health information technology and $2 billion for affiliated grants and loans to be administered by the Office of the National Coordinator for Health Information Technology. Physicians may be eligible for grants of $40,000 to $65,000 over multiple years, and hospitals for up to $11 million.
Health Resources and Services Administration	$2.5 billion, including $1.5 billion for construction, equipment, and health information technology at community health centers; $500 million for services at these centers; $300 million for the NHSC; and $200 million for other health professions training programs.
Medicare	$338 million for payments to teaching hospitals, hospice programs, and long-term care hospitals.
Medicaid and other state health programs	$87 billion for additional federal matching payments for state Medicaid programs for a 27-month period that began October 1, 2008, and $3.2 billion for additional state fiscal relief related to Medicaid and other health programs.
National Institutes of Health	$10 billion, including $8.2 billion for new grants and related activities and $1.8 billion for construction and renovation of NIH buildings and facilities, extramural research facilities, and research equipment.
Prevention and wellness	$1 billion, including $650 million for clinical and community-based prevention activities that will address rates of chronic diseases, as determined by the secretary of health and human services; $300 million to the Centers for Disease Control and Prevention for immunizations for low-income children and adults; and $50 million to states to reduce health care–associated infections.
Public Health and Social Services Emergency Fund	$50 million to the DHHS to improve the security of information technology.

SOURCE: Steinbrook, R. 2009. "Health Care and the American Recovery and Reinvestment Act." *New England Journal of Medicine* 360 (11): 1057–60. Copyright © 2009 Massachusetts Medical Society. All rights reserved. Used with permission.

Notes

1. The Library of Congress maintains a website (thomas.loc.gov), on which extensive information on federal legislation is provided. This is an excellent source of additional information on public laws that pertain to health. Information about public laws can also be accessed through www.firstgov.gov, the official United States government website, or through www.access.gpo.gov, a site maintained by the Government Printing Office.

2. Reflecting the convention adopted by Congress, acts began to be referred to by their public law numbers. These numbers reflect both the number of the enacting Congress and the sequence in which the laws are enacted. For example, Public Law (P.L.) 57-244 means the 244th law passed by the 57th Congress. Hereafter, the public law numbers of health-related federal laws in this chronology are provided.

4

NATIONAL INSTITUTE OF BIOMEDICAL IMAGING AND BIOENGINEERING ESTABLISHMENT ACT

P.L. 106-580
106th Congress

To amend the Public Health Service Act to establish the National Institute of Biomedical Imaging and Bioengineering.

Be it enacted by the Senate and House of Representatives of the United States of America in Congress assembled,

SECTION 1. SHORT TITLE.

This Act may be cited as the "National Institute of Biomedical Imaging and Bioengineering Establishment Act."

SEC. 2. FINDINGS.

The Congress makes the following findings:

(1) Basic research in imaging, bioengineering, computer science, informatics, and related fields is critical to improving health care but is fundamentally different from the research in molecular biology on which the current national research institutes at the National Institutes of Health (NIH; www.nih.gov) are based. To ensure the development of new techniques and technologies for the 21st century, these disciplines therefore require an identity and research home at the NIH that is independent of the existing institute structure.

(2) Advances based on medical research promise new, more effective treatments for a wide variety of diseases, but the development of new, noninvasive imaging techniques for earlier detection and diagnosis of disease is essential to take full advantage of such new treatments and to promote the general improvement of health care.

(3) The development of advanced genetic and molecular imaging techniques is necessary to continue the current rapid pace of discovery in molecular biology.

(4) Advances in telemedicine, and teleradiology in particular, are increasingly important in the delivery of high-quality, reliable medical care to rural citizens and other underserved populations. To fulfill the promise of telemedicine and related technologies fully, a structure is needed at the NIH to support basic research focused on the acquisition, transmission, processing, and optimal display of images.

(5) A number of Federal departments and agencies support imaging and engineering research with potential medical applications, but a central coordinating body, preferably housed at the NIH, is needed to coordinate these disparate efforts and facilitate the transfer of technologies with medical applications.

(6) Several breakthrough imaging technologies, including magnetic resonance imaging (MRI) and computed tomography (CT), have been developed primarily abroad, in large part because of the absence of a home at the NIH for basic research in imaging and related fields. The establishment of a central focus for imaging and bioengineering research at the NIH would promote both scientific advance and United States economic development.

(7) At a time when a consensus exists to add significant resources to the NIH in coming years, it is appropriate to modernize the structure of the NIH to ensure that research dollars are expended more effectively and efficiently and that the fields of medical science that have contributed the most to the detection, diagnosis, and treatment of disease in recent years receive appropriate emphasis.

(8) The establishment of a National Institute of Biomedical Imaging and Bioengineering at the NIH would accelerate the development of new technologies with clinical and research applications, improve coordination and efficiency at the NIH and throughout the Federal Government, reduce duplication and waste, lay the foundation for a new medical information age, promote economic development, and provide a structure to train the young researchers who will make the pathbreaking discoveries of the next century.

SEC. 3. ESTABLISHMENT OF NATIONAL INSTITUTE OF BIOMEDICAL IMAGING AND BIOENGINEERING.

(a) In General.—Part C of Title IV of the Public Health Service Act (42 U.S.C. 285 et seq.) is amended by adding at the end the following subpart:

Subpart 18—National Institute of Biomedical Imaging and Bioengineering

PURPOSE OF THE INSTITUTE

Sec. 464z. (a) The general purpose of the National Institute of Biomedical Imaging and Bioengineering (in this section referred to as the "Institute") is the conduct and support of research, training, the dissemination of health information, and other programs with respect to biomedical imaging, biomedical engineering, and associated technologies and modalities with biomedical applications (in this section referred to as "biomedical imaging and bioengineering").

(b)(1) The Director of the Institute, with the advice of the Institute's advisory council, shall establish a National Biomedical Imaging and Bioengineering Program (in this section referred to as the "Program.")

(2) Activities under the Program shall include the following with respect to biomedical imaging and bioengineering:

(A) Research into the development of new techniques and devices.

(B) Related research in physics, engineering, mathematics, computer science, and other disciplines.

(C) Technology assessments and outcomes studies to evaluate the effectiveness of biologics, materials, processes, devices, procedures, and informatics.

(D) Research in screening for diseases and disorders.

(E) The advancement of existing imaging and bioengineering modalities, including imaging, biomaterials, and informatics.

(F) The development of target-specific agents to enhance images and to identify and delineate disease.

(G) The development of advanced engineering and imaging technologies and techniques for research from the molecular and genetic to the whole organ and body levels.

(H) The development of new techniques and devices for more effective interventional procedures (such as image-guided interventions).

(3)(A) With respect to the Program, the Director of the Institute shall prepare and transmit to the Secretary and the Director of NIH a plan to initiate, expand, intensify, and coordinate activities of the Institute with respect to biomedical imaging and bioengineering. The plan shall include such comments and recommendations as the Director of the Institute determines appropriate. The Director of the Institute shall periodically review and revise the plan and shall transmit any revisions of the plan to the Secretary and the Director of NIH.

(B) The plan under subparagraph (A) shall include the recommendations of the Director of the Institute with respect to the following:

(i) Where appropriate, the consolidation of programs of the National Institutes of Health for the express purpose of enhancing support of activities regarding basic biomedical imaging and bioengineering research.

(ii) The coordination of the activities of the Institute with related activities of the other agencies of the National Institutes of Health and with related activities of other Federal agencies.

(c) The establishment under section 406 of an advisory council for the Institute is subject to the following:

(1) The number of members appointed by the Secretary shall be 12.

(2) Of such members—

(A) six members shall be scientists, engineers, physicians, and other health professionals who represent disciplines in biomedical imaging and bioengineering and who are not officers or employees of the United States; and

(B) six members shall be scientists, engineers, physicians, and other health professionals who represent other disciplines and are knowledgeable about the applications of biomedical imaging and bioengineering in medicine, and who are not officers or employees of the United States.

(3) In addition to the ex officio members specified in section 406(b)(2), the ex officio members of the advisory council shall include the Director of the Centers for Disease Control and Prevention, the Director of the National Science Foundation, and the Director of the National Institute of Standards and Technology (or the designees of such officers).

(d)(1) Subject to paragraph (2), for the purpose of carrying out this section:

(A) For fiscal year 2001, there is authorized to be appropriated an amount equal to the amount obligated by the National Institutes of Health during fiscal year 2000 for biomedical imaging and bioengineering, except that such amount shall be adjusted to offset any inflation occurring after October 1, 1999.

(B) For each of the fiscal years 2002 and 2003, there is authorized to be appropriated an amount equal to the amount appropriated under subparagraph (A) for fiscal year 2001, except that such amount shall be adjusted for the fiscal year involved to offset any inflation occurring after October 1, 2000.

(2) The authorization of appropriations for a fiscal year under paragraph (1) is hereby reduced by the amount of any appropriation made for such year for the conduct or support by any other national research institute of any program with respect to biomedical imaging and bioengineering.

(b) USE OF EXISTING RESOURCES.—In providing for the establishment of the National Institute of Biomedical Imaging and Bioengineering pursuant to the amendment made by subsection (a), the Director of the National Institutes of Health (referred to in this subsection as "NIH")—

(1) may transfer to the National Institute of Biomedical Imaging and Bioengineering such personnel of NIH as the Director determines to be appropriate;

(2) may, for quarters for such Institute, utilize such facilities of NIH as the Director determines to be appropriate; and

(3) may obtain administrative support for the Institute from the other agencies of NIH, including the other national research institutes.

(c) CONSTRUCTION OF FACILITIES.—None of the provisions of this Act or the amendments made by the Act may be construed as authorizing the construction of facilities, or the acquisition of land, for purposes of the establishment or operation of the National Institute of Biomedical Imaging and Bioengineering.

(d) DATE CERTAIN FOR ESTABLISHMENT OF ADVISORY COUNCIL.—Not later than 90 days after the effective date of this Act under section 4, the Secretary of Health and Human Services shall complete the establishment of an advisory council for the National Institute of Biomedical Imaging and Bioengineering in accordance with section 406 of the Public Health Service Act and in accordance with section 464z of such Act (as added by subsection (a) of this section).

(e) CONFORMING AMENDMENT.—Section 401(b)(1) of the Public Health Service Act (42 U.S.C. 281(b)(1)) is amended by adding at the end the following subparagraph:

(R) The National Institute of Biomedical Imaging and Bioengineering.

SEC. 4. EFFECTIVE DATE.

This Act takes effect October 1, 2000, or upon the date of the enactment of this Act, whichever occurs later.

Approved December 29, 2000.

SOURCE: U.S. Congress. House. *National Institute of Biomedical Imaging and Bioengineering Establishment Act.* H.R. 1795. 106th Cong. (Introduced 5/13/99.) Library of Congress THOMAS. [Online Public Law; retrieved 4/6/09.] frwebgate.access.gpo.gov/cgi-bin/getdoc.cgi?dbname=106_cong_public_laws&docid=f:publ580.106.pdf.

SUMMARIES OF A PROPOSED AND A FINAL RULE

A Proposed Rule

DEPARTMENT OF HEALTH AND HUMAN SERVICES

Centers for Medicare & Medicaid Services

42 CFR Parts 403, 411, 417, and 423

[CMS-4068-P]

RIN 0938-AN08

Medicare Program; Medicare Prescription Drug Benefit

AGENCY: Centers for Medicare & Medicaid Services (CMS), HHS.

ACTION: Proposed rule.

SUMMARY: This proposed rule would implement the new Medicare Prescription Drug Benefit. This new voluntary prescription drug benefit program was enacted into law on December 8, 2003, in section 101 of the Medicare Prescription Drug, Improvement, and Modernization Act of 2003 (MMA). The addition of a prescription drug benefit to Medicare represents a landmark change to the Medicare program that will significantly improve the healthcare coverage available to millions of Medicare beneficiaries. The MMA specifies that the prescription drug benefit program will become available to beneficiaries beginning on January 1, 2006. Please see the executive summary in the SUPPLEMENTARY INFORMATION section for further synopsis of this rule.

DATES: To be assured consideration, comments must be received at one of the addresses provided below, no later than 5:00 p.m. on October 4, 2004.

ADDRESSES: In commenting, please refer to file code CMS-4068-P. Because of staff and resource limitations, we cannot accept comments by facsimile (FAX) transmission.

You may submit comments in one of three ways (no duplicates, please):

1. Electronically. You may submit electronic comments to
   http://www.cms.hhs.gov/regulations/ecomments (attachments should
   be in Microsoft Word, WordPerfect, or Excel; however, we prefer
   Microsoft Word).
2. By mail. You may mail written comments (one original and two copies)
   to the following address only: Centers for Medicare & Medicaid
   Services, Department of Health and Human Services, Attention: CMS-
   4068-P, P.O. Box 8014, Baltimore, MD 21244-8014.
      Please allow sufficient time for mailed comments to be received
   before the close of the comment period.
3. By hand or courier. If you prefer, you may deliver (by hand or courier)
   your written comments (one original and two copies) before the close
   of the comment period to one of the following addresses. If you intend
   to deliver your comments to the Baltimore address, please call
   telephone number (410) 786-7197 in advance to schedule your arrival
   with one of our staff members.

(Because access to the interior of the HHH Building is not readily
available to persons without Federal Government identification, commenters
are encouraged to leave their comments in the CMS drop slots located in the
main lobby of the building. A stamp-in clock is available for persons wishing
to retain a proof of filing by stamping in and retaining an extra copy of the
comments being filed.)

Comments mailed to the addresses indicated as appropriate for hand or
courier delivery may be delayed and received after the comment period.

Submission of comments on paperwork requirements. You may submit
comments on this document's paperwork requirements by mailing your comments to the addresses provided at the end of the "Collection of Information
Requirements" section in this document.

For information on viewing public comments, see the beginning of the
SUPPLEMENTARY INFORMATION section.

FOR FURTHER INFORMATION CONTACT: Lynn Orlosky (410) 786-9064
or Randy Brauer (410)786-1618 (for issues related to eligibility, elections,
enrollment, including auto-enrollment of dual eligible beneficiaries, and creditable coverage).

Wendy Burger (410) 786-1566 (for issues related to marketing and
user fees).

Vanessa Duran-Scirri (214) 767-6435 (for issues related to benefits
and beneficiary protections, including Part D benefit packages, Part D covered drugs, coordination of benefits in claims processing and tracking of true-

out-of-pocket costs, pharmacy network access standards, plan information dissemination requirements, and privacy of records).

Craig Miner, RPh. (410) 786-1889 or Tony Hausner (410) 786-1093 (for issues of pharmacy benefit cost and utilization management, formulary development, quality assurance, medication therapy management, and electronic prescribing).

Mark Newsom (410) 786-3198 (for issues of submission, review, negotiation, and approval of risk and limited risk bids for PDPs [prescription drug plans] and MA-PD [Medicare Advantage prescription drug] plans; the calculation of the national average bid amount; determination and collection of enrollee premiums; calculation and payment of direct and reinsurance subsidies and risk-sharing; and retroactive adjustments and reconciliations.)

Jim Owens (410) 786-1582 (for issues of licensing and waiver of licensure, the assumption of financial risk for unsubsidized coverage, and solvency requirements for unlicensed sponsors or sponsors who are not licensed in all States in the region in which it wants to offer a PDP.)

Terese Klitenic (410) 786-5942 (for issues of coordination of Part D plans with providers of other prescription drug coverage including Medicare Advantage plans, state pharmaceutical assistance programs (SPAPs), Medicaid, and other retiree prescription drug plans; also for issues related to eligibility for and payment of subsidies for assistance with premium and cost-sharing amounts for Part D eligible individuals with lower income and resources; for rules for states on eligibility determinations for low-income subsidies and general state payment provisions including the phased-down state contribution to drug benefit costs assumed by Medicare).

Frank Szeflinski (303) 844-7119 (for issues related to conditions necessary to contract with Medicare as a PDP sponsor, as well as contract requirements, intermediate sanctions, termination procedures and change of ownership requirements; employer group waivers and options; also for issues related to cost-based HMOs and CMPs offering Part D coverage.)

John Scott (410) 786-3636 (for issues related to the procedures PDP sponsors must follow with regard to grievances, coverage determinations, and appeals.)

Tracey McCutcheon (410) 786-6715 (for issues related to solicitation, review and approval of fallback prescription drug plan proposals; fallback contract requirements; and enrollee premiums and plan payments specific to fallback plans.)

Jim Mayhew (410) 786-9244 (for issues related to the alternative retiree drug subsidy.)

Joanne Sinsheimer (410) 786-4620 (for issues related to physician self-referral prohibitions.)

Brenda Hudson (410) 786-4085 (for issues related to PACE organizations offering Part D coverage.)

Julie Walton (410) 786-4622 or Kathryn McCann (410) 786-7623 (for issues related to provisions on Medicare supplemental (Medigap) policies.)

For general questions: Please call (410) 786-1296.

SUPPLEMENTARY INFORMATION:

EXECUTIVE SUMMARY. Generally, coverage for the prescription drug benefit will be provided under private prescription drug plans (PDPs), which will offer only prescription drug coverage, or through Medicare Advantage prescription drug plans (MA-PDs), which will offer prescription drug coverage that is integrated with the healthcare coverage they provide to Medicare beneficiaries under Part C of Medicare. PDPs must offer a basic prescription drug benefit. MA-PDs must offer either a basic benefit or broader coverage for no additional cost. If this required level of coverage is offered, the PDP or MA-PD plan may also offer supplemental benefits through enhanced alternative coverage for an additional premium. All organizations offering drug plans will have flexibility in the design of the prescription drug benefit. Consistent with the MMA, this proposed rule provides for subsidy payments to sponsors of qualified retiree prescription drug plans.

We intend to implement the drug benefit to permit and encourage a range of options for Medicare beneficiaries to augment the standard Medicare coverage for drug costs above the initial coverage limit ($2250 in 2006) and below the annual out-of-pocket threshold ($5100 in 2006). In addition to the coverage established by the statute for low-income beneficiaries, we seek comments on the best way to support options for expanding beneficiaries' drug coverage. Potential options include facilitating coverage through employer plans, MA-PD plans and/or high-option PDPs, as well as through charity organizations and State pharmaceutical assistance programs. We specifically seek comments on ways to maximize the continued use of non-Medicare resources (private contributions, employer/union contributions, state contributions, health plan contributions, and other sources) that currently provide at least partial coverage for three-fourths of Medicare beneficiaries. See sections II.C, II.J, and II.P, and II R of this preamble for further details on these issues. We are also considering establishing a CMS demonstration to evaluate possible ways of achieving such extended coverage, and we welcome all suggestions in this regard.

Throughout the preamble, we identify options and alternatives to the provisions we propose. We strongly encourage comments and ideas on our approach and on alternatives to help us design the Medicare Prescription Drug Benefit Program to operate as effectively and efficiently as possible in meeting the needs of Medicare beneficiaries.

Although this proposed rule specifies most of the requirements for implementing the new prescription drug program, readers should note that we are also issuing a closely related proposed rule that concerns Medicare Advantage plans, which will usually combine medical and prescription drug coverage. In addition, although this proposed rule specifies requirements related to PDP regions it does not designate those regions. Regional boundary decisions will be made through a separate process. Additional non-regulatory guidance on this and other topics will also be forthcoming.

We have considered and, in some places, have identified how this proposed rule intersects with other Federal laws, such as the Health Insurance Portability and Accountability Act (HIPAA) of 1996 Certification of Creditable Coverage and the HIPAA Privacy Rule. We are interested in learning how this proposed rule may interact with other legal obligations to which the PDP sponsors and MA-PD plans may be subject and intend to make appropriate changes in the final rule to address such issues.

SUBMITTING COMMENTS: We welcome comments from the public on all issues set forth in this rule to assist us in fully considering issues and developing policies. Comments will be most useful if they are organized by the section of the proposed rule to which they apply. You can assist us by referencing the file code [CMS-4068-P] and the specific "issue identifier" that precedes the section on which you choose to comment.

INSPECTION OF PUBLIC COMMENTS: All comments received before the close of the comment period are available for viewing by the public, including any personally identifiable or confidential business information that is included in a comment. After the close of the comment period, CMS posts all electronic comments received before the close of the comment period on its public website. Comments received timely will be available for public inspection as they are received, generally beginning approximately 3 weeks after publication of a document, at the headquarters of the Centers for Medicare & Medicaid Services, 7500 Security Boulevard, Baltimore, Maryland 21244, Monday through Friday of each week from 8:30 a.m. to 4:00 p.m. To schedule an appointment to view public comments, phone (410) 786-7197.

COPIES: To order copies of the Federal Register containing this document, send your request to: New Orders, Superintendent of Documents, P.O. Box 371954, Pittsburgh, PA 15250-7954. Specify the date of the issue requested and enclose a check or money order payable to the Superintendent of

Documents, or enclose your Visa or Master Card number and expiration date. Credit card orders can also be placed by calling the order desk at (202) 512-1800 (or toll-free at 1-888-293-6498) or by faxing to (202) 512-2250. The cost for each copy is $10. As an alternative, you can view and photocopy the Federal Register document at most libraries designated as Federal Depository Libraries and at many other public and academic libraries throughout the country that receive the Federal Register. This Federal Register document is also available from the Federal Register online database through GPO Access, a service of the U.S. Government Printing Office. The website address is: www.access.gpo.gov/fr/index.html.

SOURCE: Reprinted from *Federal Register*. 2004. "Proposed Rules." *Federal Register* 69 (148): 46631-80.

A Final Rule

DEPARTMENT OF HEALTH AND HUMAN SERVICES

Centers for Medicare & Medicaid Services

42 CFR Parts 400, 403, 411, 417, and 423

[CMS-4068-F]

RIN 0938-AN08

Medicare Program; Medicare Prescription Drug Benefit

AGENCY: Centers for Medicare & Medicaid Services (CMS), HHS.

ACTION: Final rule.

SUMMARY: This final rule implements the provisions of the Social Security Act (the Act) establishing and regulating the Medicare Prescription Drug Benefit. The new voluntary prescription drug benefit program was enacted into law on December 8, 2003 in section 101 of Title I of the Medicare Prescription Drug, Improvement, and Modernization Act of 2003 (MMA; Pub. L. 108-173). Although this final rule specifies most of the requirements for implementing the new prescription drug program, readers should note that we are also issuing a closely related rule that concerns Medicare Advantage organizations, which, if they offer coordinated care plans, must offer at least one plan that combines medical coverage under Parts A and B with prescription drug coverage. Readers should also note that separate CMS guidance on many operational details appears or will soon appear on the CMS website, such as materials on formulary review criteria, risk plan and fallback plan solicitations, bid instructions, solvency standards and pricing tools, and plan benefit packages.

The addition of a prescription drug benefit to Medicare represents a landmark change to the Medicare program that will significantly improve the healthcare coverage available to millions of Medicare beneficiaries. The MMA specifies that the prescription drug benefit program will become available to beneficiaries beginning on January 1, 2006.

Generally, coverage for the prescription drug benefit will be provided under private prescription drug plans (PDPs), which will offer only prescription drug coverage, or through Medicare Advantage prescription drug plans (MA-PDs), which will offer prescription drug coverage that is integrated with the healthcare coverage they provide to Medicare beneficiaries under Part C of Medicare. PDPs must offer a basic prescription drug benefit. MA-PDs must offer either a basic benefit or broader coverage for no additional cost. If this required level of coverage is offered, MA-PDs or PDPs, but not fall-back PDPs, may also offer supplemental benefits through enhanced alternative coverage for an additional premium. All organizations offering drug plans will have flexibility in the design of the prescription drug benefit. Consistent with the MMA, this final rule also provides for subsidy payments to sponsors of qualified retiree prescription drug plans to encourage retention of employer-sponsored benefits.

We are implementing the drug benefit in a way that permits and encourages a range of options for Medicare beneficiaries to augment the standard Medicare coverage. These options include facilitating additional coverage through employer plans, MA-PD plans and high-option PDPs, and through charity organizations and State pharmaceutical assistance programs. See sections II.C, II.J, and II.P, and II.R of this preamble for further details on these issues.

The proposed rule identified options and alternatives to the provisions we proposed and we strongly encouraged comments and ideas on our approach and on alternatives to help us design the Medicare Prescription Drug Benefit Program to operate as effectively and efficiently as possible in meeting the needs of Medicare beneficiaries.

DATES: These regulations are effective on March 22, 2005.

FOR FURTHER INFORMATION CONTACT: *[This Final Rule contains a long list of contacts similar to the one shown above for the Proposed Rule; the list is omitted here.]*

Table of Contents [Condensed]

I. Background
    A. Medicare Prescription Drug, Improvement, and Modernization Act of 2003

B. Codification of Regulations

C. Organizational Overview of Part 423

II. Discussion of the Provisions of the Final Rule

A. General Provisions

B. Eligibility and Enrollment

C. Voluntary Prescription Benefits and Beneficiary Protections

D. Cost Control and Quality Improvement Requirements for Part D Plans

E. RESERVED

F. Submission of Bids and Monthly Beneficiary Premiums: Plan Approval

G. Payments to Part D Plan Sponsors for Qualified Prescription Drug Coverage

H. RESERVED

I. Organization Compliance with State Law and Preemption by Federal Law

J. Coordination Under Part D Plans with Other Prescription Drug Coverage

K. Application Procedures and Contracts with PDP Sponsors

L. Effect of Change of Ownership or Leasing of Facilities During the Term of Contract

M. Grievances, Coverage Determinations, and Appeals

N. Medicare Contract Determinations and Appeals

O. Intermediate Sanctions

P. Premiums and Cost-Sharing Subsidies for Low-Income Individuals

Q. Guaranteeing Access to a Choice of Coverage (Fallback Prescription Drug Plans)

R. Payments to Sponsors of Retiree Prescription Drug Plans

S. Special Rules for States-Eligibility Determinations for Low-Income Subsidies, and General Payment Provisions

T. Part D Provisions Affecting Physician Self-Referral, Cost-Based HMO, PACE, and Medigap Requirements

III. Provisions of the Final Rule

IV. Collection of Information Requirements

V. Regulatory Impact Analysis

SOURCE: Reprinted from *Federal Register.* 2005. "Rules and Regulations." *Federal Register* 70 (18): 4193-242.

PRESS RELEASE: FDA TAKES ACTION AGAINST KV PHARMACEUTICAL COMPANY

Company Making, Marketing, and Distributing Adulterated and Unapproved Drugs

March 2, 2009

The FDA announced a Consent Decree of permanent injunction filed March 2, 2009, enjoining KV Pharmaceutical Company, its subsidiaries ETHEX Corporation and Ther-Rx Corporation, and its principal officers from making and distributing adulterated and unapproved drugs. The injunction against KV and the other defendants, once entered by the court, will prevent them from manufacturing and shipping drugs until the firm obtains FDA approval. It will remain in place until the defendants sustain continuous compliance with FDA's current Good Manufacturing Practice (cGMP) and new drug approval requirements for six years.

The Consent Decree also enjoins KV's officers David A. Van Vliet, president and chief executive officer; Rita E. Bleser, president of the pharmaceutical division; Jay S. Sawardeker, vice president of corporate quality, and Marc S. Hermelin, former chief executive officer and a member of KV's Board of Directors, from manufacturing and distributing any drug at or from KV's facilities until the company's procedures and products are brought into compliance with the law.

KV Pharmaceutical manufactures, processes, packages, labels, holds, and distributes drugs from various locations in St. Louis, Mo., and the surrounding area. FDA inspected KV between December 2008 and February 2009, and found that the company had significant cGMP violations and continued to manufacture unapproved drugs. As a result of those inspections, which led to this action, KV recalled all products manufactured and distributed from its facilities.

"The FDA requires companies to manufacture drugs in accordance with the current good manufacturing practice standards and to comply with FDA approval requirements," said Janet Woodcock, MD, director of FDA's Center for Drug Evaluation and Research (CDER). "Consumers need to be confident that drugs meet our manufacturing requirements for identity, strength, purity, and quality, and have been evaluated by the FDA for safety and efficacy."

Under the terms of the Consent Decree, the defendants cannot resume manufacturing and distributing drugs until both an independent expert and FDA officials conduct inspections of their facilities and certify that they are in compliance with the Federal Food, Drug, and Cosmetic Act (the Act), its implementing regulations, and the decree. The Consent Decree also requires the defendants to destroy all drugs they recalled between May 2008 and Feb. 3, 2009. Those drugs are currently in their possession.

If the defendants fail to comply with any provision of the Consent Decree, the Act, or FDA regulations, FDA may order the firm to again stop manufacturing and distributing drugs, recall the products, or take other corrective actions.

"The FDA will carefully monitor the provisions of this injunction against the KV Pharmaceutical Company to ensure compliance," said Michael Chappell, the acting associate commissioner of FDA's Office of Regulatory Affairs. "Companies should know that FDA will investigate and take action against other marketers of unapproved drugs."

The Consent Decree subjects the defendants to liquidated damages of $15,000 per day if they fail to comply with any of the provisions of the decree, and the payment of an additional $15,000 for each violation, up to $5 million per year.

SOURCE: Reprinted from U.S. Food and Drug Administration. 2009. "FDA Takes Action Against KV Pharmaceutical Company." Press Release, March 2. [Online material; retrieved 3/30/09.] www.fda.gov/NewsEvents/Newsroom/PressAnnouncements/ucm149535.htm..

SMOKEFREE LAWS

7

Americans for Nonsmokers' Rights Foundation (www.no-smoke.org) tracks the numbers of local municipalities and states or commonwealths that have laws in effect that restrict where smoking is permitted. A state, commonwealth, or local municipality can pass a Workplace*, Restaurant**, or Bar law, or any combination of the three. As of January 4, 2009 the numbers of such laws were as follows.

Local

- A total of 2,982 municipalities in the United States have local laws in effect that restrict where smoking is allowed.
- A total of 774 of these 2,982 municipalities have a 100 percent smokefree provision in effect at the local level—either in workplaces, and/or restaurants, and/or bars.
- There are 593 municipalities with a local law in effect that requires 100 percent smokefree workplaces.
- There are 594 municipalities with a local law in effect that requires 100 percent smokefree restaurants.
- There are 464 municipalities with a local law in effect that requires 100 percent smokefree bars.
- There are 414 municipalities with a local law in effect that requires both workplaces and restaurants to be 100 percent smokefree.
- There are 460 municipalities with a local law in effect that requires both restaurants and bars to be 100 percent smokefree.
- There are 331 municipalities with a local law in effect that requires workplaces, restaurants, and bars to be 100 percent smokefree.
- There are 1,575 municipalities with a local law in effect that restricts smoking in one or more outdoor areas, including 826 that restrict smoking near entrances, windows, and ventilation systems of enclosed places; 981 that restrict smoking in public outdoor places such as parks

---

*Includes both public and private nonhospitality workplaces, including, but not limited to, offices, factories, and warehouses.

**Includes any attached bar in the restaurant.

and beaches; and 454 that restrict smoking in outdoor stadiums and other sports and entertainment venues.

Note: Since some of the above have 10 percent smokefree coverage in more than one category, *the numbers are not mutually exclusive.*

State and Local

- Across the United States, 16,505 municipalities are covered by a 100 percent smokefree provision in workplaces, and/or restaurants, and/or bars, by either a state, commonwealth, or local law, representing 70.2 percent of the U.S. population.
- 37 states and the District of Columbia have local laws in effect that require 100 percent smokefree workplaces and/or restaurants and/or bars.

State and Commonwealth

- A total of 30 states, along with Puerto Rico and the District of Columbia, have laws in effect that require 100 percent smokefree workplaces and/or restaurants and/or bars:
  - ◆ Arizona: workplaces, restaurants, and bars
  - ◆ California: restaurants and bars
  - ◆ Colorado: restaurants and bars
  - ◆ Connecticut: restaurants and bars
  - ◆ Delaware: workplaces, restaurants, and bars
  - ◆ District of Columbia: workplaces, restaurants, and bars
  - ◆ Florida: workplaces and restaurants
  - ◆ Hawaii: workplaces, restaurants, and bars
  - ◆ Idaho: restaurants
  - ◆ Illinois: workplaces, restaurants, and bars
  - ◆ Iowa: workplaces, restaurants, and bars
  - ◆ Louisiana: workplaces and restaurants
  - ◆ Maine: restaurants and bars
  - ◆ Maryland: workplaces, restaurants, and bars
  - ◆ Massachusetts: workplaces, restaurants, and bars
  - ◆ Minnesota: workplaces, restaurants and bars
  - ◆ Montana: workplaces and restaurants
  - ◆ Nevada: workplaces and restaurants
  - ◆ New Hampshire: restaurants and bars
  - ◆ New Jersey: workplaces, restaurants, and bars

- ♦ New Mexico: restaurants and bars
- ♦ New York: workplaces, restaurants, and bars
- ♦ North Dakota: workplaces
- ♦ Ohio: workplaces, restaurants, and bars
- ♦ Oregon: workplaces, restaurants, and bars
- ♦ Pennsylvania: workplaces
- ♦ Puerto Rico: workplaces, restaurants, and bars
- ♦ Rhode Island: workplaces, restaurants, and bars
- ♦ South Dakota: workplaces
- ♦ Utah: workplaces, restaurants, and bars
- ♦ Vermont: restaurants and bars
- ♦ Washington: workplaces, restaurants, and bars
- A total of 15 states, along with Puerto Rico and Washington, DC, have a state law *in effect* that requires workplaces, restaurants, and bars to be 100 percent smokefree.
- A total of 27 states, along with Puerto Rico and Washington, DC, have *enacted* some kind of 100 percent smokefree gaming law.

Note: The following state laws have been passed by legislature and signed by governor but are not yet in effect:

- Montana enacted a 100 percent smokefree bar law, which is scheduled to go into effect October 1, 2009.
- Nebraska enacted a 100 percent smokefree workplace, restaurant, and bar law, which is scheduled to go into effect June 1, 2009.

SOURCE: Reprinted with permission from American Nonsmokers' Rights Foundation. 2009. "Overview List—How Many Smokefree Laws?" [Online information; retrieved 2/2/09.] Current list can be seen at www.no-smoke.org/pdf/mediaordlist.pdf.

CONGRESSIONAL BUDGET OFFICE

The Congressional Budget Office (CBO; www.cbo.gov) produces analyses to inform Congressional policymaking. As a nonpartisan congressional agency, CBO does not make recommendations about policy. It does, however, provide analyses that can be useful to policymakers in their deliberations.

Rising healthcare costs and their consequences for Medicare and Medicaid constitute the nation's central fiscal challenge. Without changes in federal law, the government's spending on those two programs is on a path that cannot be sustained.

Over the past 30 years, total national spending on healthcare has more than doubled as a share of gross domestic product (GDP). According to CBO's latest projections in its Long-Term Outlook for Health Care Spending, that share will double again by 2035, claiming more than 30 percent of GDP. Thereafter, healthcare costs continue to account for a steadily growing share of GDP, reaching more than 40 percent by 2060 and almost 50 percent by 2082. Federal spending on Medicare and Medicaid, which accounts for 4 percent of GDP today, is projected to rise to 9 percent by 2035 and 19 percent by 2082 under current law.

Although the aging of the population is frequently cited as the major factor contributing to the large projected increase in federal spending on Medicare and Medicaid, it accounts for only a modest fraction of the growth that CBO projects. The main factor is excess cost growth—or the extent to which the increase in healthcare spending exceeds the growth of the economy. The gains from higher spending are not clear, however: Substantial evidence exists that more expensive care does not always mean higher-quality care. Consequently, embedded in the country's fiscal challenge are opportunities to reduce costs without impairing health outcomes overall.

Policymakers and the public need more analysis of the options for capturing those opportunities. CBO is therefore substantially augmenting its capabilities and work on healthcare issues.

SOURCE: Reprinted from Congressional Budget Office. 2009. *From the Director* [Online statement; retrieved 3/22/09.] www.cbo.gov/publications/collections/health.cfm.

MEDICARE REVISITED—AGAIN AND AGAIN

This chronological list contains some of the key legislative changes that have been made in the Medicare program since its enactment. The list reflects how frequently and substantively the program has been modified.

- **1965.** Medicare was enacted as Title XVIII of the Social Security Act, extending health coverage to almost all Americans aged 65 or older. Medicare was implemented and more than 19 million individuals enrolled on July 1, 1966.

- **1972.** Medicare eligibility was extended to individuals under age 65 with long-term disabilities and to individuals with end-stage renal disease (ESRD). Medicare was given the authority to conduct demonstration programs.

- **1977.** The Health Care Financing Administration (HCFA) was established to administer the Medicare program. On July 1, 2001, HCFA became the Centers for Medicare & Medicaid Services (CMS).

- **1980.** Coverage of Medicare home health services was broadened. Medicare supplemental insurance, also called "Medigap," was brought under Federal oversight.

- **1982.** The Tax Equity and Fiscal Responsibility Act made it easier and more attractive for health maintenance organizations to contract with the Medicare program. In addition, the Act expanded CMS's quality oversight efforts through Peer Review Organizations (PROs).

- **1983.** An inpatient acute hospital prospective payment system (PPS) for the Medicare program, based on patients' diagnoses, was adopted to replace cost-based payments.

- **1985.** The Emergency Medical Treatment and Labor Act (EMTALA) required hospitals participating in Medicare that operated active emergency rooms to provide appropriate medical screenings and stabilizing treatments.

- **1988.** The Medicare Catastrophic Coverage Act, which included the most significant changes since enactment of the Medicare program, improved hospital and skilled nursing facility benefits for beneficiaries, covered mammography, and included an outpatient prescription drug benefit (the Medicare Catastrophic Coverage Act) and a cap on patient liability.

The Qualified Medicare Beneficiary (QMB) program was established to pay Medicare premiums and cost-sharing charges for beneficiaries with incomes and resources below established thresholds.

- **1989.** The Medicare Catastrophic Coverage Act of 1988 was repealed after higher-income elderly protested new premiums. A new Medicare fee schedule for physician and other professional services, a resource-based relative value scale, replaced charge-based payments. Limits were placed on physician balance billing above the new fee schedule. Physicians were prohibited from referring Medicare patients to clinical laboratories in which the physicians, or physicians' family members, have a financial interest.

- **1990.** Specified Low-Income Medicare Beneficiary (SLMB) eligibility group was established for Medicaid programs to pay Medicare premiums for beneficiaries with incomes at least 100 percent but not more than 120 percent of the FPL and limited financial resources. Additional federal standards for Medicare supplemental insurance were enacted.

- **1996.** The Health Insurance Portability and Accountability Act of 1996 (HIPAA) had implications for the Medicare program. The Act created the Medicare Integrity Program, which dedicated funding to program integrity activities and allowed CMS to competitively contract for program integrity work. HIPAA also created national administrative simplification standards for electronic healthcare transactions that applied to Medicare.

- **1997.** The Balanced Budget Act of 1997 (BBA) changed Medicare in a number of ways, including the following:

  - It established an array of new Medicare managed care and other private health plan choices for beneficiaries, offered through a coordinated open enrollment process.

  - It expanded education and information to help beneficiaries make informed choices about their healthcare.

  - It required CMS to develop and implement five new prospective payment systems for Medicare services (for inpatient rehabilitation hospital or unit services, skilled nursing facility services, home health services, hospital outpatient department services, and outpatient rehabilitation services).

- ◆ It slowed the rate of growth in Medicare spending and extended the life of the trust fund for 10 years.

- ◆ It provided a broad range of beneficiary protections.

- ◆ It expanded preventive benefits.

- ◆ It called for testing other innovative approaches to payment and service delivery through research and demonstrations.

- **1998.** The Internet site www.medicare.gov was launched to provide updated information about Medicare.

- **1999.** The toll-free number 1-800-MEDICARE (1-800-633-4227) became available nationwide. The first annual *Medicare & You* handbook was mailed to all Medicare beneficiary households.

    The Ticket to Work and Work Incentives Improvements Act of 1999 (TWWIIA) expanded the availability of Medicare and Medicaid for certain disabled beneficiaries who return to work. The Balanced Budget Refinement Act of 1999 (BBRA) increased payments for some Medicare providers.

- **2000.** The Benefits Improvement and Protection Act (BIPA) further increased Medicare payments to providers and managed healthcare organizations, reduced certain Medicare beneficiary copayments, and improved Medicare's coverage of preventive services.

- **2003.** The Medicare Prescription Drug, Improvement, and Modernization Act (MMA) made the most significant changes to Medicare since the program began. MMA created a prescription drug discount card until 2006, allowed for competition among health plans to foster innovation and flexibility in coverage, covered new preventive benefits, and made numerous other changes. In 2006, the new voluntary Part D outpatient prescription drug benefit will be available to beneficiaries from private drug plans as well as Medicare Advantage plans. Employers who provide retiree drug coverage comparable to Medicare's will be eligible for a federal subsidy. Medicare will consider beneficiary income for the first time: beneficiaries with incomes less than 150 percent of the federal poverty limit will be eligible for subsidies for the new Part D prescription drug program; beneficiaries with higher incomes will pay a greater share of the Part B premium starting in 2007.

- **2004.** The Medicare-Approved Drug Discount Card Program began. It was accompanied by the transitional assistance program which provided annual credits of $600 to low-income Medicare beneficiaries who did not have prescription drug coverage in 2004–2005.

- **2005.** The "Welcome to Medicare" physical examination began to be covered. Several preventive services, including cardiovascular screening blood tests and diabetes screening tests, began to be covered for Medicare beneficiaries. Beginning on November 15, 2005, Medicare conducted the first open enrollment period for the new Part D prescription drug benefit. This permitted beneficiaries to enroll in a Medicare Prescription Drug Plan (PDP) or a Medicare Advantage Prescription Drug Plan (MAPD).

- **2006.** The Medicare Drug Benefit, which was established by the Medicare Prescription Drug, Improvement, and Modernization Act of 2003, took effect on January 1. By June 11, 2006, 22.5 million Medicare beneficiaries were enrolled in Part D plans.

- **2007.** Higher-income Medicare beneficiaries (above $80,000 for individuals or $160,000 for couples) paid higher monthly Part B premiums. The payments ranged from $105.80 to $161.40 per month and were based on income.

  The Medicare, Medicaid, and SCHIP Extension Act of 2007 prevented a 10.1 percent reduction in Medicare payments to physicians that was scheduled to take effect in 2008 and, instead, gave physicians a 0.5 increase through June 30, 2008.

- **2008.** The Medicare Improvements for Patients and Providers Act of 2008 (MIPPA) extended the planned reduction in Medicare payments to physicians through the end of 2008 and increased payment of their fees for all of 2009 by 1.1 percent. Benefit improvements for Medicare beneficiaries included reduced coinsurance payments for mental health visits and elimination of the deductibles for "Welcome to Medicare" physical examinations.

- **2009.** Although the American Recovery and Reinvestment Act of 2009, which was enacted in response to the global financial crisis that emerged in 2008, was a massive and far-reaching economic stimulus package ($787 billion), a significant amount of the resources (about $150 billion in new funds) were directed to healthcare. Of this, Medicare received a new allocation of $338 million for payments to teaching hospitals, hospice programs, and long-term care hospitals.

SOURCES: Adapted from U.S. Department of Health and Human Services. 2004. "Key Milestones in CMS Programs." [Online information; retrieved 4/10/09.] www.cms.hhs.gov/History/downloads/CMSProgramKeyMilestones.pdf.
Adapted from Henry J. Kaiser Family Foundation. 2009. "Medicare: A Timeline of Key Developments." [Online information; retrieved 4/10/09.] www.kff.org/medicare/medicaretimeline.cfm.

10

LAWS IMPLEMENTED BY EPA

The mission of the Environmental Protection Agency (EPA; www.epa.gov) is to protect human health and the environment. Established in 1970, EPA develops and enforces regulations that implement environmental laws enacted by Congress. EPA's FY 2009 Annual Performance Plan and Budget Overview includes a budget of $7.1 billion and 17,217 employees. The major pieces of legislation that EPA implements or partially implements include the following.

Atomic Energy Act (AEA; 1946)—AEA established the Atomic Energy Commission to promote the use of atomic energy for peaceful purposes to the maximum extent consistent with the common defense and security and with the health and safety of the public.

National Environmental Policy Act (NEPA; 1969)—NEPA is the basic national charter for protection of the environment. It establishes policy, sets goals, and provides means for carrying out the policy. NEPA is intended to ensure that all branches of government give proper consideration to the environment prior to undertaking any major federal action that significantly affects the environment.

Clean Air Act (CAA; 1970)—CAA is the comprehensive federal law that regulates air emissions from area, stationary, and mobile sources. This law authorizes EPA to establish national ambient air quality standards (NAAQS) to protect public health and the environment.

Clean Water Act (CWA; 1977)—Growing public awareness of and concern for controlling water pollution led to enactment of the Federal Water Pollution Control Act Amendments of 1972. As amended in 1977, this law became commonly known as the Clean Water Act. CWA established the basic structure for regulating discharges of pollutants into the waters of the United States. It gave EPA the authority to implement pollution control programs such as setting wastewater standards for industry.

Comprehensive Environmental Response, Compensation, and Liability Act (CERCLA or Superfund; 1980)—CERCLA created a tax on the chemical and petroleum industries and provided broad federal authority to respond directly to releases or threatened releases of hazardous substances that may endanger public health or the environment. Over five years, $1.6 billion was collected, and the tax went to a trust fund for cleaning up abandoned or uncontrolled hazardous waste sites. CERCLA established prohibitions and requirements concerning closed and abandoned hazardous waste sites, provided for liability of persons responsible for releases of hazardous waste at these sites, and established a trust fund to provide for cleanup when no responsible party could be identified.

Emergency Planning and Community Right-to-Know Act (EPCRA; 1986)—EPCRA was enacted by Congress as the national legislation on community safety. This law was designated to help local communities protect public health, safety, and the environment from chemical hazards. To implement EPCRA, Congress required each state to appoint a state emergency response commission (SERC). The SERCs were required to divide their states into emergency planning districts and to name a local emergency planning committee (LEPC) for each district.

Energy Policy Act (EPA; 2005)—EPA addresses energy production in the United States, including: (1) energy efficiency; (2) renewable energy; (3) oil and gas; (4) coal; (5) Tribal energy; (6) nuclear matters and security; (7) vehicles and motor fuels, including ethanol; (8) hydrogen; (9) electricity; (10) energy tax incentives; (11) hydropower and geothermal energy; and (12) climate change technology.

Endangered Species Act (ESA; 1973)—ESA provides a program for the conservation of threatened and endangered plants and animals and the habitats in which they are found. EPA's decision to register a pesticide is based on the risk of adverse effects on endangered species and on environmental fate (how a pesticide will affect habitats).

Federal Insecticide, Fungicide, and Rodenticide Act (FIFRA; 1972)—FIFRA provides for federal control of pesticide distribution, sale, and use. It gives EPA authority not only to study the consequences of pesticide usage but also to require users (farmers, utility companies, and others) to register when purchasing pesticides. Through later amendments to the law, users also must take exams for certification as applicators of pesticides. All pesticides used in the United States must be registered (licensed) by EPA.

Federal Food, Drug, and Cosmetic Act (FFDCA; 1938)—FFDCA extended federal authority to ban new drugs from the market until they were approved by the Food and Drug Administration (FDA). The law also gave the federal government more extensive power in dealing with adulterated or mislabeled food, drugs, and cosmetic products.

Food Quality Protection Act (FQPA; 1996)—FQPA amended FIFRA and FFDCA. These amendments fundamentally changed the way EPA regulates pesticides. The requirements included a new safety standard—reasonable certainty of no harm—that must be applied to all pesticides used on foods.

Marine Protection, Research, and Sanctuaries Act (MPRSA; 1988)—MPRSA, also referred to as the Ocean Dumping Act, generally prohibits (1) transportation of material from the United States for the purpose of ocean dumping; (2) transportation of material from anywhere for the purpose of ocean dumping by U.S. agencies or U.S.-flagged vessels; (3) dumping of material transported from outside the United States into the U.S. territorial sea.

Nuclear Waste Policy Act (NWPA; 1982)—NWPA supports the use of deep geologic repositories for the safe storage and/or disposal of radioactive waste. The Act establishes procedures to evaluate and select sites for geologic repositories and for the interaction of state and federal governments. It also provides a timetable of key milestones the federal agencies must meet in carrying out the program.

Occupational Safety and Health Act (OSHA; 1970)—OSHA was enacted to ensure worker and workplace safety. It requires employers to provide workers with a place of employment free from recognized hazards to safety and health, such as exposure to toxic chemicals, excessive noise levels, mechanical dangers, heat or cold stress, or unsanitary conditions.

Oil Pollution Act (OPA; 1990)—OPA streamlined and strengthened EPA's ability to prevent and respond to catastrophic oil spills. It established a trust fund, financed by a tax on oil, to fund the cleanup of spills when the responsible party is incapable of doing so or unwilling to do so.

Pollution Prevention Act (PPA; 1990)—PPA focused industry, government, and public attention on reducing the amount of pollution through cost-effective changes in production, operation, and raw materials use. Opportunities for source reduction are often not realized because existing regulations and the industrial resources required for compliance focus on treatment and disposal. Source reduction is fundamentally different than waste management or pollution control.

Resource Conservation and Recovery Act (RCRA; 1976)—RCRA gave EPA the authority to control hazardous waste from the "cradle to the grave." This includes the generation, transportation, treatment, storage, and disposal of hazardous waste.

Safe Drinking Water Act (SDWA; 1974)—SWDA was established to protect the quality of drinking water in the United States. This law focuses on all waters actually or potentially designed for drinking use, whether from aboveground or underground sources. It authorized EPA to establish safe standards of purity and required all owners or operators of public water systems to comply with primary (health-related) standards.

Superfund Amendments and Reauthorization Act (SARA; 1986)—SARA amended CERCLA to reflect EPA's experience in administering the complex Superfund program during its first six years and made several important changes and additions to the program. SARA

- stressed the importance of permanent remedies and innovative treatment technologies in cleaning up hazardous waste sites,

- required Superfund actions to consider the standards and requirements found in other state and federal environmental laws and regulations,
- provided new enforcement authorities and settlement tools,
- increased state involvement in every phase of the Superfund program,
- increased the focus on human health problems posed by hazardous waste sites,
- encouraged greater citizen participation in making decisions on how sites should be cleaned up, and
- increased the size of the trust fund to $8.5 billion.

Toxic Substances Control Act (TSCA; 1976)—TSCA gave EPA the ability to track the industrial chemicals produced or imported into the United States. EPA repeatedly screens these chemicals and can require reporting or testing of those that may pose an environmental or human-health hazard. EPA can ban the manufacture and import of those chemicals that pose an unreasonable risk.

SOURCE: Adapted from Environmental Protection Agency. 2009. "Laws that We Administer." [Online information; retrieved 3/22/09.] www.epa.gov/lawsregs/laws/index.html.

11

REDUCING MEDICAL ERRORS

Attention to medical errors escalated over five years ago with the release of a study from the Institute of Medicine (IOM), *To Err is Human*, which found that between 44,000 and 98,000 Americans die each year in U.S. hospitals due to preventable medical errors. Hospital errors rank between the fifth and eighth leading cause of death, killing more Americans than breast cancer, traffic accidents, or AIDS. Serious medication errors occur in the cases of 5 to 10 percent of patients admitted to hospitals. These numbers may understate the problem because they do not include preventable deaths due to medical treatments outside of hospitals.

Since the release of the IOM study, there has been greater focus on the quality of healthcare provided in the United States. Quality experts agree that one of the most common causes of errors is the medical system itself, not the individuals functioning within the system. Publication of the IOM report triggered substantial public and private sector activity, including the formation of the National Patient Safety Foundation by the American Medical Association, the creation of a non-punitive sentinel events reporting system by the Joint Commission for the Accreditation of Healthcare Organizations, and the establishment of new public private partnerships by the Veterans Health Administration and others.

Still, experts agree that there is much more work to do. For example, fewer than 3 percent of hospitals have implemented computerized drug ordering systems, which one study found to reduce medication errors by 86 percent. In a December 2002 Kaiser Family Foundation survey, only 5 percent of physicians identified medical errors as a top healthcare concern. Shortly after the release of the 1999 IOM report, Congress gave $50 million to the U.S. Agency for Healthcare Research and Quality for research into the causes and prevention of medical errors. Beyond that, a flurry of legislative proposals in the 106th and 107th Congress resulted in stalemate over issues such as whether error reporting should be mandatory or voluntary and confidential or publicly released. Meanwhile, controversy over how to best address medical errors has entered into other debates, incuding whether the federal government should restructure the current medical malpractice system. States have also been a part of this debate, as several now have mandatory error reporting rules and statutes with a patchwork of differing requirements.

As federal and state policymakers debate the issues related to reducing medical errors, discussion will likely focus on several key issues, including:

- What kind of standardized national reporting of medical errors should be established? Should it be voluntary or mandatory? Should it be confidential or publicly reported? In which cases?
- What agency should be designated to receive error reports? What authority should the agency have to act on reports?
- What kind of reporting may or should be required for "near miss" events? What protections should be provided to reporters of errors and near misses? What effect should this new reporting system have on existing state reporting systems?
- Should Congress set national standards for mandatory overtime by nurses and limitations on work hours for medical interns and residents, both of which have been tied to increased medical errors?
- Should Congress mandate hospitals to install computerized drug order entry systems and other technologies with proven ability to reduce errors? If so, should the federal government provide financial support to some or all hospitals to install these systems?
- Should the federal government set clear goals for the reduction of errors over a period of years, particularly for Medicare and Medicaid patients? Should penalties and/or incentives be created for providers to reduce errors?
- What steps can Congress and state legislatures take to alleviate a serious national shortage of nurses—because many medical errors have been linked with understaffing of nurses and use of temporary nurses?
- What is the role of regulatory agencies such as The Joint Commission and the National Committee on Quality Assurance in national reform on medical errors?
- Should any reports submitted under a medical errors reporting system be admissible as evidence in medical malpractice cases?

SOURCE: Reprinted with permission from Henry J. Kaiser Family Foundation. 2008. "Reducing Medical Errors: Background Brief." [Online brief; retrieved 2/11/09.] www.kaiseredu.org/topics_im.asp?id=137&parentID=70&imID=1. This information was reprinted with permission of The Henry J. Kaiser Family Foundation. The Kaiser Family Foundation, based in Menlo Park, California, is a nonprofit, independent national healthcare philanthropy and is not associated with Kaiser Permanente or Kaiser Industries.

The brief was prepared by Allison Woo, Usha Ranji, and Alina Salganicoff of the Kaiser Family Foundation. May 2008.

IDEAS FOR CLOSING THE QUALITY CHASM

12

As the nation turns to the issue of reforming our health insurance system, it is important to address simultaneously how we organize and deliver health services—to ensure that we are obtaining the best possible health outcomes for Americans and the most value for the money we spend on health care. Unfortunately, the care we receive falls short of the care it is possible to deliver, and the gap is not narrowing. According to the most recent National Scorecard published by the Commonwealth Fund Commission on a High Performance Health System, the U.S. health system in 2008 scored 65 out of 100 possible points on 37 indicators of performance capturing key dimensions of health outcomes, quality, access, equity, and efficiency.

The scorecard shows that the U.S. is not making consistent progress in reducing the variability of healthcare quality and is failing to keep pace with gains in health outcomes achieved by our industrialized peers.

- The nation now ranks last out of 19 countries on a measure of "mortality amenable to medical care"—in five years falling from 15th, as other countries raised the bar on performance.
- The widening quality chasm is having real effects on people's lives. Up to 101,000 deaths could be prevented each year if the United States raised standards of care to benchmark performance levels achieved abroad.
- While we spend more than twice what other nations spend on health, there is overwhelming evidence of inappropriate care, missed opportunities, and waste within the U.S. health system.

We are fortunate, however, that even within our imperfect system, models exist for each of the components that—if properly organized, reformed, and financed—can enable the nation to provide high-quality, affordable care to every American. The following examples of excellence from across the United States and around the world offer insight into what it takes to achieve high performance:

- A leader in innovation and quality improvement, the Geisinger Health System, on whose board I am pleased to serve, demonstrates the importance of simultaneously aligning incentives, utilizing electronic health records, and creating policies to encourage coordination of care.
- Denver Health, a comprehensive and integrated medical system that is Colorado's largest healthcare safety-net provider, has succeeded by

promoting a culture of continuous quality improvement and "lean" efficiency, adopting information technology, and providing organization-wide leadership.

- State initiatives in Iowa and Vermont have achieved better health outcomes and increased access to needed health services by encouraging adoption of the medical home model, disseminating performance information and best practices, and launching focused campaigns to cover young children.

- Regional associations like the Massachusetts Health Quality Partners and the Wisconsin Collaborative for Healthcare Quality have become leaders in quality improvement by collecting and disseminating performance data on hospitals and physician groups and by educating providers and patients to use that information to facilitate improvement activities.

- Denmark and the Netherlands have become international leaders in patient-centered, coordinated care by placing great emphasis on accessible primary care and developing information systems that assist primary care physicians in coordinating health services.

The specific policies that will both lead to better health outcomes and "bend the curve" of our nation's unsustainable healthcare spending revolve around five strategies that are amenable to action at the federal level.

- Provide affordable health coverage for all.
- Reform provider payment.
- Organize our care delivery systems.
- Invest in a modern health system.
- Ensure strong national leadership.

Congress can continue to develop the infrastructure for improving quality by making investments in health information technology and information exchange networks. If the United States is serious about closing the quality chasm, it will also need a strong primary care system, which requires fundamentally reforming provider payment, encouraging all patients to enroll in a patient-centered medical home, and supporting physician practices that serve as medical homes with information technology and technical assistance for redesigning care processes. Funding for research on comparative effectiveness and establishing a center for comparative effectiveness are also crucial to value-based purchasing and performance-improvement initiatives. Finally, the federal government can raise the bar for health system performance by setting explicit goals and priorities for improvement—particularly with regard to the most prevalent chronic conditions, which account for a large majority of healthcare costs.

By applying these policies collectively, the nation would be able to capture the synergistic benefits of specific changes that, if implemented individually, would yield more modest improvements in quality and smaller reductions in projected spending. And, to be sure, any reforms must support healthcare providers in their efforts to deliver the best care possible for their patients.

Armed with the knowledge that the status quo is no longer acceptable, we have entered a new era ripe with opportunity to close the quality chasm and improve the health and well-being of American families. Working together, we can change course and put the U.S. health system on a path to high performance.

SOURCE: Davis, K. 2009. Invited testimony by Karen Davis, PhD, President, Commonwealth Fund, given before the Senate Committee on Health, Education, Labor, and Pensions, Hearing on "Crossing the Quality Chasm in Health Care Reform," on January 29. [Online material; retrieved 3/22/09.] help.senate.gov/Hearings/2009_01_29/Davis.pdf.

ECONOMY, JOBS TRUMP ALL OTHER POLICY PRIORITIES IN 2009

As Barack Obama takes office, the public's focus is overwhelmingly on domestic policy concerns—particularly the economy. Strengthening the nation's economy and improving the job situation stand at the top of the public's list of domestic priorities for 2009. Meanwhile, the priority placed on issues such as the environment, crime, illegal immigration, and even reducing healthcare costs has fallen off from a year ago.

While it is not unusual for the public to prioritize domestic over foreign policy, the balance of opinion today is particularly one-sided. Roughly seven in ten Americans (71 percent) say that President Obama should focus on domestic policy, while just 11 percent prioritize foreign policy. By comparison, last January, 56 percent cited domestic policy as most important while 31 percent said Bush should focus on foreign policy.

The latest national survey by the Pew Research Center for the People & the Press, conducted January 7–11, 2009 among 1,503 adults on cell phones and landlines, finds that strengthening the economy and improving the job situation are higher priorities today than they have been at any point over the past decade, and the recent upward trend has been steep. The share of Americans saying that strengthening the nation's economy should be a top priority has risen from 68 percent two years ago, to 75 percent last January, to 85 percent today. Concern about jobs has risen even more sharply. The 82 percent who rate improving the job situation as a top priority represents a 21-point jump from 61 percent a year ago.

Of the 20 issues people were asked to rate in both January 2008 and January 2009, five have slipped significantly in importance as attention to the economy has surged. Protecting the environment fell the most precipitously—just 41 percent rate this as a top priority today, down from 56 percent a year ago. The percentage rating illegal immigration as a top priority has fallen from 51 percent to 41 percent over the past year, and reducing crime has fallen by a similar amount (from 54 percent to 46 percent). And while reducing healthcare costs remains a top priority to 59 percent of Americans, this is down 10 points from 69 percent one year ago.

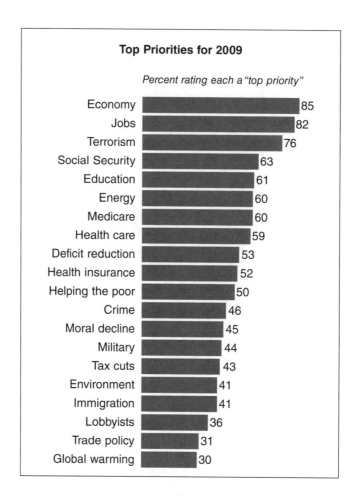

The public's interest in many other policy areas remains relatively stable, by comparison. Roughly three-quarters (76 percent) say that defending the country from future terrorist attacks should be a top priority, making it the third highest priority among the 20 issues tested in the survey. As recently as two years ago, terrorism ranked at the top of the list of policy priorities. The share of Americans who rate terrorism as a top priority has not changed substantially in recent years; the issue has simply been leapfrogged by the economy and jobs at the top of the list.

Top Domestic Priorities for Obama and Congress

Percent considering each as a "top priority"	Jan 2001	Jan 2002	Jan 2003	Jan 2004	Jan 2005	Jan 2006	Jan 2007	Jan 2008	**Jan 2009**	08–09 change
Strengthening nation's economy	81	71	73	79	75	66	68	75	**85**	+10
Improving the job situation	60	67	62	67	68	65	57	61	**82**	+21
Defending U.S. against terrorism	—	83	81	78	75	80	80	74	**76**	+2
Securing Social Security	74	62	59	65	70	64	64	64	**63**	−1
Improving educational system	78	66	62	71	70	67	69	66	**61**	−5
Dealing with U.S. energy problems	–	42	40	46	47	58	57	59	**60**	+1
Securing Medicare	71	55	56	62	67	62	63	60	**60**	0
Reducing health care costs	—	—	—	—	—	—	68	69	**59**	−10
Reducing budget deficit	—	35	40	51	56	55	53	58	**53**	−5
Providing health ins. to uninsured	61	43	45	54	60	59	56	54	**52**	−2
Dealing with problems of poor	63	44	48	50	59	55	55	51	**50**	−1
Reducing crime	76	53	47	53	53	62	62	54	**46**	−8
Dealing with moral breakdown	51	45	39	45	41	47	47	43	**45**	+2
Strengthening the military	48	52	48	48	52	42	46	42	**44**	+2
Reducing middle class taxes	66	43	—	44	48	51	48	46	**43**	−3
Protecting the environment	63	44	39	49	49	57	57	56	**41**	−15
Dealing with illegal immigration	–	–	–	–	–	–	55	51	**41**	−10
Reducing influence of lobbyists	–	–	–	–	–	–	35	39	**36**	−3
Dealing with global trade	37	25	–	32	32	30	34	37	**31**	−6
Dealing with global warming	–	–	–	–	–	–	38	35	**30**	−5

As with terrorism, public views of the importance of several other policy priorities have not changed much in recent years. Roughly six in ten continue to rate making the Social Security system (63 percent) and making the Medicare system (60 percent) more financially sound as top priorities. Dealing with the nation's energy problems also remains a top priority for six in ten, as does improving the educational system (61 percent), though the public's emphasis on the latter has slipped slightly in recent years.

SOURCE: Reprinted with permission from the Pew Research Center for the People & the Press, a project of the Pew Research Center. 2009. "Economy, Jobs Trump All Other Policy Priorities in 2009." Survey Report, January 22. Washington, DC: The Pew Research Center for the People & the Press. [Online Report; retrieved 2/12/09.] http://people-press.org/report/485/economy-top-policy-priority.

14

JOINT LETTER URGING MEDPAC TO RECOMMEND A FULL INFLATION UPDATE FOR 2010

January 5, 2009
Glenn M. Hackbarth, JD
Chairman, Medicare Payment Advisory Commission
601 New Jersey Avenue, NW
Suite 9000
Washington, DC 20001

Dear Chairman Hackbarth:

The undersigned organizations deeply appreciate that the Medicare Payment Advisory Commission (MedPAC) is preparing to recommend that the physician update for 2010 be based on the increase in the costs physicians face instead of being cut by 21 percent, as would be required by the Sustainable Growth Rate (SGR) formula. At the same time, however, we remain concerned that the Medicare Economic Index (MEI), which serves as the foundation for MedPAC's recommendation, includes a very substantial productivity adjustment which reduces the MEI by half, or even more. We strongly urge the Commission to consider recommending a 2010 update for physician services that reflects the full increase in medical practice input prices without any productivity adjustment.

The current estimate of the increase in input prices is 2.4 percent. Subtracting 1.3 percent for nonfarm multifactor productivity would reduce the update recommendation to just 1.1 percent. It took the Medicare conversion factor until 2008 to finally get back to where it was before the 2002 cut, and even now average physician payment rates are only slightly higher than in 2001, while the MEI has risen by 22 percent. A 1.1 percent increase in 2010 will not begin to make up for that gap. Besides not making up the gap, a 1.1 percent update is unlikely to even cover practice cost increases for 2010 because the MEI formula routinely understates the true cost of care.

There are two primary reasons that the MEI lags so far behind actual practice cost increases: one is that the MEI is a price index only, so the data used to calculate the physician update is based on what a medical practice looked like when the "market basket" used in the MEI was developed in 1973 and does not reflect all the costs involved in providing medical care in 2008.

333

No adjustments are made for new costs, such as computers, copiers, and additional staff, which were not present in physician offices in 1973. For example, data presented to MedPAC in October on Health Care Sector Growth indicates that just between 1999 and 2008, physician office employment increased by 27 percent. In fact, there is little about a medical practice of 2009, whether in the medical technology that is available, the office environment, the medical records processes, or the skilled clinical staff, that bears much resemblance to the medical practice of 1973, but that is the year that the inputs used in the MEI were determined. Prices have changed and weights have changed, but not the underlying inputs.

This problem is then exacerbated by an assumption that is built into the MEI and, to date, included in each year's MedPAC recommended update, that physicians, unlike any other provider group, can increase productivity year after year to the same degree as the nonfarm economy. This assumption is unrealistic. There are some ways in which physicians can and have increased productivity and efficiency but there are limits on how many minutes can be shaved off of a given service and how many services a physician can do in a day. In addition, there are often costs associated with increased efficiencies that are recognized to some extent in the relative value reviews for particular services, but there is no mechanism for increasing overall physician service funding to account for new resource inputs.

More importantly, any time that physicians may have saved by streamlining practices has been more than consumed by the time required for compliance with all the new regulatory burdens imposed on physicians over the last decade. For example, conversion to new provider identification numbers required by the Health Insurance Portability and Accountability Act (HIPAA) has led to lengthy enrollment and re-enrollment backlogs for physicians that delay payments for months, and sometimes years. During this time, physicians and their staff spend hours and hours trying to find out the status of their applications, revising and resubmitting them, and lining up loans in an increasingly tight credit market to pay their staff and other expenses. Once their enrollment is finally processed, they have to spend time making sure they get paid for all the services they provided during the months or years that the application was awaiting approval. Other tasks that have decreased physician productivity are:

- the constantly expanding list of services or durable medical equipment subject to physician certification and recertification;
- ever-changing Part D formularies and preauthorization requirements;
- compliance with HIPAA privacy and other administrative standards;
- pulling medical record information for the ever-expanding number of audits that physicians are subject to, such as Recovery Audit Contractors;

- transition to the new Medicare Administrative Contractors; and
- upcoming imaging accreditation requirements.

In the last six years, MedPAC has routinely waived or cut in half the productivity adjustment when recommending updates for inpatient and outpatient hospital services. Only once, in its recommendation for the 2004 outpatient hospital update, did MedPAC include a full productivity adjustment. The undersigned organizations urge the commission to recommend that no productivity adjustment be applied to next year's physician update. Thank you for your consideration.

Sincerely,

American Academy of Child and Adolescent Psychiatry

American Academy of Dermatology Association

American Academy of Facial Plastic and Reconstructive Surgery

American Academy of Family Physicians

American Academy of Home Care Physicians

American Academy of Hospice and Palliative Medicine

American Academy of Neurology Professional Association

American Academy of Ophthalmology

American Academy of Otolaryngology—Head and Neck Surgery

American Academy of Pain Medicine

American Academy of Pediatrics

American Academy of Physical Medicine and Rehabilitation

American Association of Clinical Endocrinologists

American Association of Clinical Urologists

American Association of Neurological Surgeons

American Association of Orthopaedic Surgeons

American College of Cardiology

American College of Chest Physicians

American College of Emergency Physicians

American College of Obstetricians and Gynecologists

American College of Osteopathic Family Physicians

American College of Osteopathic Internists

American College of Osteopathic Surgeons

American College of Physicians

American College of Radiation Oncology

American College of Radiology

American College of Rheumatology

American College of Surgeons

American Gastroenterological Association

American Geriatrics Society

American Medical Association

American Medical Directors Association

American Osteopathic Academy of Orthopedics

American Osteopathic Association

American Psychiatric Association

American Rhinologic Society

American Society for Gastrointestinal Endoscopy

American Society for Therapeutic Radiology and Oncology

American Society of Addiction Medicine

American Society of Anesthesiologists

American Society of Cataract and Refractive Surgery

American Society of Clinical Oncology

American Society of Hematology

American Society of Nephrology

American Society of Pediatric Nephrology

American Society of Plastic Surgeons

American Society of Transplant Surgeons

American Thoracic Society

American Urogynecologic Society

American Urological Association

Association of American Medical Colleges

Child Neurology Society

College of American Pathologists

Congress of Neurological Surgeons

Heart Rhythm Society

Infectious Diseases Society of America

Joint Council of Allergy, Asthma and Immunology

Medical Group Management Association

Renal Physicians Association

Society for Cardiovascular Angiography and Interventions

Society for Maternal-Fetal Medicine

Society for Vascular Surgery

Society of Critical Care Medicine

Society of Gynecologic Oncologists

Society of Hospital Medicine

Society of Interventional Radiology

Society of Thoracic Surgeons

The Endocrine Society

TYPES OF GROUPS INVOLVED IN FINANCING POLITICAL CAMPAIGNS

501(c) groups. Nonprofit, tax-exempt groups organized under section 501(c) of the Internal Revenue Code that can engage in varying amounts of political activity, depending on the type of group. For example, 501(c)(3) groups operate for religious, charitable, scientific, or educational purposes. These groups are not supposed to engage in any political activities, though some voter registration activities are permitted. 501(c)(4) groups are commonly called "social welfare" organizations that may engage in political activities, as long as these activities do not become their primary purpose. Similar restrictions apply to Section 501(c)(5) labor and agricultural groups, and to Section 501(c)(6) business leagues, chambers of commerce, real estate boards, and boards of trade.

527 group. A tax-exempt group organized under section 527 of the Internal Revenue Code to raise money for political activities including voter mobilization efforts, issue advocacy, and the like. Currently, the FEC only requires a 527 group to file regular disclosure reports if it is a political party or political action committee (PAC) that engages in either activities expressly advocating the election or defeat of a federal candidate, or in electioneering communications. Otherwise, it must file either with the government of the state in which it is located or the Internal Revenue Service. Many 527s run by special interest groups raise unlimited "soft money," which they use for voter mobilization and certain types of issue advocacy, but not for efforts that expressly advocate the election or defeat of a federal candidate or amount to electioneering communications.

Nonfederal group. A group set up to raise unlimited contributions called "soft money," which it spends on voter mobilization efforts and so-called issue ads that often criticize or tout a candidate's record just before an election in a not-so-subtle effort to influence the election's outcome. 501(c) groups and 527 groups may raise nonfederal funds.

Political action committee (PAC). A political committee that raises and spends limited "hard" money contributions for the express purpose of electing or defeating candidates. Organizations that raise soft money for issue advocacy may also set up a PAC. Most PACs represent business, such as the Microsoft PAC; labor, such as the Teamsters PAC; or ideological interests, such as the EMILY's List PAC or the National Rifle Association PAC. An organization's PAC will collect money from the group's employees or members and make contributions in the name of the PAC to candidates and political parties. Individuals contributing to a PAC may also contribute directly to candidates and political parties, even those also supported by the PAC. A PAC can give $5,000 to a candidate per election (primary, general, or special) and up to $15,000 annually to a national political party. PACs may receive up to $5,000 each from individuals, other PACs and party committees per year. A PAC must register with the Federal Election Commission within 10 days of its formation, providing the name and address of the PAC, its treasurer, and any affiliated organizations.

SOURCE: Reprinted with permission from Center for Responsive Politics. n.d. "Types of Advocacy Groups." [Online information; retrieved 2/13/09.] www.opensecrets.org/527s/types.php.

16

THE SENATE COMMITTEE SYSTEM

Due to the high volume and complexity of its work, the Senate divides its tasks among 20 committees, 68 subcommittees, and 4 joint committees. Although the Senate committee system is similar to that of the House of Representatives, it has its own guidelines, within which each committee adopts its own rules. This creates considerable variation among the panels.

Standing committees generally have legislative jurisdiction. Subcommittees handle specific areas of the committee's work. Select and joint committees generally handle oversight or housekeeping responsibilities.

The chair of each committee and a majority of its members represent the majority party. The chair primarily controls a committee's business. Each party assigns its own members to committees, and each committee distributes its members among its subcommittees. The Senate places limits on the number and types of panels any one senator may serve on and chair.

Committees receive varying levels of operating funds and employ varying numbers of aides. Each hires its own staff. The majority party controls most committee staff and resources, but a portion is shared with the minority.

Several thousand bills and resolutions are referred to committees during each two-year Congress. Committees select a small percentage for consideration, and those not addressed often receive no further action. The bills that committees report help to set the Senate's agenda.

When a committee or subcommittee favors a measure, it usually takes four actions. First, it asks relevant executive agencies for written comments on the measure. Second, it holds hearings to gather information and views from non-committee experts. At committee hearings, these witnesses summarize submitted statements and then respond to questions from the senators. Third, a committee meets to perfect the measure through amendments, and non-committee members sometimes attempt to influence the language. Fourth, when language is agreed upon, the committee sends the measure back to the full Senate, usually along with a written report describing its purposes and provisions.

A committee's influence extends to its enactment of bills into law. A committee that considers a measure will manage the full Senate's deliberation on it. Also, its members will be appointed to any conference committee created to reconcile its version of a bill with the version passed by the House of Representatives.

Other types of committees deal with the confirmation or rejection of presidential nominees. Committee hearings that focus on the implementation and investigation of programs are known as oversight hearings, whereas committee investigations examine allegations of wrongdoing.

SOURCE: Reprinted from United States Senate. n.d. *About the Senate Committee System.* [Online material; retrieved 2/16/09.] www.senate.gov/general/common/generic/about_committees.htm.

TESTIMONY ON HEART DISEASE EDUCATION, ANALYSIS RESEARCH, AND TREATMENT FOR WOMEN ACT (OR "HEART FOR WOMEN ACT")

Statement of Susan K. Bennett, MD
Clinical Director, Women's Heart Program, The George Washington University Hospital Before the House Subcommittee on Health of the Committee on Energy and Commerce

Legislative Hearing on H.R. 1014, the Heart Disease Education, Analysis Research and Treatment for Women Act

May 1, 2007

My name is Susan Bennett, and I am a practicing cardiologist; and I think first and foremost, I am one of the doctors in the trenches. I see patients five days a week, and I see men and women. About 70 percent of my practice is women, and that is primarily what I do. I am a clinical assistant professor of medicine and director of the Women's Heart Program at George Washington University Medical Center. I am also a volunteer and national spokeswoman for the American Heart Association and president of the Association of Women's Heart Programs, and I also serve on the Advisory Board of Women Heart, which is the national coalition for women with heart disease.

On behalf of the American Heart Association, or AHA, and its more than 22 million volunteers and supporters, I appreciate the opportunity to testify today on H.R. 1014, known as the HEART for Women Act. We wish to thank this House Committee on Energy and Commerce, Subcommittee on Health, for holding today's hearing on this Act, which we strongly support along with many other nonprofit health organizations.

Heart disease, stroke, and other forms of cardiovascular diseases are the number one killer of American women, claiming more than 460,000 lives each year or about a death a minute. That is more female lives than the next five causes of death combined, including deaths from lung and breast cancer. An estimated 42 million women, about one in three, are living with the chronic effects of heart disease, stroke, or some other form of cardiovascular disease.

In 1984, women achieved equality and then surpassed men in one area where they don't want it: heart disease mortality. Every year since then, more women than men have died of cardiovascular disease, or CVD. During that time, we have made good progress in reducing CVD mortality for men but the same cannot be said for women. Although mortality rates have gone down for women, the decline is not nearly as steep as it is for men.

The HEART for Women Act is intended to help close that gap by focusing on three strategies to improve diagnosis, treatment, and prevention of heart disease and stroke in women. Part of the problem is that there are not enough women or physicians who recognize heart disease as the serious health threat that it truly is. Efforts like the AHA's Go Red for Women movement and the NHLDI's Heart Truth campaign have helped to increase awareness among women about their risk of heart disease, but much more work remains.

The latest American Heart Association survey tracking women's awareness of heart disease found that 43 percent of women are still not aware that heart disease is the leading cause of death for women. Women of color are significantly less likely to know this important fact, despite being at greater risk for cardiovascular disease.

Even more alarming, especially to me, is the pervasive lack of awareness about women and heart disease among physicians. According to an American Heart Association–sponsored survey published in 2005, fewer than one in five physicians surveyed recognized that more women than men die of heart disease than other cardiovascular disease each year. Astoundingly, only 8 percent of primary care physicians knew this basic fact.

Healthcare professionals treat what they perceive to be a problem; and partially as a result of the above statistics, we see that women are often treated less aggressively. For instance, women are more likely to die within a year of their first heart attack, but are less likely to be referred for diagnostic testing ahead of time that could have caught the disease early in the preventive phase. And according to the Agency for Health Care Research and Quality's 2006 National Healthcare Disparities Report, female Medicare patients who suffer from a heart attack are less likely to receive the recommended care compared to their male counterparts.

The HEART for Women Act would help to increase awareness among populations for which there are still gaps, particularly older women and healthcare professionals. For healthcare professionals, the bill authorizes the Health Resources and Services Administration to conduct an education campaign to increase professionals' understanding about the prevalence and unique aspects of care for women in the prevention and treatment of forms of CVD.

The bill also authorizes the Secretary of Health and Human Services to develop and distribute educational materials to women 65 years and older to educate them about a woman's risk for heart attacks and strokes, risk factors, and symptoms.

Another problem that I struggle with every day in my practice is the lack of information available to us about the safety and efficacy of heart and stroke treatments for women. When a new therapy comes on the market, one of the first things I want to know is how does it work in women compared to men, and all too often that information is simply not available.

For far too long we have simply assumed that if a new drug or medical device works for a man, then it must work for a woman. Thanks to reports such as the National Institute of Medicine's landmark 2001 report "Does Sex Matter?" we know that sex really does make a difference, from womb to tomb. Researchers are learning that sex differences play an increasingly important role in prevention, diagnosis, and treatment. For instance, we have learned from the National Heart, Lung, and Blood Institute–funded WISE study that coronary artery disease may manifest itself differently in women than in men, which suggests that treatment testing regimens that work in men may not work as well in women.

Diagnostic tests, prescription drugs, and medical devices may work differently in women than men. These differences are likely due to a variety of reasons.

* * *

So in summary, for me as a practicing clinician, it is absolutely important for this Act to be passed so I can take care of women better. Thank you.

SOURCE: Reprinted from Bennett, S. K. 2007. Testimony before the House Subcommittee on Health of the Committee on Energy and Commerce Legislative Hearing on H.R. 1014, "The Heart Disease Education, Analysis Research, and Treatment for Women Act." May 1. [Online information; retrieved 2/16/09.] frwebgate.access.gpo.gov/cgi-bin/getdoc.cgi?dbname=110_house_hearings&docid=f:38951.wais.

18

CONGRESSIONAL CONFERENCE COMMITTEES

If the Senate does not accept the House's position (or the House does not agree to the Senate's position), one of the chambers may propose creation of a conference committee to negotiate and resolve the matters in disagreement between the two chambers. Typically, the Senate gets to conference with the House by adopting this standard motion: "Mr. President, I move that the Senate insist on its amendments [or "disagree to the House amendments" to the Senate-passed measure], request a conference with the House on the disagreeing votes thereon, and that the Chair be authorized to appoint conferees." This triple motion rolled into one—to insist (or disagree), request, and appoint—is commonly agreed to by unanimous consent. The presiding officer formally appoints the Senate's conferees. (The Speaker names the House conferees.) Conferees are traditionally drawn from the committee of jurisdiction, but conferees representing other Senate interests may also be appointed.

There are no formal rules that outline how conference meetings are to be organized. Routinely, the principals from each chamber or their respective staffs conduct preconference meetings so as to expedite the bargaining process when the conference formally convenes. Informal practice also determines who will be the overall conference chair (each chamber has its own leader in conference). Rotation of the chairmanship between the chambers is usually the practice when matched pairs of panels (the tax or appropriations panels, for example) convene in conference regularly. For standing committees that seldom meet in conference, the choice of who will chair the conference is generally resolved by the conference leaders from each chamber. The decision on when and where to meet and for how long are a few prerogatives of the chair, who consults on these matters with his or her counterpart from the other body.

Once the two chambers go to conference, the respective House and Senate conferees bargain and negotiate to resolve the matters in bicameral disagreement. Resolution is embodied in a conference report signed by a majority of Senate conferees and House conferees. The conference report must be agreed to by both chambers before it is cleared for presidential consideration. In the Senate, conference reports are usually brought up by unanimous consent at a time agreed to by the party leaders and floor managers. Because conference reports are privileged, if any senator objects to the unanimous consent request, a nondebatable motion can be made to take up the conference report. Approval of the conference report itself is subject to extended debate, but conference reports are not open to amendment.

Almost all of the most important measures are sent to conference, but these are only a minority of the bills that the two houses pass each year.

Exchange of Amendments Between the Houses

Differences between versions of most noncontroversial bills and some major bills that must be passed quickly are reconciled through the exchange of amendments between the houses. The two chambers may send measures back and forth, amending each other's amendments until they agree to identical language on all provisions of the legislation. Generally, the provisions of an amendment between the houses are the subject of informal negotiations, so extended exchanges of amendments are rare. But there is also a parliamentary limit on the number of times a measure may shuttle between the chambers. In general, each chamber has only two opportunities to amend the amendments of the other body because both chambers prohibit third-degree amendments. In rare instances, however, the two chambers waive or disregard the parliamentary limit and exchange amendments more than twice. The current record is nine exchanges.

At any stage of this process, a chamber may accept the position of the other body, insist on its most recent position, request a conference to resolve the remaining differences, or refuse to take further action and allow the measure to die.

The Senate normally takes action on an amendment of the House only when there is an expectation that the amendment may be disposed of readily, typically by unanimous consent. In the absence of such an expectation, the Senate will generally proceed to conference in order to negotiate a resolution to any serious disagreements within the Senate or with the House rather than attempt to resolve them on the floor.

SOURCE: Reprinted from U.S. Senate. n.d. "Senate Legislative Process." [Online information; retrieved 2/17/09.] www.senate.gov/legislative/common/briefing/Senate_legislative_process.htm#4.

19

THE FEDERAL BUDGET PROCESS

The way in which Congress develops tax and spending legislation is guided by a set of specific procedures laid out in the Congressional Budget Act of 1974. The centerpiece of the Budget Act is the requirement that Congress each year develop a "budget resolution" setting overarching limits on spending and on tax cuts. These limits apply to legislation developed by individual congressional committees as well as to any amendments offered to such legislation on the House or Senate floor.

The following is a brief overview of the federal budget process, including

- the President's budget request, which kicks off the budget process each year;
- the congressional budget resolution—how it is developed and what it contains;
- how the terms of the budget resolution are enforced by the House and Senate; and
- budget "reconciliation," a special procedure used in some years to facilitate the passage of spending and tax legislation.

Step One: The President's Budget Request

On or before the first Monday in February, the President submits to Congress a detailed budget request for the coming federal fiscal year, which begins on October 1. This budget request, developed by the President's Office of Management and Budget (OMB), plays three important roles. First, it tells Congress what the President believes overall federal fiscal policy should be, as established by three main components: (1) how much money the federal government should spend on public purposes; (2) how much it should take in as tax revenues; and (3) how much of a deficit (or surplus) the federal government should run, which is simply the difference between (1) and (2).

Second, the budget request lays out the President's relative priorities for federal programs—how much he believes should be spent on defense, agriculture, education, health, and so on. The President's budget is very specific, and recommends funding levels for individual federal programs or small groups of programs called "budget accounts." The budget typically sketches out fiscal policy and budget priorities not only for the coming year but for the next five years or more. It is also accompanied by historical tables that set out past budget figures.

The third role that the President's budget plays is to signal to Congress what spending and tax policy changes the President recommends. The President does not need to propose legislative change for those parts of the budget that are governed by permanent law if he feels none is necessary. Nearly all of the federal tax code is set in permanent law, and will not expire. Similarly, more than one-half of federal spending—including the three largest entitlement programs (Medicare, Medicaid, and Social Security)—is also permanently enacted. Interest paid on the national debt is also paid automatically, with no need for specific legislation. (There is, however, a separate "debt ceiling" which limits how much the Treasury can borrow. The debt ceiling is periodically raised through separate legislation.)

The one type of spending the President *does* have to ask for each year is:

- **Funding for "discretionary" or "appropriated" programs,** which fall under the jurisdiction of the House and Senate Appropriations Committees. Discretionary programs must have their funding renewed each year in order to continue operating. Almost all defense spending is discretionary, as are the budgets for K–12 education, health research, and housing, to name just a few examples. Altogether, discretionary programs make up about one-third of all federal spending. The President's budget spells out how much funding he recommends for each discretionary program.

The President's budget can also include:

- **Changes to "mandatory" or "entitlement" programs,** such as Social Security, Medicare, Medicaid, and certain other programs (including but not limited to food stamps, federal civilian and military retirement benefits, veterans' disability benefits, and unemployment insurance) that are not controlled by annual appropriations. For example, when the President proposed adding a prescription drug benefit to Medicare, he had to show a corresponding increase in Medicare costs in his budget, relative to what Medicare would otherwise be projected to cost. Similarly, if the President proposes a reduction in Medicaid payments to states, his budget would show lower Medicaid costs than projected under current law.
- **Changes to the tax code.** Any presidential proposal to increase or decrease taxes should be reflected in a change in the amount of federal revenue that his budget expected to be collected the next year or in future years, relative to what would otherwise be collected.

To summarize, the President's budget must request a specific funding level for appropriated programs and may also request changes in tax and entitlement law.

Step Two: The Congressional Budget Resolution

After receiving the President's budget request, Congress generally holds hearings to question administration officials about their requests and then develops its own budget resolution. This work is done by the House and Senate Budget Committees, whose primary function is to draft the budget resolution. Once the committees are done, the budget resolution goes to the House and Senate floor, where it can be amended (by a majority vote).[1] It then goes to a House–Senate conference to resolve any differences, and a conference report is passed by both houses.

The budget resolution is a "concurrent" congressional resolution, not an ordinary bill, and therefore does not go to the President for his signature or veto. It also requires only a majority vote to pass, and is one of the few pieces of legislation that cannot be filibustered in the Senate.

The budget resolution is supposed to be passed by April 15, but it often takes longer. Occasionally, Congress does not pass a budget resolution. If that happens, the previous year's resolution, which is a multiyear plan, stays in effect.

- **What is in the budget resolution?** Unlike the President's budget, which is very detailed, the congressional budget resolution is a very simple document. It consists of a set of numbers stating how much Congress is supposed to spend in each of 19 broad spending categories (known as budget "functions") and how much total revenue the government will collect, for each of the next five or more years. (The Congressional Budget Act requires that the resolution cover a minimum of five years, but Congress sometimes chooses to develop a ten-year budget.) The difference between the two totals—the spending ceiling and the revenue floor—represents the deficit (or surplus) expected for each year.
- **How spending is defined: budget authority vs. outlays.** The spending totals in the budget resolution are stated in two different ways: the total amount of "budget authority" that is to be provided, and the estimated level of expenditures, or "outlays." Budget authority is how much money Congress allows a federal agency to commit to spend; outlays are how much money actually flows out of the federal treasury in a given year. For example, a bill that appropriated $50 million for

building a bridge would provide $50 million in budget authority in the same year, but the bill might not result in $50 million in outlays until the following year, when the bridge actually is built.

Budget authority and outlays thus serve different purposes. Budget authority represents a limit on how much funding Congress will provide, and is generally what Congress focuses on in making most budgetary decisions. Outlays, because they represent actual cash flow, help determine the size of the overall deficit or surplus.

- **How committee spending limits get set: 302(a) allocations.** The report that accompanies the budget resolution includes a table called the "302(a) allocation." This table takes the total spending figures that are laid out by budget function in the budget resolution and distributes these totals by congressional committee. The House and Senate tables are slightly different from one another, since committee jurisdictions vary somewhat between the two chambers.

The Appropriations Committee receives a single 302(a) allocation for all of its programs. It then decides on its own how to divide up this funding among its 12 subcommittees, into what are known as 302(b) suballocations. The various committees with jurisdiction over mandatory programs each get an allocation that represents a total dollar ceiling for all of the legislation they produce that year.

The spending totals in the budget resolution do not apply to the "authorizing" legislation produced by most congressional committees. Authorizing legislation typically either changes the rules for a federal program or provides a limit on how much money can be appropriated for it. Unless it involves changes to an entitlement program (such as Social Security or Medicare), authorizing legislation does not actually have a budgetary impact. For example, the education committees could produce legislation that authorizes a certain amount to be spent on Title I reading and math programs for disadvantaged children. However, none of that money can be spent until the annual Labor–HHS appropriations bill—which includes education spending—sets the actual dollar level for Title I funding for the year, which is frequently less than the authorized limit.

Often the report accompanying the budget resolution contains language describing the assumptions behind it, including how much it envisions certain programs being cut or increased. These assumptions generally serve only as guidance to the other committees and are not binding on them. Sometimes, though, the budget resolution includes more complicated devices intended to ensure that particular programs receive a certain amount of funding. For example, the budget resolution could create a "reserve fund" that could be used only for a specific purpose.

The budget resolution can also include temporary or permanent changes to the congressional budget process. For example, the fiscal year 2007 budget resolution contained a provision reinstating the "pay-as-you-go rule" in the Senate (see box on page 354).

How Are the Terms of the Budget Resolution Enforced?

The main enforcement mechanism that prevents Congress from passing legislation that violates the terms of the budget resolution is the ability of a single member of the House or the Senate to raise a budget "point of order" on the floor to block such legislation. In some recent years, this point of order has not been particularly important in the House because it can be waived there by a simple majority vote on a resolution developed by the leadership-appointed Rules Committee, which sets the conditions under which each bill will be considered on the floor. However, the budget point of order is very important in the Senate, where any legislation that exceeds a committee's spending allocation—or cuts taxes below the level allowed in the budget resolution—is vulnerable to a budget point of order on the floor that requires *60 votes* to waive.

Appropriations bills (or amendments to them) must fit within the 302(a) allocation given to the Appropriations Committee as well as the Committee-determined 302(b) suballocations for the coming fiscal year. Tax or entitlement bills (or any amendments offered to them) must fit within the budget resolution's spending limit for the relevant committee or the revenue floor, both in the first year and over the total multiyear period covered by the budget resolution. The cost of a tax or entitlement bill is determined (or "scored") by the Budget Committees, nearly always by relying on the nonpartisan Congressional Budget Office, which measures it against a budgetary "baseline" that projects entitlement spending or tax receipts under current law.

The Budget "Reconciliation" Process

From time to time, Congress chooses to make use of a special procedure outlined in the Congressional Budget Act known as "reconciliation."[2] This procedure was originally designed as a deficit-reduction tool, to force committees to produce spending cuts or tax increases called for in the budget resolution.

- **What is a reconciliation bill?** A reconciliation bill is a single piece of legislation that typically includes multiple provisions (generally developed by several committees) all of which affect the federal budget—whether on the mandatory spending side, the tax side, or both.[3] A reconciliation bill is the only piece of legislation (other than

The "Pay-As-You-Go" or "PAYGO" Rule

Independent of the Congressional Budget Act, the House and Senate each have a rule requiring that all entitlement increases and tax cuts be fully offset. For example, a bill that increased Medicare spending would have to be paid for by cutting somewhere else in Medicare or another entitlement program, by raising revenues, or by a combination of the two. The rule does not apply to discretionary spending, which is limited by the allocations set in the annual budget resolution.

If legislation providing for new tax cuts or entitlement increases is not paid for, the "PAYGO" rule gives any senator the power to raise a point of order against the bill, which can only be waived by the vote of 60 senators. In the House, any member can raise a point of order, and there is no opportunity to vote to waive the PAYGO requirement—the bill is automatically defeated, unless the leadership-appointed Rules Committee has decided in advance to waive PAYGO as part of the broader measure (referred to as a rule) setting the terms of debate on the bill as a whole and the House has agreed to that rule.

PAYGO is an additional requirement, separate and apart from the terms of the budget resolution. A bill that cuts taxes or increases entitlement spending without an offset would violate the PAYGO rule even if the budget resolution had assumed the enactment of tax cuts or entitlement increases and allocated the necessary amounts to the relevant committees. (The PAYGO rule does not directly apply to the budget resolution itself or amendments to it, however.)

In order to satisfy the House and Senate PAYGO rules, a bill must be paid for over the first six years (including the current year), and over the first 11 years (including the current year). The Senate PAYGO rule does not consider the impact of a bill on Social Security and other "off-budget" items, whereas the House PAYGO rule applies to the "unified budget," which includes Social Security.

the budget resolution itself) that cannot be filibustered on the Senate floor, so it can pass by a majority vote.

- **How does the reconciliation process work?** If Congress decides to use the reconciliation process, language known as a "reconciliation directive" must be included in the budget resolution. The reconciliation directive instructs various committees to produce legislation by a specific date that meets certain spending or tax targets. (If they fail to produce this legislation, the Budget Committee Chair generally has the right to offer floor amendments to meet the reconciliation targets for them, which is enough of a threat that committees tend to comply with the directive.) The Budget Committees then package all of these bills together into one bill that goes to the floor for an up-or-down vote, with only limited opportunity for amendment. After the House and Senate resolve the differences between their competing bills, a final conference report is considered on the floor of each house and then goes to the President for his signature or veto.

- **Constraints on reconciliation: the "Byrd rule."** While reconciliation enables Congress to bundle together several different provisions affecting a broad range of programs, it faces one major constraint: the "Byrd rule," named after Senator Byrd of West Virginia. This Senate rule makes any provision of (or amendment to) the reconciliation bill that is deemed "extraneous" to the purpose of amending entitlement or tax law vulnerable to a point of order. If a point of order is raised under the Byrd rule, the offending provision is automatically stripped from the bill unless at least 60 senators vote to waive the rule. This makes it difficult, for example, to include any policy changes in the reconciliation bill unless they have direct fiscal implications. Under this rule, authorizations of discretionary appropriations are not allowed, nor are changes to civil rights or employment law, for example. Changes to Social Security also are not permitted under the Byrd rule.

  In addition, the Byrd rule bars any entitlement increases or tax cuts that cost money beyond the five (or more) years covered by the reconciliation directive, unless these "out-year" costs are fully offset by other provisions in the bill. This is a central reason why Congress made the 2001 tax cuts expire by 2010, rather than making them permanent.

End Notes

1. For more than 20 years, the House leadership has prevented the budget resolution from being subject to unlimited amendments on the floor. Instead, the Rules Committee—an arm of the leadership whose role is to develop resolutions that set the terms for floor debate—has generally allowed the consideration of only a few "substitute" amendments. These are alternative budgets, typically developed by the minority party or caucuses within the House that have a particular interest in budget policy.

2. In this context, the term "reconciliation" does not have its ordinary meaning of two parties working out their differences (for example, the House and Senate are often described as going to conference to "reconcile" competing versions of a bill). Rather, it refers to the process by which congressional committees adjust, or "reconcile," existing tax or entitlement law with the new tax or mandatory spending targets called for in the budget resolution.

3. A separate rule of the House and Senate prohibits legislation other than Appropriations Acts from providing or rescinding discretionary appropriations. On occasion this rule has been ignored and other legislation—including reconciliation bills—has included items of discretionary appropriations.

SOURCE: Reprinted with permission from Coven, M., and R. Kogan. 2007. "Introduction to the Federal Budget Process." Center for Budget and Policy Priorities. [Online information; retrieved 2/19/09.] www.cbpp.org/3-7-03bud.htm.

MICHIGAN'S BUDGET PROCESS

Introduction

The Michigan Constitution requires the Governor to propose an Executive Budget for state activities on an annual basis. By law the Executive Budget must be submitted to the Legislature within 30 days after the Legislature convenes in regular session on the second Wednesday in January. However, when a newly elected Governor is inaugurated into office, 60 days are allowed to prepare the proposal. The Executive Budget is more than a statutory requirement. It represents a statement of priorities for the policy activities of state government. Therefore, a detailed budget preparation process is necessary to provide information that will help the Governor and the Legislature allocate state resources most effectively. The budget process can be broken down into the following four stages:

- Development of the Governor's Executive Budget
- Enactment by the Legislature
- Budget Revisions
- Closing the Books

Development of the Governor's Executive Budget

Department Requests

The development of each new fiscal year budget begins in August, approximately 13 to 14 months prior to the beginning of the new fiscal year. The process starts with the State Budget Office issuing program policy guidelines to the departments. The guidelines and directions include assumptions regarding revenue changes, federal funds information, and economic adjustments. The guidelines also include instructions for the preparation of different levels of expenditures for each department. By October, departments submit their budget proposals to the State Budget Office. The State Budget Director makes preliminary budget recommendations to the Governor based on staff evaluations and funding proposals.

First Revenue Estimating Conference

These recommendations are fine-tuned during the next few months. The Revenue Estimating Conference held each January is a major part of the budget process. During the conference, national and state economic indicators are used to formulate an accurate prediction of revenue available for appropriation in the upcoming fiscal year. This conference first convened in 1992, pursuant to Act No. 72 of the Public Acts of 1991. The principal participants in the conference are the State Treasurer and the Directors of the Senate and House Fiscal Agencies or their respective designees. Other participants may include the Governor and senior officials from the Department of Treasury.

Governor's Budget Decisions

Before and after the Revenue Estimating Conference, the State Budget Office, the Executive Office, and the state departments hold briefings and hearings in order to review requests and prepare recommendations. The Governor makes final budget decisions in December prior to the presentation to the Legislature.

Executive Budget Presentation

As indicated above, Act No. 431 of Public Acts of 1984, the Management and Budget Act, requires the budget to be submitted within 30 days after the Legislature convenes in regular session on the second Wednesday in January. When a new governor is elected, 60 days are allowed.

During the budget presentation, the State Budget Director, on behalf of the Governor, presents the budget and accompanying explanations, recommendations, and legislation to the Legislature. This generally takes place in early February during a joint session of the House and Senate Appropriations Committees.

Legislative Action

By custom, all the appropriation bills are introduced in both houses of the Legislature and are divided between the houses for consideration. The bills usually receive more detailed hearings in the house of origin. Generally, all the appropriation bills are introduced by each appropriations committee chair or the ranking member of the Governor's party. Traditionally, only half of the bills are considered in each house initially. Currently, the practice is to alternate the house of origin each year. This practice allows both appropriations committees to work simultaneously on the appropriations bills.

The Appropriations Committees assign the budgets to specific subcommittees. These subcommittees then conduct a series of hearings. State department directors and their staff present an overview of the Governor's proposed budget, followed by briefings from House Fiscal Agency and Senate Fiscal Agency staff. The subcommittees may also hold public hearings in locations across the state. Finally, the subcommittee composes recommendations that are reported to the full Appropriations Committee.

During full House and Senate Committee meetings, state department directors and their staff are expected to provide explanations when their agency's appropriations are considered. A legislative fiscal analyst assigned to that bill is also present. This analyst may prepare a report or series of reports on the bill. The chair of the related subcommittee asks the legislative analyst to summarize the bill. The committee members are then free to ask questions regarding the bill. The appropriations committee may amend the bill or adopt a substitute version. Following approval, the bill is reported to the floor.

Prior to floor consideration, the Democratic and Republican members will discuss the bill during a caucus meeting. In addition to developing a party position, the caucus provides individual legislators with an opportunity to become better informed regarding policy issues incorporated in the budget.

The legislative procedure for consideration of the appropriation bills is basically the same as for other bills except that appropriation measures receive priority on the legislative calendars. In many instances, members who are going to offer amendments will propose the changes to the appropriations committees before floor debate. Floor consideration varies considerably depending on the particular subject matter, issues, and other factors. There may be minimal debate, or it may take a whole day or more for a given bill. Fiscal analysts prepare floor sheets summarizing the appropriation bill, the difference in funding from the prior year, the Governor's recommendation, or between house recommendations; new, expanded, or eliminated programs; and total FTEs (full-time equated positions) authorized.

Second Revenue Estimating Conference

A second Revenue Estimating Conference takes place in May of each year. Its purpose is to provide an updated consensus forecast of anticipated revenues for the Executive Budget. Upon completion of the revised consensus revenue estimate, legislative leadership meets with the Governor and the State Budget Director in an attempt to establish final spending targets for each state department. The process of target setting also involves discussion and attempts for agreement on other overall budget issues including boilerplate language, revenue bills, and other statutory changes to be included in the final budget.

Reports of the agreements reached during target setting are then provided to the Legislature.

Conference Committees

Differences between the two houses on each appropriations bill are resolved by a conference committee. The committee consists of six members—three members from the Senate and three members from the House. Traditionally, when differences on any of the appropriation bills necessitate a conference committee, the conferees are usually members of the respective House and Senate appropriations subcommittees. Rule 7 of the Joint Rules of the Senate and the House of Representatives provides:

> The conference committee shall not consider any matters other than matters of difference between the two Houses. When the agreement arrived at by the conferees is such that it affects other parts of the bill, the conferees may recommend amendments to conform with the agreement. The conferees may also recommend corrections to any errors in the bill or title.

Conference committees are expected to ensure that the final levels of appropriations in the conference reports are equal to the appropriations targets established by legislative leadership. This process helps ensure that the enacted appropriations bills do not exceed the consensus estimate of available revenues.

If the conference committee report is approved by both houses, the bill is enrolled and printed (final copy of a bill in the form as passed by both houses) and presented to the Governor. If the conference committee does not reach a compromise and reports that the committee cannot reach an agreement, or if the Legislature does not accept the conference report, a second conference committee may be appointed.

While there is no specific legal time requirement for passage of the budget bills, this task is accomplished prior to the beginning of the new fiscal year. Appropriations bills are usually considered and passed in April by the first house, and in early June by the second house, and usually final action is completed in July.

Governor Signs Bills and/or Vetoes

The same procedures related to gubernatorial approval of other legislation also apply to appropriation bills. However, the Governor has additional authority to veto any distinct item or items appropriating money in any appropriation bill. The parts approved become law. Vetoed items are void unless the Legislature overrules the veto by a two-thirds vote of the members elected to and serving in each house. An appropriation line item vetoed by the Governor and not subsequently overridden by the Legislature is not funded unless another appropriation for that line item is approved.

Budget Revisions

According to the Michigan Constitution, no appropriation is a mandate to spend. The Governor, by Executive Order and with the approval of the appropriations committees, can reduce expenditures whenever it appears that actual revenues for a fiscal period will fall below the revenue estimates on which the appropriations for that period are based. By statute, any recommendation for the reduction of expenditures must be approved or disapproved by both of the appropriations committees within ten days after the recommendation is made. A reduction cannot be made without approval from both committees; not later than 30 days after a proposed order is disapproved, the Governor may submit alternative recommendations for expenditure reductions to the committees for their approval or disapproval.

Since 1970, the Governor has issued 27 Executive Orders to reduce expenditures, but on 11 occasions the Executive Orders did not receive approval of the Appropriations Committees. Subsequently, the Governor issued other Executive Orders that were approved. The Governor may not reduce expenditures for the legislative or judicial branches or expenditures from funds constitutionally dedicated for specific purposes.

Each department prepares the allotment of appropriations and may request revisions, legislative or administrative transfers, or supplemental appropriations. The State Budget Office must approve revisions to allotments. Transfer of funds other than administrative transfers within a department must be submitted by the State Budget Office to the House and Senate Appropriations Committees.

Expenditure increases for a new program or for the expansion of an existing program cannot be made until the availability of money has been determined and the program has been approved and appropriated by the Legislature. The Governor and the Legislature act on supplemental appropriation bills in a manner similar to original appropriations.

Closing the Books

The fiscal year runs from October 1 to September 30 of the following year. The following January, the State Budget Office releases its initial estimates of the actual year-end balances in the General Fund and School Aid Fund. These estimates are contained in a report referred to as the Preliminary Book Closing Report.

Final book closing occurs in March. The State Budget Office releases the final accounting for the previous fiscal year revenues, expenditures, and year-end balances. These data are contained in the State of Michigan Comprehensive Annual Financial Report (CAFR).

SOURCE: Reprinted from Office of the State Budget, Michigan. n.d. "Budget Process." [Online information; retrieved 2/19/09.] www.michigan.gov/budget/0,1607,7-157-11462-34950—,00.html.

21

OVERSIGHT PLAN OF THE HOUSE COMMITTEE ON ENERGY AND COMMERCE, 111TH CONGRESS

**COMMITTEE ON ENERGY AND COMMERCE
OVERSIGHT PLAN
U.S. HOUSE OF REPRESENTATIVES
111TH CONGRESS
THE HONORABLE HENRY A. WAXMAN, CHAIRMAN**

Rule X, clause 2(d) of the Rules of the House requires each standing Committee to adopt an oversight plan for the two-year period of the Congress and to submit the plan to the Committee on Oversight and Government Reform and to the Committee on House Administration not later than February 15 of the first session of the Congress.

This is the oversight plan of the Committee on Energy and Commerce for the 111th Congress. It includes the areas in which the Committee expects to conduct oversight during the 111th Congress, subject to limits on staff and resources, but does not preclude oversight or investigation of additional matters as the need arises.

The plan outlines oversight in several areas of the committee's jurisdiction, including ENERGY AND ENVIRONMENTAL ISSUES; COMMERCE, TRADE, AND CONSUMER PROTECTION ISSUES; and COMMUNICATIONS, TECHNOLOGY AND INTERNET ISSUES; as well as HEALTH AND HEALTHCARE ISSUES. Only oversight plans in two of these areas are reproduced here. The entire oversight plan can be read at http://energycommerce.house.gov/Press_111/20090210/oversightplan.pdf.

ENERGY AND ENVIRONMENTAL ISSUES

The Committee intends to conduct oversight in the 111th Congress of numerous energy and environment-related issues to help ensure that government is working and that relevant statutes are effective and up to date.

Climate Change

Global warming and energy issues will be a key area of interest. Due to the magnitude and complexity of the task of reducing greenhouse gas emissions, the Committee expects to examine governmental and nongovernmental activities and policies in this area, and their bases. The Committee will also examine governmental and private sector policies and actions related to developing and maintaining a sustainable and affordable national energy supply, including through the efficient use of energy.

Environmental Pollution and Hazardous Waste

The Committee will examine whether the key environmental and energy laws under its jurisdiction are being implemented and followed appropriately to ensure that public health, the environment, and consumers are adequately protected. This will focus on the key issues of air pollution, drinking water contamination, hazardous waste disposal and cleanup, manufacture, use, and safety of chemical substances and pesticides on food. The Committee will examine the actions of the agencies charged with addressing these issues: the Environmental Protection Agency, the Department of Energy (DOE), and the Agency for Toxic Substances and Disease Registry.

Energy Policy

The Committee will examine U.S. policies pertaining to energy efficiency and conservation, production, and consumption of electricity, oil, natural gas, coal, hydroelectric power, nuclear power, and renewable energy. The Committee will inquire into potential opportunities for the government and private sector to enhance environmental, public health, and consumer protections (including pipeline safety), while promoting a sustainable, clean energy future. The Committee will examine the actions of agencies and offices charged with developing and implementing U.S. energy policies, including the DOE, the Federal Energy Regulatory Commission, and the Nuclear Regulatory Commission. The Committee will also examine the activities and policies of the Department of Transportation and the National Highway Traffic Safety Administration as they relate to matters within the Committee's jurisdiction.

Energy Security

The Committee will oversee management and operations issues at the DOE, including management and operations of the National Nuclear Security Administration (NNSA) and the DOE National Laboratories. The Committee will focus on DOE's management of the environment, safety, and health aspects of its policies and activities, and DOE's management of the contractors that operate the National Laboratories. In addition, the Committee will oversee the protection of nuclear materials around the globe by examining ongoing problems at both the National Labs and at nuclear power plants with respect to the security of both nuclear materials and sensitive security information and by examining nuclear detection systems at air, land, and seaports.

Bioresearch Laboratories

Building on the two hearings in the 111th Congress, the Committee will exercise continued oversight of issues related to construction and operation of high-containment bioresearch laboratories.

HEALTH AND HEALTHCARE ISSUES

Children's Health Insurance Program

The Committee will oversee the implementation of the legislation reauthorizing the Children's Health Insurance Program (CHIP) by the Department of Health and Human Services (HHS), state CHIP agencies, and their private contractors. This oversight will focus on the extent to which federal financial incentives and state outreach and enrollment activities are successful in extending coverage to low-income children who are eligible but not enrolled in Medicaid or CHIP. The Committee will also examine whether federal program funds are being used to purchase covered services efficiently in a manner that minimizes waste, fraud, and abuse.

Centers for Medicare & Medicaid Services

The Committee will review the management, operation, and activities of the Centers for Medicare & Medicaid Services (CMS), focusing on the effective provision of services under the Medicare, Medicaid, and Child Health Insurance programs and the elimination of waste, fraud, and abuse in these programs. The Committee will examine the use and oversight of private contractors by CMS in administering these programs.

Drug Safety

The Committee will review the ability of the Food and Drug Administration (FDA) to ensure the safety and effectiveness of prescription and over-the counter (OTC) drugs sold in the United States, including whether necessary safeguards for imported drugs are in place. The Committee will also examine manufacturer marketing practices for both prescription and OTC drugs.

Emergency Care Services

The Committee will review the ability of the nation's trauma centers and emergency departments to respond to the growing demand for their services. Among the areas of oversight interest are the activities of HHS to ensure that emergency rooms in cities at high risk of a terrorist attack have the capacity to handle a surge in casualties, as well as the availability of on-call specialists on a 24/7 basis.

Food Safety

The Committee will examine the causes of recent food safety problems and the effectiveness of our current regulatory system for overseeing the safety of imported foods. The Committee will review the FDA's statutory authorities for protecting the nation's food supply with a view toward identifying any gaps. The Committee will also examine whether FDA's financial and personnel resources are adequate to protect the public from unsafe food.

Health Information Technology (HIT)

The Committee will oversee the implementation of the HIT provisions of the economic recovery legislation by HHS. The Committee will focus initially on the Department's establishment of standards for interoperability, functionality, security, and privacy of electronic health records and its certification of systems that meet those standards. The Committee will also monitor the Department's HIT-related grant-making activity.

National Institutes of Health (NIH)

The NIH budget spends over $29 billion per year, largely on medical research intended to improve the health of the nation. The Committee will examine whether there is sufficient transparency and accountability to ensure that these funds are spent effectively and efficiently.

HIV/AIDS

The Committee will oversee domestic and global HIV prevention and treatment activities by HHS and the Centers for Disease Control and Prevention (CDC). Domestically, areas of concern include the scale-up of prevention efforts, the continuing implementation of CDC's routine testing recommendations, and the reach of care and treatment programs. The Committee will also monitor HHS's implementation of U.S.-funded HIV activities abroad. Particular attention will be paid to changes made by the 2008 reauthorization of the President's Emergency Plan for AIDS Relief (PEPFAR), including increased flexibility in prevention programming and an intensified emphasis on integration with other health and social services.

Hospital-Acquired Infections and Antibiotic Resistance

The Committee will oversee the actions taken by HHS, state hospital licensure agencies, and the private sector to reduce the incidence of preventable hospital-acquired infections. Among the areas of interest is checklists for use by physicians, nurses, and other hospital personnel to reduce such infections. The Committee will also review efforts to combat the spread of antibiotic resistant infections. The Committee will examine the practices that contribute to the problem, including the inappropriate use of antibiotics both by humans and in the food supply.

Preventable Medical Errors

In addition to its work on hospital-acquired infections, the Committee will also examine other preventable medical errors, which studies suggest annually cause tens of thousands of preventable deaths and cost our nation's medical system billions of dollars. The Committee will examine the practices that contribute to such preventable medical errors and review actions taken by providers, patients, insurers, and the federal government to reduce these errors.

Individual Health Insurance

The Committee will examine business practices in the individual health insurance market that may compromise the accessibility or affordability of coverage. The initial focus of this oversight will be the practice of rescission, or retroactive termination of coverage following the submission of claims by the insured individual. The Committee will review the practices of insurers, the activities of state regulatory agencies, and the enforcement of consumer protections in the individual market by HHS under the Health Insurance Portability and Accountability Act (HIPAA).

Medicaid

The Committee will oversee the implementation of the provisions of the economic recovery legislation relating to Medicaid. The Committee will review the payment of additional federal matching funds to states to ensure states deploy the funds in an efficient and effective manner. The Committee will examine whether states receiving this fiscal relief maintain adequate Medicaid reimbursement levels for providers and reimburse at an adequate rate to make services available. The Committee will also monitor the response of HHS and state Medicaid programs to the needs of uninsured, unemployed workers and their families. In addition, the Committee will examine the purchase of managed care, prescription drugs, and other covered services to determine whether greater efficiencies can be achieved for federal and state taxpayers. The Committee will review the costs and benefits of using private contractors in the administration of the Medicaid program at the federal and state level. The Committee will also review efforts to reduce waste, fraud, and abuse in the program.

Medical Device Safety

The Committee will review FDA's efforts to ensure the safety and effectiveness of medical devices. The Committee will examine the gaps in the current statutory authorities, both pre- and post-market, that FDA uses to protect patients from unsafe or ineffective devices.

Medicare

The Committee will oversee the administration and operation of the Medicare program by CMS and its contractors. Among the areas of interest is the adequacy of Medicare payment rates for primary care physicians under Part B; the appropriateness of payments to Medicare Advantage plans; the treatment of beneficiaries with chronic illness by Medicare Advantage plans, particularly private fee-for-service plans; and the business practices of Medicare Advantage plans and CMS oversight of those practices. With respect to Medicare Part D, the Committee will review the effectiveness of private plans' administration of the program; the treatment of long-term care patients; the annual reassignment of individuals who are dually eligible for Medicare and Medicaid; the treatment of long-term care patients under Part D; the availability of manufacturer rebates on drugs purchased by Medicare Part D plans; and the oversight of Part D plans by CMS. The Committee will also review efforts to reduce waste, fraud, and abuse in the program.

Navajo Nation Uranium Contamination

The Committee will monitor the cleanup of the surface and subsurface contamination of the Navajo Nation resulting from uranium mining and milling activities after World War II. Five federal agencies have developed and are implementing five-year plans to clean up the contamination and protect public health: the Bureau of Indian Affairs, DOE, the Environmental Protection Agency, the Indian Health Service, and the Nuclear Regulatory Commission.

Nursing Homes

The Committee will examine the quality of the nursing home care paid for by the Medicare and Medicaid programs. The Committee will review the monitoring and enforcement of quality standards by CMS and state survey agencies.

Off-Label Marketing

The Committee will conduct oversight of manufacturer marketing of pre-scription drugs and medical devices for uses not approved by FDA. While off-label use of drugs or devices is legal, the marketing of drugs or devices for off-label uses is not. Off-label marketing can result in unnecessary expenditures and raises potential safety and effectiveness issues for patients. The Committee will review the activities of the FDA, CMS, the Office of Inspector General, and the Justice Department to investigate and prosecute those manufacturers engaged in off-label marketing.

Privacy

The Committee will review adherence to and enforcement of the security and privacy rules under HIPAA. The Committee will also oversee the implementation of the privacy provisions in the economic recovery legislation by HHS. The Committee will focus on the use of a patient's health information by providers, health insurers, and others that receive such identifiable information.

Safety Net Hospitals and Clinics

The Committee will monitor the ability of public and private nonprofit hospitals and clinics of last resort—those that treat all patients, regardless of ability to pay—to maintain their service capacity during the recession. Of particular concern to the Committee is whether the specialized services that these facilities provide that are of community-wide benefit, such as trauma care, neonatal, intensive care, and care for burn victims, will be maintained in the face of increasing numbers of unemployed, uninsured patients.

Vaccine Policy

The Committee will oversee the various components of vaccine policy within HHS, including the development of the National Vaccine Plan; plans to procure and stockpile vaccines for use in case of an influenza pandemic, bioterror attack, or shortage of routinely administered vaccines; efforts to increase the use of vaccines among adults, including healthcare workers; and access issues associated with the Vaccines for Children program. The Committee will also review the status of the Vaccine Injury Compensation Program.

SOURCE: Reprinted from House Committee on Energy and Commerce. 2009. "Committee: Oversight Plan." [Online document; retrieved 2/20/09.] energycommerce.house.gov/Press_111/20090210/oversightplan.pdf.

22

MEDPAC

The Medicare Payment Advisory Commission (MedPAC) is an independent Congressional agency established by the Balanced Budget Act of 1997 (P.L. 105-33) to advise the U.S. Congress on issues affecting the Medicare program. The Commission's statutory mandate is quite broad: In addition to advising the Congress on payments to private health plans participating in Medicare and providers in Medicare's traditional fee-for-service program, MedPAC is also tasked with analyzing access to care, quality of care, and other issues affecting Medicare.

The Commission's 17 members bring diverse expertise in the financing and delivery of health care services. Commissioners are appointed to three-year terms (subject to renewal) by the Comptroller General and serve part time. Appointments are staggered; the terms of five or six Commissioners expire each year. The Commission is supported by an executive director and a staff of analysts, who typically have backgrounds in economics, health policy, public health, or medicine.

MedPAC meets publicly to discuss policy issues and formulate its recommendations to the Congress. In the course of these meetings, Commissioners consider the results of staff research, presentations by policy experts, and comments from interested parties. (Meeting transcripts are available at www.medpac.gov/meetings.cfm). Commission members and staff also seek input on Medicare issues through frequent meetings with individuals interested in the program, including staff from congressional committees and the Centers for Medicare & Medicaid Services (CMS), healthcare researchers, healthcare providers, and beneficiary advocates.

Two reports—issued in March and June each year—are the primary outlet for Commission recommendations. In addition to these reports and others on subjects requested by the Congress, MedPAC advises the Congress through other avenues, including comments on reports and proposed regulations issued by the Secretary of the Department of Health and Human Services, testimony, and briefings for congressional staff.

SOURCE: Reprinted from Medicare Payment Advisory Commission (MedPAC). n.d. "About MedPAC." [Online information; retrieved 2/23/09.] www.medpac.gov/about.cfm.

BILL WOULD GIVE MORE TRAINING TO MANAGERS

On March 24, 2009, Senator Daniel K. Akaka (D-HI) introduced legislation intended to improve management in the federal supervisor ranks by requiring improved management training at all agencies. The bill, S. 674, known as the Federal Supervisor Training Act of 2009, has been assigned to the Senate Homeland Security and Governmental Affairs Committee. The bill, if enacted into law, would require agencies to provide all managers with regular, ongoing training on management skills, prohibited personnel practices, employee rights, and general leadership.

Upon introducing the bill, Senator Akaka stated, "The performance of our federal employees and managers is essential to the success of our government. We will do well to invest in them through training and professional development." He also said, "Given the growing number of federal managers who are eligible to retire, it is increasingly important to train new supervisors to manage effectively. Good leadership begins with strong management training. It is time to ensure that federal managers receive appropriate training to supervise federal employees."

The proposed Federal Supervisor Training Act has three major training requirements.

1. New supervisors must receive training in the initial 12 months on the job, with mandatory retraining every three years on how to work with employees to develop performance expectations and evaluate employees. Current managers will have three years to obtain their initial training.
2. New supervisors will receive mentoring and training on how to mentor employees.
3. New supervisors will receive training on the laws governing and the procedures for enforcing whistleblower, collective bargaining, and anti-discrimination rights.

In addition, the bill

- sets standards that supervisors should meet in order to manage employees effectively,
- assesses a manager's ability to meet those standards, and
- provides training to improve areas identified in personnel assessments.

SOURCE: Reprinted from Akaka, D. K. 2009. "Akaka Introduces Bill to Improve Management, Training, and Accountability in the Federal Government." Press Release, March 24. [Online material; retrieved 3/28/09.] akaka.senate.gov/public/index.cfm?FuseAction=PressReleases.Home&month=3&year=2009&release_id=2594.

24

REMOVING BARRIERS TO RESPONSIBLE SCIENTIFIC RESEARCH INVOLVING HUMAN STEM CELLS

EXECUTIVE ORDER

- - - - - - -

REMOVING BARRIERS TO RESPONSIBLE SCIENTIFIC RESEARCH INVOLVING HUMAN STEM CELLS

By the authority vested in me as President by the Constitution and the laws of the United States of America, it is hereby ordered as follows:

Section 1. Policy. Research involving human embryonic stem cells and human non-embryonic stem cells has the potential to lead to better understanding and treatment of many disabling diseases and conditions. Advances over the past decade in this promising scientific field have been encouraging, leading to broad agreement in the scientific community that the research should be supported by Federal funds.

For the past eight years, the authority of the Department of Health and Human Services, including the National Institutes of Health (NIH), to fund and conduct human embryonic stem cell research has been limited by Presidential actions. The purpose of this order is to remove these limitations on scientific inquiry, to expand NIH support for the exploration of human stem cell research, and in so doing to enhance the contribution of America's scientists to important new discoveries and new therapies for the benefit of humankind.

Sec. 2. Research. The Secretary of Health and Human Services (Secretary), through the Director of NIH, may support and conduct responsible, scientifically worthy human stem cell research, including human embryonic stem cell research, to the extent permitted by law.

Sec. 3. Guidance. Within 120 days from the date of this order, the Secretary, through the Director of NIH, shall review existing NIH guidance and other widely recognized guidelines on human stem cell research, including provisions establishing appropriate safeguards, and issue new NIH guidance on such research that is consistent with this order. The Secretary, through NIH, shall review and update such guidance periodically, as appropriate.

Sec. 4. General Provisions.

(a) This order shall be implemented consistent with applicable law and subject to the availability of appropriations.

(b) Nothing in this order shall be construed to impair or otherwise affect:

(i) authority granted by law to an executive department, agency, or the head thereof; or

(ii) functions of the Director of the Office of Management and Budget relating to budgetary, administrative, or legislative proposals.

(c) This order is not intended to, and does not, create any right or benefit, substantive or procedural, enforceable at law or in equity, by any party against the United States, its departments, agencies, or entities, its officers, employees, or agents, or any other person.

Sec. 5. Revocations.

(a) The Presidential statement of August 9, 2001, limiting Federal funding for research involving human embryonic stem cells, shall have no further effect as a statement of governmental policy.

(b) Executive Order 13435 of June 20, 2007, which supplements the August 9, 2001, statement on human embryonic stem cell research, is revoked.

BARACK OBAMA

THE WHITE HOUSE,
March 9, 2009.

25

FEDERAL HUMAN CAPITAL SURVEY 2008

The Federal Human Capital Survey (FHCS) is conducted periodically by the U.S. Office of Personnel Management (OPM, www.opm.gov). The FHCS is a tool that measures employees' perceptions of whether, and to what extent, conditions characterizing successful organizations are present in their agencies. The first administration of this groundbreaking survey took place in 2002. It was conducted again in 2004, 2006 and 2008. The survey

- provides general indicators of how well the federal government is running its human resources management systems,
- serves as a tool for OPM to assess individual agencies, and, most importantly,
- gives senior managers critical information to answer the question, what can I do to make my agency work better?

The following table provides government-wide responses to a set of questions pertaining to Personal Work Experiences. Other categories on the survey are: Recruitment, Development, and Retention; Performance Culture; Leadership; Learning (Knowledge Management); Job Satisfaction; and Satisfaction with Benefits.

Personal Work Experiences, Items 1-10						
(1) The people I work with cooperate to get the job done.						
Strongly Agree	Agree	Neither Agree nor Disagree	Disagree	Strongly Disagree	# of Respondents	Positive Responses (Strongly Agree/Agree)
29.9%	53.9%	8.4%	6.3%	1.5%	212,197	83.9%

(2) I am given a real opportunity to improve my skills in my organization.						
Strongly Agree	Agree	Neither Agree nor Disagree	Disagree	Strongly Disagree	# of Respondents	Positive Responses (Strongly Agree/Agree)
19.7%	44.3%	17.9%	12.8%	5.3%	212,195	64.0%

(3) I have enough information to do my job well.

Strongly Agree	Agree	Neither Agree nor Disagree	Disagree	Strongly Disagree	# of Respondents	Positive Responses (Strongly Agree/Agree)
18.8%	54.6%	15.2%	9.4%	2.0%	212,194	73.4%

(4) I feel encouraged to come up with new and better ways of doing things.

Strongly Agree	Agree	Neither Agree nor Disagree	Disagree	Strongly Disagree	# of Respondents	Positive Responses (Strongly Agree/Agree)
21.7%	39.0%	19.4%	13.7%	6.1%	212,194	60.7%

(5) My work gives me a feeling of personal accomplishment.

Strongly Agree	Agree	Neither Agree nor Disagree	Disagree	Strongly Disagree	# of Respondents	Positive Responses (Strongly Agree/Agree)
28.4%	45.0%	14.9%	7.8%	3.9%	212,189	73.4%

(6) I like the kind of work I do.

Strongly Agree	Agree	Neither Agree nor Disagree	Disagree	Strongly Disagree	# of Respondents	Positive Responses (Strongly Agree/Agree)
39.2%	44.7%	11.0%	3.6%	1.6%	212,198	83.8%

(7) I have trust and confidence in my supervisor.

Strongly Agree	Agree	Neither Agree nor Disagree	Disagree	Strongly Disagree	# of Respondents	Positive Responses (Strongly Agree/Agree)
27.5%	36.7%	17.8%	10.3%	7.6%	212,190	64.2%

(8) I recommend my organization as a good place to work.

Strongly Agree	Agree	Neither Agree nor Disagree	Disagree	Strongly Disagree	# of Respondents	Positive Responses (Strongly Agree/Agree)
24.5%	40.9%	19.6%	9.0%	6.0%	212,191	65.5%

(9) Overall, how good a job do you feel is being done by your immediate supervisor/team leader?

Very Good	Good	Fair	Poor	Very Poor	# of Respondents	Positive Responses (Strongly Agree/Agree)
31.2%	35.0%	20.9%	7.8%	5.1%	212,189	66.2%

(10) How would you rate the overall quality of work done by your work group?

Very Good	Good	Fair	Poor	Very Poor	# of Respondents	Positive Responses (Strongly Agree/Agree)
37.1%	46.3%	13.5%	2.3%	0.8%	212,190	83.4%

The following table compares results from the FHCS 2008 survey to the percentage who responded favorably to the same questions collected from employees performing a range of jobs in a set of large private sector companies, primarily in the United States. The table contains a set of Personal Work Experience Items and of Job Satisfaction Items from the 2008 survey.

Personal Work Experiences Items	*Comparison of Positive Responses*	
	FHCS 2008	*Private Sector 2008*
(1) The people I work with cooperate to get the job done.	84%	80%
(2) I am given a real opportunity to improve my skills in my organization.	64%	60%
(3) I have enough information to do my job well.	73%	75%
(4) I feel encouraged to come up with new and better ways of doing things.	61%	68%
(5) My work gives me a feeling of personal accomplishment.	73%	73%
(6) I like the kind of work I do.	84%	83%
(9) Overall, how good a job do you feel is being done by your immediate supervisor/team leader?	66%	74%

Job Satisfaction Items	Comparison of Positive Responses	
	FHCS 2008	Private Sector 2008
(55) How satisfied are you with your involvement in decisions that affect your work?	53%	58%
(56) How satisfied are you with the information you receive from management on what's going on in your organization?	48%	66%
(57) How satisfied are you with the recognition you receive for doing a good job?	50%	56%
(59) How satisfied are you with your opportunity to get a better job in your organization?	39%	49%
(60) How satisfied are you with the training you receive for your present job?	55%	66%
(61) Considering everything, how satisfied are you with your job?	68%	70%
(63) Considering everything, how satisfied are you with your organization?	57%	70%

SOURCE: Reprinted from U.S. Office of Personnel Management. 2009. Federal Human Capital Survey 2008. [Online material; retrieved 3/28/09.] www.fhcs.opm.gov/.

MANAGEMENT CHALLENGES AT THE SOCIAL SECURITY ADMINISTRATION

All government agencies, as is the case in large private enterprises, face a variety of management challenges in their operations. Examples of such challenges at the Social Security Administration (SSA) are the subject of a hearing sponsored jointly by two subcommittees of the House of Representatives' Committee on Ways and Means: Income Security and Family Support, and Social Security. Testimony at the March 24, 2009 hearing included that from a representative of the U. S. Government Accountability Office (GAO).

The subcommittees had previously asked GAO to study the service delivery challenges facing SSA, particularly the substantial backlog of disability claims. Excerpts of the testimony are reprinted here illustrate the nature of some of the management challenges in a large unit of the federal government. The GAO testimony, given by Daniel Bertoni, Director of Education, Workforce, and Income Security at GAO, began as follows:

Mr. Chairmen and Members of the Subcommittees:

I am pleased to have the opportunity to discuss challenges facing the Social Security Administration (SSA) with respect to its disability claims processing and field office service delivery. SSA provides a number of services that touch many lives. In particular, each year millions of Americans who believe that they can no longer work because of severe physical or mental impairments apply for cash benefits through SSA's two disability programs—Disability Insurance (DI) and Supplemental Security Income (SSI). In addition, SSA annually processes millions of applications for retirement benefits through its Old-Age and Survivors Insurance (OASI) program, issues millions of Social Security cards, and provides many other services through its large and decentralized workforce. In fiscal year 2008, SSA had an administrative budget of over $11 billion and employed about 63,000 employees, 44 percent of whom are located in approximately 1,300 field offices across the country.

* * *

SSA has experienced a growing backlog in disability claims as well as deteriorating customer service. From fiscal years 1997 to 2006, SSA's total backlog of disability claims—the number of claims exceeding the amount that should optimally be pending at year end—doubled, reaching about 576,000 in 2006. The backlog was particularly acute at the hearings level. Backlogs, in turn, resulted in claimants waiting longer for a final decision from SSA. In addition, at field offices, SSA customers experienced longer wait times and unanswered phones. For example, between 2002 and 2006, average customer wait times in field offices increased by 40 percent, and in fiscal year 2008, more than 3 million customers waited over one hour to be served. Two key factors likely contributed to these disability claims backlogs and service delivery challenges. First, SSA experienced reductions or turnover in field office staff and key personnel involved in the disability claims process, such as disability examiners and administrative law judges (ALJ). Second, SSA experienced an increase in workloads. In particular, from 1997 to 2006, initial applications for DI and SSI disability benefits increased more than 20 percent, spurred by, among other factors, the aging of the baby boom generation, downturns in the economy, increased referrals from other programs, and changes in disability eligibility requirements in prior years. SSA projects that its workloads will continue to increase over the coming years as the baby boom generation retires.

SSA has taken steps to improve its disability claims process and reduce the backlogs as well as to manage its overall workloads, but some efforts have been hampered by poor planning and execution while others are too recent to evaluate. One of SSA's more recent efforts to improve its disability claims process—a comprehensive set of reforms called the Disability Service Improvement (DSI) initiative that was piloted in the Boston region in 2006—produced mixed results. Many aspects of DSI were ultimately suspended to focus on the hearings backlog and SSA's electronic processing system. In May 2007, SSA outlined a new plan for eliminating the hearings level backlog. We are currently evaluating the extent to which the hearings backlog reduction plan includes components of sound planning and the potential effects it may have on the hearings backlog and other SSA operations. In addition, to address overall workloads and maintain customer service in field offices, SSA shifted workloads to less busy offices and deferred work that the agency deemed as lower priority. However, deferring key workloads, such as reviews of continuing eligibility for benefits, means that beneficiaries who no longer qualify may still receive payments erroneously. More recently, in response to our recommendation that SSA develop a detailed service delivery plan, SSA is consolidating its various planning efforts into a single planning document. SSA stated this document will reflect its efforts to address service and staffing challenges related to the disability and retirement wave of the baby boom generation. However, it remains unclear how SSA will manage growing workloads with its current infrastructure of approximately 1,300 field offices and resource constraints, while minimizing the deferral of key workloads and declines in customer service.

SOURCE: Bertoni, D. 2009. "Further Actions Needed to Address Disability Claims and Service Delivery Challenges." Testimony before the Subcommittees on Income Security and Family Support and Social Security, Committee on Ways and Means, House of Representatives. GAO-09-511T. [Online document; retrieved 3/27/09.] www.gao.gov/new.items/d09511t.pdf.

OSHA PROPOSES AND THEN WITHDRAWS A RULE BASED ON OPERATION OF THE OCCUPATIONAL HEALTH AND SAFETY ACT

27

DEPARTMENT OF LABOR
Occupational Safety and Health Administration

29 CFR Part 1910
[Docket No. H-371]
RIN 1218-AB46
Occupational Exposure to Tuberculosis
AGENCY: Occupational Safety and Health Administration (OSHA), Labor.
ACTION: Proposed rule; termination of rulemaking.

SUMMARY: OSHA is withdrawing its 1997 proposed standard on Occupational Exposure to Tuberculosis (TB). Because of a broad range of Federal and community initiatives, the rate of TB has declined steadily and dramatically since OSHA began work on the proposal in 1993. Hospitals, which are the settings where workers are likely to have the highest risk of exposure to TB bacteria, have come into substantial compliance with Federal guidelines for preventing the transmission of TB. Overall reductions in TB mean that all workers are much less likely now to encounter infectious TB patients in the course of their jobs.

In addition, an OSHA standard is unlikely to result in a meaningful reduction of disease transmission caused by contact with the most significant remaining source of occupational risk: exposure to individuals with undiagnosed and unsuspected TB. Particularly outside of hospitals, workers often will not identify suspect TB cases quickly enough to implement isolation procedures and other precautions before exposure occurs.

OSHA recognizes, however, that continued vigilance is necessary to maintain the gains achieved so far. OSHA intends to provide guidance to workplaces with less medical expertise and fewer resources than hospitals, and to use cooperative relationships with employers, public health experts and other government agencies to promote TB control. OSHA will also continue to enforce the General Duty Clause of the OSH Act and relevant existing standards in situations where employers' failure to implement available precautions exposes workers to the hazard of TB infection.

DATES: This withdrawal is effective December 31, 2003.

SUPPLEMENTARY INFORMATION:

I. Background

On August 25, 1993, the Coalition to Fight TB in the Workplace petitioned OSHA to promulgate both an Emergency Temporary Standard (ETS) under section 6(c) of the Occupational Safety and Health Act (OSH Act), and a permanent occupational health standard under section 6(b) of the Act to protect workers from occupational exposure to TB (Ex.1). 29 U.S.C. 655(b), 655(c). Citing the resurgence of TB at that time and the emergence and increasing prevalence of multidrug-resistant TB (MDR-TB), the petition argued that a mandatory standard was needed to address the hazards associated with occupational exposure to TB. According to the petition, TB Guidelines developed by the Federal Centers for Disease Control and Prevention (CDC) were not an adequate response to this hazard because the guidelines were not mandatory and were not being implemented fully or rigorously in most workplaces. The petition also requested that, as an interim measure, OSHA immediately issue nationwide enforcement guidelines.

* * *

On January 26, 1994, OSHA responded to the rulemaking petition, saying that it was initiating rulemaking on a permanent standard, but would not issue an ETS. On October 17, 1997, OSHA published a Proposed Rule on Occupational Exposure to Tuberculosis (62 FR 54160). In the proposal, the Agency made a preliminary determination that workers in hospitals, nursing homes, hospices, correctional facilities, homeless shelters, and certain other work settings faced a significant risk of incurring TB infection through occupational exposure. The Agency also made a preliminary conclusion that use of established infection prevention and control measures could reduce or eliminate this significant risk. The protective measures OSHA proposed were based in large part on existing CDC guidelines, and included instituting procedures for the early identification and treatment of TB patients, isolating patients with infectious TB in rooms designed to protect others from contact with disease-causing microorganisms, requiring healthcare workers to use respirators to perform certain high-hazard procedures on infectious patients, training workers in TB recognition and control, and providing medical follow-up for occupationally exposed workers who become infected and information to their colleagues with similar exposures.

* * *

II. Reasons for Withdrawal of the Proposed Standard

OSHA has decided not to promulgate a standard addressing occupational exposure to TB because it does not believe a standard would substantially reduce the occupational risk of TB infection. Many commenters argued forcefully that the proposed rule was based on an overestimate of this risk. In addition, existing TB control efforts, initiated by the Federal government in concert with other public health agencies, have led to a dramatic decline in TB over the past decade, greatly reducing the risk of occupational exposure to TB. Because of these TB control efforts, effective infection control measures are already in place, particularly in hospitals, which is where the occupational risk of TB exposure would be most severe.

* * *

In summary, OSHA has concluded that the success of existing Federal and community programs to control TB has significantly diminished the need for a standard, and that promulgating a standard will not reduce the remaining occupational risk substantially. Under the leadership of the CDC, community, institutional, and occupational public health efforts, including OSHA's own continuing outreach and enforcement, have increased worker and employer awareness of the factors leading to TB infection and disease and led to an increased implementation of CDC's TB guidelines. OSHA also intends to continue to use its enforcement, outreach, and education resources to ensure that employers' TB control efforts remain effective.

SOURCE: Reprinted from *Federal Register*. 2003. "Occupational Exposure to Tuberculosis." *Federal Register* 68 (250): 75767—75.

MEDICAL DEVICES: FDA SHOULD TAKE STEPS TO ENSURE THAT HIGH-RISK DEVICE TYPES ARE APPROVED THROUGH THE MOST STRINGENT PREMARKET REVIEW PROCESS

Summary

The Food and Drug Administration (FDA) within the Department of Health and Human Services (HHS) is responsible for oversight of medical devices sold in the United States. Regulations place devices into three classes, with class III including those with the greatest risk to patients. Unless exempt by regulation, new devices must clear FDA premarket review via either the 510(k) premarket notification process, which determines if a new device is substantially equivalent to another legally marketed device, or the more stringent premarket approval (PMA) process, which requires the manufacturer to supply evidence providing reasonable assurance that the device is safe and effective. Class III devices must generally obtain an approved PMA, but until FDA issues regulations requiring submission of PMAs, certain types of class III devices may be cleared via the 510(k) process. The FDA Amendments Act of 2007 mandated that the Government Accountability Office (GAO) study the 510(k) process. GAO examined which premarket review process—510(k) or PMA—FDA used to review selected types of device submissions in fiscal years 2003 through 2007. GAO reviewed FDA data and regulations and interviewed FDA officials.

In fiscal years 2003 through 2007, as part of its premarket review to determine whether devices should be permitted to be marketed in the United States, FDA: (1) reviewed 13,199 submissions for class I and II devices via the 510(k) process, clearing 11,935 (90 percent) of these submissions; (2) reviewed 342 submissions for class III devices through the 510(k) process, clearing 228 (67 percent) of these submissions; and (3) reviewed 217 original and 784 supplemental PMA submissions for class III devices and approved 78 percent and 85 percent, respectively, of these submissions. Although Congress envisioned that class III devices would be approved through the more stringent PMA process, and the Safe Medical Devices Act of 1990 required that FDA either reclassify or establish a schedule for requiring PMAs for class III device types, this process remains incomplete. GAO found that in fiscal years 2003 through 2007, FDA cleared submissions for 24 types of class III devices through the 510(k) process. As of October 2008, 4 of these device types had been reclassified to class II, but 20 device types could still be cleared through the 510(k) process. FDA officials said that the agency is committed to issuing regulations either reclassifying or requiring PMAs for the class III devices currently allowed to receive clearance for marketing via the 510(k) process, but did not provide a time frame for doing so.

Recommendation

The Secretary of Health and Human Services should direct the FDA Commissioner to expeditiously take steps to issue regulations for each class III device type currently allowed to enter the market through the 510(k) process. These steps should include issuing regulations to (1) reclassify each device type into class I or class II, or requiring it to remain in class III, and (2) for those device types remaining in class III, require approval for marketing through the PMA process.

SOURCE: Reprinted from Government Accountability Office. 2009. *Medical Devices: FDA Should Take Steps to Ensure That High-Risk Device Types Are Approved Through the Most Stringent Premarket Review Process.* Report no. GAO-09-190. [Online report; retrieved 3/2/09.] www.gao.gov/products/GAO-09-190.

CBO ISSUES A COST ESTIMATE

Congressional Budget Office   February 11, 2009
Cost Estimate

H.R. 2
Children's Health Insurance Program
Reauthorization Act of 2009

H.R. 2 (enacted as Public Law 111-3) authorizes the Children's Health
Insurance Program (CHIP) through fiscal year 2013 and increases federal
funding for the program. The program provides health insurance to targeted
children of low-income families. The legislation provides performance bonus
payments to states to cover enrollment costs resulting from specified enrollment and retention efforts. H.R. 2 also establishes a child enrollment contin-
gency fund to cover state CHIP expenditures beyond the amount allotted in
statute for the 2009–2013 reauthorization period. In addition, it adds an additional state option to use CHIP funding to provide a premium assistance
subsidy for children enrolled in a qualified health insurance plan, provides additional funding for outreach grants, and will improve access to dental benefits and mental health benefits in CHIP plans.

* * *

The Congressional Budget Office (CBO) estimates that H.R. 2 will increase CHIP outlays on benefits and administrative costs by about $31.4 bil-
lion over the 2009–2014 period and by $34.5 billion over the 2009–2019
period, relative to CBO's baseline projections over that period. The increase in
CHIP outlays will be associated primarily with increased funding to maintain
current program levels and allow states the option to expand their existing
CHIP programs. Under CBO's January 2009 baseline projections, funding for
CHIP allotments was assumed to continue at approximately $5 billion each
year after the program's previously scheduled expiration on March 31, 2009.
H.R. 2 increases CHIP allotments above that level by a total of $43.9 billion
over the 2009–2013 period. In fiscal year 2013, the act will provide two semiannual allotments of $2.85 billion, which are lower than the allotment levels
in the four previous years. The first semiannual allotment in 2013 will be

accompanied by onetime funding for the program of approximately $11.7 billion. (The 2013 funding will total $17.4 billion, an increase of $12.4 billion over the January baseline projection.)

Because H.R. 2 authorizes CHIP through 2013, baseline rules established by the Balanced Budget and Emergency Deficit Control Act of 1985 call for extrapolating an annualized level of program funding at the end of authorization (in 2013) for the remainder of the baseline projection period, 2014 through 2019. Consequently, this estimate assumes that funding for CHIP will continue at the extrapolated annual amount of $5.7 billion (approximately $700 million per year more than the January baseline amount).

* * *

SOURCE: Reprinted from Congressional Budget Office. 2009. "H.R. 2: Children's Health Insurance Program Reauthorization Act of 2009." [Online document; retrieved 3/2/09.] www.cbo.gov/ftpdocs/99xx/doc9985/hr2paygo.pdf.

30

INFLUENCING THE PUBLIC POLICY ENVIRONMENT OF AN ACADEMIC HEALTH CENTER

As we discussed in Chapter 8, leaders of health-related organizations and inter-est groups have three bases of power available to them in their influencing efforts (i.e., positional power, power based on the capacity to reward or coerce, and power based on expertise). Furthermore, these leaders can focus their influencing efforts at a number of places in the policymaking process. Some of the experiences of the leaders of Academic Health Center (AHC), a part of a state university system whose identity is otherwise disguised, illustrate the variety of opportunities typi-cally available to the leaders of health-related entities who wish to influence their public policy environments.

The leaders of Academic Health Center (AHC) can and do approach the chal-lenges of influencing their public policy environment in a variety of ways. The cells in the grid shown in Exhibit 1, each identified by an alpha character, rep-resent the specific combinations of focus and power available to AHC's leaders.

EXHIBIT 1 Opportunities to Exert Influence in Public Policy Environments

	Problem Definition	*Solutions Identification*	*Political Circumstances*	*Legislation Development*	*Rule-making*	*Operation*
Power Based on Position	cell (a)	(b)	(c)	(d)	(e)	(f)
Power to Reward/ Coerce	(g)	(h)	(i)	(j)	(k)	(l)
Power Based on Expertise	(m)	(n)	(o)	(p)	(q)	(r)

In cell (a), for example, the leaders focus on how they can use their *po-sitional power* to help *define and document problems* that could be addressed through public policy. For example, as leaders of AHC, they are positioned to help policymakers understand the magnitude of the problem of the lack of health insurance among the state's citizens. These leaders are in a position to document the extent and some of the implications of the problems for policymakers. They may use their membership in the Council of Teaching Hospitals and Health Systems (COTH; www.aahc.org/members/coth) or the Alliance of Independent Academic Medical Centers (AIAMC; www.aiamc.org) to access examples from across the nation.

Furthermore, their positions as leaders of a major healthcare organization permit them to call on others for assistance in this effort. Obviously, they can call on other members of the staff at AHC. They can solicit the help of their counterparts in other health organizations in the state to buttress their documentation of the problem. In addition, they can use interest groups to which they belong, such as the State Hospital Association, to help in this process.

In cell (j), AHC's leaders focus on how their ability to *reward* or to *coerce* policymakers could be used to exert influence in the *development of legislation* that would be to the center's strategic advantage. Legislation to support a major expansion of the center's research facilities, for example, might be sponsored and championed by a legislator who receives campaign support from the center's leaders. This legislative champion of AHC's preferred policy on the issue of support for the new research facility could also be supported in a more intangible form by the leaders working with the legislator to accomplish something of importance to the legislator's district, in terms of its economy and its healthcare services, by opening an ambulatory AHC-staffed primary care center in the district.

In cell (n), the center's leaders focus on their opportunities to use the influence that derives from *expertise* to help *identify and implement policy solutions to problems.* For example, when the state legislature granted $50 million to AHC in 2010 to help establish and operate the state's only program in tissue engineering, it did so in response to the AHC's development of a proposal for the initiative as an important advance in the state's medical care and its economic base. The proposal reflected the center's considerable expertise in tissue engineering.

In cell (q), AHC's leaders focus on their opportunities to use *expertise* within the center's staff to influence the final wording on *rules or regulations* that affect the center's organizational performance. For example, the center's staff possesses expertise that would be relevant to the promulgation of federal rules pertaining to funding and operation of graduate medical education programs such as the family practice residency, Medicare reimbursement formulae and practices, and the award of National Institutes of Health research grants, as well as in many other areas. It is routine for leaders at AHC to use their expertise as a mechanism through which to influence the formulation and implementation of rules that affect their organization.

In cell (c), AHC's leaders think of ways in which their power to influence based on *position* could be used to change the *political circumstances* surrounding an issue. For example, the members of the State Board of Regents, who are part of AHC's strategic apex, by virtue of their board positions, can and do exert influence on the members of the state legislature. This influence helps determine the state's funding for the state university system, including AHC's state funding.

The examples given above are not exhaustive. They are intended only to stimulate thinking about the range of possibilities for influencing public policy that this grid illustrates.

This model does not fully capture the reality of the AHC in its public policy environment. In particular, any suggestion that the cells in Exhibit 1 can be considered independently of one another is an oversimplification. More realistically, a leader operates in several cells simultaneously even when trying to influence a single policy issue. Moreover, leaders typically focus on many issues at any given point. This complicates things considerably.

However, the grid does illustrate an important point for those who would influence an entity's public policy environment. They can legitimately and effectively focus their influence at many places in the policymaking process, and they have more than one base of power upon which to seek to influence each of these places.

REFERENCES

Aberbach, J. D., and M. A. Peterson. 2006. *The Executive Branch.* New York: Oxford University Press.

AcademyHealth. 2009. "What Is Health Services Research?" [Online information; retrieved 9/21/09.] academyhealth.org/About/content.cfm?ItemNumber=831&navItemNumber=514.

Administration on Aging (AoA). 2009a. "The Administration on Aging FY 2010 Budget Request." [Online information; retrieved 10/6/09.] www.aoa.gov/AoARoot/About/Budget/2010Justification.aspx.

———. 2009b. "AoA Programs." [Online information; retrieved 10/5/09.] www.aoa.gov/AoARoot/AoA_Programs/index.aspx.

———. 2009c. "Older Americans Act." [Online information; retrieved 10/5/09.] www.aoa.gov/AoARoot/AoA_Programs/OAA/index.aspx.

———. 2009d. "Organization." [Online information; retrieved 10/5/09.] www.aoa.gov/AoARoot/About/Organization/index.aspx.

———. 2009e. "Our Mission." [Online information; retrieved 10/5/09.] www.aoa.gov/AoARoot/About/index.aspx.

———. 2009f. "Strategic Action Plan, 2007-2012." [Online information; retrieved 10/6/09.] www.aoa.gov/AoARoot/About/Strategic_Plan/docs/AoA_Strategic_Action_Plan.pdf

Agency for Healthcare Research and Quality. 2009. "Health Services Research Core Competencies: Final Report." [Online information; retrieved 2/11/09.] www.ahrq.gov/fund/training/hsrcomp08.htm.

Alexander, J. A., T. G. Rundall, T. J. Hoff, and L. L. Morlock. 2006. "Power and Politics." In *Health Care Management: Organization Design and Behavior*, 5th ed., edited by S. M. Shortell and A. D. Kaluzny, 276–310. Clifton Park, NY: Thomson Delmar Learning.

Altmeyer, A. J. 1968. *The Formative Years of Social Security.* Madison, WI: University of Wisconsin Press.

American Heart Association (AHA). 2009. "Federal Public Policy Agenda." [Online information; retrieved 3/8/09.] www.americanheart.org/presenter.jhtml?identifier=3009617.

American Public Health Association. 2010. "The Budget and Appropriations Process." [Online document; retrieved 1/26/10.] www.apha.org/NR/rdonlyres/E68C75BA-F173-4C48-BF96-6844FBAEB35A/0/budget_101.pdf.

Anderson, G. F. 1992. "The Courts and Health Policy: Strengths and Limitations." *Health Affairs* 11 (4): 95–110.

Anderson, G. F., P. S. Hussey, B. K. Frogner, and H. R. Waters. 2005. "Health Spending in the United States and the Rest of the Industrialized World." *Health Affairs* 24 (4): 903–14.

Andres, G. J. 2009. *Lobbying Reconsidered: Politics Under the Influence.* White Plains, NY: Pearson Longman.

Atkins, D., J. Siegel, and J. Slutsky. 2005. "Making Policy When the Evidence Is in Dispute." *Health Affairs* 24 (1): 102–13.

Baumgartner, F. R., and J. C. Talbert. 1995. "From Setting a National Agenda on Health Care to Making Decisions in Congress." *Journal of Health Politics, Policy and Law* 20 (2): 437–45.

Beauchamp, T. L., and J. F. Childress. 2008. *Principles of Biomedical Ethics*, 6th ed. New York: Oxford University Press.

Bergan, D. E. 2009. "Does Grassroots Lobbying Work?" *American Politics Research* 37 (2): 327–52.

Berkman, L. F., and I. Kawachi (eds.). 2000. *Social Epidemiology*. New York: Oxford University Press.

Bircher, J. 2005. "Towards a Dynamic Definition of Health and Disease." *Medicine, Health Care and Philosophy* 8 (3): 335–41.

Birkland, T. A. 2001. *An Introduction to the Policy Process: Theories, Concepts, and Models of Public Policy Making*. Armonk, NY: M. E. Sharpe.

Blum, H. 1983. *Expanding Health Care Horizons: From a General Systems Concept of Health to a National Health Policy*, 2nd ed. Oakland, CA: Third Party Publishing.

Blumenthal, D., and J. A. Morone. 2008. "Presidents." In *Health Politics and Policy*, 4th ed., edited by J. A. Morone, T. J. Litman, and L. S. Robins, 95–126. Clifton Park, NY: Delmar Cengage Learning.

Brodie, M., and R. J. Blendon. 2008. "Public Opinion and Health Policy." In *Health Politics and Policy*, 4th ed., edited by J. A. Morone, T. J. Litman and L. S. Robins, 249–70. Clifton Park, NY: Delmar Cengage Learning.

———. 1995. "The Public's Contribution to Congressional Gridlock on Health Care Reform." *Journal of Health Politics, Policy and Law* 20 (2): 403–10.

Brown, L. D. 1991. "Knowledge and Power: Health Services Research as a Political Resource." In *Health Services Research: Key to Health Policy*, edited by E. Ginzberg, 20–45. Cambridge, MA: Harvard University Press.

Burns, J. M. 1978. *Leadership*. New York: Harper & Row.

Byrne, D. 2004. *Enabling Good Health for All: A Reflection Process for a New EU Health Strategy*. [Online report; retrieved 9/3/09.] ec.europa.eu/health/ph_overview/ Documents/pub_good_health_en.pdf.

Cass, R. S. 2008. "Judicial Partisanship Awards." *Washington Independent*, July 31. [Online material; retrieved 2/8/09.] washingtonindependent.com/350/judicial-partisanship-awards.

CDC Evaluation Working Group. 2009. "Resources." [Online material; retrieved 10/22/09.] www.cdc.gov/eval/resources.htm#logic%20model.

Center for Responsive Politics. 2009. "Lobbying Database." [Online data; retrieved 2/13/09.] www.opensecrets.org/lobby/index.php.

Centers for Disease Control and Prevention. 2006. *Deaths: Leading Causes*. [Online information; retrieved 2/2/09.] www.cdc.gov/nchs/fastats/lcod.htm.

Centers for Medicare & Medicaid Services. 2009a. "Center for Drug and Health Plan Choice." [Online information; retrieved 2/20/09.] www.cms.hhs.gov/CMSLeadership/ 05_Office_CPC.asp#TopOfPage.

———. 2009b. "Center for Medicaid and State Operations." [Online information; retrieved 2/20/09.] www.cms.hhs.gov/CMSLeadership/07_Office_CMSO.asp# TopOfPage.

———. 2009c. "Center for Medicare Management." [Online information; retrieved 2/20/09.] www.cms.hhs.gov/CMSLeadership/ 06_Office_CMM.asp#TopOPage.

———. 2009d. "National Health Expenditure Projections 2008–2018." [Online report; retrieved 4/20/09.] www.cms.hhs.gov/NationalHealthExpendData/downloads/proj2008.pdf.

———. 2009e. "Regional Office Overview." [Online information; retrieved 2/20/09.] www.cms.hhs.gov/RegionalOffices/.

Cigler, A. J., and B. A. Loomis (eds.). 2007. *Interest Group Politics*, 7th ed. Washington, DC: CQ Press.

Coalition to Protect America's Health Care. 2009. "Who We Are." [Online material; retrieved 2/14/09.] www.protecthealthcare.org/protecthealthcare/whoweare.shtml.

Cochran, C. L., and E. F. Malone. 1999. *Public Policy: Perspectives and Choices*, 2nd ed. New York: McGraw Hill.

Collins, P. M. Jr. 2008. *Friends of the Supreme Court: Interest Groups and Judicial Decision Making.* New York: Oxford University Press.

Committee on the Consequences of Uninsurance. 2004. Board on Health Care Services, Institute of Medicine. *Insuring America's Health: Principles and Recommendations*, 1–3. Washington, DC: National Academies Press.

Concept Marketing Group, Inc. 2009. *Directory of Associations.* Scottsdale, AZ: Concept Marketing Group, Inc.

Congressional Budget Office. 2009. *The Budget and Economic Outlook: Fiscal Years 2009 to 2019.* [Online information; retrieved 9/8/09.] www.cbo.gov/doc.cfm?index=9957.

———. 2008a. "Accounting for Sources of Projected Growth in Federal Spending on Medicare and Medicaid." [Online brief; retrieved 2/10/09.] www.cbo.gov/ftpdocs/93xx/doc9316/05-29-SourcesHealthCostGrowth_ Brief.pdf.

———. 2008b. "Updated Long-Term Projections for Social Security." [Online report; retrieved 2/6/09.] www.cbo.gov/ftpdocs/96xx/doc9649/08-20-SocialSecurity Update.pdf.

Congressional Research Service (CRS). 2009. "History and Mission." [Online information; retrieved 10/21/09.] www.loc.gov/crsinfo/aboutcrs.html#hismiss.

———. 2007. "Congressional Oversight Manual." [Online information; retrieved 10/5/09.] www.fas.org/sgp/crs/misc/RL30240.pdf.

———. 2006. "Summary of Public Law 109-365." [Online document; retrieved 2/26/09.] thomas.loc.gov/cgi-bin/bdquery/z?d109:HR06197.

Copeland, C. W. 2008. *The Federal Rulemaking Process: An Overview.* Congressional Research Service Report RL32240.

David, F. 2009. *Strategic Management: Concepts and Cases*, 12th ed. Englewood Cliffs, NJ: Prentice Hall.

Davidson, S. M. 1997. "Politics Matters! Health Care Policy and the Federal System." *Journal of Health Politics, Policy and Law* 22 (3): 879–96.

DeBuono, B., A. Gonzalez, and S. Rosenbaum. 2008. *Moments in Leadership: Case Studies in Public Health Policy and Practice.* New York: Pfizer, Inc.

DeNavas-Walt, C., C. B. Proctor, and J. Smith. 2008. *Income, Poverty, and Health Insurance Coverage in the United States: 2007.* Washington, DC: U.S. Census Bureau.

Diver, C. 1989. "Regulatory Precision." In *Making Regulatory Policy*, edited by K. Hawkins and J. Thomas, 199–232. Pittsburgh: University of Pittsburgh Press.

Do, D. P., and B. K. Finch. 2008. "The Link Between Neighborhood Poverty and Health: Context or Composition?" *American Journal of Epidemiology* 168 (6): 611–19.

Domhoff, G. W. 2009. *Who Rules America? Challenges to Corporate and Class Dominance*, 6th ed. Hightstown, NJ: McGraw-Hill Companies.

Dubos, R. 1959. *The Mirage of Health.* New York: Harper.

Dye, T. R. 2008. *Understanding Public Policy*, 12th ed. White Plains, NY: Pearson Longman.

Dye, T. R. 2002. *Who's Running America? The Bush Restoration*, 7th ed. White Plains, NY: Pearson Longman.

Dye, T. R., and H. Zeigler. 2009. *The Irony of Democracy: An Uncommon Introduction to American Politics*, 14th ed. Belmont, CA: Wadsworth Cengage Learning.

Edwards, G. C., M. P. Wattenberg, and R. L. Lineberry. 2009. *Government in America: People, Politics, and Policy*, Brief Study Edition, 10th ed. White Plains, NY: Pearson Longman.

Elixhauser, A., B. R. Luce, W. R. Taylor, and J. Reblando. 1993. "Health Care CBA/CEA: An Update on the Growth and Composition of the Literature." *Medical Care* 31 (7, Suppl.): JS1–JS11.

Elmendorf, D. E. 2009. Testimony Before the United States Senate Committee on the Budget, February 10. [Online information; retrieved 2/10/09.] www.cbo.gov/ftpdocs/99xx/doc9982/02-10-HealthVolumes_Testimony.pdf.

Evans, R. G., M. L. Barer, and T. R. Marmor. 1994. *Why Are Some People Healthy and Others Not? The Determinants of Health of Populations*. New York: Aldine De Gruyter.

Executive Order #2003-1, Commonwealth's Health Care Reform Agenda. 2003. [Online document; retrieved 2/24/09.] www.ohcr.state.pa.us/assets/pdfs/1-21-03-HealthCareReformExeOrder.pdf.

Feldstein, P. J. 2006. *The Politics of Health Legislation: An Economic Perspective*, 3rd ed. Chicago: Health Administration Press.

Findlaw.com. 2005. "Terri Schiavo Case: Legal Issues Involving Healthcare Directives, Death, and Dying." [Online information; retrieved 10/22/09.] news.findlaw.com/legalnews/lit/schiavo/index.html.

Fishel, J. 1985. *Presidents and Promises*. Washington, DC: Congressional Quarterly Press.

Fogler, H. S., and S. E LeBlanc. 2008. *Strategies for Creative Problem Solving*, 2nd ed. Englewood Cliffs, NJ: Prentice Hall.

French, J. R. P., and B. H. Raven. 1959. "The Basis of Social Power." In *Studies of Social Power*, edited by D. Cartwright, 150–67. Ann Arbor, MI: Institute for Social Research.

Gawande, A. 2009. "Getting There From Here: How Should Obama Reform Health Care?" *The New Yorker*, January 26.

Gluck, M. E., and R. Sorian. 2004. *Administrative Challenges in Managing the Medicare Program*. American Association of Retired People, Report #2004-15. Washington DC: American Association of Retired People.

Goodnough, A., and C. Hulse. 2005. "Despite Congress, Woman's Feeding Tube Is Removed." *New York Times*, March 19, A1.

Gormley, W. T., Jr., and C. Boccuti. 2001. "HCFA and the States: Politics and Intergovernmental Leverage." *Journal of Health Politics, Policy and Law* 26 (3): 557–80.

Gostin, L. O. 2008. *Public Health Law: Power, Duty, Restraint*, 2nd ed. Berkeley, CA: University of California Press.

Government Accountability Office (GAO). n. d. "About GAO." [Online information; retrieved 3/2/09.] www.gao.gov/about/index.html.

Green, J. 1995. "High-Court Ruling Protects Hospital-Bill Surcharges." *AHA News* 31 (18): 1.

Greenberger, D., S. Strasser, R. J. Lewicki, and T. S. Bateman. 1988. "Perception, Motivation, and Negotiation." In *Health Care Management: A Text in Organization Theory and Behavior*, 2nd ed., edited by S. M. Shortell and A. D. Kaluzny, 81–141. New York: John Wiley & Sons.

Gruber, J. 2008. "Incremental Universalism for the United States: The States Move First?" *Journal of Economic Perspectives* 22 (4): 51–68.

Hacker, J. S. 1997. *The Road to Nowhere*. Princeton, NJ: Princeton University Press.

———. 1996. "National Health Care Reform: An Idea Whose Time Came and Went." *Journal of Health Politics, Policy and Law* 21 (4): 647–96.

Hacker, J. S., and T. Skocpol. 1997. "The New Politics of U.S. Health Policy." *Journal of Health Politics, Policy and Law* 22 (2): 315–38.

Hanke, J. E., and D. Wichern. 2008. *Business Forecasting*, 9th ed. Englewood Cliffs, NJ: Prentice Hall.

Heath, R. L., and M. J. Palenchar. 2009. *Strategic Issues Management: Organizations and Public Policy Challenges*. Thousand Oaks, CA: Sage Publications.

Henry J. Kaiser Family Foundation. 2009a. *Care and Coverage of the Nation's Children: A Resource Page*. [Online material; retrieved 2/2/09.] www.kff.org/medicaid/childrenscoverageresources.cfm.

———. 2009b. *Healthcare Costs: A Primer*. [Online material; retrieved 4/20/09.] www.kff.org/insurance/upload/7670_02.pdf.

———. 2009c. *Unemployment's Impact on Uninsured and Medicaid*. [Online material; retrieved 4/20/09.] www.kff.org/charts/042808.htm.

———. 2008. "Addressing the Nursing Shortage: Background Brief." Menlo Park, CA: The Kaiser Family Foundation. [Online information; retrieved 2/5/09.] www.kaiseredu.org/topics_im.asp?imID=1&parentID=61&id=138.

Herrnson, P. S., R. G. Shaiko, and C. Wilcox. 2005. *The Interest Group Connection: Electioneering, Lobbying, and Policymaking in Washington*, 2nd ed. Washington, DC: CQ Press.

Hinckley, B. 1983. *Stability and Change in Congress*, 3rd ed. New York: Harper & Row.

Hlatky, M. A., G. D. Sanders, and D. K. Owens. 2005. "Evidence-Based Medicine and Policy: The Case of the Implantable Cardioverter Defibrillator." *Health Affairs* 24 (1): 42–51.

Hoffman, C. 2009. *National Health Insurance—A Brief History of Reform Efforts in the U.S.* Menlo Park, CA: Henry J. Kaiser Family Foundation.

Hoffman, E. D. Jr., B. S. Klees, and C. A. Curtis. 2008. "Summary of the Medicare Program." Social Security Administration's *Annual Statistical Supplement 2008*. [Online material; retrieved 3/15/09.] www.ssa.gov/policy/docs/statcomps/supplement/2008/medicare.html.

Iglehart, J. K. 1992. "The American Health Care System: Medicare." *New England Journal of Medicine* 327 (20): 1467–72.

Institute of Medicine. 2003a. *Hidden Costs, Value Lost: Uninsurance in America*. Washington, DC: The National Academies Press.

———. 2003b. *A Shared Destiny: Community Effects of Uninsurance*. Washington, DC: National Academies Press.

———. 2002a. *Care Without Coverage: Too Little, Too Late*. Washington, DC: National Academies Press.

———. 2002b. *Health Insurance Is a Family Matter*. Washington, DC: National Academies Press.

———. 2002c. *Unequal Treatment: Confronting Racial and Ethnic Disparities in Health Care*. Washington, DC: National Academies Press.

———. 2001. *Coverage Matters: Insurance and Health Care*. Washington, DC: National Academies Press.

James, C., M. Thomas, M. Lillie-Blanton, and R. Garfield. 2007. *Key Facts: Race, Ethnicity and Medical Care*. Menlo Park, CA: The Kaiser Family Foundation. [Online information; retrieved 9/25/09.] www.kff.org/minorityhealth/upload/6069-02.pdf.

Johnson, C. W. 2003. *How Our Laws Are Made*. [Online document; retrieved 2/15/09.] www.senate.gov/reference/resources/pdf/howourlawsaremade.pdf.

Johnson, L. B. 1965. *Public Papers of the Presidents of the U.S.* Vol. 2. Washington, DC: Government Printing Office.

Johnson, H., and D. S. Broder. 1996. *The System: The American Way of Politics at the Breaking Point.* Boston: Little, Brown and Company.

Jost, T. M. 2008. " 'MetLife V. Glenn': The Court Addresses a Conflict over Conflicts in ERISA Benefit Administration." *Health Affairs* 27 (5): w430–w440.

Kaiser Commission on Medicaid and the Uninsured. 2009. *The Role of Medicaid in State Economies: A Look at the Research.* [Online information; retrieved 9/25/09.] http://www.kff.org/medicaid/upload/7075_02.pdf.

Kaiser Family Foundation. 2009a. "Managed Care and Health Insurance." [Online material; retrieved 10/21/09.] www.statehealthfacts.org/comparecat.jsp?cat=7#.

———. 2009b. "Medicare: A Primer." [Online booklet; retrieved 3/11/09.] www.kff.org/medicare/upload/7615-02.pdf.

Katz, R. L. 1974. "Skills of an Effective Administrator." *Harvard Business Review* 52 (5): 90–102.

Kersh, R. 2008. "Lobbyists: Ten Myths About Power and Influence." In *Health Politics and Policy*, 4th ed., edited by J. A. Morone, T. J. Litman and L. S. Robins, 271–90. Clifton Park, NY: Delmar Cengage Learning.

Kerwin, C. M. 2003. *Rulemaking: How Government Agencies Write Law and Make Policy*, 3rd ed. Washington, DC: CQ Press.

King, M. P. 2005. *State Roles in Health: A Snapshot for State Legislators.* Denver, CO: National Conference of State Legislatures.

Kingdon, J. W. 1995. *Agendas, Alternatives, and Public Policies*, 2nd ed. New York: HarperCollins College Publishers.

Klein, H. E., and R. E. Linneman. 1984. "Environmental Assessment: An International Study of Corporate Practices." *Journal of Business Strategy* 5: 66–77.

Knowlton, L. W., and C. C. Phillips. 2008. *The Logic Model Guidebook: Strategies for Great Results.* Thousand Oaks, CA: Sage Publications, Inc.

Kravets, D. 2004. "Arizona Abortion Regulation Invades Privacy, Appeals Court Says." Associated Press, June 19.

Kravitz, R. L., M. J. Sauve, M. Hodge, P. S. Romano, M. Maher, S. Samuels, D. Harvey, V. A. Olson, J. Cahill, M. Gallagher, J. Welsh, P. Barath, S. Asch, and T. Lang. 2002. "Hospital Nursing Staff Ratios and Quality of Care. Final Report of Evidence, Administrative Data, an Expert Panel Process, and a Hospital Staffing Survey." [Online report; retrieved 6/9/09.] repositories.cdlib.org/cgi/viewcontent.cgi?article=1050&context=chsrpc.

Krieger, N. 2000. "Discrimination and Health." In *Social Epidemiology*, edited by L. F. Berkman and I. Kawachi, 36–75. New York: Oxford University Press.

Lammers, W. W. 1997. "Presidential Leadership and Health Policy." In *Health Politics and Policy*, 3rd ed., edited by T. J. Litman and L. S. Robins, 111–35. Albany, NY: Delmar Publishers, Inc.

Leichter, H. M. 2008. "State Governments: E Pluribus Multa." In *Health Politics and Policy*, 4th ed., edited by J. A. Morone, T. J. Litman, and L. S. Robins, 173–95. Clifton Park, NY: Delmar Cengage Learning.

Lindblom, C. E. 1992. *Inquiry and Change.* New Haven, CT: Yale University Press.

———. 1969. "The Sciences of 'Muddling Through.'" In *Readings in Modern Organizations*, edited by A. Etzioni, 154–65. Englewood Cliffs, NJ: Prentice Hall.

Lindgren, M., and H. Bandhold. 2009. *Scenario Planning: The Link Between Future and Strategy.* Basingstroke, Hampshire, UK: Palgrave Macmillan.

Linowes, D. F. 1998. *Creating Public Policy: The Chairman's Memoirs of Four Presidential Commissions.* Westport, CT: Praeger Publishers.

Longest, B. B., Jr. 2005. *Managing Health Programs and Projects.* San Francisco: Jossey-Bass.

———. 2004. *Managing Health Programs and Projects.* San Francisco: Jossey-Bass.

———. 2003. "Medicare: How You See It Depends on Where You Stand." *Healthcare Financial Management* (March): 88–92.

———. 1997. *Seeking Strategic Advantage Through Health Policy Analysis.* Chicago: Health Administration Press.

Longest, B. B. Jr., and K. Darr. 2008. *Managing Health Services Organizations and Systems,* 5th ed. Baltimore, MD: Health Professions Press.

Lucia, A. D., and R. Lepsinger. 1999. *The Art and Science of Competency Models: Pinpointing Critical Success Factors in Organizations.* San Francisco: Jossey-Bass/Pfeiffer.

Madison, J. 1787. "The Same Subject Continued: The Union as a Safeguard Against Domestic Faction and Insurrection." *Federalist Papers* 10.

Mark, B., D. W. Harless, and J. Spetz. 2009. "California's Minimum-Nurse-Staffing Legislation and Nurses' Wages." *Health Affairs* 28 (2): w326–w334.

McGarity, T. O., and W. E. Wagner. 2008. *Bending Science: How Special Interests Corrupt Public Health Research.* Cambridge, MA: Harvard University Press.

Medicare Payment Advisory Commission. 2003. *Report to the Congress. Medicare Payment Policy.* Washington, DC: Medicare Payment Advisory Commission.

Mesch, A. H. 1984. "Developing an Effective Environmental Assessment Function." *Managerial Planning* 32 (1): 17–22.

Moe, T. 1980. *The Organization of Interests.* Chicago: University of Chicago Press.

Moon, M. 1993. *Medicare Now and in the Future.* Washington, DC: Urban Institute.

Moran, M., M. Rein, and R. E. Goodin (eds). 2008. *The Oxford Handbook of Public Policy.* New York: Oxford University Press.

Morone, J. A. 1990. *The Democratic Wish: Popular Participation and the Limits of American Government.* New York: Basic Books.

Murray, J. E. 2007. *Origins of American Health Insurance: A History of Industrial Sickness Funds.* New Haven, CT: Yale University Press.

Nadel, M. 1995. "Congressional Oversight of Health Policy." In *Intensive Care: How Congress Shapes Health Policy,* edited by T. E. Mann and N. J. Ornstein, 127–42. Washington, DC: American Enterprise Institute and the Brookings Institution.

National Center for Health Statistics. 2007. *Health, United States, 2007 with Chartbook on Trends in the Health of Americans.* Hyattsville, MD: U.S. Department of Health and Human Services, Centers for Disease Control, National Center for Health Statistics. [Online report; retrieved 2/6/09.] www.cdc.gov/nchs/data/hus/hus07.pdf.

National Center for Health Workforce Analysis. 2009. *What Is Behind HRSA's Projected Supply, Demand, and Shortage of Registered Nurses?* Washington DC: U.S. Department of Health and Human Services, Health Resources and Services Administration, Bureau of Health Professions, National Center for Workforce Analysis. [Online report; retrieved 2/5/09.] ftp://ftp.hrsa.gov/bhpr/workforce/behindshortage.pdf.

———. 2006. *Physician Supply and Demand: Projections to 2020.* Washington, DC: U.S. Department of Health and Human Services, Health Resources and Services Administration, Bureau of Health Professions, National Center for Workforce Analysis. [Online report; retrieved 2/5/09.] ftp://ftp.hrsa.gov/bhpr/workforce/PhysicianForecastingPaperfinal.pdf.

National Governors Association and National Association of State Budget Officers. 2009. *The Fiscal Survey of States.* Washington, DC: National Association of State Budget Officers. [Online information; retrieved 9/25/09.] http://www.nasbo.org/Publications/PDFs/FSSpring2009.pdf

National Health Council, Inc. 1993. *Congress and Health: An Introduction to the Legislative Process and Its Key Participants*, 10th ed. Government Relations Handbook Series. Washington, DC: National Health Council, Inc.

National Institutes of Health. 2009. *NIH Budget.* Washington, DC: U.S. Department of Health and Human Services, National Institutes of Health. [Online information; retrieved 2/5/09.] www.nih.gov/about/budget.htm.

Naughton, K., C. Schmid, S. W. Yackee, and X. Zhan. 2009. "Understanding Commenter Influence During Agency Rule Development." *Journal of Policy Analysis and Management* 28 (2): 258–77.

Neumann, P., M. S. Kamae, and J. A. Palmer. 2008. "Medicare's National Coverage Decisions for Technologies, 1999–2007." *Health Affairs* 27 (6): 1620–31.

Newhouse, J. P. 1974. "A Design for a Health Insurance Experiment." *Inquiry* 11 (1): 5–27.

Nownes, A. J. , C. S. Thomas and, R. J. Hrebenar. 2008. "Interest Groups in the States." In *Politics in the American States*, 9th edition, edited by V. Gray and R. L. Hanson, 98–126. Washington, DC: CQ Press.

Office of the Budget. 2009. "The Budget Process in Pennsylvania." [Online booklet; retrieved 2/19/09.] www.portal.state.pa.us/portal/server.pt/gateway/PTARGS_0_113914_318373_0_0_18/BudgetProcess.pdf.

Office of Management and Budget. 2008. "Budget of the U. S. Government, FY 2009." [Online document; retrieved 2/15/09.] www.gpoaccess.gov/usbudget/index.html.

Oleszek, W. J. 2007. *Congressional Procedures and the Policy Process*, 7th ed. Washington, DC: CQ Press.

Oliver, T. R., and P. Paul-Shaheen. 1997. "Translating Ideas into Actions: Entrepreneurial Leadership in State Health Care Reforms." *Journal of Health Politics, Policy and Law* 22 (3): 721—88.

Organisation for Economic Cooperation and Development. 2008. *OECD Health Data 2008.* Paris: OECD.

Ornstein, N. J., and S. Elder. 1978. *Interest Groups, Lobbying and Policymaking.* Washington, DC: Congressional Quarterly Press.

Patton, C. V., and D. Sawicki. 1993. *Basic Methods of Policy Analysis and Planning*, 2nd ed. Englewood Cliffs, NJ: Prentice Hall.

Pennsylvania House of Representatives. 2009. *Making Law in Pennsylvania: Legislation in the PA House of Representatives* [Online information; retrieved 2/15/09.] www.legis.state.pa.us/WU01/VC/visitor_info/pdfs/makingLaw.pdf.

Peters, B. G. 2003. *American Public Policy: Promise and Performance*, 6th ed. Chappaqua, NY: Chatham House.

Peterson, M. A. 1993. "Political Influence in the 1990s: From Iron Triangles to Policy Networks." *Journal of Health Politics, Policy and Law* 18 (2): 395–438.

———. 1997. "Introduction: Health Care into the Next Century." *Journal of Health Politics, Policy and Law* 22 (2): 291–313.

Pharmaceutical Research and Manufacturers of America. 2009. *About PhRMA.* [Online information; retrieved 2/5/09.] www.phrma.org/about_phrma/.

Phipps, S. 2003. *The Impact of Poverty on Health: A Scan of Research Literature.* Ottawa, ON: Canadian Institute for Health Information.

Price, D. 1978. "Policymaking in Congressional Committees: The Impact of 'Environmental' Factors." *American Political Science Review* 72 (2): 548–75.

Ramirez, R., J. W. Selsky, and K. van der Heijden (eds). 2008. *Business Planning for Turbulent Times: New Methods for Applying Scenarios.* London: Earthscan.

Rawls, J. 1971. *A Theory of Justice.* Cambridge, MA: Belknap Press.

Reinhardt, U. E., P. S. Hussey, and G. F. Anderson. 2004. "U.S. Health Spending in an International Context." *Health Affairs* 23 (3): 10–25.

Rosenblatt, R. 2008. "The Courts." In *Health Politics and Policy*, 4th ed., edited by J. A. Morone, T. J. Litman, and L. S. Robins, 127–52. Clifton Park, NY: Delmar Cengage Learning.

Sanders, J. 2002. "Financing and Organization of National Health Systems." In *World Health Systems: Challenges and Perspectives*, edited by B. J. Fried and L.M. Gaydos, 25–38. Chicago: Health Administration Press.

Saracci, R. 1997. "The World Health Organisation Needs to Reconsider Its Definition of Health." *BMJ* 314 (7091): 1409–10.

Shadish, W. R., T. D. Cook, and D. T. Campbell. 2001. *Experimental and Quasi-Experimental Designs for Generalized Causal Inference*. Boston: Houghton Mifflin Company.

Shah, A. 2009. "Global Financial Crisis." [Online article; retrieved 5/9/09.] www .globalissues.org/article/768/global-financial-crisis.

Shewchuck, R. M., S. J. O'Connor, and D. J. Fine. 2005. "Building an Understanding of the Competencies Needed for Health Administration Practice." *Journal of Healthcare Management* 50 (1): 32–47.

Shortell, S. M., R. R. Gillies, D. A. Anderson, K. M. Erickson, and J. B. Mitchell. 2000. *Remaking Health Care in America*, 2nd ed. San Francisco: Jossey-Bass.

Shortell, S. M., and A. D. Kaluzny. 2006. *Health Care Management: Organization Design and Behavior*, 5th ed. Clifton Park, NY: Thomson Delmar Learning.

Sisko, A., C. Truffer, S. Smith, S. Keehan, J. Cylus, J. A. Poisal, M. K. Clemens, and J. Lizonitz. 2009. "Health Spending Projections Through 2018: Recession Effects Add Uncertainty to the Outlook." *Health Affairs* 28 (2): w346-w357. [Online article; retrieved 4/17/09.] content.healthaffairs.org/cgi/content/full/28/2/w346.

Skidmore, M. 1970. *Medicare and the American Rhetoric of Reconciliation*. Tuscaloosa, AL: University of Alabama Press.

Skocpol, T. 1996. *Boomerang: Clinton's Health Security Effort and the Turn Against Government in U.S. Politics*. New York: Norton.

Spetz, J., J. A. Seago, J. Coffman, E. Rosenoff, and E. O'Neil. 2000. "Minimum Nurse Staffing Ratios in California Acute Care Hospitals." [Online article; retrieved 6/9/09.] www.chcf.org/documents/hospitals/MinNurseStaffingRatios.pdf.

Spetz, J., S. Chapman, C. Herrera, J. Kaiser, J. A. Seago, and C. Dower. 2009. "Assessing the Impact of California's Nurse Staffing Ratios on Hospitals and Patient Care." [Online report; retrieved 6/9/09.] www.chcf.org/documents/hospitals/ AssessingCANurseStaffingRatios.pdf.

Starr, P. 1982. *The Social Transformation of American Medicine*. New York: Basic Books.

Starr, P., and W. A. Zelman. 1993. "Bridge to Compromise: Competition Under a Budget." *Health Affairs* 12 (Suppl.): 7–23.

Steinberg, E. P., and B. R. Luce. 2005. "Evidence Based? Caveat Emptor!" *Health Affairs* 24 (1): 80–92.

Steinbrook, R. 2009. "Health Care and the American Recovery and Reinvestment Act." *New England Journal of Medicine* 360 (11): 1057–60.

Sterman, J. D. 2006. "Learning from Evidence in a Complex World." *American Journal of Public Health* 96 (3): 505–14.

Strokoff, S. 2005. "How Our Laws Are Made: A Ghost Writer's View." [Online article; retrieved 2/15/09.] www.house.gov/legcoun/strokoff.shtml.

Swayne, L. E., W. J. Duncan, and P. M. Ginter. 2007. *Strategic Management of Health Care Organizations*, 5th ed. Malden, MA: Wiley-Blackwell Publishers.

Teitelbaum, J. B., and S. E. Wilensky. 2007. *Essentials of Health Policy and Law*. Sudbury, MA: Jones and Bartlett Publishers.

Thompson, F. J. 1997. "The Evolving Challenge of Health Policy Implementation." In *Health Politics and Policy*, 3rd ed., edited by T. J. Litman and L. S. Robins, 155–75. Albany, NY: Delmar Publishers.

Thompson, F. J. 1981. *Health Policy and the Bureaucracy: Politics and Implementation.* Cambridge, MA: Massachusetts Institute of Technology Press.

Trattner, J. H., and P. McGinnis. 2004. *The 2004 Prune Book: Top Management Challenges for Presidential Appointees.* Washington, DC: Brookings Institution Press and the Council for Excellence in Government.

Truman, D. B. 1992. *The Governmental Process,* 2nd ed. Berkeley, CA: University of California, Institute of Governmental Studies.

U.S. Census Bureau. 2009. "People QuickFacts." [Online report; retrieved 2/1/09.] quickfacts.census.gov/qfd/states/00000.html.

U.S. Department of Health and Human Services. 2008. *2007 National Healthcare Disparities Report.* Washington, DC: U.S. Department of Health and Human Services. [Online report; retrieved 1/31/09.] www.ahrq.gov/qual/nhdr07/nhdr07.pdf.

———. 2000. *Healthy People 2010: Understanding and Improving Health,* 2nd ed. [Online report; retrieved 2/1/09.] www.health.gov/healthypeople.

U.S. Department of Labor. 2009. *Career Guide to Industries.* Washington, DC: U.S. Department of Labor, Bureau of Labor Statistics. [Online publication; retrieved 2/5/09.] www.bls.gov/oco/cg/cgs035.htm.

U. S. Department of State. 2004. *Outline of the U.S. Legal System.* [Online booklet; retrieved 2/8/09.] www.america.gov/media/pdf/books/legalotln.pdf#popup.

U.S. Food and Drug Administration. 2009. *What We Do.* Washington, DC: U.S. Food and Drug Administration. [Online publication; retrieved 2/5/09.] www.fda.gov/opacom/morechoices/mission.html.

U.S. House of Representatives. 2009. "Rules of the House of Representatives, 111th Congress." [Online material; retrieved 2/20/09.] www.rules.house.gov/ruleprec/111th.pdf.

U.S. Senate. 2008. "Glossary." [Online material; retrieved 10/8/09.] www.senate.gov/reference/glossary_term/conference_committee.htm.

———. 2006. "Older Americans Act Amendments of 2006." Report 109-366. Washington, DC: Government Printing Office.

Washington State Legislature. 2009. How a Bill Becomes Law. [Online material; retrieved 2/15/09.] www.leg.wa.gov/WorkingwithLeg/bill2law.htm.

Watkins, M. 2006. *Shaping the Game: The New Leader's Guide to Effective Negotiating.* Boston: Harvard Business School Publishing.

Weissert, C. S., and W. G. Weissert. 2006. *Governing Health: The Politics of Health Policy,* 3rd ed. Baltimore, MD: Johns Hopkins University Press.

White, B., and K. Newcomer (eds.). 2005. *Getting Results: A Guide for Federal Leaders and Managers.* Vienna, VA: Management Concepts.

Wood, D. 2003. "Effects of Child and Family Poverty on Child Health in the United States." *Pediatrics* 112 (3): 707–11.

World Health Organization. 1948. Preamble to the Constitution of the World Health Organization. In *Basic Documents,* 15th ed. Geneva, Switzerland: World Health Organization.

Yankelovich, D. 1992. "How Public Opinion Really Works." *Fortune* (October 5): 102–08.

Zwick, D. I. 1978. "Initial Development of Guidelines for Health Planning." *Public Health Reports* 93 (5): 407–20.

INDEX

ABOUT THE AUTHOR

Beaufort B. Longest, Jr., is the M. Allen Pond Professor of Health Policy & Management in the Department of Health Policy & Management of the Graduate School of Public Health at the University of Pittsburgh. He is also the founding director of Pitt's Health Policy Institute.

He received his undergraduate education at Davidson College and his Master of Health Administration (MHA) and PhD from Georgia State University. He is a Fellow of the American College of Healthcare Executives and holds memberships in the Academy of Management, AcademyHealth, the American Public Health Association, and the Association for Public Policy Analysis and Management. He has the unusual distinction of having been elected to membership in the Beta Gamma Sigma Honor Society in Business and the Delta Omega Honor Society in Public Health.

His research on health policy and management issues has generated substantial grant support and has led to the publication of numerous peer-reviewed articles. His most recent article pertains to getting faculty in schools of public health more involved in policymaking. In addition, he has authored or coauthored 10 books and 30 chapters in other books. He is coauthor of *Managing Health Services Organizations and Systems,* now in its fifth edition, which is among the most widely used textbooks in graduate health management programs.

He consults with healthcare organizations and systems, universities, associations, and government agencies on health policy and management issues.